PERSONALITY
AND ORGANIZATIONAL
INFLUENCE

PERSONALITY AND ORGANIZATIONAL INFLUENCE

Edited by

BARRY M. STAW
University of California, Berkeley

L.L. CUMMINGS
University of Minnesota

 **JAI PRESS INC.**
Greenwich, Connecticut   London, England

Library of Congress Cataloging-in-Publication Data

Personality and organizational influence / edited by Barry M. Staw, L.L. Cummings.
      p.   cm.
   ISBN 1-55938-217-1
   1. Organizational behavior. I. Staw, Barry M. II. Cummings, Larry L.
HD58.7.P464   1990
658.3—dc20   90-4524
                                               CIP

Manufactured in the United States of America

CONTENTS

LIST OF CONTRIBUTORS

Seymour Adler
Stevens Institute of Technology

Robert W. Allen
University of California, Irvine

Harold L. Angle
University of Cincinnati

Chris J. Berger
Purdue University

L.L. Cummings
University of Minnesota

Jill W. Graham
Loyola University of Chicago

Robert J. House
University of Pennsylvania

Lyman W. Porter
University of California, Irvine

Edgar T. Schein
Massachusetts Institute of Technology

Benjamin Schneider
University of Maryland

John Van Maanen
Massachusetts Institute of Technology

Howard M. Weiss
Purdue University

PREFACE

The exchange of influence between individuals and organizations has become a controversial topic in recent years. One source of attention has been the resurgence of personality research, virtually forcing a reassessment of the role of individual dispositions in explaining social behavior. Another has been the broader consideration of interactions between individuals and organizations —namely,how people are affected by settings in which they work and the ways such settings can, in turn, be influenced by individuals themselves.

How individuals and organizations influence each other represents the central theme of the seven essays drawn together in this anthology. Published over a ten-year span in the annual series, *Research in Organizational Behavior*, these chapters have not lost their importance or timeliness. They speak to the issue of person–organization influence in vastly different voices, but together cover most of the major points in this controversy.

The anthology starts with an essay by Howard Weiss and Seymour Adler on the nature of personality research in organizational behavior. Written primarily as a response to—"situationalists" who had previously dismissed the role of individual dispositions in explaining behavior, these authors propose reforms in the measurement and conceptualization of personality so as to help explain greater variance in organizational research. An essay by Benjamin Schneider then attempts to move us from debates over whether the individual or the environment explains greater variance to a more interactional perspective. The interactional view is one in which both the individual's disposition and the organizational situation are mutually interdependent. The person is socialized and shaped by the organization, but the organization is itself viewed as a collection of individuals who weave its social fabric. As Schneider notes, not only do organizational environments shape people, but it is people who themselves make the place.

The next five essays in this volume move back and forth between situational and dispositional perspectives. Probably the most situational of these pieces is the essay by John Van Maanen and Edgar Schein in which a theory of organizational socialization is outlined. They not only describe a range of socialization techniques used by organizations, but also make concrete predictions about their consequences. The next essay by Lyman Porter, Robert Allen, and Harold Angle treats the individual rather than the organization as the influencing agent. It places theoretical content on the notion of upward influence, showing when and under what conditions, individual employees attempt to influence those who are more powerful in the organization. Robert House then reviews research on individual power motives, showing which individuals tend to take charge of the situation as well as the organizational conditions conducive to such power acquisition. Following these essays on power, Jill Graham writes on the issue of principled organizational dissent. Drawing from the literatures of law, group dynamics, prosocial behavior, and whistleblowing, Graham develops a theory of the determinants of individual dissent in organizations—where and when the person draws the line, refusing to accept organizational influence. The final piece in this anthology takes perhaps the broadest view of organizational influence. Berger and Cummings review the research on organizational structure (such as hierarchical level, size, complexity) and examine the impact of these macro characteristics on individual attitudes and behavior.

Many of the chapters in this volume have already achieved prominence as separate contributions to organizational research. However, it is our hope that, by pulling these essays together, further (collective) progress will be made on the duality of individual and organizational influence. The way organizations shape and control individuals, along with the mechanisms used by people to deflect and resist such efforts, are not likely to diminish as concerns of organizational research. They constitute some of the most fundamental dilemmas of the field, and, as such, are deserving of further thought and research.

L.L. Cummings
Minneapolis, Minnesota

Barry M. Staw
Berkeley, California

PERSONALITY AND ORGANIZATIONAL BEHAVIOR

Howard M. Weiss and Seymour Adler

ABSTRACT

In this paper traditional and potential roles for personality constructs in explanations of work behavior are discussed. The paper begins with an overview of the way personality has been treated in organizational research, arguing that current negative evaluations about the contributions of personality are based upon research that is conceptually and methodologically limited. It follows with a discussion of three general topics—situation strength, dependent variable analysis and interactions—to illustrate issues relevant to a more appropriate examination of personality and organizational behavior. It concludes with a discussion of the nature of personality constructs and the efficient use of personality to advance theories of individual behavior in organizations.

1

INTRODUCTION

Researchers in Organizational Psychology have not had much regard for personality constructs in recent years. Personality differences, once fundamental to the study of work motivation, attitudes, and leadership are now assigned only secondary roles in most theories of organizational behavior, if they are given any role at all. The current situation is typified by Mitchell's statement in his 1979 Annual Review of Organizational Behavior:

> We will find throughout this review that personality traits appear as predictors of attitudes (e.g. involvement) motivation (e.g. expectancies) and leadership (e.g. behavioral styles), but the central focus of that research is usually motivation, attitudes, or leadership and not personality.
>
> *This secondary role seems justified and necessary.* If Mischel's arguments are correct than we will be better served by continuing in the direction we are heading. Personality variables probably control only a minor percentage of variance in behavior when compared to situational factors (Mitchell, 1979, p. 247) (Italics added)

It is possible that Mitchell's statement may be seen as too extreme by many or even most organizational researchers. Yet there is no real evidence to suggest anything but implicit acceptance of the position. While it is true that many current models of various sorts of organizational behaviors have obligatory boxes designed to contain "individual differences," in most cases these boxes play no fundamental theoretical role and the empirical research on the models tends to focus on other issues. Some theories are even quite explicit in stating their avoidance of personality constructs. Van Maanen and Schein (1979) for example in presenting their theory of organizational socialization state "a theory of organizational socialization must not allow itself to become too preoccupied with individual characteristics . . ." (p. 216).

We disagree with those who advocate relegating personality to minor or nonexistant positions in theories of individual behavior in organizations. We are inclined to agree with their assessment of the contribution of personality to current understanding of organizational behavior. On the whole that contribution has been disappointing. We disagree however with the conclusions about personality which can be drawn from that research. Historically, personality research on organizational behavior has suffered from inadequate conceptual development and poor methodology and these factors have conspired to give personality a bad name. It is simply premature and unproductive to make any general normative statements about restricting the role of personality in organizational research. Adequate tests of the usefulness of personality must be conducted with theory based, operationally precise efforts, and past and current research on personality and OB has failed to do this.

This paper presents an overview of the way personality has been used in organizational research and suggests issues of theory and design which must be addressed if personality is to be given a fair hearing as an explanatory construct. We should state early on that we do not intend to defend, a priori, the usefulness of personality. Such a defense can only come from the outcome of adequate research. Nor do we presume to prescribe the nature of that research. Our objective is simply to raise and discuss certain issues of theory and method which bear on studying personality and work behavior.

Many readers are probably aware that the explanatory usefulness of personality constructs has once again become a popular topic in psychology. Strong attacks (Mischel, 1968; 1973) have stimulated creative responses. Clearly we have been influenced by this recent work and our discussion will rely heavily on this literature. However, this paper will not be a tutorial on current research and thinking in the field of social and personality psychology. Our objective will be the integration of relevant aspects of this work with organizational behavior.

We should also say that our discussion will focus almost totally on the use of trait conceptions of personality within a nomothetic framework. We recognize that a number of interesting nontrait approaches to personality are being examined (see Helson & Mitchell, 1978; Rychlak, 1981). However, our field has been and continues to be dominated by trait conceptions of personality and there is much of relevance being done with this approach. The limitation to traits is therefore based primarily on interest, ours and what we see as the field's. We believe that this limitation in no way inhibits the usefulness of the discussion.

Our preference for a nomothetic viewpoint is less arbitrary. We have been aware of a number of recent papers advocating idiographic approaches to organizational analyses of various sorts (e.g. Luthans & Davis, 1982). Our position is simply that in the area of personality, recurrent attempts to resurrect Allport's (1937) often referenced and often misunderstood statement about idiographic analyses have simply not been, nor will be, productive for advancing the science of individual behavior.

Frank (1982) has traced the development of idiography from the Scottish philosopher Duns Scotus through existentialist positions on scientific knowledge. He notes that the core of an idiographic position is that every individual, indeed every object, has a certain essence or "thisness" and that there can be no real understanding of the object without understanding its essence. Additionally, since each essence is unique and cannot be

resolved into class concepts, the search for scientific laws and generalizations is an impediment to real knowledge. A true idiographic position
precludes as meaningful knowledge the acceptance of lawful relationships
which generalize across individuals. We do not take this position nor do
we think that it characterizes any but a minority of organizational researchers.

We should point out that Allport's position was never so extreme. He
did not reject the meaningfulness of scientific generalizations and envi-
sioned nomothetic and idiographic "sciences" coexisting in the study of
personality. For example, in discussing the differences between the two
approaches Allport (1937) stated "the dichotomy is too sharp: it requires
a psychology divided against itself . . . It is more helpful to regard the
two methods as overlapping and contributing to each other" (p. 22). More
importantly for our position, the issues which prompted Allport to call
for an idiographic approach are easily resolved within a nomothetic framework (Frank, 1982). Allport argued that the "idiographic sciences . . .
endeavor to understand some particular event in nature or society" (Allport, 1937, p. 22). Clearly, as Frank (1982) points out, there is nothing
contradictory about explanation of particular events within the framework
of nomothetic generalizations. In fact, nomothetic science is based upon
the deduction from the general to the particular through laws and singular
observations. Finally, Frank argues that most so-called idiographic analyses are based upon hidden nomothetic principles. He cites history which
is often taken as a prototypic idiographic approach and notes that the
historian bases his analysis on unstated generalizations and assumed regularities. Similarly therapists are described as taking an idiographic approach, but essentially depend on nomothetic generalizations.

In arguing for a nomothetic viewpoint we are not denying the practical
or scientific importance of analyzing particular cases. However, we believe that this is accomplishable within a nomothetic framework. To us
it seems clear that idiographic approaches are nomothetic at heart. The
difference between the two lies in whether the matrix of generalizations
and set of categories are theory based and public or implicit and private
to the observer. Based upon these considerations we see no reason to
abandon the nomothetic approach to studying personality and work behavior.

Finally, we should note that this is not a review of personality influences
on organizational behavior. In fact we have taken great pains to avoid
discussing such findings. Extensive reviews on specific topics have been
presented elsewhere (see, for example, White, 1978, on job design or
Bass, 1981, on leadership) and we have therefore seen our task as one of
extracting underlying issues of theory and method which bear on examining personality influences. Certainly some key findings will be noted.

However, these notations will be made primarily to illustrate more general arguments.

Our paper has three major segments. The first step toward advancing new approaches and issues is an understanding of current approaches and we therefore begin with a general overview of the way personality is studied in OB research. We do this by reviewing four areas of organizational activity and drawing some common themes from these representative literatures. Our second section discusses three general issues— interactionism, dependent variable analysis and situation strength— which need to be addressed if our understanding of personality influences on organizational behavior is going to advance. Finally, we conclude with a general discussion of the explanatory nature of personality constructs and the efficient use of such constructs in theories of individual behavior in organizations.

PERSONALITY IN ORGANIZATIONAL BEHAVIOR RESEARCH

We have structured our discussion of the way personality constructs have been and are now being used in organizational research around three non-orthogonal issues; their role in theory, the types of research designs used, and the types of personality variables examined. Although these issues obviously do not capture the myriad ways in which personality has been integrated into OB research, differences in these areas struck us as particularly meaningful as we examined the nature of personality research in organizations.

Role in Theory

When personality constructs are incorporated into theories of individual behavior in organizations, the nature of that incorporation varies on two dimensions; centrality and specification of mediating processes.

1. Centrality. Theories that utilize personality variables differ in the extent to which personality is an integral component of the explanatory framework being advanced. A test of centrality would be to ask whether the theory would still exist coherently if the personality variable were removed. Theories used in OB research have clearly differed in this regard. For example, self–esteem lies at the core of Korman's (1970; 1976) theory of work motivation. Since, in his view, people are motivated to perform in a manner consistent with their self–esteem, removing self–esteem from the theory would destroy its usefulness. By contrast, in Lawler's (1971) revision of expectancy theory, self–esteem is seen as only one influence on effort—performance expectancies. While the introduction of this personality variable into the model may help enhance its comprehensiveness, removing self–esteem would basically leave the central components of the theory unaffected. Unlike Korman's self–consistency theory, the validity of Lawler's expectancy theory does not rest on the inclusion of self–esteem. We should add that centrality does not imply that the personality construct is seen as the sole influence on behavior, nor is it equivalent to a theory based upon direct as opposed to interactive effects. For example, need for Achievement and Fear of Failure are both central to the theory of achievement motivation (Atkinson, 1964), but without additional knowledge about the probability and incentive values of success and failure, specific predictions about motivation and behavior cannot be derived.

2. *Specification of Mediating Processes.*   Theories also differ in the extent to which the links between personality and criteria are specified. Obviously much of the personality research in our field is not systematically derived from theory, personnel selection research for example, and in such research, personality–criteria links are rarely elaborated on. While this is certainly more likely to occur in research that is not theory driven, theoretical perspectives which incorporate personality also vary on this dimension. For example, the mediating processes linking LPC and group performance are not specified in Fiedler's (1967) contingency theory of leadership. By contrast, other theories systematically work through the linkages between personality and the other variables being studied. To return to Lawler's (1971) revised expectancy theory, self esteem is hypothesized specifically to affect effort—performance expectancies, which in turn interact with performance—outcome beliefs and valences to influence motivation. While one might expect centrality to be positively associated with specification of mediating processes, it is clear by looking at these two examples that this is not always the case. LPC is central to Fiedler's theory while self esteem is peripheral to Lawler's.

Role in Design

We have drawn on Magnusson and Endler (1977), Howard (1979), Terborg (1981) and others to identify four ways that personality can be treated in the design of research. These different design treatments correspond to differences in expected personality-behavior relationships.

1. *Direct Effects.*   Here the direct effect of a personality variable on some relevant dependent variable is examined. In such research, the effects of other personality and situational variables are seen as irrelevant to interpretation of the effects of the personality variable in question and

are either ignored, controlled or reported separately. While much of the OB research fitting this design is cross–sectional, the research generally is interpreted in terms of the personality variable having a direct causal influence on levels of the criterion in question.

2. *Mechanistic Interaction.* In mechanistic interaction designs, the effects of a personality variable on a criterion are considered at least partially dependent on other situational and/or personal factors. Included in this category would be those studies in the analysis of variance tradition, in which main effects of personality and situational variables, as well as their interactive effects, are isolated. Also included would be those studies in the correlational tradition, in which personality is seen to moderate the relationship between a situational variable and the criterion, or in which the situation is seen to moderate the relationship between personality and the criterion. The mechanistic interaction design, like the direct design, implies a clear distinction between independent and dependent variables (Magnusson & Endler, 1977; Olweus, 1977). While most mechanistic interactions in OB examine the interactive effects of persons and situations, interactive effects of multiple personality constructs can and have been studied in the same way (see for example, McClelland & Boyatzis, 1982). In contrast with the direct design which examines single bivariate relationships (what Mischel, 1968, calls "personality coefficients"), mechanistic interaction designs are used to investigate more complex multivariate relationships.

3. *Reciprocal Effects.* In both the direct and interaction designs described above, personality is studied as an independent variable. Studies which look at reciprocal effects are those in which personality is treated as the dependent variable. Personality has been conceptualized as the dependent variable in studies on the effects of job ambiguity (Brousseau & Prince, 1981), rural and urban upbringing on adult work needs (Adler, Aranya & Amernic, 1981), and job mobility on locus of control (Hammer & Vardi, 1981). As with studies using the designs described above, most of the studies of reciprocal effects in the OB literature have, in fact, relied on data collected cross-sectionally.

4. *Dynamic Interaction.* While the direct effects design conceptualizes personality as the independent variable, and the reciprocal effect design treats personality as the dependent variable, the dynamic interaction design "stresses an interaction process in which persons and situations form an inextricably interwoven structure (Magnusson & Endler, 1977, p. 18)." In this view, personality, situations and behavior are continuously influencing each other in a process that Bandura (1978) calls reciprocal determinism. Examples of research examining dynamic interactions include

the work of Duncan and Fiske (1978) on verbal interaction, Bales and Cohen (1979) on the development of Symlog to analyze group interactions, and the 10 year longitudinal study on the mutual influences of job conditions and personality reported by Kohn and Schooler (1982). While the conceptual emphasis in these designs is on the ongoing reciprocal influences of personality and on personality (Endler & Magnusson, 1976; Schneider, 1983), statistically, in any given analysis, personality is temporarily treated as the dependent or independent variable.

Type of Personality Variable

Personality constructs employed in OB research can be grouped into two broad categories, although some constructs have components of both of these categories.

1. Cognitive. These refer to characteristic properties of the individual's perceptual and thought processes, how the individual processes information. Such cognitive style variables (Goldstein & Blackman, 1978) as cognitive complexity, reflectivity–impulsitivity, dogmatism, and locus of control would be included in this category. Also included would be stable differences in the manner in which people perceive the world around them. Well known examples of such perceptual personality constructs would be field articulation or field dependence-independence (Witkin & Goodenough, 1977), cognitive complexity (Goldstein and Blackman, 1978) and self–monitoring (Snyder, 1974).

2. Motivational. Those stable individual differences in the why, when, where and how behavior is energized and maintained comprise the motivational personality variables. Needs, motives, and values all fall into this category. Stable affective or drive–related variables, like trait anxiety, would be included here as well.

Overview of Literature

In order to capture a sense of how personality constructs have been employed, research in four representative areas will be described within a framework of the descriptive categories just discussed.

Job Scope

The extensive use of individual difference variables in the job scope literature has its roots in the classic studies by Turner and Lawrence (1965) and Hulin and Blood (1968). These early studies utilized the sociological constructs of urban–rural upbringing and alienation from middle class norms to explain different worker reactions to jobs. Since the important research of Hackman and Lawler (1971), the subsequent development of the Job Characteristics Model by Hackman and Oldham (1975; 1980) and the construction of the Job Diagnostic Survey (Hackman & Oldham, 1976), personality variables have been included in most studies of job scope. This extensive use of personality makes the job scope literature instructive for examining how personality has been studied when it is considered important and its importance follows from theory. As stated previously, our review will describe how personality is treated rather than the nature and extent of personality effects. Reviews of this latter issue are available in Hackman and Oldham (1980), Roberts and Glick (1981), and White (1978).

Although personality constructs have been widely used in research on job scope, personality typically plays a peripheral role in the theories being tested. The best–developed and most frequently employed theory of job scope, the Job Characteristics Model (Hackman & Oldham, 1975), has as its prime focus a description of the influence of core job characteristics on the psychological states and subsequent behavioral reactions of workers. Personality is introduced into the theory to specify the type of person for whom the model is more or less likely to be predictive. The function of personality, then, is to establish some boundary conditions for the effectiveness of the model, to "fine–tune" (Mitchell, 1979) the model. It is assumed that for people in general, the model will be valid. Were personality to be removed, the Job Characteristic Model would still stand as a coherent theory of job scope.

The Job Characteristics Model says relatively little about the linkages between the aspect of personality considered and the other components of the theory. In Hackman and Lawlers' (1971) original paper, they did provide a brief discussion of the nature of the linkage. Their initial position was that enriched jobs provide intrinsic rewards related to higher order need fulfillment and therefore enrichment should work only for those for whom these needs are salient. Essentially, in trying to use an expectancy framework to understand the effects of task characteristics, they imply that higher order need strength affects the valences of outcomes provided by working on enriched jobs. This was a reasonable starting point. However, it should be noted that neither instrumentalities nor valences are presented as specific components of the model and no discussion of how HONS might effect, in a unique way, any of the three key psychological states is provided. As research on the model has progressed, the linkages have become, if anything, less precise. Recent statements of the theory (Hackman & Oldham, 1980) make no systematic use of expectancy theory to derive a role for Growth Need Strength and GNS is now hypothesized to moderate a number of relationships less predictable from valence differences within an expectancy framework (Hackman & Oldham, 1980). No research has been conducted which tries to explicate the way moderator or main effects of GNS on perceptions, psychological states or outcomes might occur and linkages to antecedent or consequent components are left unclear.

In the job scope literature, personality is almost always studied using mechanistic interaction designs, with personality variables analyzed as moderators of task characteristics—criteria relationships. The mechanistic interaction design so dominates the thinking of researchers that many often neglect to report the direct zero order correlations of personality and the dependent variables or the job scope measures. Historically, the rigid use of the mechanistic interaction framework can be traced directly to Turner and Lawrence's (1965) study of moderating influences on reactions to task characteristics. The use of the approach was solidified by the work of Hackman and Lawler (1971) which has served as a model for subsequent research on job scope. So influential was Hackman's and Lawler's original design that through much of the 1970s, research continued to use their subgrouping approach to moderator analysis, with many researchers going as far as using the same arbitrary top–third, bottom–third split (Roberts & Glick, 1981). Although we now see more use of the moderated regression approach (Abdel-Halim, 1979; Arnold & House, 1980; Champoux & Peters, 1980), this is simply a more appropriate way of examining mechanistic interactions and does not represent a change in thinking about the nature of personality effects.

A peripheral role for personality in a mechanistic interaction framework was logical as an initial approach to studying personality and job scope. Peripheral was logical because the essential issue was the general effect of some property of the environment (tasks). Mechanistic interaction was logical within the context of an experimental tradition which, because of the direct manipulation of stimuli and the random assignment of subjects to conditions, directed thinking towards persons and situations as separate causal variables [$B = f(P, E)$] that, while independent, could have interactive effects on some dependent measure [$B = f(P, E, P \times E)$].

Strict adherence to this conceptualization of persons and situations as independent now seems limiting with the recognition that people can choose the situations they encounter, they can modify their tasks to fit their needs, their behavior is a function of their perceptions and their perceptions are only partly determined by objective task properties, etc. As a result, we see more attempts to move away from the traditional approach. Examples include Salancik and Pfeffer's (1977, 1978) work, the research by Stone (1979) and Jones and Butler (1980) on the direct effects of personality on perceptions of job characteristics and the interesting work on dynamic interactions by James and Jones (1980) and Kohn and Schooler (1982).

Personality constructs used in job scope research are almost exclusively motivational. The reason for this is best understood by again examining the historical context of personality research in this area. Turner and Lawrence's (1965) original moderator results were based on demographic analyses and explained by the authors using sociological constructs. There soon ensued a concerted effort to provide a more psychological explanation of these original results and that effort focused primarily on motivational variables in the form of needs or values.

Blood and Hulin (1968) offered an explanation in terms of individual differences in a constellation of variables they labeled as "middle class norms." Although their empirical research was conducted at a community level of analysis and many of their construct labels had a sociological ring, their explanation was primarily psychological, focusing on differences at the individual level, and motivational, referring to variations in work values and needs. Research stimulated by this work has been more explicit in examining individual differences in motivational personality constructs (see for example, Stone 1976).

The explanation provided by Hackman and Lawler (1971), the next influential attempt to translate the Turner and Lawrence (1965) findings into psychological constructs, was fundamentally quite similar to Hulin and Blood (1968). To be sure, the Hackman and Lawler position was substantially better grounded in psychological theory, derived essentially from a combination of expectancy theory and Maslow's hierarchy of needs. It also was initially more thorough in explicating the mediating processes. Yet their construct of Higher Order Need Strength was and remains, in the more recent form of Growth Need Strength (Hackman & Oldham, 1975), motivational in character. The development of operationalizations of the Hackman and Oldham constructs has contributed to the domination of motivational personality constructs, specifically Growth Need Strength, in research on personality effects. Not only has much of the job scope research conceptualized personality in terms of this specific variable, measurement of GNS has been almost exclusively limited to the GNS scales included in the Job Diagnostic Survey (Hackman & Oldham, 1975) or close variants of these scales (e.g., the measure of self-actualization need strength used by Sims & Szilagyi, 1976). As a result, findings in this area may not only be construct-bound (motivational variables), they are to a large extent measure-bound, with an instrument whose construct validity has been seriously questioned (Aldag & Brief, 1975; Stone, Ganster, Woodman & Fusilier, 1979) and whose personality construct is drawn from a theory (Maslow's) which has been appropriately criticized both for its conceptual fuzziness and its lack of empirical support (Wahba & Bridwell, 1976).

While recent work in the area has begun to pay attention to more cognitive personality variables (Sims & Szilagyi, 1976; Stone, 1979; Weiss & Shaw, 1979), motivational approaches continue to be dominant. As a result, it is fair to say that discussions of research on personality and job scope are limited to the effects of motivational variables of a very circumscribed type.

After reviewing personality–job scope findings, White (1978) concluded that this whole line of research would best be abandoned. Our review of the way personality has been treated would suggest that White's conclusion is premature. We have seen that designs other than mechanistic interaction and personality variables that are non–motivational have scarcely been employed. Too often the use of personality has been based not on theory but on the availability of the Job Diagnostic Survey, a clear manifestation of what Kaplan (1964) calls the Law of the Instrument.

Our conclusions about the effects of the original research by Hulin and Blood or Hackman, Lawler and Oldham should not be read as a criticism of these early efforts. That work was, in a way, too stimulating. Particularly in the case of the Job Characteristics Model, the comparative comprehensiveness of the theory, the development of theory–based instrumentation and the initial empirical payoffs created a compelling paradigm for studying job characteristics. Unfortunately, the initial success of that paradigm restricted thinking about alternative ways of incorporating personality into job scope theory. We are now seeing some movement in other directions. For example, Salancik's and Pfeffer's (1978) Social Information Processing approach suggests alternative ways in which personality might influence perceptions and evaluations of task characteristics. Activation Arousal Theory reference might be useful in suggesting more complex and well defined roles for personality variables related to characteristic arousal or anxiety levels. In any case, our examination of the limited way in which personality has been studied in job scope research to date makes it clear that contrary to White's (1978) assessment, the potential contribution of personality in this area has scarcely been explored.

Leadership

In contrast with the job scope area, leadership research has not been dominated by any one approach. Yet, by and large, when personality has been introduced into leadership theory, it has played a central role. Trait theories of leadership (i.e., Ghiselli, 1971), explicitly argue that leaders can be distinguished from followers, and successful leaders from unsuccessful leaders, on the basis of specific personality traits. While, it is often the case that theory is not employed to make specific a priori predictions about which trait will be important, trait approaches clearly place personality, along with demographic and ability variables, at the core of leadership theory.

The centrality of personality constructs is also exhibited in the leadership research out of the Ohio State tradition (Fleishman, 1953; Halpin & Winer, 1957). This work is often seen as a major break from the trait approach which characterized the area before 1950. Indeed in his 1973 retrospective Fleishman quite explicitly talks of the sense of excitement felt in moving away from traits and focusing on leader behaviors. Yet actual analysis of the nature of the constructs and measures indicates that this movement was more apparent than real. Consideration and Initiating Structure are nothing if they are not dispositional constructs. The LBDQ, SBDQ and LOQ clearly are meant to assess broad cross–situational behavioral tendencies. That the Ohio State researchers were reluctant to use these labels to refer to supposed internal entities or personal characteristics does not alter the fact that the constructs are operationalized and utilized in the same way as are other trait variables. The absence, until recently, of any significant research on the determinants of these "behaviors" further indicates that their development was less of a break from the personality tradition than is usually believed.

The centrality of personality traits in leadership research is not limited to main–effect conceptualizations. In Fielder's (1967) Contingency Model of leadership, the effects of LPC, which is often conceptualized as a stable personality trait (Fiedler, 1967; Rice, 1978; Strube & Garcia, 1981), can only be predicted with knowledge of the situation. Yet LPC is, of course, a central rather than peripheral component of Fiedler's theory of leadership.

This tendency for personality to play a more central role in leadership research is not, however, manifested in more recent work on perceptions of leader behavior (Lord, Foti & Phillips, 1981), the symbolic nature of leadership (Pfeffer, 1981) or leader attributions (Mitchell, Green & Wood, 1981). Yet, these would appear to be areas where differences in perceptual and processing variables could make a contribution (see, for example, Weiss & Adler, 1981).

While research and theory on leadership frequently consider personality as central to understanding leader behavior and effectiveness, too often the linkages between personality and other components of the theory remain unexplicated. Even the contingency model, which made a significant contribution by advocating the importance of the interaction between persons and situations, has very little to say about the links between LPC and group outcomes. In fact, the history of the model is partially a story of attempts to derive a meaningful mediating process to explain inductively derived LPC-situation interactions, with the explanations offered over the years being less than satisfying. This lack of attention to mediation is also generally true for leadership style research, although path–goal theory (Evans, 1970; House, 1971) has attempted to specify some of the links between Consideration and Initiating Structure on the one hand and follower motivation and satisfaction on the other.

While most of the Industrial/Organizational research on leader traits has left linkages unspecified, there are noteworthy exceptions in small group work. Here, for instance, researchers have offered models that link specific traits (e.g., extroversion or energy) to behaviors (e.g., rate of talking), leader behavior to group acceptance, and acceptance, in turn, to group performance (e.g., see Bass, 1981, Chapter 6).

Classic research on personality and leadership was clearly dominated by direct effects designs (see Bass, 1981, for a review). Much research using the direct effect design is still being conducted (for example, Anderson & Schneier, 1978, on locus of control and leader effectiveness and Miner's, 1978, work on managerial motivation) particularly when the focus is on managerial selection and training. However, generally the main effect design has given way to the mechanistic interaction design. Fiedler's (1967) Contingency Model is, of course, specifically structured to reflect the mechanistic interaction of persons and situations and research on the model typically analyzes the pattern of personality outcome correlations across varying situational conditions. In fact, Fielder explicitly dismisses the possibility of any meaningful reciprocal effects of the situation on leader personality. Path goal theory (House, 1971) and work on substitutes for leadership (Kerr & Jermier, 1978) are additional examples of this design. Mechanistic interaction in leadership research is not limited to person–situation effects as some work has focused on multiple trait effects as well. Examples include Fleishman and Harris (1962), O'Reilly and Roberts (1978) and Larson, Hunt and Osborne (1976) in the Ohio State tradition and McClelland's work on the Leadership Motive Pattern (McClelland & Boyatzis, 1982).

Recently, leadership research has begun to examine reciprocal effects on leader behavior (Podsakoff, 1982), but only a few studies have addressed whether these reciprocal effects generalize to leader personality. One such study is Bons, Bass and Komorita's (1970) longitudinal examination of how years and type of military experience affect the LPC of military leaders. Overall though, while reciprocal effects on leadership have begun to receive well–deserved attention, systematic exploration has yet to be made on reciprocal effects on leader personality, or on dynamic interactions between leader personality and the leadership situation.

Research following the trait model has often used the "shotgun" approach in the choice of personality variables. While generally this research has neither been guided by nor contributed to leadership theory, it has generated data over a broad array of motivational, cognitive, and perceptual constructs. New personality measures are quickly incorporated into leadership trait research. At the same time, it is interesting to note the difficulty in classifying the traits used in some of the more systematic research on leader characteristics. LPC, for instance, has alternatively been understood as a motivational variable reflecting differences in primary or secondary needs, a cognitive variable reflecting differences in cognitive complexity and an attitudinal variable, simply reflecting beliefs about one's least preferred co-worker (Rice, 1978). This has contributed to the inability to find a reasonable theoretical explanation for the pattern of data described by the model. Consideration and Initiating Structure are similarly difficult to classify. While, operationalized as overt behavioral dispositions, it is possible that these dispositions may result from latent cognitive or motivational constructs (or their interaction), although the use of these variables suggests that they are generally considered more motivational than cognitive.

Research on personality and leadership generally has shown personality to have statistically significant, though not strong, direct and interactive effects (Bass, 1981). Reactions to Stodgdill's famous 1948 review article (Stogdill, 1948), as Stogdill himself later pointed out, disproportionally "over-emphasized the situational, and underemphasized the personal, nature of leadership (Stogdill, 1974, p. 72)." While personality effects have been found, understanding of leadership processes has not advanced as a result. Our belief is that this is because not enough attention has been paid to building theories that systematically examine the mediating links between leader behavior and relevant outcome variables. At the simplest level we assume that some traits have their effect by influencing leader behaviors that influence, in turn, follower goal-directed behavior. However, leader behaviors are not the only links between leader traits and subordinate reactions. Research by Lord and his associates on leader categorization (Lord, Foti and Phillips, 1981) suggests that leader traits may affect subordinate reactions in ways apart from the mediating influence of leader behavior. So, for example, a particular characteristic may be one element of a perceptual category whose other elements are relevant to the acceptance of influence (i.e., perceived competence, reward power). Perception of the initial characteristic may lead to classification of the leader in this category and the inference of the existence of these other elements. This research only highlights the importance of specifying the mediating processes between traits and leader effectiveness if the study of personality and leadership is to progress.

Employee Withdrawal

Until recently there has been little theory in the area of withdrawal behavior (turnover, absenteeism, and lateness). However, models of various forms of withdrawal are now being presented (Steers & Rhodes, 1978; Mobley, 1977; Mowday, Porter & Steers, 1982). These models all include a role for personality, suggesting that personality research in this area may soon be conducted more systematically than in the past. Steers and Rhodes (1978) specifically talk about a person's work ethic as an influence on attendance pressures. Both Steers and Rhodes and Mobley (1977) see individual values as key influences in employee dissatisfaction which in turn may lead to absenteeism or quitting. Further, the Mobley model includes such factors as the tendency to seek immediate versus delayed reinforcement, impulsive behavior and work centrality as influences on turnover. It is, however, unclear whether these later factors are being conceptualized as personality constructs. The consideration of personality in these areas could potentially be productive as there are well–developed literatures on a number of constructs relevant to these issues (see, for example, the work on reflexivity–impulsivity, Messer, 1976). Interestingly, while personality is included in these models, its role is quite peripheral. In both the Steers model of turnover and the Mobley model of absenteeism, the removal of personality variables would not substantially alter the processes postulated.

Given that so much research on withdrawal was until recently non-theoretical and stimulated mostly by applied problems, it is not surprising that direct effects studies are most often encountered. In their review of the turnover literature, Porter and Steers (1973) found weak–to–moderate correlations for such factors as achievement orientation, anxiety, independence and self-confidence. Muchinsky and Tuttle (1979), after surveying the available data, concluded that the effect of personality on turnover is marginal. Very few studies exist that examine the influence of personality on other forms of withdrawal behavior (Muchinsky, 1977).

In an interesting departure, Porter and Steers (1973) suggested that direct effects of personality might be manifested as curvilinear rather than linear relationships. In the one study testing this idea, however, Bernardin (1977) found little evidence of higher turnover or absenteeism from those at either end of the continuum of several personality traits when compared with those not at the extremes.

A recent exception to studies using direct effects designs was reported by Mowday and Spencer (1981) in which moderated regression was used to test both the direct and interactive effects of autonomy and achievement needs on turnover and absenteeism. Personality and job scope interacted significantly in determining absenteeism, but not turnover. However, the pattern of those interactions was not consistently in line with predictions.

Though little actually has been done on personality and withdrawal, the recent development of more theoretical approaches which include personality suggest that more research will be forthcoming. Analysis of the role of personality in these models suggests, however, that future work is likely to concentrate on direct effects and mechanistic interactions and focus primarily on a few motivational variables, presumed to influence values. Perhaps some of the recent attention given to the consequences of absenteeism and turnover (Mowday, Porter & Steers, 1982) will stimulate research on reciprocal and dynamic interactions. As yet, discussions of these consequences have not contained effects on personality.

Goal-Setting

Locke's (1968) major statement of goal-setting theory makes little mention of personality as a determinant of goal-setting behavior. Locke (1968) does imply that an individual's conscious desires (p. 183) or preferences (p. 185) could mediate the effects of incentives on the choice of goals. Beyond this, however, no specific role for personality is discussed. The absence of any integration of personality constructs into the theory is surprising since goal setting has its conceptual roots in Lewin's work on level of aspiration. In that original research, the choice of task difficulty levels was seen as partly a reflection of stable personality dispositions (Campbell, 1982). After reviewing the empirical literature on level of aspiration, much of which appeared over 40 years ago, Campbell concludes that "the evidence suggesting that level of aspiration (i.e., level of goal difficulty) is partially a personality characteristic is quite impressive." (p. 89). Relating these findings to contemporary goal setting research, Campbell speculates about personality influences in goal setting. None the less, in spite of relevant existing literature, a systematic role of personality, either central or peripheral, within contemporary goal setting theory has yet to be worked out.

Consistent with this lack of theoretical consideration, the research on personality reported in the goal setting literature has been somewhat haphazard. Almost universally, personality is treated as a moderator within a mechanistic interaction design. The predominance of the mechanistic moderator design is in keeping with the emphasis on goal setting as an external intervention rather than an internal self regulatory process. While much has been done on examining the effects of externally set goals, less attention has been paid to self-set-goals. (Rakestraw & Weiss, 1981).

Attention to this later issue would necessitate a broader approach to examining personality effects—emphasizing research on direct and particularly reciprocal effects.

Even within the mechanistic framework, the role of personality is of marginal interest in studies on goal setting. When personality is examined, measures are typically "tacked on" to research on other issues. Locke, Shaw, Saari and Latham (1981) describe how severe weaknesses in these studies with respect to the treatment of personality make it impossible to draw any conclusions about personality and goal setting. Among the weaknesses they cite are inconsistencies in the measures used for a given construct, administration of personality scales after experimental manipulation of goals, performance or both, reported interactions that are not subjected to appropriate statistical tests, and the assignment of goals which inhibits the emergence of individual differences.

Why include a discussion of personality and goal setting when relatively little has been done and the results have been discouraging? Our answer involves more than the fact that this is an important area of current organizational research. In significant ways, the use of personality in this area is more widely generalizable. The study of personality in goal setting has been of secondary importance with personality hypotheses much less firmly grounded in theory than other aspects of the research. The choices of personality variables seem very haphazard with little written about the reasons for choosing the particular variables or measures. The research is almost always conducted in the context of attempting to find effects for goal setting interventions, creating very "strong" situations likely to overwhelm individual differences. When goals are assigned, researchers have not considered the reciprocal effects this manipulation might have on personality. Yet in spite of these restricted uses of personality, researchers in the area are beginning to conclude that personality is unimportant here. This may in fact be true, but certainly we should reserve judgment until more systematic work is conducted.

Conclusions

A number of themes emerge from this review. First, it is obvious that few of the available ways of conceptualizing and studying personality effects on organizational behavior have been used in empirical research. Few studies of reciprocal or dynamic interaction effects have been reported. Research has been very mechanistic, assuming a clear distinction between independent and dependent variables. Few studies have employed longitudinal designs, emphasizing correlational studies or relatively short term experimentation. Scholars in our field have long been aware that the prevalence of cross-sectional research generally limits the construction of strong causal models of work behavior. It is sometimes assumed, however, that this problem is less critical for personality research, given the presumption of causal precedence for fixed personality traits. Our recent awareness of organizational influences on personality traits and values (see, for example, Weiss, 1978) and of attributional processes in which personality is inferred from outcomes, suggests that our early complacency about interpreting cross–sectional personality research is no longer justified. Movement away from main effects and mechanistic interaction will require longitudinal analyses. In addition, as will be discussed later, personality effects may vary over time indicating that even studies still focusing on main or interactive effects will have to become more cognizant of processes that occur and change over time. Further illustrating the limitations of previous work is the fact that the personality variables we have used are overwhelmingly motivational. This may reflect an earlier emphasis on motivational traits among personality researchers, an emphasis that was a legacy of psychodynamic roots in the development of personality theory. This emphasis is becoming less and less true of personality research outside of OB.

A second theme which emerges concerns the general homogeneity of approach within areas. While we have pointed out that diversity certainly does not characterize the field as a whole, we are particularly struck by the homogeneity of constructs, designs and instruments within each area. It is interesting to note that against this backdrop of similarity, modest changes in measurement, design or theory in any one area are seen as quite innovative. Substituting Growth Need Strength for Protestant Ethic or moderated regression for subgroup analyses within the job scope area are examples. From outside the job scope area, these changes seem more like minor variations. Job scope research remains limited to motivational variables studied from a mechanistic interaction perspective. Similarly, the change from focusing on traits to focusing on behavioral dispositions in the leadership area was really less of a change than the researchers believed it to be at the time. It seems that as a field develops, the range of alternatives explored often begins to narrow. This is no doubt due to the influence of one or a few key studies which excite the field (e.g., Turner & Lawrence, 1965, and Hackman & Lawler, 1971, in job scope, the Ohio State work in leadership).

A final theme which emerges is the superficial thought given to personality in our theory and research. This is manifested in a number of ways. First, linkages between personality and the other components of our theories are given substantially less theoretical specification than are those related to situational variables. Second, much of the data collected on personality effects is collected as part of larger studies where other issues are given theoretical procedence. This is particularly true in those areas where there is an important applied issue being analyzed. In such research, the creation of effective interventions is of primary importance and dominates the researcher's attention. Third, we tend to draw on personality variables in isolation, lifting them out of their nomological networks, neither building upon nor feeding back to their theoretical underpinnings. Indeed we too frequently ignore the nature and extent of those construct–relevant data. This point goes beyond our frequently choosing measures with little construct validity (which is, unfortunately, true). It means that even where good construct validity evidence exists, we rarely use it to enlighten us on the issue at hand. Our use of personality measures is too often intended to account for a little more variance and too seldom intended to extend explanation.

ISSUES OF PERSONALITY ANALYSIS

If the usefulness of personality is going to be adequately evaluated, organizational researchers will need to give greater thought to the nature of personality effects. In this section we discuss three important topics for consideration in personality—OB research, situational strength, dependent variable analysis and interactionism.

Situational Strength

Mischel (1977) has suggested that situations can be characterized by their relative "strength" and he and other personality researchers (Monson, Hesley & Chernick, 1982; Snyder & Ickes, in press; Stagner, 1977); have argued that situational strength moderates trait-behavior relationships. Essentially their position is that certain situations have well recognized and widely accepted rules of conduct which constrain and direct behavior. In such situations interindividual variability in behavior is low and personality differences are likely to have little predictive power. Other situations are more ambiguously structured, allowing for variation in meaning and behavior and better prediction from personality constructs.

Mischel (1977) has provided the clearest specification of differences between the two types of situations. For Mischel strong (powerful) situations:

1. Lead everyone to construe the situation the same way.
2. Induce uniform expectancies regarding appropriate response patterns.
3. Provide adequate incentives for the performance of that response pattern.
4. Require skills that everyone has.

In contrast, weak situations:

1. Are not uniformly encoded.
2. Do not generate uniform expectancies.
3. Do not offer incentives for performance.
4. Fail to provide the learning conditions necessary for successful genesis of the behavior.

To illustrate the effects of situational strength, Monson et al. (1982) have examined the relationship between extroversion and talkativeness in strong and weak situations they created in the laboratory. In two strong situation conditions, confederates conversing with a volunteer subject directed their conversation toward or away from topics which were known, by prior assessment, to interest the subject. In a weak situation condition, confederates neither encouraged nor discouraged conversation. As predicted, the correlation between extroversion and talkativeness was r = .56 in the weak situation but averaged only r = .24 in the two strong situations.

Differences between strong and weak situations raise a number of issues relevant to analyzing personality effects on organizational behavior. Perhaps most obvious is the problem of interpreting personality findings generated in typical laboratory studies. The laboratory is a place for testing theory–derived predictions under controlled conditions. As such, it can be and has been a useful setting for studying personality and work behavior. However, that usefulness is often attenuated by failure to consider the strength of the laboratory situation and the importance of representative design.

It is easy to recognize that in any experiment, the variance attributable to persons, situations, and interactions is as much a function of the researcher's ingenuity as it is the validity of theoretical propositions. Yet, laboratory research on personality and organizational behavior has frequently ignored the implications of this basic point. In the experimental tradition, as Cronbach noted some years ago (Cronbach, 1957), individual differences are an annoyance and substantial effort is devoted to the maximization of variance due to experimental conditions. Essentially, the aim of the typical laboratory experiment is the creation of strong situations guided by theoretical propositions, and success is gauged by whether the situations are as strong as theory would suggest they should be. As a result, the typical laboratory experiment is a situation where personality effects are going to be minimized. This is clearly appropriate for certain types of hypotheses. Frequently however, researchers interested in studying personality and personality-situation interactions have unthinkingly tried to graft personality hypotheses onto typical experimental procedures, creating artificially strong manipulations and using homogeneous samples with restricted variance on the individual difference variable. The potential for misrepresentation of personality effects in such experimental situations is obvious. This is not to say that laboratory settings are inappropriate for testing general theoretical propositions about personality effects. Ickes' (in press) weak situation paradigm in which spontaneous behavior among interactants is assessed and predicted with good success in an unstructured laboratory situation well illustrates that point.

We have so far limited our discussion to problems associated with examining general theoretical propositions. However, frequently our laboratory studies are implicitly intended to describe the effects of personality in some target situation, even if that target is more conceptual than real. Under these conditions, our research becomes more particularistic than universalistic (Kruglanski, 1975) and we must be careful to create settings which are representative (Brunswick, 1956) of the target. This obviously does not imply the inappropriateness of laboratory abstractions. It does imply that those abstractions must be operationalized with manipulations which approximate differences manifested in the situation to which we wish to generalize. Similar considerations of representativeness must be applied to the personality variable (not necessarily the persons) as well.

Organizational settings are characterized by neither Ickes' "weak situation" nor the strong conditions of typical laboratory experiments. Organizational settings do, however, differ in situational strength and laboratory researchers should pay more attention to the parameters of "real world" strength in designing their experimental conditions. Failure to do so can easily lead to misinterpretation of results.

A clear illustration of this point is provided by Ganster's (1980) laboratory experiment investigating the moderating influences of various personality dimensions on perceptions of, and reactions to, task characteristics. Using a between–groups design, subjects were assigned to either a "fairly complex electronic assembly operation" (high scope task) or a parts identification and sorting task (low scope task). Protestant Ethic, Growth Need Strength, Need for Achievement and Sensation Seeking Tendency were examined as predictors of task satisfaction and perceptions of task characteristics and as moderators of the relationships among task manipulations, perceptions and satisfaction. The results of the study showed weak and generally inconsistent personality effects. Across experimental conditions, very small main effects on satisfaction and perception were found. Only one moderating influence was shown and this was in the direction opposite to what was predicted.

Ganster's findings suggest the relative unimportance of personality for predicting reactions to task design interventions. However, this conclusion must be tempered in light of the extremely strong, nonrepresentative manipulations. The difference between an electronic assembly task and a parts sorting task seems particularly nonrepresentative of probable job changes in organizations. Indeed, Ganster notes that the extremely strong manipulations were created to deliberately represent a wide range of core dimensions. The strength of the manipulations is seen by their accounting for between 45% and 74% of the variance in task perceptions and 58% of the variance in satisfaction. Using perceptions of the four core dimensions as predictors of satisfaction resulted in a multiple correlation of R = .84.

Clearly, Ganster produced an extremely strong manipulation of task differences which could easily eliminate the possibility for more than trivial personality main or moderator effects. While his attempt to break away from the correlational design which has characterized the job scope literature is laudable, his failure to consider the impact of the strength or the representativeness of his manipulations reduces the meaningfulness of his results. This seems particularly unfortunate and unnecessary in the task design area where so much parametric data is available to the researcher. JDS scores are available for many different jobs. It should be possible to examine the representativeness of laboratory manipulations by comparing the JDS scores of experimental tasks, or at least JDS differences between tasks, with scores from actual jobs or reported score changes after real redesign interventions. Group differences in the laboratory would then represent the changes likely to occur as a result of typical task redesign efforts. Such representative designs would take advantage of experimental control while, at the same time, providing more meaningful information about the importance of personality effects outside the laboratory.

Although the topic of situational strength quite naturally leads to a discussion of appropriate experimental design, it should not be forgotten that this is more than a methodological issue. It is also a conceptual issue of the extent of behavioral constraint in organizations and the relative importance of personality differences in organizational situations characterized by more or less constraint. Theoretically, it should be possible to scale work situations in terms of underlying strength and thereby predict personality-behavior relationships. The ability to do this will help us learn about the way both personality and situations influence behavior. However, operationalizing the theoretical construct of situational strength in an organizationally relevant way seems to us to be a particularly difficult task, one which will require extensive work on three distinct problems.

First, a clear specification of the differences between strong and weak situations at the theoretical level is needed. While Mischel's delineation is a useful beginning, it is ambiguous and uninformative in places. For manipulations. The difference between an electronic assembly task and a parts sorting task seems particularly nonrepresentative of probable job changes in organizations. Indeed, Ganster notes that the extremely strong manipulations were created to deliberately represent a wide range of core dimensions. The strength of the manipulations is seen by their accounting for between 45% and 74% of the variance in task perceptions and 58% of the variance in satisfaction. Using perceptions of the four core dimensions as predictors of satisfaction resulted in a multiple correlation of R = .84.

Clearly, Ganster produced an extremely strong manipulation of task differences which could easily eliminate the possibility for more than trivial personality main or moderator effects. While his attempt to break away from the correlational design which has characterized the job scope literature is laudable, his failure to consider the impact of the strength or the representativeness of his manipulations reduces the meaningfulness of his results. This seems particularly unfortunate and unnecessary in the task design area where so much parametric data is available to the researcher. JDS scores are available for many different jobs. It should be possible to examine the representativeness of laboratory manipulations by comparing the JDS scores of experimental tasks, or at least JDS differences between tasks, with scores from actual jobs or reported score changes after real redesign interventions. Group differences in the laboratory would then represent the changes likely to occur as a result of typical task redesign efforts. Such representative designs would take advantage of experimental control while, at the same time, providing more meaningful information about the importance of personality effects outside the laboratory.

Although the topic of situational strength quite naturally leads to a discussion of appropriate experimental design, it should not be forgotten that this is more than a methodological issue. It is also a conceptual issue of the extent of behavioral constraint in organizations and the relative importance of personality differences in organizational situations characterized by more or less constraint. Theoretically, it should be possible to scale work situations in terms of underlying strength and thereby predict personality-behavior relationships. The ability to do this will help us learn about the way both personality and situations influence behavior. However, operationalizing the theoretical construct of situational strength in an organizationally relevant way seems to us to be a particularly difficult task, one which will require extensive work on three distinct problems.

First, a clear specification of the differences between strong and weak situations at the theoretical level is needed. While Mischel's delineation is a useful beginning, it is ambiguous and uninformative in places. For

Dependent Variables Analysis

Any attempt to integrate personality constructs into theories of organizational behavior must pay particular attention to certain critical dimensions of the dependent variables. Generally organizational researchers are only superficially aware of the way differences in their dependent variables influence differences in the types of explanatory constructs which will be useful. Obviously certain behaviors are likely to be predictable by some personality constructs and not others. However this simply scratches the surface of the dependent variable issue. We will illustrate by discussing the relevance of three general dimensions of dependent variable analysis—aggregation, differences between means and variance in behavior and time of collection. The first issue has generated the most research in the personality literature and will therefore be discussed at length. The latter two will be more briefly presented in the hope of stimulating work on the general problem of dependent variable analysis.

Aggregation. Implicit in the definition of traits is consistency. It is therefore not suprising that the most persuasive argument against the usefulness of traits has centered on the prevalence of cross-situational variability in behavior (Mischel, 1968; 1973). It is also not surprising that defenders of traits have expended much effort in analyzing the issue of consistency and trying to demonstrate the logical and empirical weaknesses of Mischel's position.

Mischel argued that personality traits are thought of as broad underlying dispositions that exert a generalized influence on behavior. As a result, "data that demonstrate strong generality in the behavior of the same person across many situations are critical for trait and state personality theories; the construct of personality itself rests on the belief that individual behavior consistencies exist widely and account for much of variance in behavior" (Mischel, 1968, p. 13). However, Mischel argued, existing evidence for consistency in behavior, particularly across situations and measurement modes, is weak, indicating the lack of explanatory and predictive utility of trait constructs.

Responses to Mischel's critique have taken many forms. The most cogent logical arguments have revolved around the multiple meanings of "consistency" and the restrictive nature of Mischel's use of the term. So, for example, a number of researchers have drawn distinctions between absolute consistency (low within person variance in behavior across situations) and relative consistency (stable rank orderings among people across situations) suggesting that it is the latter rather than the former which is implied by trait concepts. Still others have pointed to the distinction between constructs and the behaviors they are meant to explain. According to this position, the utility of traits is not assessed by the degree of behavioral consistency but rather by the explanatory power of theoretical systems in which these constructs are embedded. Traits at the mediating level can be stable yet interact with other traits and situational factors to produce behavioral diversity (Endler & Magnusson, 1977).

In a series of influential papers, Epstein (1977, 1979, 1980) has empirically examined the issue of consistency in a manner which he believes to be more appropriate to a dispositional conception of personality than that used in studies cited by Mischel. Epstein points out that traits are aggregate concepts. They focus on consistent patterns or tendencies in behavior. However, consistency has typically been inappropriately evaluated by correlating data (behaviors, personality measures, etc.) at two points in time. The resulting correlation, usually no higher than r = .30, has then been unjustifiably taken to indicate behavioral inconsistency. For Epstein, a more appropriate test of consistency is to examine correlations between behavior indices aggregated across multiple occasions. Such aggregations have greater reliability and better operationalize the dispositional quality of traits. Epstein (1977) supports his argument with data showing that when behavioral measures are collected over several occasions and aggregated into composite scores, their stability increases and so do their correlations with personality predictors.

Jaccard (1977), building on work by Fishbein and Ajzen (1974), has advanced a taxonomy of behavioral measures that extends Epstein's aggregation concepts and specifies the types of criteria most likely to be predictable from personality variables. Jaccard begins by presenting a matrix of behaviors (rows) and occasions (columns) and uses it to distinguish among a number of different behavioral criteria. The simplist type in Jaccard's taxonomy consists of single–act, single observation criteria. As Epstein (1979) notes, personality variables are unlikely to predict criteria of this sort. Jaccard's second type of criterion involves aggregation of observations of the same behavior repeated over multiple occasions (single–act repeated observation). These multiple occasions can be homogeneous, the same behavior in the same replicated situation, or heterogeneous, the same behavior in different situations. Epstein's operations use this approach to criterion measurement—aggregating observations collected over a period of several days. Jaccard then extends single–act/repeated–observation measures to describe multiple act criteria. In his matrix, the rows represent separate behaviors that are viewed as being different manifestations of the same trait. Multiple–act criteria are aggregated across these different behaviors and thereby operationalize "behavioral patterns" consistent with the underlying trait. Again, these multiple–act criteria can be aggregated across homogeneous and heterogeneous occasions, producing multiple–act/repeated–observation criteria. Jaccard argues that multiple act criteria are operationalizations most compatable with the definition of traits as broad underlying dispositions. He suggests therefore that multiple–act/repeated–observation criteria would be most appropriate for personality research.

The logic of Epstein's and Jaccard's position clearly suggests that personality should be a better predictor of aggregated behavioral indices than of measurement of single behaviors or behaviors over a short period of time. Data supporting the increased predictability of aggregated indices by personality is provided by McGowan and Gormly (1976) and Jaccard (1974). McGowan and Gormly obtained peer ratings of students' energy levels and then collected observations on five energy–related behaviors (i.e. walking speed, posture adjustments during class). The energy ratings correlated r = .70 with the multiple–act criterion aggregated over the five behaviors but averaged only r = .43 with the five components. Jaccard (1974) created a "dominance" relevant multiple-act criterion by asking undergraduates to generate a list of behaviors they thought "dominant" and "non dominant" females would perform. A second group of undergraduates filled out the resulting 40 behavior checklist and three different measures of dominance. For each of these measures the correlation with the multiple-act criterion was substantially greater than the average correlation with the individual behaviors. So, for example, one measure of dominance correlated r = .64 with the multiple-act criterion but averaged r = .20 with the individual behaviors.

The relevance of this work on criterion aggregation to organizational behavior is clear. Criteria of interest to organizations vary in their degree of aggregation over time and situations. For example, one can think of a dimension anchored by task performance at a single time or day and career performance or progress. The latter aggregated criteria are likely to be more predictable from personality than the former criteria. Yet often only short term criteria are used to examine personality effects on organizational behavior.

Research on goal setting and individual differences well illustrates this point. In this area, as in others, studies of personality effects have typically relied on single act measures. One can distinguish, however, between the goal an individual might set for a specific task versus the general level of goals he has set for the many tasks he has performed on his job over an extended period, a year, for example, or a career. Often organizations are interested in the latter while research on personality and goal setting typically uses the former. The results of that research might therefore provide a distorted picture of the role of personality.

We have recently examined this issue with regard to self esteem and goal setting (Adler & Weiss, Note 1). Subjects set goals for each of three trials on anagram and creativity tasks. Single–act/single–observation criteria of goals set and performance on single trials were assessed. Single–act/repeated–observation criteria in homogeneous situations were operationalized by averaging goals over trials and performance over trials for each task. Single–act/repeated–observation criteria in heterogeneous situations were measured by aggregating across trials and tasks for both goals and performance. The effects of aggregation can be seen in the correlations presented in Table 1. Interestingly, aggregation over repeated wrials of the same task (homogeneous situations) had only a negligible effect on the correlations with self esteem. On the other hand, aggregation across different tasks (heterogeneous situations) produced substantially stronger correlations (r = .46 for self esteem and goals and r = .50 for self esteem and performance). We note that these correlations are much higher than those usually found in laboratory studies of goal setting and personality.

For conceptual as well as psychometric (see Ghiselli, Campbell & Zedeck, 1981) reasons, organizational researchers should pay particular attention to the level of aggregation in their dependent variable. However, we caution that researchers not treat aggregation as a gimmick designed to improve prediction from personality. They should instead remain cognizant of the meaning and the importance of criteria created by different types of aggregation. Certainly our operationalizations must be understood as simply "slices" from an ongoing stream of behavior. Different researchers create units of varying size depending on needs and objectives (Turner, 1965). For the experimental psychologist, a blink of the eye is a unit of relevance. For the organizational researcher, career progress may be the cut of greatest interest. However, the fact that our criterion

Table 1. Correlations of Self Esteem with Goals
and Performance as a Function of Criterion
Aggregation

Criteria	Goals	Performance
Single Observation		
Anagram	.30[1]	.16[1]
Creativity	.24[1]	.27[1]
Multiple Observation—Homogenous Situations		
Anagram	.34	.18
Creativity	.30	.34
Multiple Observation—Heterogeneous Situations		
Anagram and Creativity	.46	.50

[1] Average Correlations.

units are creations of the researcher does not in any sense suggest that these units are arbitrary. We can aggregate behaviors and increase reliability and predictability but we should not do this if there is a cost in meaningfulness.

We believe that personality researchers who have studied the issue of aggregation have been deficient in this regard, often implicitly inverting the typical research problem. That is, the appropriate question of whether personality predicts a particular criterion chosen on the basis of practical or theoretical importance is often reversed to become "how can we operationalize behavior so that it is predictable from personality?" While advocating aggregation, they have ignored the key issue of the conceptual importance of the newly created dependent variable.

Jaccard's (1977) typology is illustrative. Jaccard argues that multiple-act/repeated–observation criteria come closest to operationalizing the dispositional quality of traits and they should therefore be used in evaluating the usefulness of personality. Jaccard is probably right when he suggests that multiple–act criteria are more closely related to personality than other criteria. Yet this is exactly the wrong reason for choosing dependent variables. We would argue that for most (but not all) organizational problems, single–act/repeated–observations across heterogeneous situations are more likely to be theoretically relevant aggregations. Goal setting, conformity and information search may all be organizational manifestations of self esteem, yet an aggregate of all these behaviors would be less than meaningful for most organizational problems. More meaningful would be goal setting over time and situations or conformity over time and situations.

Additionally, even when we focus on single behaviors we must be vigilant in questioning the relevance of aggregation. Sometimes we are interested in operationalizing longer term trends, patterns or averages. Our example of career performance is relevant here. In other cases we are less interested in understanding response trends than we are in predicting single instances. So, for example, aggregating responses to emergencies would make little sense since we are more interested in knowing how a person will respond in each instance. Analysis of this issue suggests to us that legitimately aggregated variables are typically ones where higher values at one time can compensate for lower values of at another. Variables which do not lend themselves to aggregation do not allow for compensation across instances. This, as well as other ways of distinguishing between legitimate and nonlegitimate aggregation, should be explored.

A final point regarding aggregation needs to be made. Often, ratings are used as dependent variables in organizational research involving personality. Since raters implicitly average performance observations collected over time and occasions one might argue that these operationalizations are aggregations and should therefore be more predictable from personality than other types of criteria. We would submit that while ratings are aggregations, they are haphazard aggregations produced by unequal weighting of poorly sampled observations (Ilgen & Feldman, 1983). In these aggregations, the independence of observations is questionable and the effect of time (recency, primacy) is uncontrolled. Equating performance ratings with the type of aggregation implied by this discussion would be inappropriate given current appraisal procedures.

Performance Distributions. The assessment of inconsistency in performance has recently been advocated by Kane and Lawler (1979). While their discussion focuses on subjective appraisals, much of what they say applies to any type of performance measurement system. Essentially their point is that most appraisal systems require that a distribution of performance relevant behavioral instances be summarized with a single index representing average or typical performance, much as a mean is used to represent the central tendency of an array of scores. However, just as score arrays have other parameters, so too do distributions of performance instances. Kane and Lawler argue that organizations should expand their performance measurement systems to include characteristics of performance distributions in addition to central tendencies. Specifically, they argue that for many situations, the variation in performance—signaling unpredictability—is a relevant performance parameter. Presumably meaningful differences exist among employees in the distribution of their performances across instances in addition to differences in average performance levels. In many cases, organizations would be well advised to pay attention to these differences in performance variance.

The debate among personality researchers over behavioral consistency has generated a great deal of research on individual differences in consistency that has relevance for understanding variations in performance distributions. This research has taken two distinct paths. One path begins with the work reported by Bem and Allen (1974). They argue that the lack of consistency among supposed trait indicators may result from a fallacious assumption that each trait dimension is equally relevant for describing all assessees. They argue that not all traits are relevant to all individuals and therefore the utility of any particular trait is limited to that subgroup to whom the trait applies. For those individuals, and only for those individuals, consistency among trait indicators is expected. Bem and Allen provided empirical support for their position by simply asking people how consistently friendly they were from situation to situation. Answers to this simple question were used to form subgroups of consistent and nonconsistent respondents, presumably reflecting differences in trait relevance. Subgroup analyses indicated that reports of friendliness from various observers (mother, father, peers, etc.) showed higher correlations among those who described themselves as consistent than among those who did not. Similarly for the group characterized as consistent, friendliness behavior was substantially more predictable from standardized measures of friendliness and extroversion.

Bem and Allen are often mistakenly understood as suggesting that there are individual differences in consistency. In fact, they do not suggest that people differ in their level of behavioral consistency but rather that what appears to be inconsistency reflects instead a difference between the researcher's and respondent's definition of consistency. The Bem and Allen position rests on a constructual nature of traits, regarding traits as researcher–created constructs formed by an "investigator's partitioning of behaviors into the same equivalence class" (p. 509). According to Bem and Allen, individuals can be quite consistent "within themselves" but be inconsistent in terms of the investigator's construct. This latter inconsistency neither invalidates the concept of personality nor the usefulness of the investigator's trait. It does however limit that trait's usefulness to certain individuals.

In contrast to the Bem and Allen position, a number of researchers have suggested the existence of stable, predictable differences in behavioral consistency. In their view, some people are more dispositional; more influenced by internal personality factors and others are more situational; responsive to demands and differences among situations. Dispositional individuals are more likely to demonstrate cross–situational consistency and their behavior is more likely to be predictable from standard trait measures than situational individuals. In effect, what is being suggested is a personality trait of the most general kind—individual differences in the degree of dispositional behavior. Some researchers, in fact, have had a fair amount of success classifying people into these two types. The most extensive and successful work in this area has been done by Snyder and his colleagues using the personality dimension of self–monitoring (Snyder, 1974). High self–monitors are guided more by situational cues than low self–monitors and their behaviors are generally less consistent across situations and less predictable from personality traits than low self–monitors. A similar pattern of results has been found using the personality dimension of private self–consciousness (Fenigstein, Scheier, & Buss, 1975). (A recent review of the work on both dimensions as moderators of personality behavior relationships is found in Snyder & Ickes, in press.)

While theoretical differences exist between the Bem and Allen position and the consistency–as–trait position, the results of the research guided by both positions has demonstrated the same thing—individual differences in cross situational consistency exist and can be predicted. In the Bem and Allen case, these differences are quite trait–specific. In the cases of self–monitoring and self–consciousness, the differences at least are presented as being quite general.

The recognition of performance variability as an important criterion of work behavior quite naturally leads to an appreciation of the personality research on differences in behavioral consistency. However, the translation of that research to the study of performance distributions is substantially more complex than any surface similarity would suggest. The major complicating factor is, of course, the difference between performance and behavior. Performance results from the interaction of behavior and task demands. If task demands or behavioral requirements were constant over all potential performance instances, behavioral variability might translate into performance variability. Obviously such is not the case, and therefore the extent to which predictors of behavioral consistency also predict performance variability will depend upon the variance in behavioral requirements across the potential performance instances of a job. In certain jobs, behavioral consistency will produce wide variations in performance as individuals respond with a characteristic behavior pattern in both appropriate and inappropriate situations. For other jobs, the behavioral requirements for efficient performance may be similar across seemingly disparate situations. Here, behavioral consistency might directly translate to performance consistency. On the first job, we might expect self–monitoring or self–consciousness to be negatively correlated with performance variance. On the second job, our expectation would be for a positive correlation.

To summarize: in our opinion, performance consistency is a potentially important dependent variable for organizational research. As researchers begin to analyze differences in this type of criterion, they might profitably look to the personality research on behavioral consistency. However, in doing so they would be advised to remember the distinction between behavior and performance and not expect simple predictability of performance consistency paralleling the predictions of behavioral consistency in the personality research. Analyses of task requirements, situational variability and expected intercorrelations among trait indicators will be necessary and, as with other personality effects, interactions are more likely than main effects.

Time.   Finally, the time at which the dependent variable is collected is a critical issue for the explanatory usefulness of personality. An old, generally ignored, but insightful paper by Weitz (1966) first raised this issue in the context of selection and criterion evaluation. It has relevance to organizational phenomena as well. Weitz' major point was that different types of predictors will be more or less valid (predictive of the criterion) depending upon when the criterion is measured. If measured early in the workers' tenure, aptitude differences will be more predictive and personality less predictive. If measured later, aptitude differences will account for less variance (job experience will wash out meaningful initial aptitude differences) and personality, as an influence on motivation in Weitz's discussion, will explain more variance.

Recent papers by Katz (1980) and Organ (1981) have raised this issue again in the context of individual and situational influences at different career points. Both discussions suggest that situational factors have a greater influence on the behavior of new workers than do individual difference variables such as personality. This proposition follows from the idea (expressed also by Louis, 1980; Weiss, 1977, 1978) that the new work situation generates a good deal of uncertainty with prior experience providing insufficient cues for behavioral guidance. Under such conditions, individuals become particularly attentive to external sources of information, making them susceptible to what Katz refers to as "situational control."

We believe that this description of the psychological state and behavioral requirements of new workers, along with the contrasting views of the states and requirements of more advanced workers, is essentially correct and has important implications for personality research and the likelihood of discovering personality effects. However, we think that the implications of career stage differences for personality research lie less with expected differences in the global role of "personality" than with the relevance of different types of personality variables at different points in the worker's job tenure. It would be a mistake to assume that the conceptual distinction between strong and weak situations can easily be mapped onto career stages. While Katz' description might suggest that "strength" is greatest earlier in one's career, decreases in the ambiguity of reward structures and greater acceptance of norms over time might suggest the opposite (Note 2). Forcing an artificial correspondence between tenure and situational strength will close our thinking to important personality and situational effects at all career stages.

For example, Katz's discussion about the prevalence of uncertainty and the search for informational cues among new workers suggests not so much the absence of important personality effects as that those effects might be found among variables assessing differences in uncertainty (self-esteem, for example,) or reflecting differences in the weight given to various types of information likely to be encountered during search. In this vein, Weiss (1977, 1978) has found that self-esteem predicts the degree of imitation of role models among workers and has suggested that this effect results from differences in uncertainty and uncertainty inspired search (Weiss & Knight, 1980). In addition, Weiss and Shaw (1979) have shown that field independence predicts the weight given to social information in judgments of task characteristics. Katz' own work (Katz, 1978) on the different issues which concern workers at different career points also suggests the relevance of career stages to understanding the importance of different aspects of personality. We therefore agree with Katz that the combining of respondents at different career points may well mask important differences in individual and situational influences on behavior. We believe, however, that the problem is which personality variables are operating not whether personality is operating.

Adequate evaluation of personality influences on reactions to organizational interventions also requires awareness of temporal effects. Manipulation strength may dissipate over time, turning initially strong situations into weaker ones and allowing both main and interactive effects of personality to emerge.

Finally, time is a critical issue for any analysis of dynamic interaction. If individuals to any extent modify and influence the situations they encounter, that process must be studied longitudinally. Cross–sectional analyses will not capture the dynamic interaction process. In addition, if one suspects that interventions are likely to be modified as a result of individual dispositions, not an unreasonable suspicion, research must be conducted with appropriate time intervals built into the design. Similar sensitivity to appropriate intervals must characterize those studies which examine long-term personality changes that occur as a result of organizational experiences. We must admit that we have no guidelines to offer about appropriate time frames for studying these issues. We would simply advise researchers to be cognizant and active on this issue.

Personality—Situation Interactionism

Much of the creativity in personality theory over the past decade and a half was stimulated by Mischel's (1968) critique of personality research. The ensuing controversy over whether personality or situation is the more important determinant of behavior is now generally recognized as a pseudoissue. This controversy revolved around the percentage of criterion variance accounted for by personality and situational factors. However, we have seen that in any given study these percentages may be affected by restrictions of range in the personality variable, level of criterion aggregation, situationally imposed constraints on behavior and other factors unrelated to the relative importance of personality or situation as a determinant of behavior.

The personality-situation debate has been an important stimulus to the development of a new model of personality: interactionism (Endler & Magnusson, 1976). Interactional psychology sees behavior as being determined by "a complex interplay of situations and persons" (Magnusson

& Endler, 1977). In a previous volume of this series, Schneider (1983) has noted some important implications of interactionism for the field of organizational behavior. Rather than restating the basic propositions of interactional psychology, the reader is referred to Schneider's (1983) summary or to more extensive discussions in Endler and Magnusson (1976), Magnusson and Endler (1977) or Pervin and Lewis (1978). Our purpose here is to focus on two key aspects of interactionism and discuss their implications for the study of personality and organizational behavior.

Person and Situation Inextrixably Linked in Determining Behavior. As we have seen, OB theory and research generally treat personality and situational variables as independent from one another. Personality-situation interaction, when studied at all, is defined as mechanistic interaction, the nonadditive joint contribution of a personality-situation interaction term within the general least squares (ANOVA or moderated regression) model (Terborg, 1981). The assumption is that the distinct contributions of personality and situations can be individually identified. In contrast, interactionists argue that personality and situation are inherently inseparable. This is true in two important senses.

For one, as Weick (1979) has argued, situations are enacted: that is they are our cognitive constructions of the environment. The actor brackets the ongoing stream of experience, imposes structure, and attaches meaning to the components of that structure. For each individual, his construal of the environment is the situation. In this way of thinking it makes little sense to speak of the situation as being apart from personality. A basic element of interactionism then is that "on the situation side, the psychological meaning of situations for the individual is the important determining factor (Magnusson & Endler, 1977, p. 4)."

A second sense of personality-situation linkage relates to the dynamic interaction designs that we have been discussing all along, the notion of continuous reciprocal influence. In Weick's (1979) words, "the actor does something that produces an ecological change, which change then constrains what he does next, which in turn produces a further ecological change, and so on (p. 130)." Green's (1976) analysis of role-making and Porter, Lawler and Hackman's (1975) discussion of the complementary processes of organizational socialization and individualism capture this sense of dynamic interactionism. In these approaches, the organizational environment is seen to exert pressures toward change on the new member while the new member in turn seeks to place his stamp on the organizational environment. As opposed to person-job matching which is conceived as a one-time fit, the interactionist view is of ongoing change, mutual influence and person-situation accomodation (Schneider, 1983). Although the importance of dynamic interactionism has been recognized in theory, we have seen little use of the dynamic interaction design in research, as our earlier review indicated. To move ahead in this area, we need to see more programatic longitudinal research. Programatic because, while our theory may speak of bidirectional influence, any one study might choose to focus on specific, directional effects. It is only through the systemic accumulation of studies of this sort that the dynamic interplay of personality, situation, and behavior can be fully captured (Magnusson & Endler, 1977). Longitudinal, since personality is by definition relatively stable and will be affected only gradually. Sudden enduring changes in personality traits are not to be expected.

Recent developments in statistical analysis may help us better examine such dynamic interactive phenomena. Wolfle and Robertshaw (1982), for example, used LISREL to investigate the interplay of personality and environment in a recent longitudinal study of the effects of college attendance on locus of control. The correlation between college attendance and locus of control measured at a later point was shown to be significant. However, LISREL analysis demonstrated that only 20% of this relation was due to the effects of the college experience on locus of control. Some 80% of the correlation was attributable to the influences of an earlier locus of control score and to ability—both on the decision to attend college and on later locus of control. Kohn and Schooler (1982) used a similar analytic approach called MILS, to estimate the relative influences of personality and job conditions on each other over a ten year period. Through their analysis, the authors were able to identify contemporaneous and lagged effects of personality on job conditions, and job conditions on personality, as well as lagged effects of some personality traits on other traits. These analytical tools may become invaluable to us in our study of such interactions in organizational behavior.

Coherence of Behavior.   One argument against the usefulness of personality traits rests, as we have noted, on the lack of consistency in behavior from situation to situation. According to the interactionist response (Magnusson and Endler, 1977) this argument confuses two classes of variables, mediating variables and reaction variables. Personality dispositions are hypothetical contructs that are seen to act as mediating variables in explaining overt reactions or behavior. The interactionists argue that a lack of consistency at the behavioral level may not reflect a lack of consistency at the mediating level. Inconsistencies in an employee's level of effort from task to task, for example, do not necessarily mean that behavior is wholly determined by situational factors. Nor do Magnusson and Endler (1977), in developing this argument, imply that there is always consistency at the mediating level; merely that there is no simple correspondence between these two levels. Rather than focus on consistency in behavior, we should focus on coherence. Coherence in behavior means that "behavior is inherently lawful and hence predictable without necessarily being stable in either relative or absolute terms. We are referring to patterns of behavior that may vary across situations of various kinds but in which the behavior is coherent and lawful all the same (Magnusson & Endler, 1977, p. 7)." This, then, is a key message of interactionism for the study of personality in organizational behavior. We need to search for coherence of behavior at the mediating level and should not be deterred by inconsistency at the reaction level.

Nygard (1981) gives us a good illustration of the critical role of personality in understanding behavioral coherence in his analysis of Atkinsons's (Atkinson & Raynor, 1978) theory of achievement motivation. The components of this theory include two motivational personality variables: the need for achievement and the motive to avoid failure. Another crucial variable, from which the remaining components of the theory can be derived, is the individual's perception of his probability of succeeding in a particular situation. As Nygard (1981) points out, Atkinson's theory is interactionist par excellence; strong need for achievement does not mean strong effort for all tasks. Rather, the theory specifically predicts little difference in effort between those high and low in need achievement when the perceived probability of task success is close to either 0 or 1. The difference in effort between those with different need for achievement grows as the probability of task success moves toward the .5 level of difficulty. What is important for this discussion, then, is that achievement behavior is lawful, specific behavioral predictions can be made and tested, and that this behavior cannot be understood without considering personality. We believe that this is the role we should be building for personality in our theories of organizational behavior.

EFFICIENT USE OF PERSONALITY CONSTRUCTS

Analysis of the literature on personality and organizational behavior suggests to us that efficient use of personality constructs will require more than a consideration of aggregation or situational strength or dynamic interactionism. Efficient use of personality, in the sense of enhancing theory, will require systematic understanding of the nature of personality constructs and the role these constructs play in explanatory systems. We have neither the space nor the expertise to fully discuss all the relevant philosophical details. The reader is directed toward Alston (1975) and Ryle (1949) for discussions of dispositional concepts and to Beck (1953), Messick (1981), and of course MacCorquodale and Meehl (1948), for discussions on the nature of psychological constructs. However, we do believe that a few issues are worth mentioning in the context of the objectives of this paper.

Personality traits are frequently defined as dispositions to behave in certain ways. That is, as Alston (1975) notes, they are seen as probabilistic "if-then" relationships with the then component referring to a class of multiple, co-varying responses. "To say that X has a certain disposition is to assert a hypothetical proposition, a proposition that if X is in a certain type of situation (S) X will emit a certain type of response (R)." (Alston, 1975, p. 19) Often, to move personality traits beyond being solely inductive summaries of stimulus–response relationships, the concep of "underlying state" is added to the definition.

Mischel (1968, 1973) uses this type of definition in formulating his attack on traits. He states:

> Personality comprises broad underlying dispositions which pervasively influence the individual's behavior across many situations and lead to consistency in his behavior.
>
> Mischel, 1973, p. 253

Aside from the problem of operationally defining "broad' or "consistency" such a dispositional definition is misleading because it does not capture how personality concepts are actually used by personality theorists, it confuses the explanatory construct (trait) with the phenomenon being explained (behavior patterns) and, in so doing, restricts the nature of confirming and disconfirming evidence. So, for example, by including cross–situational consistency in his definition of traits, Mischel is able to argue against their validity by reporting evidence of inconsistency. We might respond by arguing that Mischel's data regarding consistency was inappropriate (following Epstein, 1977, or Jaccard, 1977). However, such a response would not be necessary because, as we have seen in our discussion of interactionism, trait concepts do not necessarily imply cross–situational consistency.

Personality traits are theoretical constructs. These constructs are used to refer to attributes of people. They are presumed to be stable but not necessarily unchangeable. Like all theoretical constructs, they are inferred from observables or sets of observables but are not equivalent to these operationalizations (MacCorquodale & Meehl, 1948). They derive their meaning from their position in larger theoretical systems.

Obviously, if these constructs are to be of any value they must enter into lawful functional relationships with other theoretical and observable variables. But to say that they have lawful relations with observable behavior is not to say that the relationships are of the cross–situational consistency variety outlined by Mischel. It is to say that from operational assessments of the theoretical construct and from knowledge of the functional relationships of that construct to other constructs in the system and from operationalizations of those other constructs, one can derive behavioral predictions for specific settings. The predictions can be used to test the theoretical propositions, including those related to the personality construct, and the explanatory usefulness of the system and its components can be assessed.

We should note that organizational researchers use many types of theoretical constructs that have no greater logical claim to usefulness than do personality constructs. Skills, abilities and aptitudes are notable examples. These are also unobservable hypothetical constructs inferred from overt behavior and deriving their meaning from their position in theoretical systems. Yet we have rarely questioned the legitimacy of these constructs in explanatory systems. Why? To us, the answer lies more in the current empirical rather than logical superiority of ability constructs.

In thinking about appropriate constructs, it is useful to remember that it makes little sense to worry about the "reality" of personality traits. Reality is, of course, impossible to determine and a personality trait, like any theoretical construct, can be judged only in terms of the explanatory usefulness of the theoretical system of which it is a part. This is not to say that a presumption of reality cannot sometimes be helpful. Such a presumption can result in the discovery of more basic processes. Additionally, thinking in terms of analogous "real" structures can help us cognitively by allowing us to think about personality in the same way we like to think about environments. However, such thinking can just as easily be disruptive when it restricts theory to mechanistic process orientations or leads to extensive unproductive searches for microstructures. We should note, parenthetically, that the environmental characteristics we include in our theories—such things as skill variety, role conflict, and reward structure—have no better claim to reality than personality traits. Essentially, both personal and situational characteristics are constructs that are understandable only in terms of theory (Turner, 1965). This is not to argue for or against the ultimate reality of some constructs but simply to say that reality is not a criterion of scientific explanation. As Einstein (1938) stated:

> In our endeavor to understand reality we are somewhat like a man trying to understand the mechanism of a closed watch. He sees the face and the moving hands, even hears the ticking, but he has no way of opening the case. (p. 31)

If theoretical constructs derive their meaning from the interlocking set of theoretical and empirical laws in which they play a part, then a "necessary condition for a construct to be scientifically admissable is that it occur in a nomological net at least some of whose laws involve observables" (Cronbach & Meehl, 1955). While personality constructs all have the same theoretical status, clearly there are differences in the extensiveness of the networks and therefore the meaningfulness of the constructs.

To us, recognition of the importance of theoretical systems in the meaning of constructs is the critical issue for the productive use of personality in organizational behavior. Specifically, we see three critical implications. Obviously, we need to use personality indices that have good construct validity. This is so well understood by the field that it is simply astounding how frequently it is ignored. Even a cursory examination of the literature indicates that the choice of measures is less a function of its construct validity than its use in previous studies, reported coefficient alpha levels, or the availability of enough copies of the instrument.

However, the issue of adequate theoretical systems suggests more than choosing measures with adequate construct validity. It means we have to stop treating construct validity as if it were a property of the measure only and use the construct validity evidence, the whole network, as an aid to our thinking about organizational phenomena. Every time we find a personality effect, we tie two sets of laws together: those that relate to the organizational problem and those that relate to the personality construct. The nomological network that is provided to us by the personality construct can become an invaluable tool in helping derive an appropriate explanatory system for our organizational problem. An empirical finding of a relationship between a personality construct and an organizational behavior (be it main effect or interactive) puts that behavior into the nomological network of the personality construct, suggesting new potential relationships and ways of expanding the explanatory system for the organizational phenomenon of interest. Similarly, although less efficiently, the absence of an effect suggests areas where explanation is less likely to be found. It makes sense therefore in developing our theories and choosing our personality variables to focus on constructs and measures with well worked out nomological nets and use those nets to our advantage.

In our opinion, this use of personality constructs is rarely done in organizational research. Too often, a personality variable is created solely for use within a particular theory of work behavior (Growth Need Strength for job scope or LPC for leadership) and its network therefore contains only relationships within the theory. In such a case, the personality variable may help account for more variance but it will not provide additional heuristic information. Other times, an external personality variable, often with reasonably extensive construct validity evidence, is brought into a theoretical system, either conceptually or empirically, but the construct validity evidence is only superficially alluded to or ignored. Examples are the use of self-esteem and need achievement in goal-setting research. Treating the variable in isolation of its theoretical context expands neither the network of the personality construct nor the organizational behavior.

Finally, a third implication for efficient use of personality in OB is derived from analysis of the constructual nature of personality. Theoretical constructs are unobservables that are inferred from observable indicants. For any theoretical system, a set of correspondence rules exists by which a theoretical term is translated to an observable or set of observables so that theoretical laws can be used to derive empirical relationships. We know that our measures obviously are not equivalent to our constructs and we also know that as signs of the constructs, they are often flawed. Recognition of this should, but rarely does, lead to the use of multiple indicants. As we have already discussed, much of our personality research in OB is instrument–bound. Progress will require using multiple operationalizations within and across studies.

Our reading of the OB literature suggests that the most critical need in creating a more productive role for personality is to begin thinking more deeply and creatively about where personality fits in our individual theories of organizational behavior and about the personality constructs we use. We are not arguing that personality must always occupy a central role. We are arguing against the continued treatment of personality as ad hoc, scattered, shotgun attempts to predict behavior or as appendages to existing research designs.

Part of the discipline of thinking through the role assigned to personality involves the specification of the linkages between the personality construct and other theoretical constructs. Even when the ultimate purpose of our research is pure prediction, as in the selection context, our efforts will be more efficient if we analyze the steps by which personality ultimately influences performance in a particular job over a given period of time. We suspect that had researchers invested in such thought more often, many of the negative or inconsistent findings that have emerged from personality research would have been avoided. How can we do a better job of thinking through the role of personality in our theories of work behavior? Obviously, all of the issues we have discussed are relevant. However, two additional points need to be made:

1. Theory before Design. We should not commit ourselves to a particular design for the study of personality until we have first developed our preliminary conceptual ideas about the influence of personality constructs. For a long while, the direct–effects design dominated research. Disappointment with the results of simple bivariate research, an increasing appreciation for the complexity of factors determining work behavior and advances in computer technology that have facilitated application of multivariate analyses have led to an increased commitment to the mechanistic interaction design. The inclusion of more independent variables, however, does not inevitably lead to more careful thinking about the role played by personality factors. Once we have freed ourselves from a commitment to a particular design, we can think creatively about where personality should fit within a useful explanatory system, (e.g., centrally, peripherally, direct effect, interactive effect). Theory before design also means that we cannot productively study personality effects in contexts designed to examine other issues. Research settings must be appropriate for personality manifestations as suggested by our theories.

2. *Theory before Measurement.* As we have seen in our review, personality research in specific areas is often dominated by particular types of constructs and specific measures. Clearly, personality constructs are of various sorts with different expected effects on behavior. It might be useful to think first in terms of types of constructs before focusing on any particular construct. In any case, as discussed earlier, we should be attracted to personality constructs with well developed nomological nets. Drawing from such constructs will improve our chances of attaining meaningful findings and, in turn, our research will extend existing nomological nets to include work related behaviors. Obviously the choice of constructs must precede the choice of personality measures. As we stated before, researchers in OB are often guilty of grasping available popular personality measures, measures that presumably come with reliable short forms or which assess many different constructs simultaneously, and include them in research because of convenience. Our choice of measures, as well as design, must be more carefully considered.

CONCLUSIONS

We began our paper by noting the tarnished reputation of personality constructs among organizational researchers. This reputation has developed from years of research which has produced comparatively little insight into organizational behavior. It has also developed from the awareness among OB researchers of the criticisms being leveled at personality in more basic areas of psychology.

These criticisms have been based upon both empirical data and logical analysis. We have noted, however, that reasonable objections come more from empirical rather than logical considerations. In fact, most of the criticisms offered by personally researchers place greater emphasis on the inability of personality constructs to predict behavior patterns then from the question of construct legitimacy. Even Mischel (1973), who provides logical arguments against the explanatory usefulness of personality, suggests we examine a set of cognitive individual difference variables which are similar to the kinds of mediating traits discussed by Endler and Magnusson (1977).

Organizational researchers also have based their criticisms of personality more on empirical than logical problems. As we have stated, we do not disagree with those who argue that the contribution of personality to organizational behavior has been disappointing. We do, however, disagree with the conclusions about the usefulness of personality that can be drawn from this data. The reasons for this disagreement, which should now be apparent, center on two general issues.

First, once we accept the legitimate, logical status of personality constructs, it no longer makes any sense to discuss the usefulness of "personality" in global terms. Personality traits come in all sizes and shapes. Some relate to cognitive styles, some relate to motivational principles. Some constructs in use are well developed. Others are poorly conceptualized. Some have reasonable measurement procedures. Others do not. It is simply inappropriate to think in terms of the overall utility of "personality." We must instead recognize that usefulness relates to particular constructs, particular situations and particular issues. We have no right to make inductive statements about the whole class of constructs when we have not sampled systematically from that class or from a class of problems where personality might be useful theoretically.

Our second general point relates to this last statement. Our review suggests that OB researchers have barely scratched the surface of the ways in which personality constructs may enter into theoretical systems. It is interesting to note that the large number of empirical studies of organizational behavior incorporating personality variables does not translate into a wide variety of designs, constructs, or conceptualizations. Reasonable inference always involves the ruling out of plausible alternative hypotheses. Before we use the existing data to infer that personality research is not likely to be productive, we must entertain the plausible rival hypothesis that we have not adequately studied the issues.

In this paper we have tried to offer suggestions on how research examining personality effects might be more adequately conducted. These suggestions were not designed to serve as a shopping list of do's and don'ts. Rather they were offered in the hope of encouraging OB researchers to study personality in a more systematic way. The results of more systematic attention may, in fact, lead to the same conclusions which are now being entertained. We think not. However, if they do, these conclusions will be based upon a substantially sounder set of evidence.

NOTES

1.   Adler, S., and Weiss, H. M. Criterion aggregation in personality research: Self esteem and goal setting. Paper presented at the 90th annual convention of the American Psychological Association, Washington, D.C., August, 1982.

2.   We wish to thank Larry Cummings for suggesting this alternative.

REFERENCES

Abdel-Halim, A. A. Individual and interpersonal moderators of employee reactions to job characteristics: A reexamination. *Personnel Psychology*, 1979, *32*, 121–137.

Adler, S., Aranya, N., & Amernic, J. Community size, socialization, and the work needs of professionals. *Academy of Management Journal*, 1981, *24*, 504–511.

Adler, S., & Coolan, J. Lateness as a withdrawal behavioral. *Journal of Applied Psychology*, 1981, *61*, 544–554.

Aldag, R. J., & Brief, A. P. Some correlates of work values. *Journal of Applied Psychology*, 1975, *60*, 757–760.

Allport, G. W. *Personality: A Psychological Interpretation*. N.Y.: Holt, Rinehart and Winston, 1937.

Alston, W. P. Traits, consistency and conceptual alternatives for personality theory. *Journal for the Theory of Social Behavior*, 1975, *5*, 17–47.

Anderson, C. R., & Schneier, C. E. Locus of control, leader behavior and leader performance among management students. *Academy of Management Journal*, 1978, *21*, 690–698.

Andrisani, P., & Nestel, G. Internal-external control as a contribution to and outcome of work experience. *Journal of Applied Psychology*, 1976, *61*, 156–165.

Arnold, H. J., & House, R. J. Methodological and substantive extensions to the job characteristics model of motivation. *Organizational Behavior and Human Performance*, 1980, *25*, 161–183.

Ashour, A. S. The contingency model of leadership effectiveness: An evaluation. *Organizational Behavior and Human Performance*, 1973, *9*, 339–355.

Atkinson, J. W. *An Introduction to Motivation*. Princeton, NJ: Van Nostrand, 1964.

Atkinson, J. W., & Raynor, J. O. (Eds.), *Personality, Motivation and Achievement*. New York: Wiley & Sons, 1978.

Bales, R. F., & Cohen, S. P. *SYMLOG: A System for the Multiple Level Observation of Groups*, N.Y.: Free Press, 1979.

Bandura, A. The self system in reciprocal determinism. *American Psychologist*, 1978, *33*, 344–358.

Bass, B. M. Leadership opinions as forecasts of supervisory success. *Journal of Applied Psychology*, 1956, *40*, 345–346.

Bass, B. M. *Stogdill's Handbook of Leadership*. New York: The Free Press, 1981.

Beck, L. W. Constructions and inferred entities. In H. Feigl and M. Brodbeck (Eds.), *Readings in the Philosophy of Science*. New York: Appleton-Century-Crofts, 1953.

Bem, D. J., & Allen, A. On predicting some of the people some of the time: The search for cross-situational consistencies in behavior. *Psychological Review*, 1974, *81*, 506–520.

Bernardin, H. J. The relationship of personality variables to organizational withdrawal. *Personnel Psychology*, 1977, *30*, 17–27.

Blood, M. R. Work values and job satisfaction. *Journal of Applied Psychology*, 1969, *53*, 456–459.

Blood, M. R., & Hulin, C. L. Alienation, environmental characteristics, and worker responses. *Journal of Applied Psychology*, 1967, *51*, 284–290.

Bons, P. M., Bass, A. R., & Komorita, S. S. Changes in leadership style as a function of military experience and type of command. *Personnel Psychology*, 1970, *23*, 551–561.

Brousseau, K. R., & Prince, J. B. Job-person dynamics: An extension of longitudinal research. *Journal of Applied Psychology*, 1981, *66*, 59–62.

Brunswick, E. *Perception and the Representative Design of Psychological Experiments*. Berkeley, CA: University of California Press, 1956.

Caldwell, D. F., & O'Reilly, C. A. Boundary spanning and individual performance: The impact of self-monitoring. *Journal of Applied Psychology*, 1982, *67*, 124–127.

Campbell, D. J. Determinants of choice of goal difficulty level: A review of situational and personality influences. *Journal of Occupational Psychology*, 1982, *55*, 79–95.

Champoux, J. E., & Peters, W. S. Applications of moderated regression in job design research. *Personnel Psychology*, 1980, *33*, 759–783.

Cronbach, L. J. The two disciplines of scientific psychology. *American Psychologist*, 1957, *12*, 671–684.

Cronbach, L. J., & Meehl, P. E. Construct validation in psychological tests. *Psychological Bulletin*, 1955, *52*, 281–302.

Dossett, D. L., Latham, G. P., & Mitchell, T. R. The effects of assigned versus participatively set goals, KR, and individual differences when goal difficulty is held constant. *Journal of Applied Psychology*, 1979, *64*, 291–298.

Duncan, S., & Fiske, D. W. *Face-to-Face Interaction: Research, Methods, and Theory*. Hillsdale, NJ: Lawrence Erlbaum Associates, 1976.

Einstein, A., & Infeld, L. *The Evolution of Physics*. N.Y.: Simon and Schuster, 1938.

Endler, N. S., & Magnusson, D. Toward an interactional psychology of personality. *Psychological Bulletin*, 1976, *83*, 956–974.

Epstein, S. Traits are alive and well. In D. Magnusson and S. Endler (Eds.) *Personality at the Crossroads: Current Issues in Interactional Psychology*. Hillsdale, N.J.: Erlbaum, 1977.

Epstein, S. The stability of behavior: I. On predicting most of the people much of the time. *Journal of Personality and Social Psychology*, 1979, *37*, 1097–1126.

Epstein, S. The stability of behavior: II. Implications for psychological research. *American Psychologist*, 1980, *35*, 790–806.

Evans, M. G. The effects of supervisory behavior on the path goal relationship. *Organizational Behavior and Human Performance*, 1970, *5*, 277–298.

Fenigstein, A., Scheier, M. F., & Buss, A. H. Public and private self-consciousness: Assessment and theory. *Journal of Consulting and Clinical Psychology*, 1975, *43*, 522–527.

Fiedler, F. E. *A Theory of Leadership Effectiveness*. New York: McGraw-Hill, 1967.

Fiedler, F. E., & Chemers, M. M. Leadership and Effective Management. Glenview, Ill.: Scott, Foresman, 1974.

Fishbein, M., & Ajzen, I. Attitudes toward objects as predictors of single and multiple behavioral criteria. *Psychological Review*, 1974, *81*, 59–74.

Fleishman, E. A. The measurement of leadership attitudes in industry. *Journal of Applied Psychology*, 1953, *37*, 153–158.

Fleishman, E. A. Twenty years of consideration and structure. In E. A. Fleishman and J. G. Hunt (Eds.) *Current Developments in the Study of Leadership*, Carbondale, IL.: SIU Press, 1973.

Fleishman, E. A., & Harris, E. F. Patterns of leadership behavior related to employee grievances and turnover. *Personnel Psychology*, 1962, *15*, 43–56.

Frank, I. Psychology as a science: Resolving the idiographic-nomothetic controversy. *Journal for the Theory of Social Behavior*, 1982, *12*, 1–20.

Ganster, D. C. Individual differences and task design: A laboratory experiment. *Organizational Behavior and Human Performance*, 1980, *26*, 131–148.

Ghiselli, E. E. The prediction of predictability. *Educational and Psychological Measurement*, 1960, *20*, 3–8.

Ghiselli, E. E. *Explorations in Managerial Talent*. Pacific Palisades, CA: Goodyear, 1971.

Ghiselli, E. E., Campbell, J. P., & Zedeck, S. *Measurement Theory for the Behavioral Sciences*. San Francisco: W. H. Freeman, 1981.

Goldstein, K. M., & Blackman, S. *Cognitive Style: Five Approaches and Relevant Research.* New York: Wiley, 1978.

Graen, G. Role making processes within complex organizations. In M. D. Dunnette (Ed.) *Handbook of Industrial and Organizational Psychology.* Chicago: Rand-McNally, 1976.

Gruenfeld, L. W. Field dependence and field independence in a framework for the study of task and social orientations in organizational leadership. In D. Graues (Ed.), *Management Research: A Cross-Cultural Perspective.* Amsterdam, The Netherlands: Elsevien-North Holland Biomedical Press, 1973.

Gruenfeld, L. W., & MacEachron, A. E. A cross-national study of cognitive style among managers and technicians. *International Journal of Psychology,* 1975, *10,* 27–55.

Guion, R. M., & Gottier, R. F. Validity of personality measures in personnel selection. *Personnel Psychology,* 1965, *18,* 135–164.

Hackman, J. R., & Lawler, E. E. Employee reactions to job characteristics. *Journal of Applied Psychology,* 1971, *55,* 259–286.

Hackman, J. R., & Oldham, G. R. Development of the Job Diagnostic Survey. *Journal of Applied Psychology,* 1975, *60,* 159–170.

Hackman, J. R., & Oldham, G. R. Motivation through the design of work: Test of a theory. *Organizational Behavior of Human Performance,* 1976, *16,* 250–279.

Hackman, J. R., & Oldham, G. R. *Work Redesign.* Reading, Mass.: Addison-Wesley, 1980.

Halpin, A. W., & Winer, B. J. A factorial study of the leader behavior descriptions. In R. M. Stogdill & A. E. Coons (Eds.) *Leader Behavior: Its Description and Measurement.* Columbus: Ohio State University, Bureau of Business Researchers, 1957.

Hammer, T. H., & Vardi, Y. Locus of control and career self-management among non-supervisory employees in industrial settings. *Journal of Vocational Behavior,* 1981, *18,* 13–29.

Helson, R., & Mitchell, V. Personality. In M. R. Rosenzweig and L. W. Porter (Eds.) *Annual Review of Psychology,* Vol. 29, Palo Alto, CA: Annual Reviews, Inc., 1978.

Hemphill, J. K., & Coons, A. E. Development of the leader behavior description questionnaire. In R. M. Stogdill & A. E. Coons (Eds.), *Leader Behavior: Its Description and Measurement.* Columbus: Ohio State University, Bureau of Business Research, 1957.

House, R. J. A path-goal theory of leader effectiveness. *Administrative Science Quarterly,* 1971, *16,* 321–338.

Howard, J. A. Person-situation interaction models. *Personality and Social Psychology Bulletin,* 1979, *5,* 191–195.

Hulin, C. L., & Blood, M. R. Job enlargement, individual differences, and worker responses. *Psychological Bulletin,* 1968, *69,* 41–55.

Ickes, W. A basic paradigm for the study of personality roles and social behavior. In W. Ickes and S. Knowles (Eds.) *Personality, Roles and Social Behavior.* N.Y.: Springer-Verlay, in press.

Ilgen, D. R. & Feldman, J. M. Performance appraisal: A process focus. In B. M. Staw & L. L. Cummings (Eds.) *Research in Organizational Behavior, (Vol. 5).* Greenwich, CT: JAI Press, 1983.

Jaccard, J. J. Predicting social behavior from personality traits. *Journal of Research in Personality,* 1974, *7,* 358–367.

Jaccard, J. J. Personality and behavioral predictions. An analysis of behavioral criterion measures. In L. Kahle and D. Fiske (Eds.) *Methods for Studying Person-Situation Interactions.* San Francisco: Jossey-Bass, 1977.

James, L. R., & Jones, A. P. Perceived job characteristics and job satisfaction: An examination of reciprocal causation. *Personnel Psychology,* 1980, *33,* 97–135.

Jones, A. P., & Butler, M. L. Influences of cognitive complexity on the dimensions underlying perceptions of the work environment. *Motivation and Emotion,* 1980, *4,* 1–19.

Kane, J. S., & Lawler, E. E. III. Performance appraisal effectiveness: Its assessment and determinants. In B. M. Staw (Ed.) *Research in Organizational Behavior*, Vol. *1*. Greenwich, CT: JAI Press, 1979.

Kaplan, A. *The Conduct of Inquiry*. San Francisco: Crowell, 1964.

Katz, R. The influence of job longevity on employee reactions to task characteristics. *Human Relations*, 1978, *31*, 703–725.

Katz, R. Time and work: Toward an integrative perspective. In B. M. Staw and L. L. Cummings (Eds.) *Research in Organizational Behavior*, Vol. *2*. Greenwich, CT: JAI Press, 1980.

Kerr, S., & Jermier, J. M. Substitutes for leadership: Their meaning and measurement. *Organizational Behavior and Human Performance*, 1978, *22*, 375–403.

Kerr, S., Schriesheim, C. A., Murphy, C. J., & Stogdill, R. M. Toward a contingency theory of leadership based upon the consideration and initiating structure literature. *Organizational Behavior and Human Performance*, 1974, *12*, 62–82.

Kerr, S., & Schriesheim, C. Consideration, initiating structure, and organizational criteria: An update of Korman's 1966 review. *Personnel Psychology*, 1974, *27*, 555–568.

Kohn, M. L., & Schooler, C. Job conditions and personality: A longitudinal assessment of their reciprocal effects. *American Journal of Sociology*, 1982, *87*, 1257–1286.

Korman, A. K. "Consideration," "Initiating Structure," and organizational criteria. *Personnel Psychology*, 1966, *18*, 349–360.

Korman, A. K. The prediction of managerial performance: A review. *Personnel Psychology*, 1968, *21*, 295–322.

Korman, A. K. Toward an hypothesis of work behavior. *Journal of Applied Psychology*, 1970, *54*, 31–41.

Korman, A. K. Hypothesis of work behavior revisited and an extension. *Academy of Management Review*, 1976, *1*, 50–63.

Kruglanski, A. W. The human subject in the psychology experiment: Fact and artifact. In L. Berkowitz (Ed.) *Advances in Experimental Social Psychology*, Vol. 8. N.Y.: Academic Press, 1975.

Larson, L. L., Hunt, J. G., & Osborn, R. N. The great hi-hi leader behavior myth: A lesson from Occam's razor. *Academy of Management Journal*, 1976, *19*, 628–641.

Lawler, E. E. *Pay and Organizational Effectiveness*. New York: McGraw-Hill, 1971.

Locke, E. A. Toward a theory of task motivation and incentives. *Organizational Behavior and Human Performance*, 1968, *3*, 157–189.

Locke, E. A., Shaw, K. N., Saari, L. M., & Latham, G. Goal setting and task performance: 1969–1980. *Psychological Bulletin*, 1981, *90*, 125–152.

Lord, R. G., Foti, R. J., & Phillips, J. S. A theory of leadership categorization. In J. G. Hunt, U. Sekaran & C. Schriesheim (Eds.), *Leadership: Beyond Establishment Views*. Carbondale, Ill.: Southern Illinois University Press, 1981.

Louis, M. R. Surprise and sense making: What newcomers experience in entering unfamiliar organizational settings. *Administrative Science Quarterly*, 1980, *35*, 226–251.

Luthans, F. & Davis, T. R. V. An idiographic approach to organizational behavior research: The use of single case experimental designs and direct measures. *Academy of Management Review*, 1982, 7, 380–391.

MacCorquodale, K., & Meehl, P. E. On a distinction between hypothetical constructs and intervening variables. *Psychological Review*, 1948, *55*, 95–107.

McGowan, J., & Gormly, J. Validation of personality traits: A multi-criteria approach. *Journal of Personality and Social Psychology*, 1976, *34*, 791–795.

Magnusson, D., & Ekehammer, B. Similar situations—similar behaviors? A study of the intraindividual congruence between situation perceptions and situation reaction. *Journal of Research in Personality*, 1978, *12*, 41–48.

Magnusson, D., & Endler, N. S. Interactional psychology: Present status and future prospects. In D. Magnusson & N. N. S. Endler (Eds.) *Personality at the Crossroads: Current Issues in Interactional Psychology*. Hillsdale, NJ: Lawrence Erlbaum, 1977.

Maslow, A. H. *Motivation and Personality*. New York: Harper, 1954.

McClelland, D. C. & Boyatzis, R. E. Leadership motive pattern and long term success in management. *Journal of Applied Psychology*, 1982, *67*, 737–743.

Messer, S. B. Reflection–impulsivity: A review, *Psychological Bulletin*, 1976, *83*, 1026–1052.

Messick, S. Constructs and their vicissitudes. *Psychological Bulletin*, 1981, *89*, 575–588.

Middleton, W. L. Personality qualities predominant in campus leaders. *Journal of Social Psychology*, 1941, *13*, 199–201.

Miller, D., De Vries, M. F. R., & Toulouse, J. M. Top executive locus of control and its relationship to strategy-making, structure, and environment. *Academy of Management Review*, 1982, *25*, 237–253.

Miner, J. B. Twenty years of research on role-motivation theory of managerial effectiveness. *Personnel Psychology*, 1978, *31*, 739–760.

Mischel, W. *Personality and Assessment*, N.Y.: Wiley, 1968.

Mischel, W. Toward a cognitive social learning reconceptualization of personality. *Psychological Review*, 1973, *80*, 252–283.

Mischel, W. The interaction of person and situation. In D. Magnusson and N. S. Endler (Eds.), *Personality at the Crossroads: Current Issues in Interactional Psychology*. Hillsdale, N.J.: Erlbaum, 1977.

Mitchell, T. R. Organizational Behavior in M. R. Rosenzweig and L. W. Porter (eds.) *Annual Review of Psychology* Vol. *30* Palo Alto, CA: Annual Reviews Inc., 1979

Mitchell, T. R., Green, S. G., & Wood, R. An attributional model of leadership and the poor performing subordinate. In L. L. Cummings and B. M. Staw, *Research in Organizational Behavior*, Vol. *3*, Greenwich, CT: JAI Press, 1981.

Mobley, W. H. Intermediate linkages in the relationship between job satisfaction and employee turnover. *Journal of Applied Psychology*, 1977, *62*, 237–240.

Mobley, W. H., Griffeth, R. W., Hand, H. H., & Meglino, B. M. Review and conceptual analyses of the employee turnover process. *Psychological Bulletin*, 1979, *86*, 493–522.

Monson, T. C., Hesley, J. W., & Chernick, L. Specifying when personality traits can and cannot predict behavior: An alternative to abandoning the attempt to predict single act criteria. *Journal of Personality and Social Psychology*, 1982, *43*, 385–399.

Moskowitz, D. S. Coherence and cross-situational generality in personality: A new analysis of old problems. *Journal of Personality and Social Psychology*, 1982, *43*, 754–768.

Mowday, R. T., Porter, L. W., & Steers, R. M. *Employee Organization Linkages. The Psychology of Commitment, Absenteeism and Turnover*. N.Y.: Academic Press, 1982.

Mowday, R. T., & Spencer, D. G. The influence of task and personality characteristics on employee turnover and absenteeism incidents. *Academy of Management Journal*, 1981, *24*, 634–642.

Muchinsky, P. M., & Tuttle, M. L. Employee turnover: An empirical and methodological assessment. *Journal of Vocational Behavior*, 1979, *14*, 43–77.

Muchinsky, P. M. Employee absenteeism: A review of the literature. *Journal of Vocational Behavior*, 1977, *10*, 316–340.

Nygard, R. Toward an interactional psychology: Models from achievement research. *Journal of Personality*, 1981, *49*, 363–387.

Olweus, D. Aggression and peer acceptance in preadolescent boys: Two short term longitudinal studies of ratings. *Child Development*, 1977, *48*, 1301–1313.

O'Reilly, C. Personality–job fit: Implications for individual attitudes and performance. *Organizational Behavior and Human Performance*, 1977, *18*, 36–46.

Organ, D. W. Direct, indirect, and trace effects of personality variables on role adjustment. *Human Relations*, 1981, *34*, 573–587.

Payne, R. L., Fineman, S., & Jackson, P. R. An interactionist approach to measuring anxiety at work. *Journal of Occupational Psychology,* 1982, *55,* 13–25.

Pervin, L. A., & Lewis, M. *Perspectives in Interactional Psychology.* N.Y.: Plenum, 1978.

Pfeffer, J. Management as symbolic action: The creation and maintenance of organizational paradigms. In L. L. Cummings and B. M. Staw (Eds.) *Research in Organizational Behavior,* Vol. *3.* Greenwich, CT: JAI Press, 1981.

Podsakoff, P. M. Determinants of a supervisor's use of rewards and punishments: A literature review and suggestions for further research. *Organizational Behavior and Human Performance,* 1982, *29,* 58–83.

Porter, L. W., & Steers, R. M. Organizational, work and personal factors in employee turnover and absenteeism. *Psychological Bulletin,* 1973, *80,* 151–176.

Porter, L. W., Lawler, E. E. III & Hackman, J. R. *Behavior in Organizations,* N.Y.: McGraw-Hill, 1975.

Price, R. H., & Bouffard, D. L. Behavioral appropriateness and situational constraint as dimensions of social behavior. *Journal of Personality and Social Psychology,* 1974, *30,* 579–586.

Rabinowitz, S., Hall, D. T., & Goodale, J. G. Job scope and individual differences as predictors of job involvement: Independent or interactive? *Academy of Management Journal,* 1977, *20,* 273–281.

Rakestraw, T. L., Jr. & Weiss, H. M. The interaction of social influences and task experience on goals, performance, and performance satisfaction. *Organizational Behavior & Human Performance,* 1981, *27,* 326–344.

Rice, R. W. Construct validity of the least preferred coworker score. *Psychological Bulletin,* 1978, *85,* 1199–1237.

Roberts, K. H., & Glick, W. The job characteristics approach to task design: A critical review. *Journal of Applied Psychology,* 1981, *66,* 193–217.

Rotter, J. B. Generalized expectancies for internal versus external control of reinforcement. *Psychological Monographs,* 1966, *80* (1, Whole No. 609).

Rychlak, J. F. *Introduction to Personality and Psychotherapy.* Boston: Houghton-Mifflin, 1981.

Ryle, G. *The Concept of Mind.* N.Y.: Barnes and Noble, 1949.

Salancik, G. R., & Pfeffer, J. An examination of need satisfaction models of job attitudes. *Administrative Science Quarterly,* 1977, *22,* 427–456.

Salancik, G. R., & Pfeffer, J. A social information processing approach to job attitudes and task design. *Administrative Science Quarterly,* 1978, *23,* 224–253.

Schneider, B. An interactionist perspective on organizational effectiveness. In K. Cameron & D. Whetten (Eds.) *Organizational Effectiveness.* New York: Academic Press, 1982.

Schneider, B. Interactional psychology and organizational behavior. In L. L. Cummings & B. M. Staw (Eds.) *Research in Organizational Behavior,* Vol. *5.* Greenwich, CT: JAI Press, 1983.

Sims, H. P., & Szilagyi, A. D. Job characteristic relationships: Individual and structural moderators. *Organizational Behavior and Human Performance,* 1976, *17,* 211–230.

Snyder, M. The self-monitoring of expressive behavior. *Journal of Personality and Social Psychology,* 1974, *30,* 526–537.

Spector, P. E. Behavior in organizations as a function of employee's locus of control. *Psychological Bulletin,* 1982, *91,* 482–497.

Stagner, R. On the reality and relevance of traits. *Journal of General Psychology,* 1977, *96,* 185–207.

Steers, R. M., & Rhodes, S. R. Major influences on employee attendance: A process model. *Journal of Applied Psychology,* 1978, *63,* 391–407.

Stogdill, R. M. Personal factors associated with leadership: A survey of the literature. *Journal of Psychology,* 1948, *25,* 35–71.

Stogdill, R. M. *Handbook of Leadership.* N.Y.: Free Press, 1974.

Stone, E. F. The moderating effect of work related values on the job scope-job satisfaction relationship. *Organizational Behavior and Human Performance,* 1976, *15,* 147–167.

Stone, E. F. Field independence and perceptions of task characteristics: A laboratory investigation. *Journal of Applied Psychology,* 1979, *64,* 305–310.

Stone, E. F., Ganster, D. L., Woodman, R. W., & Fusilier, M. R. Relationships between Growth Need Strength and selected individual differences measures employed in job design research. *Journal of Vocational Behavior,* 1979, *14,* 329–340.

Strube, J. J., & Garcia, J. E. A meta-analytic investigation of Fiedler's model of leadership effectiveness. *Psychological Bulletin,* 1981, *90,* 307–321.

Snyder, M., & Ickes, W. J. Personality and social behavior. In G. Lindzey and E. Aronson (Eds.) *Handbook of Social Psychology (3rd Edition).* Reading, MA: Addison-Wesley, in press.

Terborg, J. R. Interactional psychology and research on human behavior in organizations. *Academy of Management Review,* 1981, *6,* 569–576.

Turner, A. N., & Lawrence, P. R. *Industrial Jobs and The Worker.* Cambridge, MA: Harvard Graduate School of Business Administration, 1965.

Turner, M. B. *Philosophy and the Science of Behavior.* N.Y.: Appleton-Century-Crofts, 1965.

Van Maanen, J., & Schein, E. H. Toward a theory of organizational socialization. In B. M. Staw (Eds.) *Research in Organizational Behavior,* Vol. *1.* Greenwich, CT: JAI Press, 1979.

Wahba, M. A., & Bridwell, L. G. Maslow reconsidered: A review of research on the need hierarchy theory. *Organizational Behavior and Human Performance,* 1976, *15,* 212–240.

Weick, K. E. *The Social Psychology of Organizing (2nd ed.).* Reading, Mass.: Addison-Wesley, 1979.

Weiss, H. M. Subordinate imitation of supervisor behavior: The role of modeling in organizational socialization. *Organizational Behavior and Human Performance,* 1977, *19,* 89–105.

Weiss, H. M. Social learning of work values in organizations. *Journal of Applied Psychology,* 1978, *63,* 711–718.

Weiss, H. M., & Adler, S. Cognitive complexity and the structure of implicit leadership theories. *Journal of Applied Psychology,* 1981, *66,* 69–78.

Weiss, H. M., & Knight, P. A. The utility of humility: Self esteem, information search and problem solving efficiency. *Organizational Behavior and Human Performance,* 1980, *25,* 216–223.

Weiss, H. M., & Shaw, J. B. Social influences on judgments about tasks. *Organizational Behavior and Human Performance,* 1979, *24,* 126–140.

Weissenberg, P., & Kavanagh, M. J. The independence of initiating structure and consideration: A review of the evidence. *Personnel Psychology,* 1972, *25,* 119–1961.

Weitz, J. Criteria and transfer of training. *Psychological Reports* 1966, *19,* 195–210.

White, J. K. Individual differences in the job quality-worker response relationship: Review, integration and comments. *Academy of Management Review,* 1978, *3,* 267–280.

Witkin, H. A., & Goodenough, D. R. Field dependence and interpersonal behavior. *Psychological Bulletin,* 1977, *84,* 661–689.

Wolfle, L. M., & Shaw, R. D. Effects of college attendance on locus of control. *Journal of Personality and Social Psychology,* 1982, *43,* 802–810.

Zedeck, S. Problems with the use of "moderator" variable. *Psychological Bulletin,* 1971, *76,* 295–310.

INTERACTIONAL PSYCHOLOGY AND ORGANIZATIONAL BEHAVIOR

Benjamin Schneider

ABSTRACT

This paper first reviews some of the classic recent writings on interactional psychology and then presents an interpretation of current thinking about job attitudes, socialization to work, and leadership from the interactionist perspective. In the review, the debate between Mischel and Bowers is discussed, the former representing the situationist, the latter the interactionist position. Then, a summary of other interactionist writers is organized around three key interactionist themes: (1) human behavior is both internally and externally controlled, with the person as well as the situation playing an active role in the resultant observed behavior; (2) there is no one best way to collect data on human behavior but the laboratory experiment has inherent problems in that it fails to allow for naturally occurring person-situation interactions and the unfolding of behavior *in situ;* and (3) the term "interaction" has many conceptual and statistical meanings only one of which is captured by the ANOVA "X" as in "A X B interaction."

After exploring each of these three themes, the research on job attitudes, socialization, and leadership is shown to be quite situationist in perspective with a concentration, respectively, on socially constructed rather than interactionist realities, what the organization does to newcomers, rather than how newcomers and settings influence each other, and how behavior is a function of the decision situation rather than how leader attributes and setting interact. Thus, it is shown, human behavior at work has been overwhelmingly assumed to be situationally rather than personally determined. Finally, some perspectives for a more trait- or person-oriented approach are presented and it is concluded that the interactionist position seems to most accurately represent the emergent nature of the real world of work organizations.

The major purpose of this essay is to introduce the student of organizational behavior to the thinking of interactional psychologists. To accomplish this goal, first some background on the views of interactional psychologists is presented, then a summary of some ideas about integrating interactionism and organizational behavior is presented. Finally, the potential relevance of this integration and interactional psychology to three key OB areas of research is suggested.

BACKGROUND

The Mischel-Bowers Debate

Interactional psychology represents a rapprochement between trait- and dynamic-oriented personality theorists (personologists) on the one hand and social learning and behavioral psychologists (situationists) on the other hand. Until the middle 1960s personologists and situationists functioned independently under a kind of implicit truce with neither casting public aspersion on the other. This changed in 1968 when Mischel (1968) published a book particularly critical of trait theorists. The following lengthy quotation summarizes the extreme case of Mischel's (1968, pp. 295–296) position:

> The trait position leads one to infer enduring generalized attributes in persons and to predict from the inferred trait to behavior in various situations. This would be an appropriate procedure if it could be done reliably and provide predictive power. The problem is that the heuristic yield from the trait approach over the last five or more decades has been . . . remarkably slim.
> . . . Although it is evident that persons are the source from which human responses are evoked, it is situational stimuli that evoke them, and it is changes in conditions that alter them. Since the assumption of massive behavioral similarity across diverse situations no longer is tenable, it becomes essential to study the differences in the behaviors of a given person as a function of the conditions in which they occur. . . . The notion of "typical" behavior, which is fundamental to trait conceptualizations, has led psychometricians and trait theorists to view situational variability as "error." The social behavior position, however, construes what the psychometrician considers error to actually be critical determinants of behavior.

Most of the criticisms of Mischel's position that followed concentrated on his extreme social learning perspective, as set forth in the above quotation. While clearly a *part* of his book, he seems to have used the extreme social learning perspective more as a frame of reference than as a total representation of his own position. Thus, conclusions like the following also exist:

> it is important to include the subjects' own phenomenology and constructs as data sources since he construes, abstracts and experiences behavior, as well as performing overtly, just as much as the psychologists who try to study him (1968, p. 300).

Indeed, in later works (e.g., Mischel, 1973) more of the cognitive flavor of his position comes through; these will be noted below. So much of his book focused on the external control of behavior, however, that retorts to that position were not long in appearing.

Perhaps the most insightful of these was a paper by Bowers (1973) in which the interactionist perspective was presented. Thus, rather than arguing *for* traits or *against* situationism, Bowers presented the interactionist perspective (1973, p. 307):

> It is my argument that both the trait and the situationist positions are inaccurate and misleading and that a position stressing the interaction of the person and the situation is both conceptually satisfying and empirically warranted.

Bowers's paper is a tour de force with two major themes: (1) a refutation of the metaphysical, psychological, and methodological underpinnings of situationism, and (2) the presentation of the interactionist perspective.

For purposes of the present paper, Bowers's major refutation of situationism is its dependence on the experimental method as the source of data for drawing conclusions about (1) the power of situations to control behavior and (2) the non-validity and non-utility of the trait approach. As Bowers notes, situationists have "subtly coopted [the] prestige of the experimental method" and used the assumed superiority of the *method* as a basis for claims regarding the strength of *findings*. The crux of Bowers's argument is that experimentalists play with experimental conditions until the manipulation has the desired effect and then argue, persuasively, that situations control behavior. The fact that actual experimental treatments are typically nonrepresentative of the potential range of treatments (i.e., there is no random assignment of treatments to participants) is not recognized by researchers themselves nor by reviewers of research who are already disposed to view the world through situationist lenses.

Bowers's perspective on interactionism is that "*situations are as much a function of the person as the person's behavior is a function of the situation*" (1973, p. 327, italics in original). He argues from the Piagetian assimilation-accommodation framework that situations for persons exist as a result of the means and methods used for knowing them. The situation, then, is a function of the perceiver in the sense that perceivers' cognitive schemas filter and organize situations; situations, then, are not separable from persons.

Why are person and situation typically not separable? Because people tend to choose to locate themselves in environments that are compatible with their own behavior tendencies. That is, as Wachtel (1973) noted, much about the nature of the environments in which people behave is an outcome of the behavior of the people in those environments. This yields similarity in the kinds of situations similar people create for themselves. It follows, then, that if people foster environments that are consistent with their own inclinations, those environments will be isomorphic with, not separable from, the people in them.

It should be obvious that Bowers argues that the experimental method, through rigid controls on behavior and short time perspective, does not permit for the definition of situation by persons. He notes how the "enormous constraints" imposed on variability in behavior in the typical experiment vitiate the potential for the variance in people to play a role in the emergent nature of situation. In summary, then, he argues for more flexibility in research designs and more attention to the reciprocation of person and situation in defining one another as the key to understanding the nature of person and situation. In McGuire's (1973, p. 448) terms:

> [S]imple a-affects-b hypotheses fail to catch the complexities of parallel processing, bi-directional causality, and reverberating feedback that characterize cognitive and social organization.

Of course Mischel and Bowers are not the only parties to a discussion of the nature of the personal and situational correlates of behavior. Indeed in the past five years at least three books of readings on interactional psychology have appeared (Endler & Magnusson, 1976a; Magnusson & Endler, 1977a; Pervin & Lewis, 1978a). Although some writers on personality theory think interest in interactional psychology may have peaked (Maddi, 1980) a consideration of the major themes of interactionism reveals as yet unrealized potential for insight into a number of contemporary topics in OB.

Interactional Psychology: The Major Questions

Table 1 summarizes the three major questions in interactional psychology. The table is a condensation of the writings of Endler and Magnusson (1976b), Magnusson and Endler (1977b) and Pervin and Lewis (1978b), as well as Ekehammar's (1974) review of the history of research on interactionism.

The Internal-External Question. As revealed in the discussion of the Mischel-Bowers debate, a core question in understanding human behavior is the attribution of cause. This seems only logical given the proclivity of humans to want to make such attributions (e.g., Kelley, 1971). Interactionists, and most contemporary personologists, would agree that behavior is a function of both internal and external causative agents, but that for different people different kinds of behavior in different kinds of situations may be expected.

Table 1.   Three Major Questions in Interactional Psychology

1. *The Internal-External Question:*
    Is human behavior controlled internally (inner; person), externally (outer; situation) or both internally *and* externally? One corollary to this issue is whether behavior is the result of proactivity or passivity on the part of the behaver. A second corollary concerns the conceptualization of the external world, i.e., is the physical or psychological environment the important situation in person-situation research?

2. *The Data Collection Question:*
    Is the appropriate data collection strategy self-report, experimental or observations or combinations of these? A corollary to this issue concerns time perspective: Should we be freezing behavior or witnessing it unfold?

3. *The Data Analysis Question:*
    Is the appropriate data analysis strategy based on correlation/regression, analysis of variance, or some combination? A corollary issue here is the variety of meanings given the term "interaction" and whether the focus of analysis should be on traits, situations, or the interaction.

While this appears to support Mischel's negative conclusions about behavioral stability and the predictability of behavior, the interactionists' concept of coherence in behavior provides the vehicle for avoiding Mischel's conclusion. Coherence

> refers to behavior that is inherently lawful and hence predictable without necessarily being stable in either absolute or relative terms. . . . Coherence means that the individual's pattern of stable and changing behavior across situations of different kinds is characteristic of him or her (Magnusson & Endler, 1977b, p. 7).

The concept of coherence exists in contrast to ideas regarding absolute consistency in behavior (i.e., a particuar individual will behave the same way across all situations) or even relative consistency (i.e., a group of individuals ranked with respect to a particular behavior in situation A will retain the same rank in situation B even though the average level of behavior may have changed). Absolute and relative consistency were the criteria Mischel used in denying the predictability of the behavior of individuals based on trait assessments. Coherence, on the other hand, suggests that individuals may exhibit neither absolute nor relative consistency yet still be predictable, because the way they are inconsistent from situation to situation is consistent (reliable) for them.

What accounts for coherence? The consensus among interactionists is that it results from information processing. Thus, interactionists view humans as generally proactive perceivers who, through their perceptions and cognitions, actively structure the external world. Essentially no interactionist, then, construes the situation in person-situation research in terms of the physical situation:

> In the two prevailing views man is to be viewed either as a passive recipient, being acted upon or alternatively, one who models his world and who by his actions affects his perceptions and cognitions. The former passive model is compatible with the position that there exists a real world and the function of man's perceptions and cognitions is to uncover the world while in the active model the world of experience and knowledge is the result of the interaction between the external world, however defined, and man himself (Pervin & Lewis, 1978b, p. 8).

What is critical here is the idea of active involvement in a situation, through perception and other behaviors, as the way people come to understand situations. While it is true that such variables as past experiences, preferences, needs, and values, play a role in assisting individuals' understanding of a situation, interactionists emphasize actual behavior *in situ* as the main vehicle. This belief in the way individuals come to understand situations places interactionists on common philosophical grounds with action researchers (Sanford, 1970) or action scientists (Argyris, 1980) or ticklers (Salancik, 1979). All believe that one comes to understand a situation by making it, the situation, behave.

In summary, then, interactionists believe in the coherence of behavior which, in turn, is thought to be a function of the active psychological construction of situations through perception and based on experience. Because situations are actively constructed, the separation of person from situation is difficult. This is especially true in the long run, since assessing coherence in people requires a relatively long period of time with a number of observations of different people in different settings.

The Data Collection Question. It is clear that personologists have tended to focus on self-report measures as their trait data (predictors) and observations as their criteria (usually some form of rating of behavior by an observer). In contrast, situationists have depended upon manipulations of situational contingencies as their predictors and observation as their dependent variables.

As noted earlier, while situationists most often subscribe to the concept of random assignment of participants to treatments, some situationists do focus on case studies (one participant in many treatments). However, none practice random assignment of treatments to participants, and they rarely recognize that humans select themselves into particular situations, that is, into treatment conditions.

Bowers (1973) made the issue of random assignment of treatments to individuals a major weapon in his arsenal for attacking the situationists' tendency to depend upon laboratory experiments as support for inter-situational instability. There are two major reasons for suspecting the utility of laboratory experiments for understanding coherence in behavior. First, as already mentioned, assessing coherence in people requires observing behavior across many situations so that the kinds of changes in behavior that characterize a person as s/he moves from situation to situation can be documented. On this first reason, Pervin and Lewis (1978b, pp. 18–19) note that:

> Much of our research to date has involved a freezing of behavior rather than a witnessing of the unfolding of behavior. . . . Processes such as regulation, adaptation, and exchange seem to be at the core of organismic behavior and an understanding of such processes would appear to require long-term observations and a longer time perspective than is often the case in psychology today. Observation of behavior as process suggests that variables often indeed have a reciprocal effect upon one another and that the determinants of action at one point in the process can be very different from and understood only in the light of determinants of action at another point in the process.

Pervin and Lewis praise the research procedures practiced by ethologists (behavioral biologists) as an example of the kind of processual research required to illuminate the unfolding of behavior. Ethologists study complex social behavior as the result of the interactions among variables such as hormone level, prior learning experience, eliciting stimuli in the environment, and surrounding cues.

The second reason why dependency upon laboratory experimentation may not be useful as a vehicle for understanding naturally occurring behavior concerns the self-selection of situations. Situationists, as active manipulators of the environments for randomly assigned "subjects" completely deny participants the opportunity to self-select themselves into situations. In this process, situationists completely obscure the data regarding the nonrandomness by which people come to be in situations:

> The situations that an individual encounters are not a random selection of all possible situations. Many of the situations in which we participate are chosen by ourselves (*selected situations*) but some seem to be imposed on us (*required situations*). . . . The result of this process of selection of situations that one encounters is that each individual appears in a restricted set of situations and these types of situations are a function of and have relevance for the person concerned (Magnusson & Endler, 1977b, p. 20).

Both the issues of time perspective and the idea of self-selection into situations argue against dependence upon laboratory experimentation as a basis for conclusions about the stability, coherence, or situation-dependence of human behavior. Both issues suggest the necessity for long-term observational/correlational research and for inclusion of prior experience/history as important issues in understanding today's, and in predicting tomorrow's behavior (on the latter point see also Mischel, 1973).[1]

The Data Analysis Question. Situationists have typically analyzed their data using ANOVA strategies, while personologists of the trait (compared to dynamic) persuasion have employed regression techniques. This difference in analytic preference fits well with underlying assumptions about the causes of behavior and the choice of the locus for research (i.e., laboratory or field).

In both kinds of analytic techniques, the potential for observing person-situation interaction effects is minimal. Paradoxically, then, both ANOVA and moderated multiple regression procedures for testing for the significance of algebraic interaction terms (i.e., A X B interactions) are frequently inappropriate and nonuseful in interactional studies. Especially in laboratory studies this is true, because to obtain a significant interaction term, there must be extremes of the variables, and rarely in laboratory research are there any extremes on measures of the person. Thus, even when some "personality" measure is employed in a laboratory study, because of the nature of such research (e.g., male college sophomores), extremes of personality are unlikely.

Indeed, the issue of extremes applies not only to findings of significant algebraic interaction effects but also to the question of the relative stability of persons across situations. Epstein (1979, p. 1102) puts this issue as follows:

> It has been falsely argued that if there were stability in personality, individual differences would necessarily account for a relatively large proportion of total variance. This argument is fallacious for two reasons. First, the proportion of variance attributable to any one factor, such as individuals, is always influenced by the range of variability represented by the other factors. Thus, if situations are selected over a wide range of variability and individuals over a narrow range, the proportion of variance for individuals will be smaller than for situations. . . . Second, the analysis of variance has been misused in obtaining estimates of stability, for instead of using the appropriate error term for obtaining estimates of stability coefficients, the variance for individual differences has been compared to total variance.

Even in field studies, when techniques like moderated multiple regression (e.g., Zedeck, 1971) are used, significant effects for the interaction term are rarely observed (Schneider, 1978a). In field settings as in laboratory settings, extremes of person variables are not typically observed. If in both laboratory and field research significant algebraic interaction terms for person and situation cannot be expected, how can we pursue the issue of an interactional psychology? The answer is that algebraic interaction is but one way to think about interaction. Indeed, Pervin and Lewis (1978b, pp. 13–16) describe at least five variations on the interpretation of the meaning of interaction: descriptive interaction, statistical interaction, additive interaction, interdependent interaction, and reciprocal action-transaction. Their descriptions of these are paraphrased below and then discussed:

1. Descriptive interaction—refers to the mere description or codification of interpersonal relationships rather than an explanation of the interaction in terms of personal, situational, and reciprocal attributes. Pervin and Lewis provide the example of investigating how schizophrenic disorders manifest themselves in interpersonal behavior and note that such a study would only be interactional if designed to examine how the observed behavior reflects characteristics of the participants and the context.

2. Statistical interaction—refers to what was previously termed "algebraic interaction," that is, the traditional two (A X B) or three-way (A X B X C) interaction term in ANOVA, or the interaction term as a variable in multiple regression. If the interaction term's β weight is significant, the interaction is thought to be significant. It is important to note that inclusion of an interaction term in data analysis does not make a piece of research interactional, nor does *lack* of such a term make the effort non-interactional. Thus, statistical or algebraic interaction terms which fail to include as one element in the interaction term data on person attributes or contexts are not considered truly interactionist.

There are very few studies of a statistical or algebraic interaction sort in organizational behavior, and those that do exist typically fail to find support for the significance of the interaction term (Schneider, 1978a, in press; Terborg, 1977). I have already noted that the failure to obtain significance of these terms in work organizations can be attributed to the fact that the extremes of persons and situations rarely exist together; this absence of extremes mitigates against the possibilities for significance. Magnusson and Endler's (1977b) concept of the selected setting is useful here—people select themselves into settings they fit and out of settings they do not fit. Extensive literatures in vocational psychology (e.g., Crites, 1969) and the psychology of turnover (e.g., Mobley, 1982) can be cited to support this fundamental principle. This principle, in turn, produces the restriction in range of persons/situations which at best produce linear (additive) effects for person and situation in the prediction of work behavior (Schneider, 1978a).

3. Additive interaction—refers, as noted, to the case where two or more variables combine linearly, but not interactively, in the prediction

and understanding of some criterion of interest. While the idea of additive interaction makes little statistical sense, conceptually it is appealing as a way to understand the real world in which manipulations are not so extreme as to produce the kinds of reactions required for the significance of an interaction term. Additive interaction argues, for example, that conditions at work can be established which facilitate job performance for the people who work in a particular setting and that, regardless of their personal ability level, the setting itself will make an independent positive contribution to their performance. Much of the literature reviewed by Schneider (1978a, 1978b) on ability and situation interaction at work and by Cronbach and Snow (1977) on aptitude and learning mode interaction seems to be best characterized as representing the additive interaction model. In these kinds of research, then, a typical result would be that ability correlates positively with performance, but that the level of the scatterplot of that relationship is related to leadership style, reward system, job enrichment, goal setting condition, and so on, producing a significant linear combination of ability and situation in the prediction of performance (cf. Locke, Mento, & Katcher, 1978).

4.   Interdependent interaction—refers to the case when two or more person and situation variables can be independently measured but the effects of those variables can only be understood in relation to one another. Pervin and Lewis (1978b, p. 140) say:

> When a phenomenon is conceived of in terms of the effect of many interdependent variables, we are faced with the problem of a system, a complex network of interdependent variables such that a change in the status of one variable may have varying consequences for all other related variables. This kind of interaction would appear to be the essence of the view that we can never understand persons in isolation from situations or situations in isolation from persons.

5.   Adding Pervin and Lewis's fifth way of understanding interaction, "reciprocal action-transaction," completes the list by contributing the concept of time or process and the idea that a causative variable may also be affected by the very process of having an effect.

Of these five ways of characterizing interaction, interdependent interaction and reciprocal action-transaction best capture the essence of the interactionist perspective. They suggest that the natural ebb and flow of people and settings are continually affected by each other, and that one-way causal inferences fail to adequately represent the reality of most work settings. These views of interaction also indicate that the internal-external, data collection, and data analysis issues are inseparable from one another. Finally, even surface attention to the implications of these views of person-situation interaction yield relatively dramatic insights into the kinds of research necessary to capture the richness of interdependence that obviously exists in the world of work.

Summary   By way of summarizing this exploration into the concerns and issues of interactional psychology, three principles of interactional psychology are presented as answers to the three questions presented in Table 1. Each principle is followed by a brief note which will be useful in Part II of this paper, Application of the Principles to OB.

1.   *The Internal-External Question:* Human behavior is both internally and externally controlled. The control is reciprocal in form because in the real world persons select themselves into and out of settings. Human behavior in natural settings is an outcome of the active perception of situations by relatively similar self-selected people, rather than the result of the imposition of required situations; the emergent environment as perceived by active members is the important situation in person-situation research.

This first principle emphasizes the real-time nature of most real world human behavior, thus denying the relevance of the typical laboratory experiment to issues concerned with an understanding of person-situation interaction. It also notes that people tend to select settings. This is a critical issue for understanding the psychology of situations and the inseparability of person from setting in the world of work. Thus, it follows from this principle that because people enact settings, people and settings are difficult to separate. Finally the principle specifies that behavior in settings is a function of the perceived setting, i.e., the psychological environment is the important element in understanding the relationships between settings, persons, and behavior.

2.   *The Data Collection Question:* Any data collection strategy which allows for documenting the natural process of interaction between person and setting and which includes data on person, setting, and their inter-action is legitimate in interactional research. Long-term experiments, then, are certainly reasonable so long as they are conducted in the real world, employ reasonable interventions as the experimental manipulations (cf. Fairweather & Tornatzky, 1977 for a review of such efforts), include theoretically relevant data on persons, and function in a process evaluation (continuous monitoring of change) mode (Goldstein, 1979).

The importance of the first two conditions (realistic interventions and theoretically relevant data on persons) has been accurately documented recently by Locke and his colleagues (Locke, Shaw, Saari, & Latham, 1981, p. 142) in their review of individual differences in goal-setting research:

> The only consistent thing about the studies of individual differences in goal setting is their inconsistency. A number of reasons for this can be offered. First, the studies were not specifically designed to look for individual differences effects. The very fact that most studies assigned goals to the subjects means that any individual differences that did exist were masked by the demand characteristics of the design. . . . The best design for revealing individual differences would be one in which there is free (or a considerable amount of) goal choice rather than assigned goals. . . .

Second, most of the individual difference variables included in the studies were not based on any clear theoretical rationale; thus, even when differences were found, they were hard to explain.

The importance of reasonable interventions, process evaluation, and theoretically relevant data is difficult to overemphasize. Natural interaction can probably only be observed if process, rather than only outcome, evaluation is practiced. Thus *how* outcomes emerge after intervention or manipulation is as important as *which* outcomes and the *levels* of outcomes that are observed; the unfolding of behavior is important. On the principle of a reasonable intervention, most situationist studies present required situations (demand conditions) to research participants (called subjects) in ways that all but eliminate individual differences when they do exist, and which deny the concept of coherence in behavior. Returning then to Bowers's position, it becomes quite obvious in reviewing much of the social psychological situationist-oriented literature that published research is replete with demonstrations rather than investigations; research is more of the "*watch this*" than "*I wonder*" sort (see Argyris, 1968; Orne, 1962; Weick, 1967 for varying perspectives on this point).

3.   *The Data Analysis Question:* There is no such thing as *the* appropriate data analysis strategy. However, it is clear that the usual conceptualization of the word interaction as representing an algebraic term in ANOVA is quite narrow. The word interaction in interactional psychology connotes reciprocal causation of person and situation. The idea of reciprocal causation implies people interacting in naturalistic settings over extended periods of time. The central data analytic problem appears to be the analysis of data collected over many (observational) (survey) (experimental) periods and relating earlier observations to later behaviors of interest.

Recently Epstein (1979, 1980) has been grappling with this problem and has argued forcefully for the utility of data aggregation over time for individuals. In contrast, then, to the usual procedure of aggregating across individuals at one point in time, he suggests that a way to study coherence in behavior is to aggregate over time both predictor and criterion data for each individual in a data set. Indeed, Epstein (1979) showed that for the major studies supportive of stability in personality, all had taken steps to reduce errors of measurement (unreliability) in individual level data by obtaining relatively extensive samples of behavior and then aggregating prior to calculating correlations. He proceeded to support this idea in three of his own studies.

In conclusion, interactional psychology promotes a conceptualization of human behavior which is supportive of the idea that humans are proactive in perceiving situations into which they select themselves, that naturally occurring behavior is frequently the result of long-term reciprocal transaction between person and setting, that short-term laboratory experiments are futile as vehicles for understanding person-situation interaction, and that an interpretation of the word interaction need not include only an X (Terborg, 1981).

APPLICATIONS

In this section of the paper, some principles of interactional psychology will be used as vehicles for examining three different OB topics, namely job attitudes, socialization to work, and leadership. While no grand theoretical scheme led to selection of these particular topics for discussion, for each a reason existed. Job attitudes was selected because of the traditional implicit assumption in the literature that attitudes at and towards work are a function of what happens to and around people at work rather than correlates of attributes people bring with them. For example, there exist precious few studies predicting job satisfaction or other job attitudes using selection procedures (Schneider, Hall & Nygren, 1972). Recently, the implicit assumption has been made explicit and theories about attitudes at work have become quite situationist in character; this will be the focus of the job attitudes section.

Socialization to work was chosen because it is a topic that requires a longitudinal perspective and, indeed, has frequently been studied with longitudinal methodologies. However, little work has been accomplished on conceptualizing or studying the role of person variables in socialization. This failure seems to be particularly acute when one notes that the way people in an organization behave is obviously a function of contextual factors which, predominantly, are other people. *Why* most people become socialized to a setting has not been so frequently questioned as *How* they become socialized. A focus on persons provides some insight into the *Why*.

Finally the study of leadership is included because it is potentially the most exciting topic in OB. Yet we have managed to study this topic for 25 or more years now without saying much about the attributes of those who lead. There are, of course, exceptions to this conclusion and a focus on those exceptions provides some suggestions for research that may help clarify the nature of leadership, and management, at work.

Examination of these three topics will be based on the following set of assumptions derived from Part I:

1. People select themselves into and out of situations based on the general fit of themselves to the situation.

2. Self-selection of people into and out of settings results in relatively homogeneous settings, yielding people interacting with relatively similar people. Over time it is the interactions of people with similar others that defines work settings as we find them; work settings emerge more than they are created (Schneider, in press).
3. While the general debate over the stability of personality vs. the effect of situations on behavior may be theoretically interesting, the interactionist position seems to best capture the world of work. This is so because of self-selection which mitigates against people encountering random situations. Thus, the oft-made observation that people appear more stable than Mischel's (1968) conclusions would suggest is probably true because we typically observe people in a relatively narrow range of situations and, then, over many observational periods (Epstein, 1979).

In terms of these principles, it is interesting to note that none of the prominent interactionists or even others who are interested in documenting the stability or coherency of personality (e.g., Epstein, 1980) have attended to the extensive literature in OB on the utility of trait measures for predicting long-term vocational behavior. For example, the Strong-Campbell Interest Inventory (Campbell & Hansen, 1981) has revealed quite remarkable stability in individuals' interest patterns over 30 or more years as well as good accuracy in predicting occupational choice (Anastasi, 1976). With respect to managerial behavior, Campbell, Dunnette, Lawler, and Weick (1970), report on the validity of various trait approaches to the prediction of managerial effectiveness. For example, they noted how the Guilford-Zimmerman Temperament Survey and various biographical information blanks were capable of making accurate predictions of managerial success as defined by such indices as job level achieved or relative salary level (correlations of .60 or so are not unusual). Thus, it appears to be true that, as Epstein (1979, 1980) would suggest, traits and predictions of behavior over the long run can be stable and valid. The secret here, as in Epstein's own work, appears to be the use of criteria which are, in fact, aggregates of individual samples of behavior (job or salary level) rather than point predictions of specific time-bounded behavior. Fishbein and Ajzen (1975) call these aggregates "multiple-act" criteria; opportunity is provided for individuals to display a range of behaviors and, thus, for coherence to emerge.

Personologists and interactionists have also ignored the findings in vocational and industrial psychology supporting the conclusions that relatively similar people select themselves into settings and, if they are dissimilar, select themselves out. On the former point, Holland's (1966, 1973, 1976) and Lofquist and Dawis' (1969) theories of vocational choice clearly support the idea of person-environment match. These scholars have marshalled an enormous arsenal of data to document self-choice tendencies. Similarly, the turnover literature reveals how self-selection, this time out of settings, works to narrow the range of people one would expect to find in a setting (cf. Mobley, 1982; Porter & Steers, 1973; Schneider, in press; Schneider & Mitchell, Note 1).

In the next three sections these ideas about self-selection, the natural emergence of settings, coherence in behavior, and the various ways of conceptualizing person-situation interaction are employed as lenses through which to examine the research on job attitudes, socialization to work and leadership.

Attitudes at and towards Work.

The major theme of this section will be an interactional interpretation of research on job attitudes. The focus of the interpretation will be the situationist-oriented papers of Salancik and Pfeffer (1977, 1978). These are convenient foci because of the care with which their arguments have been presented. The key point made by Salancik and Pfeffer (1978, p. 226) is that:

> The social information processing approach proceeds from the fundamental premise that individuals, as adaptive organisms, adapt attitudes, behavior, and beliefs to their social context and to the reality of their own past and present behavior and situation. This premise leads inexorably to the conclusion that one can learn most about individual behavior by studying the informational and social environment within which that behavior occurs and to which it adapts.

In their first paper, Salancik and Pfeffer (1977) were concerned with the relevance of need theories for understanding job attitudes, especially job satisfaction. In that paper they presented a considerable amount of evidence regarding the inadequacy of need theories that is remarkably reminiscent of the Mischel (1968) treatise on trait theories of personality. Indeed, one of the central themes in the Salancik and Pfeffer (1977) essay was the instability or inconsistency of the need state of individuals. The later paper (1978) completes the conclusion of the first: the social environment of individuals, not their need states nor their need state/environmental match, predicts job satisfaction. Job satisfaction, then, is a reaction to a socially constructed reality, which in turn depends upon the cues and clues of the environment for data. This retort to need/dominated theories of job satisfaction is reminiscent (though not remarkably so) of Mischel's (1973) later position regarding a definition of personality that is grounded in individual differences in social construction competencies. Parenthetically it must be noted that research on need theories at work has been almost totally dominated by the field survey/

correlational procedure while the studies used by Salancik and Pfeffer in support of their position have been almost exclusively laboratory experiments.

From an interactionist perspective, both need theories and the social information processing approaches to understanding job attitudes suffer from theoretical, methodological, and data analysis problems. Some of these flaws have been outlined by Calder and Schurr (1981) but their alternative, the cognitive psychological or information processing view, appears to yield little more than the idea that attitudes are the result of "a constructive process in which incoming information is interpreted in terms of relevant stored information" (p. 290). Indeed, by emphasizing the role of organizational procedures (e.g., group inclusion) rather than individual characteristics (e.g., internal-external control) as the causes of particular attitudes, Calder and Schurr seem to place themselves squarely in the situationist camp.

Simply stated, no current conceptualization of job attitudes addresses the process by which individual attributes and organizational attributes in natural interaction yield job attitudes, nor does any theory specify *which* individual attributes when in interaction with *which* situational attributes will, over time, yield *which* job attitudes. Finally, no theory addresses the fact that different kinds of people are typically found in different kinds of work situations. Thus, over time, as people select themselves in and out of settings, the effect of homogenization of people types should yield relatively similar job attitudes among those remaining.

This latter thought suggests that the similarity of people *in the way they construct reality* rather than some "rationalization" or "attribution" accounts for many of the field-collected effects presented by Salancik and Pfeffer and others who have studied the relative contribution of individual and situational variables to job attitudes (e.g., Oldham & Hackman, 1981). Self-selection in and out of settings, rather than attribution, would also account for the finding that long-term employees have more positive job attitudes (Sheldon, 1971). Indeed self-selection and the tendency of settings to be defined similarly by relatively similar kinds of people leads to the interesting hypothesis that different organizations are likely to encounter different kinds of environmental pressures (e.g., a turbulent environment), and that they should have characteristic ways of responding to the environments they do encounter. Thus, as Lawrence and Lorsch (1969) and others have shown, there is no one best way for an organization to respond to all environments. What is an appropriate response depends on many factors including, I would maintain, the kinds of people in the organization.

While it is not yet clear how organizations should be typed with respect to people attributes, some preliminary work in this direction has been accomplished by Holland (1966, 1973). He has categorized careers into six types and shown, over hundreds of studies, that people tend to enter career environments that fit their career interests. A most interesting feature of Holland's work is the manner in which he defines a career environment: Career environments are determined by the kinds of people in them.

If career environments are defined by the kinds of people in them, and if people select themselves in and out of organizations and jobs, for any one person and any one organization one would expect, over time, a settling out or stabilizing effect. In fact we find that most turnover in organizations at the individual level is early (Wanous, 1980) and, at least theoretically, turnover rates will be higher in less stable (i.e., younger) organizations than in more stable or older ones (Schneider, in press).

These conclusions suggest that the job attitudes of people in an organization are a function of the kinds of people attracted to, selected by, and retained there. The problem is that research designs, especially of the short-term laboratory experiment type *and* of the single organization sort, would fail to illuminate this hypothesis.

For example, research on higher-order need strengths (HNS) as a moderator of the job characteristic-job satisfaction relationship has been plagued by inconsistent findings (Roberts & Glick, 1981; Salancik & Pfeffer, 1977). One hypothesis not presented for these inconsistencies concerns the single-organization problem. Briefly stated, field research conducted in single organizations that attempts to use person variables as moderators of any relationship are doomed to lack generalizabilitiy and to reflect inconsistency across settings. This is true because of the homogeneity of people within settings, also known as the restriction of range problem. As noted earlier, homogeneity vitiates the probability of finding significant algebraic interaction terms, and those are precisely what moderators are (Zedeck, 1971). Indeed, not only are moderators unlikely, but individual differences as direct correlates of attitudes should also not be expected, again because of restriction of range.

Thus, while it should be obvious now why laboratory experiments are a poor source for hypotheses about what yields particular job attitudes at work, it should also be clear why single organization studies also cannot be depended upon as a source for generalizable findings. What is clear is that job attitude research needs to be field-oriented, longitudinal, multi-situational (with respect to industry, job-type, etc.), and include psychologically relevant data on persons (career interests, need for achievement, etc.), before we will begin to have an understanding of how job attitudes come to be what they are.

Finally, some mention of the correlates of job attitude research needs to be made. That is, in research using job attitudes as predictors of some other form of behavior, consideration of the issue posed by Epstein (1979, 1980) as data aggregation in the criterion, and by Fishbein and Ajzen (1975) as multiple act criteria is required. It is of interest to note that both personality (Epstein) and attitude theorists (Fishbein & Ajzen) have reached a similar conclusion with respect to the prediction of behavior: use cumulative data or multiple instances of the behavior as the criterion or dependent variable. As noted earlier, industrial psychologists have employed this dictum with considerable success by utilizing such cumulative data as managerial level or salary as criteria in the prediction of managerial effectiveness.

Multiple act or aggregate behaviors are useful as criteria because they are reliable and because they, in fact, represent the typical behavior of people. What is critical here is that personality and attitude measures are frequently called "typical behavior" measures (cf. Anastasi, 1976), yet evaluations of their utility in predicting behavior have been based on the prediction of single instances of behavior. The assumption of coherency in behavior introduced earlier suggests that the appropriate data for evaluating the validity of attitude measures are of the multiple act kind.

In summary, job attitude researchers have tended to ignore a number of the key assumptions of interactional psychology; namely, that people select situations (both on the entry and exit side), that situational variance in research is a function of the people in the situation, that single organization studies and laboratory experiments each make generalizability very difficult if not impossible, and that coherence in behavior dictates the use of multiple act or aggregate data as criteria in predictive studies (see also Fisher, 1980).

Socialization to Work

Socialization to the world, i.e., to becoming an adult member of a society, has been studied by all kinds of behavioral scientists, including sociologists, anthropologists, and psychologists. Except for developmental psychologists, however, socialization has been the study of how humans come to take on the behavioral and spiritual norms and values of their society. Indeed the study of socialization might be called the study of passage rites, the careful documentation of how societies mold their members to the status quo of the society.

For the most part this situationist orientation to the study of socialization has dominated studies of socialization to work. Indeed, scholars have been so enamored of the societal metaphor when studying socialization to work that the classic studies have tended to be accomplished in highly structured settings—settings which are almost "total organization" (Etzioni, 1975) in form. That is, many of the concepts that pervade the socialization literature derive from observations of relatively rigid and formalized, uniformed, people-processing programs (e.g., police [VanMaanen, 1976], priests [Potvin & Suziedelis, 1969], military recruits [Janowitz, 1960], physicians [Becker, Geer, Hughes & Strauss, 1961], forest rangers [Kaufman, 1960]). The relevance of this observation is that the uniformed professions (Becker et al., who studied physicians, called their book *Boys in White*) represent only a small proportion of all workers and even then, are representative of more extreme and, perhaps, homogeneous work cultures.

It follows that socialization to work in less rigidly defined roles should take more forms and, indeed, this seems to be true. For example, early research by Berlew and Hall (1966) on the socialization of managers and by Schein (1964) on the early experiences of M.B.A.s illuminated the *differences* in newcomer experiences, especially as regards early job challenge. The long-term study of AT&T managers (Bray, Campbell, & Grant, 1974) has continued this tradition by examining the joint influences of personal attributes (assessed via the assessment center method) and job challenge on the outcomes of socialization. As the role/ organization becomes less rigid, then, more types of people and more types of socialization experiences emerge requiring the scholar to note them.

There are suprisingly few studies which attempt to integrate theories about the various ways in which different individuals encounter different situations with theories about the ways situations may influence people. Interestingly, much of the work that has been accomplished has been done by occupational sociologists and it has been summarized by Mortimer and Lorence (1979).

Mortimer and Lorence cite a number of longitudinal studies revealing the kind of reciprocal person-situation relationships between individual and occupational attributes that interactional psychologists might predict: (1) Kohn and Schooner (1978) showed how people's intellectual flexibility predicted job complexity ten years later and the reciprocal effect was also observed; (2) Andrisani and Nestel (1976) noted how upward occupational mobility seems to lead to increased self-efficacy and that different levels of perceived self-efficacy predict later success in work (as indicated by annual salary); (3) Mortimer and Lorence themselves showed how, over a ten-year period, rewarding occupational experiences tend to reinforce the same values that constituted the basis of earlier work selection. As would be predicted on the basis of earlier discussions regarding self-selection into environments of a type similar to one's own, Mortimer and Lorence show *both* selection and socialization factors affecting worker values, present and future. Indeed they are explicit in their treatment of these effects as being reciprocal in nature (p. 138): "work satisfaction should also increase as a result of this continuing reciprocal process." Further, consistent with hypotheses noted earlier with respect to job attitudes, Mortimer and Lorence hypothesize that the positive relationships between age and work satisfaction and the relatively high level of job satisfaction expressed in all occupational groups (even under objectively poor working conditions) are attributable to the same continuing reciprocal process.

Yet, VanMaanen and Schein (1979, p.216) in their very comprehensive view of the socialization literature take the following position:

> [W]e assume here that a theory of organizational socialization must not allow itself to become too preoccupied with individual characteristics (age, background, personality characteristics, etc.), specific organizations (public, private, voluntary, coercive, etc.) or particular occupational roles (doctor, lawyer, crook, banker, etc.). . . . Our concern is therefore with "*people processing*" devices. The frequency and substantive outcome of the use of these devices across particular types of people, organizations, and occupations are then peripheral to our analytic concern.

The central conceptual problem with this theoretical stance is the implicit assumption that individual characteristics, specific types of organizations, and particular occupational roles are somehow independent of each other *and* of the specific form of people-processing devices observed in a particular setting. The interactionist perspective developed here suggests that specific types of organizations and occupational roles are likely to be characterized by individuals with particular characteristics yielding characteristic people-processing or socialization devices. Only when one entertains this natural selectivity of individuals for roles and organizations with concomitant differences in socialization programs will findings across studies be understandable.

Thus, one of the perplexing problems in the socialization literature has been the lack of consistency in findings across studies. All studies find that some socialization processes are at work and that there seem to be stages of the socialization experience (cf. Wanous, 1980), but what the processes are and how they are experienced varies, and the role of the individual in the process is ignored. As Jones (Note 2, p. 5) has recently stated:

> [Socialization research] . . . is predicated on the notion of the naive newcomer, and there is a paucity of research which deals with the socialization process from the newcomers' perspective. Even at the processual, cognitive level, accounts of newcomers "making sense" of their new situation frequently emphasize the primary effect of the *organizational* context on newcomer perception, rather than what newcomers, themselves, add to the process or situation.

Jones goes on to show how past experience, self-efficacy and individual differences in attributional tendencies (i.e., to self or others) may all affect the power of organizational devices to effect individual behavior and socialization experiences.

But even Jones fails to entertain the idea that different organizations and/or roles will, themselves, have different kinds of people-processing devices as a function of the kinds of people who occupy those organizations and/or roles. That is, should it be surprising when one discovers that a paramilitary organization like a police department employs military tactics in socializing recruits who, in any case, have frequently had prior military experience? Or, is it surprising to find that scholars studying the socialization of newcomers to different kinds of organizations require specification of a different number of stages with different names in order to capture the socialization experience of the people they studied (Louis, 1980)?

The point here is not to deny the contributions of a situationist orientation to socialization but to note that single organization or single role studies have built in self-selection bias, especially when the people studied are entering a relatively rigid and formally defined role. Such roles are almost guaranteed to require careful preselection by self and organization and, when studied, will appear to leave little room for individual initiative. These kinds of situations, in other words, fulfill all of the reasons for not using laboratory experiments as data for generalizing to the world of natural interaction. Parenthetically, it should be noted that all theoretical perspectives (e.g., Louis, 1980) which implicitly make the assumption of random assignment of person types to roles/organizations will similarly suffer from lack of generalizability.

Conversely, the AT&T studies of managerial lives (Bray et al., 1974) reveal how different kinds of socialization experiences linearly contribute to managerial success over and above individual attributes. Such studies are indeed rare (Schneider, 1978b), probably because personologists have tended to only look at traits while situationists have concentrated on various job variables. Hopefully we will in the future gain some clarity on what the important individual variables are for a more complete understanding of the effective socialization of different kinds of people in different kinds of roles and organizations (Reichers, Note 3).

Leadership at Work

For about 25 years organizational researchers and social psychologists have perpetuated the myth that traits fail to predict leadership accession and effectiveness. This is of course a myth because many early studies of leaders showed that traits were useful predictors of leadership acquisition and effectiveness. The confusion in interpretation of findings arose because the same traits were not particularly useful in distinguishing a collection of leaders from a collection of nonleaders, and because different traits were accurate at identifying leaders in different situations. Yukl (1981) hypothesizes that it was Stogdill's (1948) accurate report of the contingency nature of trait correlates of leadership that suppressed leadership trait research in the following decades.

For whatever the reason, the study of the personal traits of leaders has received scant attention when judged against the probably thousands of studies using just the LBDQ (Leadership Behavior Description Questionnaire; cf. Fleishman, 1957). As Stogdill (1974, p. 72) noted in his *Handbook of Leadership*:

> [R]eviews . . . have been cited as evidence in support of the view that leadership is entirely situational in origin and that no personal characteristics are predictive of leadership. This view seems to overemphasize the situational, and underemphasize the personal, nature of leadership.

Recent reviews of the relevance of trait approaches to the understanding and prediction of leadership effectiveness in managerial roles has been impressive, with different traits apparently useful in different kinds of settings. For example, Yukl (1981, p. 77) notes that studies of Miner's (1978) six motives to manage reveal stronger predictive power for managers in larger, more bureaucratically structured settings than for managers in less hierarchical organizations. Similarly, one can compare Bentz's (1967) description of the successful Sears executive to the one provided by Bray et al. (1974) for AT&T. The former has an emphasis on power, competitive drive for eminence and authority, and the need to be recognized, while the latter appears to emphasize the more general success-at-work theme, success in a monetary/financial sense, and an interest in self-development (especially towards innovation and adaptation). The power and influence theme at AT&T, when it appears, is focused not only on work but also externally to the community.

In the same contingency vein, McClelland's work (cf. Brown, 1965) with the three needs for achievement (nAch), power (nPow), and affiliation (nAff) can be cited. For example, nAch predicts success positively in innovative firms but negatively in bureaucratic firms, while with nPow the reverse is true (Andrews, 1967). Similar findings regarding the role of nAch in smaller, more entrepreneurial firms has been reported (Hundal, 1971), and the role of nPow in more traditional bureaucracies is well documented (McClelland, 1975). Some laboratory experiments (albeit relatively long ones in which people in working groups *had* to interact) have also revealed these kinds of contingency effects. Here reference is made to the innovative studies of nAch, nPow, and nAff conducted by Litwin and Stringer (1968).

Following hypotheses presented earlier, it is appropriate to suggest that the kinds of people in different kinds of organizations will yield attraction-selection-socialization-attrition cycles appropriate for those kinds of settings. This will yield people with more or less appropriate trait or motive patterns, and those with the most appropriate managerial or leadership motive pattern for that setting will become leaders.

It was precisely this line of thinking that led Fiedler (cf. 1967) to his contingency theory. This theory postulates that people are predominantly either task or relationship oriented. Fiedler found that his measure of task or relationship orientation failed to produce consistent predictive results and that prediction effectiveness seemed to depend on three situational variables: Leader-member relations (most important), position power, and task structure.

Years of research suggest considerable merit and robustness to the conceptualization, with most criticisms of the theory being attacks of the Least Preferred Co-worker (LPC) measure of task achievement or affiliation orientation (see Strube & Garcia, 1981, for support of the theory and Yukl, 1981, p. 139 for a full listing of the critiques). If it is true that some of the weak support for Fiedler is attributable to the LPC, it might prove worthwhile to employ McClelland's use of the T.A.T. projective measure of nAch, nAff, and nPow or Miner's Sentence Completion Blank in research using Fiedler's tripartite index of situational favorability.

An interactional interpretation, however, would focus not only on the trait measure but on the natural interaction of person and setting as a basis for cues to inconsistent results, even when the results come out of an obviously interactionist position. One clue here is Fiedler's consistent success in accounting for military leadership with more inconsistency in the industrial sector. Perhaps one can trace this to the model's origins which were based on inconsistent findings from military teams (bomber, tank, and artillery crew commanders) or other formally organized teams (basketball) with designated leaders. Is it possible that in accounting for the inconsistencies in predictive results among these small formal groups that Fiedler chose the attributes he did to serve as contingency effects?

Such questioning suggests the conclusion that even Fiedler's theory may not be complex enough to account for who may become a leader in a specific setting for a relatively narrowly defined point in time. This conclusion is meant to suggest that the more micro the prediction desired, that is, the more narrowly defined the situation is, the more detailed the conceptualization needs to be. In brief, predicting and understanding who will be an effective tank commander in the next 6 to 12 months is a much more difficult problem than predicting who will achieve a high level in an organization 8 or 10 years in the future. Three factors enhance prediction in the latter case: (1) the micro features of the various mini-settings of natural and reciprocal interaction have a chance to cancel each other out and/or accumulate; (2) the dependent variable is an aggregate which capitalizes on behavioral coherence and is thus more reliable, and (3) the passage of time serves to both make the setting more homogeneous and reify the personal attributes of those who remain.

Predicting leadership in more time-bounded situations fails to consider the coherence of behavior and the fact that people tend to move in and out of differentially favorable situations so far as leadership possibilities are concerned. In fact, attempting to predict leadership through trait measures in a time-bounded situation is almost the equivalent of trying to employ trait measures as predictors in laboratory experiments especially when the situation may not be one the (potential) leader has *chosen*.

It is important to note that other conceptualizations of leadership sometimes called contingency or situational theories are, in fact, the latter. Thus, they typically specify what a leader should do if they have particular types of subordinates (e.g., House & Mitchell, 1974), if they encounter different kinds of group situations (e.g., Yukl, 1981), or when they need to make a decision about subordinate participation in decisions (Vroom & Yetton, 1973). No attention is paid to the personal attributes of the leader in these theories.

From an interactionist perspective a potentially very interesting conceptualization of leadership is tne Vertical Dyadic Linkage Theory (VDL) proposed by Graen and his colleagues (Graen & Cashman, 1975; Dansereau, Graen & Haga, 1975). This theory explains leadership in dyadic terms, that is, in terms of the pair relationships existing between people in leadership roles and *each* of their subordinates. The micro levels of analysis used in this research include data on actual dyadic interaction patterns. If Graen and his coworkers could illuminate the personal attributes of leaders and the various attributes of situations that converge to be reflected in particular leader-subordinate interaction patterns, we would have the opportunity to conduct true interactionist research on leadership. Hollander's (1978) transactional theory and Hersey and Blanchard's (1982) situationist theory, if they included relevant data on the attributes of the leader (e.g., self-perceived competence or own maturity), could also yield important information about the conceptualization and prediction of leader behavior.

All three theories present an opportunity to understand the coherence of behavior, that is, a chance to discover the characteristically different ways different leaders behave when confronted by different subordinates/situations. Such documentation, it can be hypothesized, would reveal that different leaders have *profiles* of behavior and it is those profiles which distinguish them from other leaders and nonleaders. The challenge is to specify the personal and situational correlates of these varying profiles of behavior.

The message in this section on leadership is simply one of revealing how an interactionist position can help illuminate potentially interesting questions. Two such questions are posed: (1) Given the established effectiveness of trait predictions of leadership ascension and effectiveness at work, why do almost all theories of leadership fail to consider the personal attributes of leaders as part of their conceptualization? and (2) Would thinking about leadership effectiveness in different situations as being characterized by different *profiles* of behavior enhance the probability that scholars could identify the personal and situational correlates of those profiles?

SUMMARY AND CONCLUSIONS

The goal of this essay was to introduce the central issues in interactional psychology. Two paths to this goal were used: A summary of the recent history and thinking in interactionism, and the application of interactional thinking to studies of job attitudes, socialization to work, and leadership.

The review of recent history and thinking revealed a number of major themes that characterize interactional psychology. These themes can be characterized as the causal, methodological, and data analytic. Briefly, it was shown that interactionists believe in the primacy of interaction between persons and setting as the cause of behavior, that short-term laboratory experiments which fail to capture person-situation reciprocity are ineffective as sources of information about real-time behavior, and that the ANOVA concept of algebraic interaction is but one way to conceptualize the meaning of interaction.

More specifically, the focus on person and setting as relatively inseparable due to continual reciprocal interaction was instrumental in dismantling the oft-assumed superiority of the short-term laboratory experiment as a method. In addition, the idea that people actively choose settings effectively eliminated the belief that random assignment to treatments was the sure path to the *experimentum crucix*.

The arguments against the superiority of the lab experiment were shown to be critical for supporting the interactionist position. This was so because only if it can be shown that situationists (experimentalists) essentially insure desired behavior by eliminating the possibility of individual differences, can their attacks on the trait and dynamic positions be rebuked. Of special importance were situationist attacks on the stability of traits and trait-based predictions of behavior.

The major ideas derived from this review concerned: Self-selection into (and out of) situations yielding relatively homogeneous settings; coherence in human behavior, meaning that different people have different *profiles* of behavior, i.e., that a person's typical behavior may have variability as s/he moves from setting to setting; that point predictions of behavior (behavior in one setting at one time) are very difficult, but aggregate or multiple act criteria are predictable; and, that settings are characterized by the people in them.

These major ideas were then applied to current thinking in OB about job attitudes, socialization to work, and leadership. In all three the major insight offered by the interactional psychology perspective was self-selection into and out of situations. This insight was useful as an alternative explanation for the Salancik and Pfeffer (1977, 1978) critiques of need theories and job attitudes; it served as a vehicle for specifying the absence of thinking about how different kinds of people get socialized in different kinds of work settings; and it revealed an almost slavish concern for the leader's situation as a determinant of leader behavior to the exclusion of traits and/or trait-situation reciprocation.

Additional insights were gained from consideration of the laboratory experiment as the source of most data supporting a social constructionist view of job attitudes. But perhaps equally important was the finding that in socialization, job attitude, and leadership research, single organization studies might suffer from external validity problems as much as laboratory experiments. Thus it was shown that failure to take person type into account in research also leads to ignoring the role of organization type. By ignoring person and organization variability in research (let alone their interaction), one is forced to be cautious about the generalizability and utility of OB theories and applications. Indeed single organization studies may suffer from lack of internal validity as well as external validity.

Methodologically, the perspective presented here would encourage long-term studies of the growth and development of people and their organizations where both person and organization attributes are known prior to their interaction. How people and settings unfold and emerge is the great mystery, and we sorely need such research (Kimberly & Miles, 1980). In a more practical vein, documentation of the methodological benefits of accumulating criterion data for individuals as suggested by Epstein (1979) and Fishbein and Ajzen (1975), (and demonstrated so well by industrial psychologists in predicting managerial success [Campbell et al., 1980]) supports both the concept of coherence in behavior and traditional concern for personality and attitude measures as indicants of typical behavior.

Finally, interactional psychology opens a new window on old problems and yields a host of interesting questions about the emergence of settings. In contrast, then, to "creationists," interactionism questions how settings come to evolve as they do. It's a really interesting question!

ACKNOWLEDGMENTS

The writing of this paper was partially supported by the Organizational Effectiveness Research Group, Psychological Sciences Division, Office of Naval Research under Contract No. N00014-79-C-0781, Contract Authority Identification Number NR 170-894, Benjamin Schneider, Principal Investigator.

I have profited from helpful comments on an earlier version of this paper by Dave Bowen, Arnon Reichers, John Wanous, and Ken Wexley. This paper was written while the author was at Michigan State University.

NOTE

1. The "volunteer subject" phenomenon (Rosenthal & Rosnow, 1969) suggests that many laboratory experiments are themselves being conducted on self-selected participants of a particular type: e.g., higher need for social approval, more intelligent, more sociable than non-volunteers. This phenomenon yields, then, research on a restricted range of people, who are then randomly assigned to demanding situations.

REFERENCE NOTES

1. Schneider, B., & Mitchell, T. M. *Work and career considerations in understanding employee turnover intentions: Development of the turnover diagnostic.* Unpublished manuscript, Department of Psychology, Michigan State University, 1981.
2. Jones, G. R. *Psychological orientation and the process of organizational socialization.* Unpublished manuscript, Department of Management, Michigan State University, 1981.
3. Reichers, A. E. *Personality, socialization, and adjustment to work.* Unpublished manuscript, Department of Management, Michigan State University, 1981.

REFERENCES

Anastasi, A. *Psychological testing* (4th ed.). New York: Macmillan, 1976.
Andrews, J. D. W. The achievement motive and advancement in two types of organizations. *Journal of Personality and Social Psychology,* 1967, *6,* 163–168.
Andrisani, P. J., & Nestel, G. Internal-external control as contributor to and outcome of work experience. *Journal of Applied Psychology,* 1976, *61,* 156–165.
Argyris, C. Some unintended consequences of rigorous research. *Psychological Bulletin,* 1968, *70,* 185–197.
Argyris, C. *Inner contradictions of rigorous research.* New York: Academic Press, 1980.
Becker, H., Geer, B., Hughes, E., & Strauss, A. *Boys in white.* Chicago: University of Chicago Press, 1961.

Bentz, V. J. The Sears experience in the investigation, description, and prediction of executive behavior. In F. R. Wickert & D. E. McFarland (Eds.), *Measuring executive effectiveness*. New York: Appleton-Century-Crofts, 1967.

Berlew, D. E., & Hall, D. T. The socialization of managers: Effects of expectations on performance. *Administrative Science Quarterly*, 1966, *11*, 207–223.

Bowers, K. S. Situationism in psychology: An analysis and critique. *Psychological Bulletin*, 1973, *80*, 307–336.

Bray, D. W., Campbell, R. J., & Grant, D. L. *Formative years in business: A long-term A.T.&T. study of managerial lives*. New York: Wiley, 1974.

Brown, R. *Social psychology*. New York: The Free Press, 1965.

Calder, B. J., & Schurr, P. H. Attitudinal processes in organization. In L. L. Cummings & B. Staw (Eds.), *Research in organizational behavior*, Vol. 3. Greenwich, CT: JAI Press, 1981.

Campbell, D. P., & Hansen, J. C. *Manual for the SVIB-SCII*. Stanford: Stanford University Press, 1981.

Campbell, J. P., Dunnette, M. D., Lawler, E. E. III, & Weick, K. E., Jr. *Managerial behavior, performance, and effectiveness*. New York: McGraw-Hill, 1970.

Crites, J. O. *Vocational psychology*. New York: McGraw-Hill, 1969.

Cronbach, L. J., & Snow, R. E. *Aptitudes and instructional methods: A handbook for research on interactions*. New York: Irvington, 1977.

Dansereau, F., Jr., Graen, G., & Haga, W. J. A vertical dyad linkage approach to leadership within formal organizations: A longitudinal investigation of the role making process. *Organizational Behavior and Human Performance*, 1975, *13*, 46–78.

Ekehammar, B. Interactionism in personality from a historical perspective. *Psychological Bulletin*, 1974, *81*, 1026–1048.

Endler, N. S., & Magnusson, D. (Eds.). *Interactional psychology and personality*. New York: Hemisphere, 1976a.

Endler, N. S., & Magnusson, D. Personality and person by situation interactions. In N. S. Endler & D. Magnusson (Eds.), *Interactional psychology and personality*. New York: Hemisphere, 1976b.

Epstein, S. The stability of behavior: I. On predicting most of the people much of the time. *Journal of Personality and Social Psychology*, 1979, *37*, 1097–1126.

Epstein, S. The stability of behavior: II. Implications for psychological research. *American Psychologist*, 1980, *35*, 790–806.

Etzioni, A. *A comparative analysis of complex organizations* (Rev. ed.). New York: Free Press, 1975.

Fairweather, G. W., & Tornatzky, L. G. *Experimental methods for social policy research*. Oxford: Pergamon Press, 1977.

Fiedler, F. E. *A theory of leadership effectiveness*. New York: McGraw-Hill, 1967.

Fishbein, M., & Ajzen, I. *Belief, attitude, intention, and behavior: An introduction tc theory and research*. Reading, MA: Addison-Wesley, 1975.

Fisher, C. D. On the dubious wisdom of expecting job satisfaction to correlate witl performance. *Academy of Management Review*, 1980, *5*, 607–612.

Fleishman, E. A. A leader behavior description for industry. In R. M. Stogdill & A. E Coons (Eds.), *Leader behavior: Its description and measurement*. Columbus, OH Bureau of Business Research, Ohio State University, 1957.

Goldstein, I. L. Training in work organizations. In M. R. Rosenzweig & L. W. Porte (Eds.), *Annual review of psychology*, Vol. 31. Palo Alto: Annual Reviews, Inc., 197ᶜ

Graen, G., & Cashman, J. F. A role-making model of leadership in formal organization: A developmental approach. In J. G. Hunt & L. L. Larson (Eds.), *Leadership frontier: Kent, OH: Kent State University Press, 1975.

Hersey, P., & Blanchard, K. H. *Management of organizational behavior* (4th. ed.). Englewood Cliffs, NJ: Prentice Hall, 1982.

Holland, J. L. *The psychology of vocational choice.* Waltham, MA: Blaisdell, 1966.

Holland, J. L. *The psychology of vocational choice* (Rev. ed.). Waltham, MA: Blaisdell, 1973.

Holland, J. L. Vocational preferences. In M. D. Dunnette (Ed.), *Handbook of industrial and organizational psychology.* Chicago: Rand McNally, 1976.

Hollander, E. P. *Leadership dynamics: A practical guide to effective relationships.* New York: Free Press, 1978.

House, R. J., & Mitchell, T. R. Path-goal theory of leadership. *Contemporary Business,* 1974, *3,* 81–98.

Hundal, P. S. A study of entrepreneurial motivation: Comparison of fast and slow progressing small scale industrial entrepreneurs in Punjab, India. *Journal of Applied Psychology,* 1971, *55,* 317–323.

Janowitz, M. *The professional solider.* Glencoe, IL: The Free Press, 1960.

Kaufman, H. *The forest ranger.* Baltimore: Johns Hopkins Press, 1960.

Kelley, H. *Attribution in social interaction.* Morristown, NJ: General Learning Press, 1971.

Kimberly, J. R., & Miles, R. H. (Eds.). *The organizational life cycle.* San Francisco: Jossey-Bass, 1980.

Kohn, M. L., & Schooner, C. The reciprocal effects of the substantive complexity of work and intellectual flexibility: A longitudinal assessment. *American Journal of Sociology,* 1978, *84,* 24–52.

Lawrence, P. R., & Lorsch, J. W. *Organization and environment: Managing differentiation and integration.* Homewood, IL: Irwin, 1969.

Litwin, G. H., & Stringer, R. A. *Motivation and organizational climate.* Boston: Harvard Business School, Division of Research, 1968.

Locke, E. A., Mento, A. J., & Katcher, B. L. The interaction of ability and motivation in performance: An exploration of the meaning of moderators. *Personnel Psychology,* 1978, *31,* 269–280.

Locke, E. A., Shaw, K. N., Saari, L. M., & Latham, G. P. Goal setting and task performance: 1969–1980. *Psychological Bulletin,* 1981, *90,* 125–152.

Lofquist, L. H., & Dawis, R. V. *Adjustment to work.* New York: Appleton-Century, 1969.

Louis, M. R. Surprise and sense making: What newcomers experience in entering unfamiliar organizational settings. *Administrative Science Quarterly,* 1980, *25,* 226–251.

Maddi, S. R. *Personality theories: A comparative analysis* (4th ed.). Homewood, IL: The Dorsey Press, 1980.

Magnusson, D., & Endler, N. S. (Eds.). *Personality at the crossroads: Current issues in interactional psychology.* Hillsdale, NJ: Erlbaum, 1977a.

Magnusson, D., & Endler, N. S. Interactional psychology: Present status and future prospects. In D. Magnusson & N. S. Endler (Eds.), *Personality at the crossroads: Current issues in interactional psychology.* Hillsdale, NJ: Erlbaum, 1977b.

McClelland, D. *Power: The inner experience.* New York: Irvington, 1975.

McGuire, W. J. The Yin and Yang of progress in social psychology: Seven Koan. *Journal of Personality and Social Psychology,* 1973, *26,* 446–456.

Miner, J. B. Twenty years of research on role motivation theory of managerial effectiveness. *Personnel Psychology,* 1978, *31,* 739–760.

Mischel, W. *Personality and assessment.* New York: Wiley, 1968.

Mischel, W. Toward a cognitive social learning reconceptualization of personlity. *Psychological Review,* 1973, *80,* 252–283.

Mobley, W. H. *Employee turnover in organizations.* Reading, MA: Addison-Wesley, 1982.

Mortimer, J. T., & Lorence, J. Work experience and occupational value socialization: A longitudinal study. *American Journal of Sociology*, 1979, *84*, 1361–1385.

Oldham, G. R., & Hackman, J. R. Relationships between organizational structure and employee reactions: Comparing alternative frameworks. *Administrative Science Quarterly*, 1981, *26*, 66–83.

Orne, M. T. On the social psychology of the psychological experiment: With particular reference to their demand characteristics and their implication. *American Psychologist*, 1962, *17*, 776–783.

Pervin, L. A., & Lewis, M. (Eds.). *Perspectives in interactional psychology*. New York: Plenum, 1978a.

Pervin, L. A., & Lewis, M. Overview of the internal-external issue. In L. A. Pervin & M. Lewis (Eds.), *Perspectives in interactional psychology*. New York: Plenum, 1978b.

Porter, L. W., & Steers, R. M. Organizational, work and personal factors in employee turnover and absenteeism. *Psychological Bulletin*, 1973, *80*, 151–176.

Potvin, R. H., & Suziedelis, A. *Seminarians of the sixties*. Washington, D. C.: Center for Applied Research in the Apostolate, 1969.

Roberts, K. H., & Glick, W. The job characteristics approach to task design: A critical review. *Journal of Applied Psychology*, 1981, *66*, 193–217.

Rosenthal, R., & Rosnow, R. L. *Artifacts in behavioral research*. New York: Academic Press, 1969.

Salancik, G. R. Field stimulations for organization behavior research. *Administrative Science Quarterly*, 1979, *24*, 638–649.

Salancik, G. R., & Pfeffer, J. An examination of need satisfaction models of job attitudes. *Administrative Science Quarterly*, 1977, *22*, 427–456.

Salancik, G. R., & Pfeffer, J. A social information processing approach to job attitudes and task design. *Administrative Science Quarterly*, 1978, *23*, 224–253.

Sanford, N. Whatever happened to action research? *Journal of Social Issues*, 1970, *26*, 3–23.

Schein, E. H. How to break in the college graduate. *Harvard Business Review*, 1964, *42*, 68–76.

Schneider, B. Implications of the conference: A personal view. *Personnel Psychology*, 1978, *31*, 299–304a.

Schneider, B. Person-situation selection: A review of some ability-situation interaction research. *Personnel Psychology*, 1978, *31*, 281–297b.

Schneider, B. Organizational effectiveness: An interactionist perspective. In D. Whetten & K. S. Cameron (Eds.), *Organizational effectiveness: A comparison of multiple models*. New York: Academic Press, in press.

Schneider, B., Hall, D. T., & Nygren, H. T. Self-image and job characteristics as correlates of changing organizational identification. *Human Relations*, 1972, *24*, 397–416.

Sheldon, M. E. Investments and involvements as mechanisms producing commitment to organizations. *Administrative Science Quarterly*, 1971, *16*, 143–150.

Stogdill, R. M. Personal factors associated with leadership: A survey of the literature. *Journal of Psychology*, 1948, *25*, 35–71.

Stogdill, R. M. *Handbook of leadership: A survey of theory and research*. New York: Free Press, 1974.

Strube, J. J., & Garcia, J. E. A meta-analytic investigation of Fiedler's model of leadership effectiveness. *Psychological Bulletin*, 1981, *90*, 307–321.

Terborg, J. R. Validation and extension of an individual differences model of work performance. *Organizational Behavior and Human Performance*, 1977, *18*, 188–216.

Terborg, J. R. Interactional psychology and research on human behavior in organizations. *Academy of Management Review*, 1981, *6*, 569–576.

VanMaanen, J. Breaking in: Socialization at work. In R. Dubin, (Ed.), *Handbook of work, organization, and society.* Chicago: Rand McNally, 1976.

VanMaanen, J., & Schein, E. H. Toward a theory of organizational socialization. In B. Staw (Ed.), *Research in organizational behavior,* Vol. 1. Greenwich, CT: JAI Press, 1979.

Vroom, V. H., & Yetton, P. W. *Leadership and decision-making.* Pittsburgh: University of Pittsburgh Press, 1973.

Wachtel, P. Psychodynamics, behavior therapy and the implacable experimenter: An inquiry into the consistency of personality. *Journal of Abnormal Psychology,* 1973, *82,* 324–334.

Wanous, J. P. *Organizational entry: Recruitment, selection and socialization of newcomers.* Reading, MA: Addison-Wesley, 1980.

Weick, K. E. Organizations in the laboratory. In V. H. Vroom (Ed.), *Methods of organizational research.* Pittsburgh: University of Pittsburgh Press, 1967.

Yukl, G. A. *Leadership in organizations.* Englewood Cliffs, NJ: Prentice Hall, 1981.

Zedeck, S. Problems with the use of "moderator" variables. *Psychological Bulletin,* 1971, *76,* 295–310.

TOWARD A THEORY OF ORGANIZATIONAL SOCIALIZATION

John Van Maanen and Edgar H. Schein

ABSTRACT

The process of organizational socialization is examined in terms of the strategic forms it typically assumes. Attention is also directed to those specific organizational boundaries crossed by persons when acquiring a new work role. A set of propositions is then derived which attempts to link a particular organizational socialization tactic to the behavioral responses of individuals subjected to that tactic during a boundary passage. An underlying theme of the essay is simply that *what* people learn about their work roles in organizations is often a direct result of *how* they learn it.

I. ORGANIZATIONAL SOCIALIZATION

Introduction
Work organizations offer a person far more than merely a job. Indeed, from the time individuals first enter a workplace to the time they leave their membership behind, they experience and often commit themselves to a distinct way of life complete with its own rhythms, rewards, relationships, demands, and potentials. To be sure, the differences to be found within and between organizations range from the barely discernible to the starkly dramatic. But, social research has yet to discover a work setting which leaves people unmarked by their participation.

By and large, studies of work behavior have, to date, focused primarily upon the ahistorical or "here and now" behavior and attitudes assumed by individual members of an organization that are associated with various institutional, group, interactional, and situational attributes. Relatively less attention has given to the manner in which these responses are thought to arise. In particular, the question of how it is that only certain patterns of thought and action are passed from one generation of organizational members to the next has been neglected. Since such a process of socialization necessarily involves the transmission of information and values, it is fundamentally a cultural matter.[1]

Any organizational culture consists broadly of long-standing rules of thumb, a somewhat special language, an ideology that helps edit a member's everyday experience, shared standards of relevance as to the critical aspects of the work that is being accomplished, matter-of-fact prejudices, models for social etiquette and demeanor, certain customs and rituals suggestive of how members are to relate to colleagues, subordinates, superiors, and outsiders, and a sort of residual category of some rather plain "horse sense" regarding what is appropriate and "smart" behavior within the organization and what is not. All of these cultural modes of thinking, feeling, and doing are, of course, fragmented to some degree, giving rise within large organizations to various "subcultures" or "organizational segments."[2]

Such cultural forms are so rooted in the recurrent problems and common experiences of the membership in an organizational segment that once learned they become viewed by insiders as perfectly "natural" responses to the world of work they inhabit. This is merely to say that organizational cultures arise and are maintained as a way of coping with and making sense of a given problematic environment. That organizations survive the lifetimes of their founders suggests that the culture established by the original membership displays at least some stability through time. Metaphorically, just as biologists sometimes argue that "gene pools" exploit individuals in the interest of their own survival, organizations, as sociocultural forms, do the same. Thus, the devout believer is the Church's way of ensuring the survival of the Church; the loyal citizen is the State's way of ensuring the survival of the State; the scientific apprentice is Physics' way of ensuring the survival of Physics; and the productive employee is the Corporation's way of ensuring the survival of the Corporation.

This is not to say, however, that the transfer of a particular work culture from generation to generation of organizational participants occurs smoothly, quickly, and without evolutionary difficulty. New members always bring with them at least the potential for change. They may, for example, question old assumptions about how the work is to be performed, be ignorant of some rather sacred interpersonal conventions that define authority relationships within the workplace, or fail to properly appreciate the work ideology or organizational mandate shared by the more experienced members present on the scene. Novices bring with them different backgrounds, faulty preconceptions of the jobs to be performed within the setting, including their own, and perhaps values and ends that are at odds with those of the working membership.

The more experienced members must therefore find ways to insure that the newcomer does not disrupt the ongoing activity on the scene, embarrass or cast a disparaging light on others, or question too many of the established cultural solutions worked out previously. Put bluntly, new members must be taught to see the organizational world as do their more experienced colleagues if the traditions of the organization are to survive. The manner in which this teaching/learning occurs is referred to here as the *organizational socialization process*.

What Is Organizational Socialization?

At heart, organizational socialization is a jejune phrase used by social scientists to refer to the process by which one is taught and learns "the ropes" of a particular organizational role. In its most general sense, organizational socialization is the process by which an individual acquires the social knowledge and skills necessary to assume an organizational role. Across the roles, the process may appear in many forms, ranging from a relatively quick, self-guided, trial-and-error process to a far more elaborate one requiring a lengthy preparation period of education and training followed by an equally drawn-out period of official apprenticeship.[3] In fact, if one takes seriously the notion that learning itself is a continuous and life-long process, the entire organizational career of an individual can be characterized as a socialization process (Schein,1971a; Van Maanen, 1977a). At any rate, given a particular role, organizational socialization refers minimally, though, as we shall see, not maximally, to the fashion in which an individual is taught and learns what behaviors and perspectives are customary and desirable within the work setting as well as what ones are not.

Insofar as the individual is concerned, the results of an organizational socialization process include, for instance, a readiness to select certain events for attention over others, a stylized stance toward one's routine activities, some ideas as to how one's various behavioral responses to recurrent situations are viewed by others, and so forth. In short, socialization entails the learning of a cultural perspective that can be brought to bear on both commonplace and unusual matters going on in the workplace. To come to know an organizational situation and act within it implies that a person has developed some commonsensical beliefs, principles, and understandings, or in shorthand notation, a *perspective* for interpreting one's experiences in a given sphere of the work world. As Shibutani (1962) suggests, it provides the individual with an ordered view of the work life that runs ahead and guides experience, orders and shapes personal relationships in the work setting, and provides the ground rules under which everyday conduct is to be managed. Once developed, a perspective provides a person with the conventional wisdom that governs a particular context as to the typical features of everyday life.

To illustrate this highly contingent and contextual process, consider the following hypothetical but completely plausible exchange between an experienced patrolman and a colleague in a police department. When asked about what happened to him on a given shift, the veteran officer might well respond by saying, "We didn't do any police work, just wrote a couple of movers and brought in a body, a stand-up you know." The raw recruit could hardly know of such things, for the description given clearly presumes a special kind of knowledge shared by experienced organizational members as to the typical features of their work and how such knowledge is used when going about and talking about their job. The rookie must learn of these understandings and eventually come to make use of them in an entirely matter-of-fact way if he is to continue as a member of the organization. At root, this is the cultural material with which organizational socialization is concerned.

At this point, however, it is important to note that not all organizational socialization can be assumed to be functional for either the individual or the organization. Organizations are created and sustained by people often for other people and are also embedded deeply within a larger and continually changing environment. They invent as well as provide the means by which individual and collective needs are fulfilled. Whereas learning the orgnaizational culture may always be immediately *adjustive* for an individual in that such learning will reduce the tension associated with entering an unfamiliar situation, such learning, in the long run, may not always be adaptive, since certain cultural forms may persist long after they have ceased to be of individual value. Consider, for example, the pervasive practice in many relatively stable orgnaizations of encouraging most lower and middle managerial employees to aspire to high position within the organization despite the fact that there will be very few positions open at these levels. Perhaps the discontent of the so-called "plateaued manager" can then be seen as a result of a socialization practice that has outlived its usefulness.

Consider also that what may be adjustive for the individual may not be adaptive for the organization.[4] Situations in which the careless assignment of an eager and talented newcomer to an indifferent, disgruntled, or abrasively cantankerous supervisor may represent such a case wherein the adjustive solution seized upon by the new member is to leave the organization as soon as employment elsewhere has been secured. Socialization practices must not therefore be taken for granted or, worse, ignored on the basis that all cultural learning is fundamentally functional. The sieve that is history operates in often capricious and accidental ways and there is little reason to believe that all aspects of a culture that are manufactured and passed on by members of an organization to other incoming members are necessarily useful at either the individual or collective levels.

We must note also that the problems of organizational socialization refer to any and all passages undergone by members of an organization. From beginning to end, a person's career within an organization represents a potential series of transitions from one position to another (Van Maanen, 1977b; Glaser, 1968; Hall, 1976; Schein, 1971a). These transitions may be few in number or many, they may entail upward, downward, or lateral movement, and demand relatively mild to severe adjustments on the part of the individual. Of course, the intensity, importance, and visibility of a given passage will vary across a person's career. It is probably most obvious (both to the individual and to others on the scene) when a person first enters the organization—the outsider to insider passage. It is perhaps least obvious when an experienced member of an organization undergoes a simple change of assignment, shift, or job location. Nevertheless, a period of socialization accompanies each passage. From this standpoint, organizational socialization is ubiquitous, persistent, and forever problematic.

II. BACKGROUND AND UNDERLYING ASSUMPTIONS

With few exceptions, observers of organizations have failed to give systematic attention to the problem of how specific bits of culture are transmitted within an organization. The empirical materials that do exist are

scattered widely across all disciplines found in the social sciences and
hence do not share a common focus or a set of similar concepts.[5] Even
within sociology and anthropology, the disciplines most concerned with
cultural matters, the published studies devoted to socialization practices
of groups, organizations, subcultures, societies, tribes, and so forth tend
to be more often than not anecdotal, noncomparative, and based upon
retrospective informant accounts of the process rather than the observation of the process *in situ.* Indeed, then, general statements about the
process, content, agents, and targets of organizational socialization are
grossly impressionistic. In other words, a total conceptual scheme for
attacking the problem may be said to be presently nonexistent.

In this and the sections to follow, we offer the beginnings of a *descriptive* conceptual scheme which we feel will be useful in guiding some
much-needed research in this crucial area. Our efforts are directed toward
building a sound theoretical base for the study of organizational socialization and not toward proffering any normative theory as to the "effectiveness" or "ineffectiveness" of any given organizational form. We are interested consequently in generating a set of interrelated theoretical propositions about the structure and outcome of organizational socialization
processes. Such a theory, to be analytically sound, must accomplish at
least three things. *First,* it must tell us where to look within an organization to observe socialization in its most salient and critical forms. *Second,*
such a thoery must describe, in a fashion generally applicable to a large
number of organizational contexts, the various cultural forms organizational socialization can take. And, *third,* the theory must offer some explanation as to why a particular form of a socialization occurring at a given
location within an organization tends to result in certain kinds of individual or collective outcomes rather than others. Only in this fashion will
it be possible to build a testable theory to direct research in the area.[6]

Some Assumptions

There are, of course, many assumptions that undergird our theory
building efforts in this regard. *First,* and perhaps of most importance, is
the well-grounded assumption that individuals undergoing any organizational transition are in an anxiety-producing situation. In the main, they
are more or less motivated to reduce this anxiety by learning the functional and social requirements of their newly assumed role as quickly as
possible. The sources of this anxiety are many. To wit, psychological
tensions are promoted no doubt by the feelings of loneliness and isolation
that are associated initially with a new location in an organization as well
as the performance anxieties a person may have when assuming new
duties. Gone also is the learned social situation with its established and
comfortable routines for handling interaction and predicting the responses

of others to oneself. Thus, stress is likely because newcomers to a particular organizational role will initially feel a lack of identification with the various activities observed to be going on about them. Needless to say, different kinds of transitions will invoke different levels of anxiety, but any passage from the familiar to the less familiar will create some difficulties for the person moving on.

Second, organizational socialization and the learning that is associated with it does not occur in a social vacuum strictly on the basis of the official and available versions of the new role requirements. Any person crossing into a new organizational region is vulnerable to clues on how to proceed that originate within the interactional zone that immediately surrounds him. Colleagues, superiors, subordinates, clients, and other associates support and guide the individual in learning the new role. Indeed, they help to interpret the events one experiences such that one can eventually take action in one's altered situation. Ultimately, they provide the individual with a sense of accomplishment and competence (or failure and incompetence).

Third, the stability and productivity of any organization depends in large measure upon the ways newcomers to various positions come eventually to carry out their tasks. When the passing of positions from generation to generation of incumbents is accomplished smoothly with a minimum of disruption, the continuity of the organization's mission is maintained, the predictability of the organization's performance is left intact. And, assuming the organizational environment remains reasonably stable, the survival of the organization is assured—at least in the short run. It could be said that the various socialization processes carried out within an organization represent the glue which holds together the various interlocking parts of an ongoing social concern.

Fourth, the way in which individuals adjust to novel circumstances is remarkably similar though there is no doubt great variation in the particular content and type of adjustments achieved (or not achieved). In some cases, a shift into a new work situation may result in a sharply altered organizational and personal identity for an individual, as often occurs when a factory worker becomes a foreman or a staff analyst becomes a line manager. In other cases, the shift may result in only minor and insignificant changes in a person's organizational and personal identity, as perhaps is the case when a craftsman is rotated to a new department or a fireman changes from working the hook-and-ladder to a rescue squad. Yet, in any of these shifts there is still likely to be at least some surprise or what Hughes (1958) calls "reality shock" in store for the individual involved when he first encounters the new working context. When persons undergo a transition, regardless of the information they already possess about the new role, their a priori understandings of that role will undoub-

tedly change.[7] In short rarely, if ever, can such learning be complete
until a newcomer has endured a period of initiation within the new role.
As Barnard (1938) noted with characteristic clarity, "There is no instant
replacement, there is always a period of adjustment."

Fifth, the analysis that follows makes no so-called functional assumptions about the necessity of organizations to socialize individuals to particular kinds of roles. Indeed, we reject any implicit or explicit notions
that certain organizationally relevant rules, values, or motivations must
be internalized by people as "blueprints for behavior" if they are to
participate and contribute to the organization's continued survival. Such a
view leaves little room for individual uniqueness and ignores the always
problematic contextual nature of the various ways organizational roles
can be filled. While, there are no doubt reasons why certain socialization
tactics are used more frequently by one organization than another, these
reasons are to be located at the human level of analysis, not at the structural or functional levels. From this perspective, we are very much com-
mitted to a symbolic interactionist view of social life, one that suggests
that individuals, not organizations, create and sustain beliefs and what is
and is not functional (Strauss, 1959). And, as in all matters individual,
what is functional for one actor may be dysfunctional for another.

Sixth, and finally, we assume here that a theory of organizational
socialization must not allow itself to become too preoccupied with individual characteristics (age, background, personality characteristics, etc.),
specific organizations (public, private, voluntary, coercive, etc.), or particular occupational roles (doctor, lawyer, crook, banker, etc.). To be of
value to researchers and laymen alike, the theory must transcend the
particular and peculiar and aim for the general and typical. At least at this
stage in the construction of a theory, there are, as we will show, some
rather recognizable and pervasive socialization processes used across virtually all organizational settings and all kinds of individuals that can be
understood far more quickly and directly if we do not bog ourselves down
in the examination of every dimension that conceivably could influence
the outcome of a given process. In other words, the theory we sketch out
below does not seek to specify its own applications or uniqueness. What
we attempt to accomplish here is the identification of the likely effects
upon individuals who have been processed into a general organizational
location through certain identified means. Our concern is therefore with
the effects of what can be called *"people processing"* devices. The frequency and substantive outcome of the use of these devices across particular types of people, organizations, and occupations are then peripheral
to our analytic concern and properly lie beyond the scope of this paper,
for these are questions best handled by detailed empirical study.

Plan of This Paper

Given this rather lengthy presentation of introductory matters, the following section, Part III, provides a model of the general setting in which organizational socialization takes place. As such, it is a theoretical depiction of an organization within which certain boundaries exist and therefore demark particular transition points where socialization can be expected to occur. In Part IV, several types of individual responses or outcomes to the socialization process are described in terms we believe to be both organizationally and theoretically revevant. That is, these outcomes are potential effects of a given socialization process and are considered largely in terms of how an individual actually behaves in the new organizational role, not in terms of how an individual may or may not feel toward the new role. It is, therefore, the performance or action of a person that concerns us in this section and not attitudes, motives, beliefs, or values that may or may not be associated with an individual's handling of a given organizational role. In Part V, we present the basic propositions which comprise the core analytic materials of this paper and specify a set of strategic or tactical means by which organizational socialization is typically accomplished. Each strategy or tactic is discussed generally and then related systematically to its probable absence or presence at a given boundary as well as its probable effect upon individuals who are crossing a particular boundary. Part VI concludes the paper with a brief overview and guide to future research in this area.

III. THE ORGANIZATIONAL SETTING: SEGMENTS AND BOUNDARIES

Perhaps the best way to view an organization follows the anthropological line suggesting that any group of people who interact regularly over an extended period of time will develop a sort of unexplicated or tacit mandate concerning what is correct and proper for a member of the group to undertake as well as what is the correct and proper way to go about such an undertaking. At a high level of abstraction, then, members of ongoing business organizations, for example, orient their efforts toward "making money" in socially prescribed ways just as members of governmental agencies orient their efforts toward "doing public service" in socially prescribed ways. More concretely, however, organizations are made up of people each following ends that are to some degree unique. But, since these people interact with one another and share information, purposes, and approaches to the various everyday problems they face, organizations can be viewed as arenas in which an almost infinite series of negotiated situations arise over who will do what, when, where, and in what fashion. Over time, these negotiations result in an emerging set of *organizationally defined roles* for people to fill (Manning, 1970). These roles may or may not be formalized and fully sanctioned throughout the organization, yet they nonetheless appear to have some rather stable properties associated with them which tend to be passed on from role taker to role taker. Of course, these organizationally defined roles hardly coerce each role taker to perform in identical ways. Certainly, whenever a novel problem arises, people come together acting within their roles to confront and make sense of the shared event. Such events, if serious enough, give rise to altered definitions of both the organizational role and the organizational situation in which the role is carried out. From this standpoint, an organization is little more than a situated activity space in which various individuals come together and base their efforts upon a somewhat shared, but continually problematic, version of what it is they are to do, both collectively and individually.[8]

The problem we face here concerns the manner in which these versions of what people are to do—organizationally defined roles—are passed on and interpreted from one role occupant to the next. To do so, however, requires a model of the organization such that members can be distinguished from one another and from outsiders on the basis of as few organizational variables as possible. Furthermore, we need a model that is flexible enough to allow for as much descriptive validity as possible across a wide variety of organizational contexts.

Schein (1971a) has developed a model of the organization that provides a quite useful description of an organizationally defined role in terms of three dimensions that are discernible empirically. The first dimension is a *functional* one and refers to the various tasks performed by members of an organization. Thus, most organizations have departmental structures, which for enterprises located in the business sector of the economy might include the functions of marketing, finance, production, administrative staff, personnel, research and development, and so forth. In the public sector, an organization such as a police department might have functional divisions corresponding to patrol, investigations, communications, planning, records, custody, and the like. Visually, we can map the functional domains of an organization along departmental and subdepartmental or program lines as if each function and subfunction occupied a part of a circle or pie-shaped figure. Each function then covers a particular portion of the circumference of the circle depending upon its proportionate size within the organization. Consider, for example, the XYZ Widget Company as depicted in Figure 1.

Each slice in the figurative representation is a functional division with relatively distinct boundaries such that most persons in the organization

XYZ WIDGET CO.

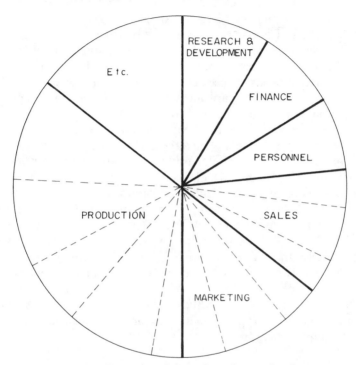

RESEARCH & DEVELOPMENT

Etc.

FINANCE

PERSONNEL

PRODUCTION

SALES

MARKETING

Figure 1.   Functional domains of organizations.

could easily locate themselves and others within a slice of the circle. Clearly, no two organizations would be precisely the same, because even if the department and subdepartment structures were identical, the numbers of people contained within each slice would no doubt differ.

The second dimension identified by Schein concerns the *hierarchical* distribution of rank within an organization. This is essentially a matter of who, on paper, is responsible for the actions of whom. It reflects the official lines of supervisory authority within an organization, but does not presume that such authority carries with it the power to direct the behavior of underlings.

According to the model, very decentralized organizations will have, for example, relatively few hierarchical distinctions, whereas very centralized organizations will have many. Mapping this dimension on paper, it would typically make a triangular shape (the traditional organizational pyramid) wherein the highest ranks are held by relatively few people located at the apex. For example, Figure 2 illustrates the hierarchical dimension in five hypothetical, but possible, organizations.

As Figure 2 suggests, a vast number of hierarchical possibilities exist. The XYZ Widget Company (2-A) is perhaps the most typical in that it fits textbook models of a management structure wherein increasing rank is assumed by decreasing numbers of people in a relatively smooth way. The Metropolitan Police Department (2-B) is representative of a large number of service bureaucracies. These agencies have been tagged "street level" organizations, because, in part, most of their membership occupies positions that carry low rank. To wit, over 75 percent of the employees in most police organizations work as patrolmen or investigators, the lowest-ranked positions in these organizations (Van Maanen, 1974; Lipsky, 1971). Zipper Sales, Inc. (2-C) illustrates an organization with a very steep authority structure within which each rank supervises relatively few people but there are many ranks. Pyramid sales organizations and peacetime armies are good examples in this regard. The Zero Research Institute (2-D) displays what a relatively flat hierarchical structure looks like in this scheme. Here there are few ranks for members to seek to ascend. Finally, the Stuffed Mattress Corporation (2-E) is included here to demonstrate something of the range of possibilities available to describe the hierarchical spread which potentially can characterize an organization. As can be seen, the Stuffed Mattress Company has a bulging number of middle managers. In fact, there are more managers than workers in this hypothetical firm.

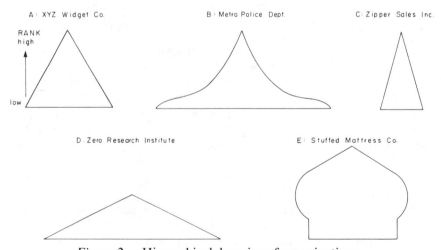

Figure 2.   Hierarchical domains of organizations.

The third dimension in Schein's model is the most difficult to conceptualize and concerns the social fabric or interpersonal domain of organizational life. This is fundamentally an interactional dimension and refers to a person's *inclusion* within the organization. It can be depicted as if it were a radial dimension extending from the membership edge of a slice of organizational members in toward the middle of the functional circle. As Figure 3 indicates, movement along this dimension implies that a member's relationship with others in some segment of the organization changes. One moves toward the "center of things" or away toward the "periphery." When examining this dimension, the question must be

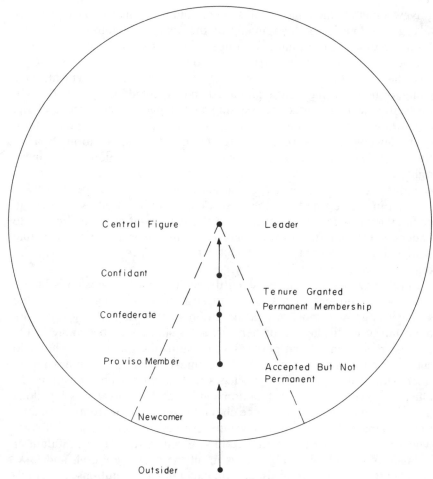

Figure 3. Inclusionary domains of organizations.

asked how important to others on the immediate sense is a given member's role in the workings of a particular group, department, or organization? Thus, this radial dimension must involve the social rules, norms, and values through which a person's worthiness to a group is judged by members of that group. It concerns in part, then, the shared notions of what the "realwork" of any organizational segment is at any given time. To move along this dimension is to become accepted by others as a central and working member of the particular organizational segment and this can normally not be accomplished unless the member-in-transition demonstrates that he or she too shares the same assumptions as others in the setting as to what is organizationally important and what is not.

Newcomers to most hierarchical levels and functional areas in virtually all organizations inevitably remain "on the edge" of organizational affairs for some time after entrance for a host of reasons. They may not yet be deemed trustworthy by other members on the scene. They may not yet have had time to develop and present the sort of affable, cynical, easy going, or hard-driving front maintained and expected by critical others in the setting which marks membership in the particular segment of the organization to which the newcomer has been assigned. Or, quite typically, newcomers must first be tested either informally or formally as to their abilities, motives, and values before being granted inclusionary rights which then permit them: (1) to share organizational secrets, (2) to separate the *presentational* rhetoric used on outsiders to speak of what goes on in the setting from the *operational* rhetoric used by insiders to communicate with one another as to the matters-at-hand, and/or (3) to understand the unofficial yet recognized norms associated with the actual work going on and the moral conduct expected of people in the particular organizational segment.

In other words, movement along the inclusionary dimension is analogous to the entrance of a stranger to any group. If things go well, the stranger is granted more say in the group's activities and is given more opportunity to display his or her particular skills, thus becoming in the process more central and perhaps valuable to the group as a whole. In short, to cross inclusionary boundaries means that one becomes an *insider* with all the rights and privileges that go with such a position. To illustrate, given a particular function and hierarchical level, passing along the inclusionary dimension can be characterized as going from an outsider to a marginally accepted novice group member, to a confederate of sorts who assists other members on certain selected matters, to a confidant or intimate of others who fully shares in all the social, cultural, and task-related affairs of the group. In certain educational institutions, the granting of university tenure represents the formal recognition of crossing a major inclusionary boundary, as well as the more obvious hierarchical passage.

When the three dimensions—functional, hierarchical, and inclusionary—are combined, the model of the organization becomes analytically most useful and interesting. From a Weberian, ideal-type perspective, organizations are conical in shape and contain within them three generic types of boundaries across which a member may pass (see Figure 4-A). And, as Schein suggests, these boundaries will differ within and between organizations as to both their number and permeability (i.e., the ease or difficulty associated with a boundary passage). Relatively tall organizations (4-B) may have, for example, many hierarchical boundaries yet relatively few functional and inclusionary ones. By implication, members moving up or down in such organizations must orient themselves more to rank and level distinctions among the membership than to the distinctions which result from either functional specialization or social status within a given rank. Military organizations and the elaborate pageantry that surrounds the hierarchical realms within them are unusually good examples of this type. On the other hand, flat organizations (4-C) such as some consulting firms have few hierarchical boundaries but many functional and inclusionary ones. Indeed, in such firms, turnover is high and few members are allowed (or necessarily desire) to pass across the relatively stringent radial dimensions to become central and permanent fixtures within the organization. Prestigious universities represent

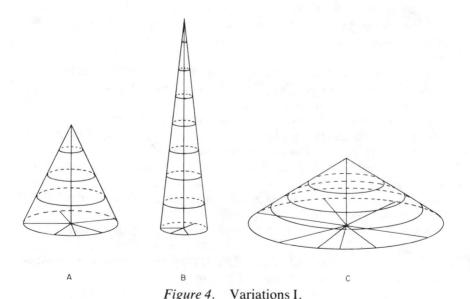

A   B   C

Figure 4. Variations I.

another good illustration in which functional boundaries are exceedingly difficult to rotate through and inclusionary boundaries are guarded by the most rigorous of tenuring policies.

Organizations also differ in the sorts of filtering processes they use to screen, select, and process those members who pass across particular boundaries. Hierarchical boundaries crossed by persons moving upward are associated usually with filtering processes carrying notions of merit, potential, and judged past performance, although age and length of service are often utilized as surrogate measures of "readiness" to move upward in an organization. Functional boundaries usually filter people on the basis of their demonstrated skill or assumed aptitude to handle a particular task. However, when functional boundaries are relatively permeable, as they often are, the filtering process may operate on the premise that there are people in the organization who "need" or "wish" to broaden their work experiences. Finally, inclusionary filters, in the main, represent evaluations made by others on the scene as to another's "fitness" for membership. Of course, such evaluations may be formal, informal, or both. Consider the new patrolman in a large urban police department who must not only serve out a period of official probation successfully, but also must pass a number of unofficial colleague-initiated tests on the street before others in the department will view him as a desirable member of the patrol division (and assigned squad within that division) within the organization (Van Maanen, 1973; Rubenstein, 1973).[9]

Given this model, some key postulates about the socialization process in organizations can be stated.

First, socialization, although continuous throughout one's career within an organization, is no doubt more intense and problematic for a member (and others) just before and just after a particular boundary passage. That is, an individual's anxiety and hence vulnerability to organizational influence are likely to be highest during the anticipatory and initiation phases of an organizational boundary passage. Similarly, the more boundaries that are crossed by a person at any one time, the more profound the experience is likely to be for the person. This is one reason why the outsider-to-insider passage in which an individual crosses over all three organizational boundaries at once is so often marked by dramatic changes in a person, changes of a sort that are rarely matched again during other internal passages of the individual's career (Van Maanen, 1976; Glaser, 1968; Becker et al., 1961; Hughes, 1958).

Second, a person is likely to have the most impact upon others in the organization, what Porter, Lawler, and Hackman (1975) call the "individualization" process and what Schein (1971a) refers to as the "innovation" process, at points furthest from any boundary crossing. In other words, the influence of the organization upon the individual peaks during passage, whereas the individual's influence upon the organization peaks well after and well before any further movement.

Third, because of the conical shape typically displayed by organizations, socialization along the inclusionary dimension is likely to be more critical to lower-placed members than higher-placed members since, according to the model, to move up in the organization indicates that some, perhaps considerable movement has already occurred inward. This presumes, however, an ideal-type, symmetrically shaped organization in which central members from the top to the bottom of the organization all share roughly the same norms and values. In fact, as Figure 5-A shows, organizations may be nonsymmetrically skewed, thus, hierarchically favoring the movement up of only those persons coming from a particular functional or inclusionary location. Consider, for example, those business concerns whose top executives invariably come from only certain functional areas of the organization. Similarly, organizations may also be tipped radically to the side (Figure 5-B). In such cases, certain inclusionary prerequisites for career movements and their associated boundary passages have been more or less altered because "insiders" at one level are "outsiders" at another. Nor are "insiders" in a favorable position to move upward in the organization, as might be the case in more symmetrically shaped firms where certain key values are shared by all "insiders" regardless of level. To take an example, certain organizations headed by reform-minded top officials may make "mountain climbers" out of some members who literally scale the vertical dimension of the organization from an outsider's or noninclusionary position. Yet, it is probably also true that during such a climb the climber has little effect upon any of the various groups in which he or she may have claimed membership, since the climber will never have developed a persuasive or influential position within these organizational segments.[10]

We have now reached the stage where it makes sense to return to the

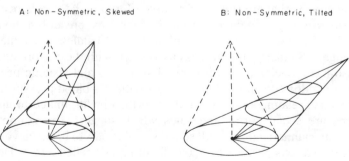

A: Non−Symmetric, Skewed   B: Non−Symmetric, Tilted

Figure 5.   Variations II.

individual level of analysis for a time and consider the ways in which people can respond to an organizational socialization process. And, after considering this problem briefly, we can then proceed to the central matters of our concern, the examination of various processes through which organizationally defined roles (consisting of hierarchical, functional, and inclusionary properties) are passed on from generation to generation of organizational members.

IV. INDIVIDUAL RESPONSES TO ORGANIZATIONAL SOCIALIZATION ROLE COMPONENTS—KNOWLEDGE, STRATEGY, AND MISSION

Any organizationally defined role includes what Hughes (1958) called a "bundle of tasks." Whether one is a lathe operator, dentist, beauty operator, or computer programmer, each role includes many specific actions and tasks to be performed, ranging from perhaps sweeping the floor to mediating disputes between colleagues, or, from filling in for an absent coworker to utilizing one's own somewhat special and unique skills in the performance of a given task. In general, then, a role is merely the set of often diverse behaviors that are more or less expected of persons who occupy a certain defined position within a particular social system, in this case, an organization (Parsons, 1951; Newcomb, 1952; Biddle and Thomas, 1966). Moreover, it usually follows that if these expectations are met or exceeded, certain organizational rights and rewards are passed on to the person performing the role. If not, however, is usually follows that certain remedial actions are taken or punishments meted out.

All roles which are created, sustained, and transmitted by people include both content characteristics (i.e., what it is people should do) and process characteristics (i.e., how it is they should do it). The content of a particular role can be depicted both in terms of a general, almost ideological mandate that goes with it and in terms of the general set of mandate-fulfilling actions that are supposed to be performed by the role occupant. Thus, doctors are thought to "heal the sick" by prescribing available "cures" to be found somewhere within the vast catalogue of "medical" knowledge." Similarly, the process associated with the performance of a role also has associated with it general strategies and specific practices. The doctor "does diagnosis" by taking a patient's blood pressure, eliciting a history, reading an X-ray, and so forth. Finally, linked to all these concerns are social norms and rules which suggest, for example, the appropriate mannerisms, attitudes, and social rituals to be displayed when performing various parts of the "bundle of tasks" called a role. Doctors, to continue our illustration, have "bedside manners," often assume a pose of distance or remoteness toward certain emotionally trying events in the lives of their patients, and take a characteristically "all knowing" stance toward most of the nursing personnel with whom they come into contact.

Putting these conceptual matters together, organizationally defined roles can be seen to possess, *first,* a *content or knowledge base* which, if accepted by the role occupant, indicates the range of existing solutions to the given problems encountered regularly on the job. Engineers know, for instance, the heat limits to which certain metals can be exposed before the molecules of the materials rearrange themselves. *Second,* an organizationally defined role includes a *strategic base,* which suggests the ground rules for the choosing of particular solutions. Hence, the engineers may be out to "cut costs" or "beat the competition" in some organizations when designing a particular product or piece of machinery. *Third,* organizationally defined roles are invested historically with something of an *explicit and implicit mission, purpose, or mandate* which is, in part, traceable to the knowledge and strategy bases of the roles, but also is grounded in the total organizational mission and in the relationships that a particular role has with other roles within and outside the organization. Engineering roles, to wit, are defined and supported by other managerial, technical support, and sales roles in both organizational and client contexts, and hence are influenced by their relative position in the overall scheme of things. While the professionalization of a particular occupational role can be viewed as an attempt to reduce such dependencies through the claim made by role practitioners to have an autonomous and special knowledge base, such professionalization in an orgnaizational society such as our is very incomplete.[11] At any rate, the missions associated with organizationally defined roles serve to legitimate, justify, and define the ends pursued by role occupants and, thus, support to some degree the various strategies and norms followed by those presently performing the role.

These three features of an organizationally defined role—knowledge base, strategy, and mission—and the norms that surround them are, of course, highly intertwined. A change in the knowledge base of a given role may alter the means and ends followed by practitioners. Indeed, the recognized failure to achieve a given end may provoke the development of new knowledge. Strategic failures are not unknown either and may lead to disenchantment and change in the mission and knowledge bases of a particular role. Nevertheless, given the situation in which a newcomer is asked to take on an organizationally defined role, that newcomer must respond in some fashion to these three elements.

Responses to Socialization

Custodianship, content innovation, and role innovation   Perhaps the easiest or most expedient response of a newcomer to a given role is to assume a custodial or caretaker stance toward the knowledge, strategies, and missions associated with the role (Schein, 1971b). Taking such a stance, the newcomer does not question but accepts the status quo. Certainly, there are powerful reasons for adopting such a custodial or conforming orientation. First and foremost among them is the plain fact that the inherited past assumed by the newcomer may have much to recommend it in terms of functional achievement. If the enterprise has been successful, why "rock the boat"? One simply learns the substantive requirements of the job and the customary strategies that have been developed to meet these requirements (and the norms of use that surround them) and the successful accomplishment of the mission is assured.

On the other hand, as a newcomer one may feel for a variety of reasons somewhat impatient with or uneasy about the knowledge base of a particular organizational role that is transmitted and, hence, be unwilling to limit oneself to the use of such knowledge in the performance of the role. A newly promoted marketing manager may, for instance, take issue with the quality of some of the regional reports used by his predecessor to inform his decision making. The new manager may then aggressively seek out other information on which to base his decisions. As a result, new strategies and perhaps even new objectives may eventually develop in this department. Similarly, tactical alternatives as to the means to certain ends may be sought out by individuals after assuming a new role. The new marketing manager may decide to involve more salesmen and engineers in group meetings devoted to developing new product lines instead of relying only on his or her own marketing people.

Schein (1971b) refers to this response as "content innovation." It is marked by the development of substantive improvements or changes in the knowledge base or strategic practices of a particular role. The "reformer" in public service agencies, for example, rarely seeks to change the stated objectives of the agency mission, but rather seeks to improve, make more efficient or less corrupt the existing practices by which given ends are collectively sought. In such cases, traditional ends and norms of practice are accepted by the newcomer, but the person is troubled by the existing strategies or technologies-in-use for the achievement of these ends and perhaps is troubled too by the degree to which the traditional norms are circumvented in practice.

Pushing the analysis one more step, an individual may seek to redefine the entire role by attacking and attempting to change the *mission* associated traditionally with that role. This response is characterized by a complete rejection of most of the norms governing the conduct and performance of a particular role. The "Rebel" or "Guerrilla" or "Insurgent" are popular tags we attach to and associate with such responses. Take, for example, Ralph Nader's attempts within certain communities of lawyers who work for the federal government to create and sustain an organizationally defined role of consumer advocate, industrial safety proponent, or even whistleblower. Also note the recent questioning raised by health care officials as to the appropriate aims of medical practice. Some doctors have in fact argued vigorously in both words and deeds for professional roles that are proactive and preventive-centered rather than the historically fixed reactive and treatment-centered roles. Schein (1971b) has called this response "role innovation in that a genuine attempt is made by a role holder to redefine the ends to which the role functions.

Thus, there are two poles toward which a newcomer's response to an organizationally defined role can gravitate. At one extreme is the caretaking response, marked by an acceptance of the role as presented and traditionally practiced by role occupants. We will label this response and the various forms it can take as "custodial." At the other extreme, we can group responses of an "innovative" nature. Perhaps most extreme are those responses which display a rejection and redefinition of the major premises concerning missions and strategies followed by the majority of the role occupants to both practice and justify their present role—what we label here "role innovation." Less extreme, but perhaps equally as innovative in some cases are those responses indicative of an effort to locate new knowledge on which to base the organizationally defined role or improved means to perform it—what we label here "content innovation." Of course, such new knowledge, if discovered, may lead only to a further rationalization of the present practices and goals, but, nevertheless, the search itself, to differing degrees, represents something of an innovative response. For our purposes, then, those individuals who after assuming a given role seek actively to alter its knowledge base, strategic practices, or historically established ends display a generic response type we will label "innovative," which can be further broken down into role innovation and content innovation.

The central but still nagging question remains, of course, as to the reasons that provoke one or the other response types. Certainly, individuals vary in their backgrounds, value systems, and predispositions to calmly accept things as they are or to vigorously strive to alter them. It is true too that changes in the larger environment within which organizationally defined roles are played out may force certain changes upon role occupants despite perhaps vehement resistance or whatever particular backgrounds, values, or predispositions define those who presently perform a given role. But, these factors go well beyond our interests here, for they essentially lie outside an organizational analysis. *The causal mechanism we seek to examine here is the organizational socialization process itself.* Therefore, the argument to follow suggests that there are particular forms of socialization that can enhance or retard the likelihood of an innovative or custodial response to an organizationally defined role no matter what the attributes of the people being processed or how the particular environment is characterized within which the process occurs. What these forms are and how they work is the topic now to be addressed.

V. PEOPLE PROCESSING—THE TACTICAL DIMENSIONS OF ORGANIZATIONAL SOCIALIZATION AND THEIR EFFECTS

The phrase "tactics of organizational socialization" refers to the ways in which the experiences of individuals in transition from one role to another are structured for them by others in the organization (Van Maanen, 1978). These tactics may be selected consciously by the management of an organization, such as the requirement that all newcomers attend a formal training session or orientation program of some kind before assuming the duties of a particular role. Or they may be selected "unconsciously" by management, representing merely precedents established in the dim past of an organization's history, such as the proverbial "sink or swim" method of socialization used on certain jobs by which individuals must learn how to perform the new role on their own. From the perspective of those learning the role, the selection of teaching methods is often made by persons not of their own situation but rather by those long gone. Yet, these choices may still bind contemporary members of the organization. Or, teaching methods may arise simply from certain latent and unexamined premises or assumptions underlying present practices. However, regardless of the manner of choice, any given tactic represents a distinguishable set of events which influence the individual in transition and which may make innovative responses from that individual more likely than custodial (or vice-versa). It is possible, therefore, to denote the various tactics used by organizations and then to explore the differential results of their own use upon the people to whom they are directed.

The analysis presented in this section explores these tactics from primarily a structural standpoint. That is, we are interested in describing various forms and results of socialization as they occur when persons move across hierarchical, functional, and inclusionary boundaries. The main focus is consequently upon the external or structural properties peculiar to a specified tactic. The tactics are essentially process variables akin to but more specific than such general transitional processes as education, training, apprenticeship, or sponsorship. Furthermore, the process variables themselves are not tied to any particular type of organization. Theoretically, at least, they can be used in virtually any setting in which individual careers are played out, be they business careers, school careers, political careers, service careers, blue-, white-, or pink-collar careers, civil service careers, and so on. The analysis follows, then, the most fundamental premise that people respond to particular organizationally defined roles differently not only because people and organizations differ, but also because socialization processes differ. And, like a sculptor's mold, certain forms of socialization can produce remarkably similar outcomes no matter what individual ingredients are used to fill the mold or no matter where the mold is typically set down.

Each tactic we discuss below operates in a way that somewhat uniquely organizes the learning experiences of a newcomer to a particular role. Although much of the evidence presented here on the effects of a given strategy comes from studies conducted on the outsider-to-insider passage wherein a person first becomes a member of the organization, the analysis seems to go beyond these transitions by examining the effects of each tactic across the three organizational boundaries separately, reinforcing, at the same time, the proposition that socialization occurs periodically throughout the organizational careers of individuals.

The various tactics we will describe are not mutually exclusive. Indeed, they are usually combined in sundry and sometimes inventive ways. The effects of the tactics upon people are consequently cumulative. Except for a short summary section, we discuss each tactic in relative isolation. However, the reader should be aware that any recruit to an organizational position often encounters all the listed tactics simultaneously. Additionally, each tactic is discussed along with its counterpart or opposing tactic. In other words, each can be thought of as existing on a continuum where there is a considerable range between the two poles.

The term "tactic" is used here to describe each of the listed processes, because the degree to which any one tactic is used by an organization is not in any sense a "natural" or prerequisite condition necessary for socialization to occur. In other words, socialization itself always takes place at boundary transitions by some means or other. And, whether the tactics used are selected by design or accident, they are at least theoretically subject to rapid and complete change at the direction of the management of an organization. In other words, the relative use of a particular tactic upon persons crossing given organizational boundaries can be, by and large, a choice made by organizational decision makers on functional, economic, technical, humanistic, expedient, traditional, or perhaps purely arbitrary grounds. This is an important point, for it suggests that we can be far more self-conscious about employing certain "people processing techniques" than we have been in the past. In fact, a major purpose of this paper is to heighten and cultivate a broader awareness of what it is we do to people under the guise of "breaking them in" to an organizationally defined role. Presumably, if we gain a greater understanding and appreciation for the sometimes unintended consequences of a particular tactic, we can alter the strategy for the betterment of both the individual and the organization.

Van Maanen (1978) has identified at least six major tactical dimensions which characterize the structural side of organizational socialization. These dimensions or processes were deduced logically from empirical observations and from accounts found in the social science literature. We do not assert here that this list is exhaustive or that the processes are presented in any order or relevance to a particular organization or occupation. These are fundamentally empirical questions that can be answered only by further research. We do assert, however, and attempt to demonstrate that these tactics are quite common to a given boundary passage and of substantial consequence to people in the organization in that they partially determine the degree to which the response of the newcomer will be custodial or innovative.

Lastly, we should note that there is seemingly no logical or conclusive end to a list of organizational socialization tactics. The list may well be infinite, for these are essentially cultural forms that are continually subject to invention and modification as well as stabilization and continuity. At least at this juncture in the development of theory, questions concerning the use of and change in the various tactics of socialization are just beginning to be answered by carefully designed research. Our reasons for choosing these particular tactics are simply the visible presence (or omnipresence) of a tactic across what appears to be a wide variety of organizations as well as the seeming importance and power of that tactic on persons who are subjected to it.

The six dimensions we will analyze are:
1. Collective vs. individual socialization processes.
2. Formal vs. informal socialization processes.
3. Sequential vs. variable socialization processes.
4. Fixed vs. variable socialization processes.
5. Serial vs. disjunctive socialization processes.
6. Investiture vs. diversiture socialization processes.

Collective vs. Individual Socialization Processes

Definition *Collective socialization* refers to the tactic of taking a group of recruits who are facing a given boundary passage and putting them through a common set of experiences together. A number of good examples of this process is readily available: basic training or boot camp in military organizations, pledging in fraternal orders, education in graduate schools for the scholarly and professional trades, intensive group training for salesmen in business firms, management training courses to which groups of prospective or practicing managers are sent for an extended period of common education, and so forth.

At the other extreme, socialization in the *individual* mode refers to the tactic of processing recruits singly and in isolation from one another through a more or less unique set of experiences, Apprenticeship programs, specific intern or trainee assignments, and a plain "on-the-job training" wherein a recruit is expected to learn a given organizationally defined role on his or her own accord are typical examples. As Wheeler (1977) notes, the difference between the two tactical forms is analogous to the batch versus unit styles of production. In the batch- or mass-production case, recruits are bunched together at the outset and channeled through an identical set of events with the results being relatively uniform. In the unit or made-to-order case, recruits are processed individually through a rather different series of events, with the results being relatively variable.

As Becker (1964) and others have argued quite persuasively, when individuals experience a socialization program collectively, the thoughts, feelings, and actions of those in the recruit group almost always reflect an "in the same boat" consciousness. Individual changes in perspective are therefore built upon an understanding of the problems faced by all group members. In Becker's words, "As the group shares problems, various members experiment with possible solutions and report back to the group. In the course of collective discussions, the members arrive at a definition of their situation and develop a consensus."

Collective socialization processes often promote and intensify the demands of the socialization agents. Indeed, army recruits socialize each other in ways the army could never do, or, for that matter, would not officially be permitted to do. Similarly, graduate students are often said to learn more from one another than from the faculty. And, while the socialization agents may have the power to define the nature of the collective problem, the recruits often have more resources available to them to define the solution—time, expereince, motivation, expertise, and patience (or lack thereof). In many cases, collective tactics result in formation of an almost separate subworld within the organization comprised solely of recruits, complete with its own argot, areas of discourse, and unique understandings. A cultural perspective is developed that can be brought to bear upon common problems faced by the group.[13] Dornbush (1955) suggested, for example, that a "union of sympathy" developed among recruits in a Coast Guard Academy as a result of the enforced regimentation associated with the training program. Sharing similar difficulties and working out collective solutions clearly dramatized to the recruits the worth and usefulness of colleagial relationships.

Individual strategies also induce personal change. But the views adopted by people processed individually are likely to be far less homogeneous than the views of those processed collectively. In psychoanalytic training, for example, the vocabulary of motives a recruit-patient develops to interpret his or her situation is quite personal and specific compared to the vocabulary that develops in group therapy (Laing, 1960). Of course, such socialization can result in deep individual changes—what Burke (1950) refers to as "secular conversion"—but they are lonely changes and are dependent solely upon the particular relationship which exists between agent and recruit.

Apprenticeship modes of work socialization are sometimes quite similar to the therapist-patient relationship. If the responsibility for transforming an individual to a given status within the organization is delegated to only one person, an intense, value-oriented process is most likely to follow. This practice is common whenever a role incumbent is viewed by others in the organization as being the only member capable of shaping the recruit. Caplow (1964) notes the prevalence of this practice in the upper levels of bureaucratic organizations. Since the responsibility is given to only one organizational member, the person so designated often becomes a role model whose thoughts and actions the recruit emulates. Police departments, craftlike trades, and architectural firms all make extensive use of the individual socialization strategy. Outcomes in these one-on-one efforts are dependent primarily upon the affective relationships which may or may not develop between the apprentice and master. In cases of high affect, the new member is liable to quickly and fully appreciate and accept the skills, beliefs, and values of his or her mentor and the process works relatively well. However, when there are few affective bonds, the socialization process may break down and the hoped-for transition will not take place.

From this standpoint, individual socialization processes are most likely to be associated with complex roles. Further, such modes are most frequently followed when there are relatively few incumbents compared to many aspirants for a given role and when a collective identity among recruits is viewed as less important than the recruit's learning of the operational specifics of the given role.

On the other hand, collective socialization programs are usually found in organizations where there are a large number of recruits to be processed into the same organizationally defined role; where the content of this role can be fairly clearly specified; and, where the organization desires to build a collective sense of identity, solidarity, and loyalty within the cohort group being socialized. Overall, the individual processes are expensive both in time and money. Failures cannot be easily recycled or rescued by reassignment. And, with growing bureaucratic structures, collective socialization tactics, because of their economy, ease, efficiency, and predictability, have tended to replace the more traditional individual modes of specialization such as apprenticeship and "on-the-job training" in the modern organization (Salaman, 1973; Perrow, 1972; Blau and Schoenherr, 1971).

Given these considerations, we can now derive some propositions about the relationship of this socialization dimension to boundary passages and recruit responses.

Propositions

1. Collective socialization is most likely to be associated with functional boundaries (where new skills of a technical or functional nature have to be learned) or with the external—nonmember to member—inclusionary boundary of a given organizational segment (where some period of orientation or training is required before it is felt recruits are capable of entering into even the simplest of role relations associated with the new role).

2. Individual socialization is most likely to be associated with hierarchical boundaries where preparation for promotion requires the complex learning of skills, attitudes, and values, and where specific judgments of a given individual must be made by certain others in the organization as to the person's "fitness" for promotion (or demotion). Similarly, one would expect individual socialization to precede passage through the innermost inclusionary boundaries within an organizational segment. To be granted tenure or a very central position in any organizational segment implies that the individual has been evaluated by others on the scene as to his or her trustworthiness and readiness to defend the common interests of other "insiders." Clearly, such delicate evaluations can only be accomplished on a relatively personal and case-by-case basis.

3. Whatever the boundary being passed, collective socialization is most likely to produce a custodial (or, at best, a content innovative) orientation among newcomers. It is least likely to produce role-innovative outcomes, because the group perspective which develops as a result of collective socialization acts as a constraint upon the individual.[14] The likelihood of rebellion must be mentioned, however, because the consensual character of the solutions to the boundary passage problems worked out by the group may allow the members to collectively deviate more from the standards set by the agents than is possible under the individual mode of socialization. Collective processes provide a potential base for recruit resistance.

Classic illustrations of the dilemma raised by the use of the collective strategy can be found in both educational and work environments. In educational settings, the faculty may beseech a student to study hard while the student's compatriots exhort him to relax and have a good time. In many work settings, supervisors attempt to insure that each employee works up to his level of competence while the worker's peers try to impress hupon him that he must not be a "rate buster." To the degree that recruits are backed into the proverbial corner and can not satisfy both demands at the same time, they will typically follow the dicta of those with whom they spend most of their time. Thus, in collective modes, the congruence between agent objectives and the actual perspectives and practices adopted by the group is always problematic. "Beating the system" by selectively ignoring or disobeying certain agent demands is far more likely to occur in a collective socialization process than in an individualized one wherein agent surveillance is closer at hand to correct whatever "wrongs" the newcomer may be learning.

4. Individual socialization is most likely to produce the specific outcomes desired by the socialization agent(s). Because of the relatively greater control an agent has over a recruit in the individual mode, these outcomes can be custodial, content innovative, or role innovative.

The implication here is simply that if one is attempting to train for content or role innovation (i.e., set up socialization situations which will maximize the likelihood of innovative responses, it is probably essential to minimize as much as possible any collective processes, thus avoiding the formation of recruit group norms based on a common or shared fate. More so than individual norms, group norms are likely to be both traditional and custodial in orientation (often reflected by the popular idioms, "the path of least resistance" or the "lowest common denominator"), which serves to severely limit the newcomers' potential responses to their novel work situation.

Formal vs. Informal Socialization Processes

Definition   Formal socialization refers to those processes in which a newcomer is more or less segregated from regular organizational members while being put through a set of experiences tailored explicitly for the newcomer. Formal processes, then, leave no doubt as to the recruit's "special" role of the scheme of things organizational (Wheeler, 1966), These processes are illustrated by such socialization programs as police academies, professional schools, various sorts of internships, and apprenticeships in which the activities that are to be engaged in by the apprentice are prescribed officially and clearly.

Informal socialization processes, in contrast, do not distinguish the newcomer's role specifically, nor is there an effort made in such programs to rigidly differentiate the recruit from the other more experienced organizational members. As such, informal tactics provide a sort of laissez-faire socialization for recruits whereby new roles are learned, it is said, through trial and error. Examples here include those proverbial "on-the-job-training" assignments, apprenticeship programs in which the apprentice's role is not tightly specified, and, more generally, any situation where the newcomer is accepted from the outset as at least a provisional member of a work group and not officially placed into a recruit role by the use of specific labels, uniforms, assignments, or other symbolic devices designed to distinguish newcomers from others on the scene.

This dimension is related closely to the collective-individual dimension, but it is, in principle, different. While most collective socialization processes are also formal ones, there are some which are informal. To wit, there are those situations where a cohort of new employees is brought into an organization together, where meetings are held periodically to assess how the group is collectively getting along, but where the work assignments of each member of the cohort are to different departments within which each member of the cohort is trained through informal means. On the other hand, one can also imagine a very formal socialization program existing for an individual which entails the labeling of the person as a recruit and also specifies quite minutely a series of activities that must be performed as part of the training regime. Would-be partners in law firms are often subject to such socialization tactics whereby they must first handle the "dirty work" of the firm for some period. Certainly this sort of "pledge class of one" is not that uncommon in many occupational spheres.

Formal socialization processes are typically found in organizations where specific preparation for new status is involved and where it is deemed important that a newcomer learn the "correct" attitudes, values, and protocol associated with the new role. To put the matter bluntly, the more formal the process, the more concern there is likely to be shown for the recruit's absorption of the appropriate demeanor and stance associated with the target role—that one begins to think and feel like a United States Marine, an I.B.M. executive, or a Catholic priest.

The greater the separation of the recruit from the day-to-day reality of the work setting, the less the newcomer will be able to carry over and generalize any abilities or skills learned in the socialization setting (Bidwell, 1962; Schein and Bennis, 1965). Formal processes concentrate, therefore, more upon attitude than act. Such results may be implicit or unintended, however. Consider, for example, the research which suggests

that police recruits, student nurses, and sales trainees commonly de-
nounce their formal training as irrelevant, abstract, and dull. Paradoxically, these newcomers are also expressing in their attitude precisely
those components of the valued subcultural ethos that characterizes their
particular occupation—autonomy, pragmatism, and the concern for personal style (Van Maanen, 1974; Shafer, 1975; Olesen and Whittaker, 1968).

It is important to note too that formal periods of socialization not only
serve to prepare recruits to assume particular statuses in an organizational
world, they also serve to provide an intensive period in which others in
the organization can rather closely judge the newcomer's commitment
and deference to the critical values of the occupation. Recruits in police
academies are, for example, assessed quite thoroughly by staff members
as to their loyalty not only to the organization, but to their fellow recruits
as well. And, those who do not adhere to particular norms thought crucial
to the trade (e.g., the "no rat rule") are ushered as unceremoniously out
of police departments as they were rushed ceremoniously in (Manning
and Van Maanen, 1978). It is true, of course, that merely passing through
a rigorous formal process serves also as a test of the recruit's willingness
to assume the new role. Often, simply the sacrifice and hard work it takes
a recruit to complete a very long formal process serves effectively to fuse
the newcomer to the prepared-for role. Thus, given a lengthy and demanding formal process, it is unlikely that one will later wish to jeopardize the
practical value of such a course by quitting or appearing to forget occupational lessons once learned.

Learning through experience in the informal socialization mode is an
entirely different matter. First, such tactics place recruits in the position
where they must select their own socialization agents. The value of this
mode to the newcomer is then determined largely by the relevant knowledge possessed by an agent and, of course, the agent's ability to transfer
such knowledge. The freedom of choice afforded recruits in the more
informal processes has therefore a price: They must force others in the
setting to teach them.[15] Second, mistakes or errors made by recruits in an
informal socialization process must be regarded as more costly and serious than mistakes occurring in formal processes. Because real work is
interfered with, a recruit who makes a mistake may create considerable
trouble for both himself and others. The rookie patrolman who "freezes"
while he and his partner strive to settle a tavern brawl on the street rather
than in an academy role-playing exercise may find himself ostracized from
the inner circle of his squad. The forgetful novice beautician who pro-
vokes a customer by dyeing her hair the wrong color may be forced to
look elsewhere for an organization in which to complete the mandatory
licensing requirement of the trade. Experienced organizational members
know full well that "mistakes happen," but a recruit is under a special

pressure to perform well during an informal initiation period—or to at least ask before acting.

With these considerations in mind, the following general propositions can now be stated.

Propositions

1. Formal socialization is most likely to be associated with hierarchical and inclusionary boundary passages wherein a newcomer is expected to assume a new *status* or *rank* in the organization (complete with the values, attitudes, and demeanor that go with such new status). Informal socialization, on the other hand, is most likely to be associated with functional boundary passages wherein the newcomer must learn new skills, methods, or practical abilities. If, however, the new skills to be learned also require a new knowledge base, a formal training period dealing specifically with such knowledge and its use may precede the boundary passage. Since the teaching of such knowledge is likely to occur in idealized or "theoretical" situations in a formal process, an informal process of socialization dealing with the applications of the knowledge will still be required upon the recruit's entrance into the new role.[16]

In effect, this proposition alerts us to the apparent functional necessity for the use of formal socialization tactics when there exists a cultural gap between the organizational segments to be traversed by the individual. For example, a company sending an American manager to head an overseas subsidiary should probably allow for a formal period of socialization, including perhaps language training, briefings on the new culture, guided tours of the key areas, and so forth. All of this must occur under the formal tutelage of someone who knows what sorts of culture shocks are likely to be encouraged during the transition. Such movements are not limited theoretically to hierarchical or inclusionary boundaries, but rather reflect the size of the cultural differences that exist at any boundary. In some organizations, a move from engineering to sales may involve as much culture shock for an individual as a promotion from project leader to group supervisor or a transfer from staff analyst to line manager.

2. Formal socialization tactics are most likely to be found where the nature of the work and/or the values surrounding the work to be performed in the target role are seen to involve high levels of risk for the newcomer, colleagues of the newcomer, the organization itself, and/or clients of the organization.

Thus the training of doctors, professional pickpockets, lawyers, and airline pilots involves long periods of formal socialization largely because the work involved in all these cases is complex, difficult, and usually entails a very high penalty for making a mistake. Formal training for electricians, soldiers, and machinists is also predicated on the need to minimize the minimizable risks—human or otherwise—such as damaging expensive equipment.Where the cost of a mistake is relatively low, informal socialization processes are more likely to be found.

3. Whatever the boundary passage, formal socialization is most likely to produce a custodial orientation.

As implied above, formal tactics tend to emphasize the "proper" or "accepted" ways to accomplish things in an organization. Even the fact that the target role can be presented in isolation from its everyday performance implies that there are available various traditional means of accomplishing the task. However, a caveat is appropriate here, for it is often the case that once recruits have begun to perform the role in an official capacity, they "unlearn" much of what they learned in the formal process and begin to substitute "practical" or "smart" ways of doing things for the "proper" or "standard" strategies they were once taught. From this standpoint, formal socialization processes represent frequently only the "first wave" of socialization and are followed by a "second wave" of informal socialization once the newcomer is located in a particular organizational slot and begins to discover the actual practices that go on there (Inkeles, 1966).[17] Whereas the first wave stresses a broad stance toward the job, the second wave emphasizes specific actions, unique applications of the general rules, and the odd nuances thought necessary by others on the scene to perform the role in the work setting. When the gap separating the two sorts of learning is rather large, disillusionment with the first wave may set in, causing the newcomer to disregard virtually everything learned in the formal socialization process. Thus, while formal processes tend to produce custodial orientations among recruits, these orientations may not be all too stable unless the lessons of the formal process are reasonably congruent with those of the informal process which may follow.

4. Informal socialization, like individual socialization, carries with it the potential for producing more extreme responses in either the custodial or innovative directions than formal socialization.

If, for example, a recruit is assigned in the informal mode to a work group or a boss characterized by an "organization man" orientation, he or she is likely to become very custodial in orientation—at least in the short run. On the other hand, if that same recruit is assigned to a work group or boss characterized by an innovative orientation, he or she might then become quite innovative too. What we are saying, in effect, is that individual and informal socialization are potentially more powerful techniques of shaping work behavior than formal and collective modes, because they involve on-the-job contingencies as well as teaching by people who are clearly doing the work. In contrast, formal processes artificially divide up concerns that must be approached simultaneously on the job and are often under the control of instructors (agents) whose credibility is lacking. It would appear then that if formal and collective processes are to "succeed" from an agent's perspective, first, they must be long enough to almost force recruits to learn their lessons well and perhaps practice them too and, second, they must be run by persons who have considerable legitimacy in the eyes of the recruits.

Sequential vs. Random Steps in the Socialization Process

Definition The degree of formality and the degree to which the process of socialization is collective are, as indicated, associated with major boundary passages, with basic orientation activities, and, most often, with the initial entry of a recruit into the organization. However, for some roles in an organization, the socialization process may cover a broad spectrum of assignments and experiences, taking sometimes many years of preparation. The person wishing to become a medical specialist has, for instance, to go through an undergraduate premed program, medical school, internship, and residency before becoming eligible to simply take the specialist board examinations. Similarly, a person being groomed for a general manager position may have to rotate through several staff positions as a junior analyst, through various functional divisions in order to learn the "areas of the business," and through various supervisory levels to build up experiences and a so-called "good track record" which would then warrant the ultimate "goal job" (Gordon, 1977).

Sequential socialization refers to the degree to which the organization or occupation specifies a given sequence of discrete and identifiable steps leading to the target role. *Random socialization* occurs when the sequence of steps leading to the target role is unknown, ambiguous, or continually changing. In the case of most professional training such as medicine, we have a very sequential process in that the steps leading to the professional role must be negotiated in a specific order. In the case of the general manager, however, we have a sequential process only with respect to supervisory or rank levels, but the sequence of rotating through functional positions and divisions is often unspecified and, in some organizations, left more or less to "random" events. Thus, in random processes, while there may be a number of steps or stages leading to the taking of certain organizational roles, there is no necessary order specified in terms of the steps that are to be taken.

When examining sequential strategies, it is crucial to note the degree to which each stage builds or expands upon the preceding stage. For example, the courses in most technical training programs are arranged in what is thought to be a simple-to-complex progression. On the other hand, some sequential processes seem to follow no internal logic. Management education is, for instance, quite often disjointed, with the curriculum jumping from topic to topic with little integration across stages. In such cases, what is learned by a recruit in the program is dependent simply upon what is liked best in the sequence. If, however, the flow of topics or courses is harmonious and connected functionally or logically in some fashion, what may seem like minor alterations required of an individual at each sequential stage will accumulate so that at the end persons will "discover" themselves to be considerably different than when they began (e.g., in training for a specific skill). One sees this effect most clearly in the acquisition of complex skill or in the complete "professional" perspective or in the value systems built up after many years of graduate study.[18]

Relatedly, if several agents handle various portions of a sequential process, the degree to which the aims of the agents are common is very important. For example, in some officer's training schools of peacetime military organizations, the agents responsible for physical and weapons training tend to have very different perspectives toward their jobs and toward the recruits than those agents who are in charge of classroom instruction (Wamsley, 1972). Recruits quickly spot such conflicts when they exist and sometimes exploit them, playing agents off against one another. Such incongruities often lead to a more relaxed situation for the recruits, one in which they enjoy watching their instructors pay more attention to each other than they pay to the training program.

We should note that many of these concerns apply to random processes as well. In both random and sequential arrangements, agents may be unknown to one another, they may be quite far apart spatially, and may have thoroughly different images of their respective tasks. Both Merton (1957) and Glaser (1964) have remarked upon the difficulty many scientists apparently have when moving from a university to an industrial setting to practice their trade (a random socialization process). The pattern is seemingly quite disconcerting for many scientists when they discover that their academic training emphasized a far different set of skills, interests, and values than is required in the corporate environment. As Avery (1968) observed, to become a "good" industrial scientist, the individual has to learn the painful lesson that to be able to sell an idea is at least as important as having one in the first place. From this standpoint, empathy must certainly be extended to the so-called juvenile delinquent who receives "guidance" at various times from the police, probation officers, judges, social workers, psychiatrists, and correctional officials. Such a process, sometimes sequential but typically random, evocatively suggests that the person may well learn to be only whatever the immediate situation demands.

In a sequential process, there is likely to be a strong *bias* in the presentation by each agent to make the next stage appear benign. Thus, a recruit is told that if he will just "buckle down and apply himself" in Stage A, Stages B, C, D. and E will be easy. Agents usually mask, unwittingly or wittingly, the true nature of the stage to follow, for, if recruits feel that the future is bright, rewarding, and assured, they will be most cooperative at the stage they are in, not wishing to risk the future they think awaits them. To wit, note the tactics of high school mathematics teachers who tell their students that if they will just work hard in algebra, geometry will be a "cinch." An extreme case of this sequential "betrayal" occurs in state executions, where condemned persons are usually told by their "coaches" on the scene that their demise will be quick, painless, and likely to speed them on their way to a "better place" (Eshelman, 1962).

Given these sensitizing definitions and the qualifications that apply to this socialization tactic, some theoretical propositions can now be stated.

Propositions

1. Sequential socialization is most likely to be associated with hierarchical boundaries.

Hierarchies are typically organized from the outset on the assumption that higher-level positions cannot be fulfilled adequately until lower-level ones have first been fulfilled. Such an assumption is not built into functional or inclusion boundaries where a person can demonstrate a readiness for passage at any given time. At least in part, hierarchies preserve sequential socialization processes in order to maintain the image that the hierarchy itself is a valid base for the distribution of authority. If one could skip levels, the whole concept of authority, it is thought, would be undermined. Of course, in some executive promotions, skipping is accomplished for all practical purposes through the extremely rapid advancement of someone viewed as unusually talented, "fast tracked," fortuitously connected, just plain lucky, or all of these attributes together.

To pass inclusion boundaries may take a long time while one is proving oneself to be trustworthy to many different people, but the process typically does not specify a sequence in which such a test can or must be passed. In the case of functional boundaries, there may be many specific steps associated with the education or training activities involved in preparing to cross the boundary, but, sometimes at least, one may be given a job on the basis of education received at a much earlier time or on the basis of certain experiences which are seen as "equivalent" to education or training. Inclusionary and functional boundary passages are, therefore, associated more with various sorts of random socialization processes.

2. Sequential socialization is more likely to produce custodial orientations among recruits than innovative orientations because the recruits remain "locked in," as it were, to the conforming demands of others in the organization for a long period of time before the target role is achieved. Even the ability of the organization to specify a sequence implies a set of fairly clear norms about what is required to perform the target role. And, the clearer the role, the more likely it is that the training for that role will produce custodial response.

On the other hand, recruits who encounter various socialization experiences in a *random* fashion may find themselves exposed to a wide and diverse variety of views and perceptions of the target role which would make it more likely than is true of sequential socialization to lead to innovative orientations. It would seem therefore that a company who wishes to groom innovative general managers would do well to avoid sequential prcesses and encourage more *ad hoc* decision-making procedures in the organization concerning managerial job moves and training experiences.

Fixed vs. Variable Socialization Processes

Definition This dimension refers to the degree to which the steps involved in a socialization process have a *timetable* associated with them that is both adhered to by the organization and communicated to the recruit. *Fixed socialization* processes provide a recruit with the precise knowledge of the time it will take to complete a given passage (Roth, 1963). Thus, while organizations may specify various career paths having different timetables, all of these paths may be more or less fixed in terms of the degree to which the recruit must follow the determined timetable. Some management trainees, for instance, are put on so-called "fast tracks" and required to accept new rotational assignments every year or so despite their own wishes. Similarly, others said to be on "slow" or "regular" tracks may be forewarned not to expect an assignment shift for at least 4 or 5 years. Consider also that promotional policies in most universities explicitly specify the number of years a person can be appointed to a given rank. They also spell out precisely when a tenure decision must be reached on a given individual. The process can sometimes be speeded up.

Variable socialization processes give a recruit few clues as to when to expect a given boundary passage. Thus, both the prisoner of war who is told by his captors that he will be released only when he has "learned the truth" and the patient in a psychiatric hospital who cannot return home until he is again judged "normal" are in pure versions of the variable process. On a more mundane level, most upwardly mobile careers in business organizations are marked by variable socialization processes rather than fixed ones, because many uncontrolled factors such as the state of the economy and the turnover rates in the upper echelons of management may partially determine whether and when any given person will be promoted to the next higher level.

Furthermore, what may be true for one person is not true for another in variable socialization processes. Such a situation requires a recruit to search out clues as to the future. To wit, apprenticeship programs often specify only the minimum number of years a person must remain in the apprentice role and leave open the time a person can be expected to be advanced into the journeyman classification. However, since the rates of passage across any organizational boundary are a matter of some concern to people, transitional timetables may be developed by recruits anyway on the most flimsy and fragmentary information. Rumors and innuendos about who is going where and when they are going characterize situations marked by the presence of the variable strategy of socialization. Indeed, the would-be general manager often pushes quite hard to discover the signs of a coming promotion (or demotion). The individual listens closely to stories concerning the time it takes one to advance in the organization, observes as carefully as possible the experiences of others, and, in general, develops an age consciousness delineating the range of appropriate ages for given positions. And, whether or not this age consciousness is accurate, the individual will measure his or her progress against such beliefs.

Relatedly, Roth (1963) suggests that a special category of "chronic sidetrack" may be created for certain types of role failures. Thus, in the fixed socialization processes of public schools, the retarded are shunted off to distinct classes where the notion of progress does not exist. Similarly, in some police agencies, recruits unable to meet certain agent demands, particularly during that portion of the socialization process which is fixed and takes recruits typically through the academy to the patrol division, are provided long-term assignments as city jailers or traffic controllers, not as patrolmen. Such assignments serve as a signal to the recruit and others in the organization that the individual has left the normal career path. To the extent that such organizational "Siberias" exist and can be identified with certainty by those in the setting, chronic sidetracking from which there is rarely a return is a distinct possibility in fixed socialization processes. On the other hand, sidetracking is usually more subtle and problematic to a recruit operating in a variable socialization track. Indeed, many people who are working in the middle levels of management are often unable to judge just where they are, where they are going, or how they are doing. Consequently, variable processes are likely to create much anxiety and perhaps frustration for individuals who are unable to construct reasonably valid timetables to inform them of the appropriateness of their movement (or lack of movement) in the organization.

It also should be noted that variable processes are a very powerful antidote in the formation of group solidarity among potential recruits to certain organizationally defined roles. The movement of people at different rates and according to different patterns makes it virtually impossible for a cohort group to remain cohesive and loyal to one another. Indeed, in highly competitive situations, recruits being processed in a variable mode tend to differentiate themselves, both socially and psychologically, from each other. Furthermore, they often are obsequious to authority, suspicious of colleagues, and, more generally, adopt strategies of passage that ·minimize risk. Therefore, if, from the organization's point of view, peer group solidarity in a recruit is desirable, care should be taken to use only fixed timetables in the socialization processes.

We now look to certain propositions which arise on the basis of this discussion of fixed and variable socialization tactic.

Propositions

1. Fixed timetables for socialization processes are most likely to be associated with hierarchical boundary passages and least likely to be used with inclusionary boundary passages; functional boundaries present a mixed case.

Thus, in some organizations, one can almost guarantee that after a certain number of years to the day, one will be promoted to a higher rank. Consider here the military and certain civil service bureaucracies. To the contrary, one cannot guarantee that after a certain length of time a person will have learned what is necessary to make a functional move or will have acquired the trust and support required to move closer to the core of the organization. Those latter moves are more likely to be made on the basis of situational or *in situ* assessments and can involve very long or very short periods of time.

2. Fixed socialization processes are most likely to produce innovative responses; *variable socialization* processes are most likely to produce custodial responses.

The logic behind this proposition is simply that a variable situation leads to maximum anxiety and this anxiety operates as a strong motivator toward conformity. Intuitively, most managers utilize this principle when they attempt, for example, to control their most rebellious or difficult subordinates by telling them that their next career move "may or may not happen" within a given time frame. Doctors too use this tactic to induce patients to "get well" by refusing to provide them with any kind of timetable for their release from the hospital. And, of course, interrogators in police organizations and prison camps use the vagueness that surrounds one's expected length of sentence to pressure prisoners to make confessions and change attitudes (Schein, 1961; Goffman, 1961).

Variable socialization processes keep a recruit maximally off balance and at the mercy of socialization agents. In effect, the agent says to a recruit, "I will pass you along to the next stage when you are ready, but I will decide when you are ready." In fixed processes, such as a 4-year medical school program, a 3-month boot-camp, a 1-year apprenticeship, a set 2-year tour of duty to another geographical district of a business firm, persons can usually gear themselves to the situation better than in the variable case and therefore can plan innovative activities to fit the time-table. It should also be noted, however, that a fixed process may undermine the power of the innovator vis-à-vis the group of which he is a part. This is particularly the case near the end of a given stage, since others in the organization typically also know that the innovator is now in a "lame duck" period. Consequently, from the point of view of the innovator in certain roles, it is desirable to be in a position to know one's own time-table but to conceal this knowledge from others.

Serial vs. Disjunctive Socialization Processes

Definition A *serial socialization* process is one in which experienced members of the organization groom newcomers who are about to assume similar kinds of positions in the organization. In effect, these experienced members serve as role models for recruits. In the police world, for exam-ple, the serial mode—whereby rookies are assigned only older veteran officers as their first working partners on patrol—is virtually taken for granted, and some observers have suggested that it is this aspect of polic-ing that accounts for the remarkable intergenerational stability of patrol-men behavior patterns (Westley, 1970; Rubenstein, 1973; Manning and Van Maanen, 1978). Serial modes create something analogous to Mead's (1956) notion of a postfigurative culture. Just as children in stable societies are able to gain a sure sense of the future that awaits them by seeing in their parents and grandparents an image of themselves grown older, employees in organizations can gain a surer sense of the future by seeing in their more experienced elders an image of themselves further along in the organization. A danger exists, of course, that this image will be neither flattering nor desirable from the perspective of the recruits and many newcomers may leave the organization rather than face what ap-pears to be an agonizing future. In industrial setings where worker morale is low and turnover is high, a serial pattern of initiating newcomers into the organization would maintain and perhaps amplify an already poor situation.

When newcomers are not following the footsteps of immediate or re-cent predecessors, and when no role models are available to recruits to inform them as to how they are to proceed in the new role, the socializa-tion process is a *disjunctive* one. Many examples can be cited. Take, for instance, the case of a black firefighter entering a previously all-white engine company or a woman entering managerial ranks in a firm in which such ranks had previously been occupied only by males. In these cases, there are few, if any, persons on the scene who have shared the unique problems faced by the recruit. Certainly such situations make things extremely difficult and anxiety-provoking for the newcomer. An interesting illustration is also provided by the "heroic myth" to be found in many cultures and presented by Campbell (1956). In most versions of this saga, a young man is deliberately sent away from his homeland and "suffers" through a series of trials and tribulations in order to discover new ways of thinking about and doing things. Typically, after some most disjunctive adventures and misadventures, the hero is given some sort of magic gift and brings it back to his home society as a way of revitalizing it. Such disjunctive themes are also central ones in western fairy tales (Bettelheim 1976).[19]

The analytic distinction between serial and disjunctive socialization processes is sometimes brought into sharp focus when an organization undertakes a "house cleaning" whereby old members are swept out of the back door and new members brought in the front door to replace them. In extreme cases, an entire organization can be thrown into a disjunctive mode of socialization with the result that the organization will no longer resemble its former self. It is also true that occasionally the person who is presumably being socialized by another organizational member has more experience and knowledge than the one doing the socializing. To wit, in colleges where faculty members are constantly entering and exiting, long-term students exert much control over the institution. Certainly, in other organizations such as prisons and mental hospitals, recruit turnover is often considerably smaller than staff turnover. It should not be surprising then that these organizations are often literally run by the inmates.

Sometimes, what appears to be a serial process is actually disjunctive. In many work organizations, it is the case that if someone is exceptionally good and is promoted to project leader by age 25, that same person must be exceptionally mediocre to be in that same position at age 50 or 55. Because of such circumstances, the age-graded stereotype of the youthful, naive, and passive junior member of the firm being coached wisely by a mature, informed, and active mentor is frequently false. The process may have been designed as a serial one, but, to the recruit, the process may be disjunctive if he or she is unwilling to take the mentor seriously. Roth (1963) labels this problem "gapping" and it appears to be a serious one associated with serial strategies. Gapping refers to the historical, social, or ideological distance between recruits and agents. And, when the past experiences, reference groups, or values of the agents are quite removed from those of the recruits, good intentions aside, the serial process may become a disjunctive one.

In summary, it is generally true that recruits representing the first class will set the tone for the classes to follow. It is not suggested that those who follow are paginated *seriatim,* but simply that for those to come, it is easier to learn from others already on hand than it is to learn on their own as originators. As long as there are others available in the socialization setting whom the newcomers consider to be "like them," these others will act as guides, passing on consensual solutions to the typical problems faced by a recruit. Mental patients, for example, often report that they were only able to survive and gain their release because other more experienced patients "set them wise" as to what the psychiatric staff deemed appropriate behavior and indicative of improvement (Stanton and Schwartz, 1959; Goffman, 1961).

We can now state some propositions which relate these above considerations to the theoretical variables of interest.

Propositions

1. Serial socialization is most likely to be associated with inclusionary boundary passages.

This association results because to become a central member of any organizational segment normally requires that others consider one to be affable, trustworthy, and, of course, central as well. This is unlikely to occur unless these others perceive the newcomer to be, in most respects, similar to themselves. Recruits must at least seem to be taking those with whom they work seriously or risk being labeled deviant in the situation and hence not allowed across inclusionary boundaries.

2. Serial socialization processes are likely to be found only at those functional or hierarchical boundary passages which are seen by those in control of the process as requiring a continuity of skills, values, and attitudes. *Disjunctive* processes are most likely to be found at those functional and hierarchical boundary passages which are seen as not requiring such continuity. In other words, there is no a priori reason why serial or disjunctive processes would be found at either of these two types of boundaries. Organizations seemingly can arrange for a serial or disjunctive process at these locations according to criteria of their own making.

3. Serial socialization processes are most likely to produce a custodial orientation; disjunctive processes are most likely to produce an innovative orientation.

Whereas the serial process risks stagnation and contamination, the disjunctive process risks complication and confusion. But, the disjunctive pattern also creates the opportunity for a recruit to be inventive and original. Certainly newcomers left to their own devices may rely on inappropriate others for definitions of their tasks. Without an old guard around to hamper the development of a fresh perspective, the conformity and lockstep pressures created by the serial mode are absent. Entrepreneurs, for example, almost automatically fall into a disjunctive process of socialization as do those who fill newly created organizational roles. In both cases, there are few role models available to the individual who have had similar experiences and could therefore coach the newcomer in light of the lessons they have learned. Consequently, if innovation is to be stimulated, for whatever reason, the socialization process should minimize the possibility of allowing incumbents to form relationships with their likely successors, for these role incumbents will typically teach the recruit the "old" ways of doing things. Instead, the process should maximize either a very broad range of role models such as might be created through the use of individual, informal, and random tactics of socialization or deliberately create situations where gaps occur between role model and recruit, or construct brand-new roles to keep the recruits "loose" in their orientation.

Investiture vs. Divestiture Socialization Processes

Definition   The final strategy to be discussed here concerns the degree to which a socialization process is constructed to either confirm or disconfirm the entering identity of the recruit. *Investiture socialization* processes ratify and document for recruits the viability and usefulness of those personal characteristics they bring with them to the organization. An investiture process says to the newcomer, "We like you just as you are." Indeed, the organization through the use of this tactic does not wish to change the recruit. Rather, it wishes to take advantage of and build upon the skills, values, and attitudes the recruit is thought to possess. From this perspective, investiture processes substantiate and perhaps enhance the newcomer's view of himself. To wit, most young business school graduates are on an investiture path, though at certain boundaries they may run into certain disconfirming expereinces. At times, positions on the bottom rungs of organizational ladders are filled by the use of this tactic wherein newcomers to these positions are handled with a great deal of concern. Investiture processes attempt to make entrance into a given organizationally defined role as smooth and trouble free as possible. Orientation programs, career counseling, relocation assistance, social functions, even a visit to the president's office with the perfunctory handshake and good wishes systematically suggest to newcomers that they are valuable to the organization.

Divestiture socialization processes, in contrast, seek to deny and strip away certain personal characteristics of a recruit. Many occupational and organizational communities almost require a recruit to sever old friendships, undergo extensive harassment from experienced members, and engage for long periods of time in doing the "dirty work" of the trade typified by its low pay, low status, low interest value, and low skill requirements. Many aspects of professional training such as the first year of medical school and the novitiate period associated with religious orders are organized explicitly to disconfirm many aspects of the recruit's entering self-image, thus beginning the process of rebuilding the individual's self-image based upon new assumptions. Often these new assumptions arise from the recruits' own discovery, gradual or dramatic, that they have an ability to do things they had not thought themselves able to do previously.

Ordinarily, the degree to which the recruit experiences the socialization process as an ordeal indicates the degree to which divestiture processes are operating. Goffman's (1961) "total institutions" are commonly thought typical in this regard in the deliberate "mortifications to self" which entry into them entails. But, even in total institutions, socialization processes will have different meaning to different recruits. Thus, the degree to which the process is one of devestiture or investiture to a recruit is, in part, a function of the recruit's entering characteristics and orientation toward the role. Perhaps Goffman and others have been overimpressed with the degree of humiliation and profanation of self that occurs in certain organizations. Even the harshest of institutional settings, some recruits will undergo a brutal divestiture process with a calculated indifference and stoic nonchalance. Some recruits too will have been through divestiture processes so frequently that new socialization attempts can be undergone rather matter-of-factly. Furthermore, "total institutions" sometimes offer a recruit a sort of home-away-from-home that more or less complements the recruit's entering self-image. Thus, for convicted robbers, becoming a member of, say, a thief subculture in a prison acts more as an investiture than a divestiture process. In such situations, one's preinstitutional identity can be sustained, if not enhanced, with ease.

Yet, the fact remains that many organizations consciously promote ordeals designed to make the recruit whatever the organization deems appropriate, what Schein has described as "up-ending" experiences (Schein, 1964). In extreme circumstances, recruits are forced to abstain from certain types of behavior, must publicly degrade themselves and others, and must follow a rigid set of rules and regulations. Furthermore, measures are often taken to isolate recruits from former associates who presumably would continue to confirm the recruit's old identity. The process, when voluntarily undergone, serves to commit and bind the person to the organization and is typically premised upon a strong desire on the part of the recruit to become an accepted member of the organization (or an organizational segment). In brief, the recruit's entrance into the role or system is aided by his or her "awe" of the institution and this "awe" then sustains the individual's motivation through subsequent ordeals of divestiture. Consider here, first-year law students at elite universities (Turow, 1977) or young women entering religious orders (Hulme, 1956).

There are many familiar illustrations of organizations in this society that require a recruit to pass robust tests in order to gain privileged access into their realms: religious cults, elite law schools, self-realization groups, professional athletic teams, many law enforcement agencies, military organizations, and so on. Even some business occupations such as certified public accounting have stiff licensing requirements which, to many recruits, appear much like a divestiture process. It should be kept in mind, however, that these stern tactics provide an identity-bestowing as well as an identity-destroying process. Coercion is not necessarily a damaging assault on the person. Indeed, it can be a device for stimulating many personal changes that are evaluated positively by the person and others. What is, of course, problematic with coercion is its nonvoluntary aspects and the possibility of misuse in the hands of irresponsible agents.

Given these concerns, some propositions can now be presented which seek to further explicate the workings of this socialization tactic in organizational settings.

Propositions

1. Divestiture processes are most likely to be found (1) at the point of initial entry into an organization or occupation, and (2) prior to the crossing of major inclusionary boundaries where a recruit must pass some basic test of worthiness for membership in an organizational segment.

Once the person has passed these initial boundaries, subsequent boundary passages are much more likely to be of an investiture nature unless movement from one segment of the organization to another involves a major change of skills, value, or self-image. For example, one can imagine the college graduate engineer going into an engineering department of a company and experiencing this process as basically an investiture one. If, at a later time, this person decides to move into line management and goes through an extensive formal or informal management training process, such training may well be experienced as a divestiture process, because it may challenge many of the individual's cherished values which were associated with and rooted in the old engineering role.

2. Divestiture processes are most likely to lead to a custodial orientation: investiture processes are most likely to lead to an innovative orientation (unless the recruit enters and is rewarded for holding a custodial orientation at the outset).

Divestiture processes, in effect, remold the person and, therefore, are powerful ways for organizations and occupations to control the values of incoming members. Such processes lie at the heart of most professional training, thus helping to explain why professionals appear to be so deeply and permanently socialized. For, once a person has successfully completed a difficult divestiture process and has constructed something of a new identity based on the role to which the divestiture process was directed, there are strong forces toward the maintenance of the new identity. The strongest of these forces is perhaps the fact that the sacrifice involved in building the new identity must be justified, consequently making any disclaimers placed on the new identity extremely difficult for the person to accomplish. Furthermore, since the person's self-esteem following the successful completion of a divestiture process comes to rest on the new self-image, the individual will organize his present and future experiences to insure that his self-esteem can be enhanced or at least maintained (Goffman, 1959; Schein, 1961; Schein and Bennis, 1965). In short, the image becomes self-fulfilling.

Interaction of the Socialization Tactics

In the preceding portions of this "people processing" discussion, we identified some of the major tactical dimensions of socialization processes. These tactics were presented as logically independent of each other. Furthermore, we examined, through a series of propositional acts, the likelihood that each tactic would be associated with certain kinds of organizational boundary passages and the likelihood that each tactic would lead to either a custodial or innovative response. On examining real organizations, it is empirically obvious that these tactical dimensions are associated with one another and that the actual impact of organizational socialization upon a recruit is a cumulative one, the result of a combination of socialization tactics which perhaps enhance and reinforce or conflict and neutralize each other. It is also obvious that awareness of these tactical dimensions makes it possible for managers to design socialization processes which maximize the probabilities of certain outcomes. In the following section, we suggest some propositions about strategic combinations of socialization tactics in relation to the critical search for the conditions under which an organization can expect to promote from its recruits custodial, content-innovative, or role-innovative responses.[20]

Propositions

1. A *custodial* response will be most likely to result from a socialization process which is (1) sequential, (2) variable, (3) serial, and (4) involves divestiture processes.

In other words, the conditions which stimulate a custodial orientation derive from processes which involve the recruit in a definite series of cumulative stages (sequential); without set timetables for matriculation from one stage to the next, thus implying that boundary passages will be denied the recruit unless certain criteria have been met (variable); involving role models who set the "correct" example for the recruit (serial); and processes which, through various means, involve the recruit's redefinition of self around certain recognized organizational values (divestiture).

2. Content innovation is most likely to occur through a socialization process which is (1) collective, (2) formal, (3) random, (4) fixed, and (5) disjunctive.

In other words, for content innovation to occur in a role, it is desirable to train the role recruits as a formal group in which new ideas or technologies are specifically taught such that the value of innovation is stressed. Furthermore, it is desirable to avoid training sequences which might reinforce traditional ways of doing things but also to avoid variable timetables which might induce anxiety and promote divisive competition among recruits in which the best way to succeed is to "play it safe." Finally, the more the role models are themselves innovative (or absent altogether), the more the recruit will be encouraged (or forced) to innovate.

3. Role innovation, the redefining of the mission or goals of the role itself, is the most extreme form of innovation and is most likely to occur through a socialization process which is (1) individual, (2) informal, (3) random, (4) disjunctive, and (5) involves investiture processes.

In other words, for an individual to have the motivation and strength to be a role innovator, it is necessary for that person to be reinforced individually by various other members of the organization (which must be an informal process since it implies disloyalty to the role, group, organizational segment, or total organization itself), to be free of sequential stages which might inhibit innovative efforts, to be exposed to innovative role models or none at all, and to experience an affirmation of self throughout the process. It is very difficult indeed to change norms surrounding the mission or goals of an organizationally defined role. Therefore, it will probably only occur when an individual who is innovative in orientation at the outset encounters an essentially benign socialization process which not only does not discourage role innovation, but genuinely encourages it.

VI. SUMMARY AND CONCLUSIONS

What we have presented in this paper includes: a model of the organization and its major internal boundaries; a concept of role and role learning; the notions of custodial or innovative responses to socialization experiences; and a detailed analysis of six different dimensions of the socialization process which can be thought of as distinct "tactics" which managers (agents) can employ when socializing new recruits into the organization or at various boundary passages.

We have attempted to spell out, through a series of propositions, the likelihood that any given tactic would or would not be associated with any particular kind of organizational boundary passage. Also, we have developed several propositions about the likelihood of any given tactic leading to custodial, content-innovative, or role-innovative responses. Finally, we have proposed a combination of tactics which one might hypothesize as being most likely to produce each of the specific organizational responses.

We do not consider this a completed theory in that we do not as yet have enough empirical evidence to determine in a more tightly arranged and logical scheme how the various socialization tactics can be more or less ordered in terms of their effects upon recruits being initiated into organizational roles. We do feel, however, that the six analytically distinct dimensions of the socialization process represent a first and important step in this direction. We believe, then, that we have displayed some theory which can now be tested empirically.

In any event, we feel that the specification of the dimensions themselves at least opens up—both for researchers and managers in organizations—an analytic framework for considering the actual processes by which people are brought into new roles in the workplace. Indeed, it is time to become more conscious of the choices and consequences of the ways in which we "process people." Uninspired custodianship, recalcitrance, and even organizational stagnation are often the direct result of how employees are processed into the organization. Role innovation and ultimately organizational revitalization, at the other extreme, can also be a direct result of how people were processed. From this perspective, organizational results are not simply the consequences of the work accomplished by people brought into the organization; rather, they are the consequences of the work these people accomplish after the organization itself has completed its work on them.

FOOTNOTES

1. The view of social action taken in this paper is based essentially upon Meadian social psychology and is expressed most succinctly by the symbolic interactionists (see, for example, the work of Mead, 1930; Goffman, 1959; Blumer, 1969; Hughes, 1971; Becker, 1970). Personal change within this framework always requires the analytic occasion of "surprise." Such surprise prompts, even if only momentarily, a kind of disengagement from the concerns of the moment and perhaps the apprehension of those affairs that the person has not hitherto noticed at all. Philosophically, the perspective is related closely to that of phenomenology. For some groundings here, see Schutz, 1970; Lyman and Scott, 1970; Psathas, 1972; and, especially, Zaner, 1970.

2. We use the phrase "organizational segment" quite broadly in this paper. We mean by the phrase simply the joining of actions undertaken by different organizational members in the pursuit of certain ends. Departments are, therefore, organizational segments, as are work groups or project teams. Vertical and horizontal cliques, cabals, and conspiracies also fall under this rubric, for their existence implies an unofficial, though nonetheless real, merging of individual efforts. See Manning (1977) and Burns (1955, 1958, 1961) for a more elaborate use of this concept.

3. In general, any form of adult socialization, including the organizational variety, is analogous to that of childhood socialization, but an adult socialization process must contend with the individual's "culture of orientation," which may stand in the way of the organization's efforts. For an introduction to the various forms of adult and organizational socialization, see, for example, Becker and Strauss, 1956; Schein, 1961, 1964, 1968; Becker, 1964; Caplow, 1964; Brim and Wheeler, 1966; Roth, 1963; Moore, 1969; Inkeles, 1966; Manning, 1970; and Van Maanen, 1976. For an earlier statement of some of the ideas in this paper, see Van Maanen and Schein, 1977. Another introduction to the topic can be located in Porter, Lawler, and Hackman (1975) under the partially misleading chapter title "Adaptation Processes."

4. To some extent, those adjustments that turn out to be nonadaptive fall under the classification of what Platt (1972) calls a "social trap." In brief, such traps may involve, first, a time delay before the ill effects of a particular adjustment are felt as is the case with smoking and lung cancer or industrial pollution and environmental decay. Second, social traps also describe situations wherein strong individual incentives (or disincentives) seemingly prohibit people from acting in their collective best interest as exemplified by the infamous Kitty Genovese slaying in New York City or in game situations marked by the "Prisoner's Dilemma."

5. To wit, psychologists of a developmental stripe emphasize cognitive learning (e.g., Erikson, 1959, 1968; Piaget, 1962, 1969; Kroll et al., 1970; Keen, 1977) whereas psychologists more concerned with individual differences emphasize the matching of persons and setting in their socialization studies (e.g., Holland, 1966; Roe, 1957; Super et al., 1963). On the other hand, political scientists seem most concerned with how newcomers gain "control of things" (e.g., Hyman, 1959; Bell and Price, 1975; Edelman, 1967). Students of complex organizations nearly always focus on the effectiveness of the newcomer (e.g., Berlew and Hall, 1966; Feldman, 1976; Schein, 1978). Anthropologists, when they consider *adult* socialization at all, tend to be far more interested in transitions across particular societies than those occurring within a society (e.g., Taft, 1975; Kimball and Watson, 1972; Stonequist, 1937) or with those passages within a society that mark a youth's transitition into adulthood (Van Gennep, 1960; LeVine, 1973). All this is to say that these diverse studies provide some very rich descriptive materials but rarely do the theoretical accounts of the socialization process go beyond disciplinary boundaries. We have tried at least in small measure to transcend these boundaries in this paper.

6. To be sure, even if we accomplished these ends fully, our theory would still be of only the middle range (Merton, 1957). A comprehensive theory must also consider the origins and alterations in the historical patterns of organizational socialization as well as the differential effects of the process upon people of widely diverse backgrounds, cultures, and situations. The importance of a comparative and historical approach to the design of socialization studies cannot be underestimated. While we have a number of longitudinal accounts of the process as it occurs in a particular organization or occupation (e.g., Dornbush, 1955; Lieberman, 1956; Evan, 1963; Light, 1972; Van Maanen, 1973; Rosenbaum, 1976), these remain solitary case studies complete with their own idiosyncratic conceptual frameworks. Some good examples of the type of comparative and historical empirical work needed in this regard are provided by Lortie, 1975; Faulkner, 1974; and Kanter, 1968.

7. The most general process model of socialization is the Lewinian model with its three phases of "unfreezing, changing, and refreezing." Both Schein (1961a,b; 1968) and Van Maanen (1976) have relied extensively on this general formulation when describing the organizational socialization process from the individual's perspective.

8. This is, of course, taking an anthropological or cultural perspective on complex organizations, which requires the suspension of belief in formal pronouncements or inductive fiats

as to what organizations are about until detailed empirical study has been conducted into the workings of any given organization. Such an approach has much to recommend it. Indeed, the various studies which refer to the differences between the intentional and unintentional consequences, the manifest and latent goals, the theory-in-use and theory-in-practice, and the explicit and implicit objectives of an organization all would seem to point in this direction (e.g., Gouldner, 1954; Blau, 1955; Crozier, 1964; Burns, 1961; Schein, 1970; Argyris and Schön, 1974; Blankenship, 1977).

9. Looking to the functional and hierarchical boundaries, this would appear to be the case because immediately after entrance to a new position, the individual is too wrapped up in learning the requirements of the job to have much, if any, influence upon those requirements themselves. And, just before passage, the person is probably too caught up in the transition itself to have (or desire to have) much influence on the position being left behind. Across the inclusionary boundaries, the situation is similar though perhaps less clear. Immediately after entry, the person knows few people and will have developed little of the sort of interpersonal trust with others on the scene which is necessary to exert meaningful influence. But, after having achieved a central and visible position within the particular setting, it is likely that such a position is premised upon the individual's almost total acceptance of the norms and values of the group. As anthropologists are prone to say, the person may have "gone native" and has consequently lost the sort of marginality and detachment necessary to suggest critical alterations in the social scheme of things.

10. A more specific example is useful here. Police organizations come to mind, for there are some interesting case examples: Newly appointed so-called "progressive" or "reform" chiefs of police have, after purging the top administrative ranks and inserting personnel who were sympathetic to their preconceptions of what the organization should be about, tried to insure that only the "right types" (those who were also likely to share the chief's vision) would be promoted in the system. Thus, "old timers" who had very central and influential positions within their respective ranks and functions were no longer in favorable positions to rise in the organization. Policy changes around the structure of the promotion board, oral examinations, and the educational requirements for particular ranks seemingly worked in this regard. Yet, given the short-lived tenure of the instigators of these reforms and the short-lived period of the reforms themselves, moving these departments from the top down proved to be quite difficult, if not impossible. Indeed, lower-placed members in these departments were able (through a variety of inventive means) to block reform in the long run by either forcing the new chief out entirely or by "snapping" the chief back into a position where the values of organizational members once again fell more or less along a plumb line dropped from the top of the organizational cone. See Daley, 1973; Fishgrund, 1977; Beigel and Beigel, 1977 for case materials bearing on the rather remarkable resistance to change exhibited in police organizations.

11. For some further treatments of this role, position, and claims made by occupations commonly thought to be "professional," see Wilensky, 194; Goode, 1969; Vollmer and Mills, 1966; Hughes, 1958; and especially, Blankenship, 1977.

12. Aside from the strategic matters considered directly in the text, the poles of each tactical dimension represent differences in the amount of prior planning engaged in by members of the organization, differences in the level of commitment of organizational resources to a given socialization pattern, and differences in the number of agents actively involved in the process. However, situational and historical considerations unique to any given occupation or organization limit the kind of generalizations we can make on these matters. In other words, in some lines of work, the choice of an *individual* mode of socialization may require more planning, be more costly, and require more agents than the choice of a *collective* mode. In other endeavors, however, the case may be reversed. "Quality control"

may be a crucial aspect of the organization's choice of tactics wherein due to the exacting, dangerous, or consequential nature of the task to be performed by a newcomer to the field, standardized outcomes (promoted by collective processes—see following section) are, if not required, at least socially desirable, as is the case in medicine or firefighting. Needless to say, comparative studies are crucial in this regard.

13. The strength of group understandings depends, of course, upon the degree to which all members actually share the same fate. In highly competitive collective settings, group members know that their own success is increased through the failure of others; hence, the social support networks necessary to maintain cohesion in the group may break down. Consensual understandings will develop, but they will buttress individual modes of adjustment. Junior faculty members in publication-minded universities, for instance, follow group standards, although such standards nearly always stress individual scholarship, the collective standard being, as it is, an individual one.

14. A corollary to this proposition can also be suggested. Namely, the longer recruits remain together as a collective entity, the less likely role-innovative responses become. Van Maanen (1978) refers to such lengthy collective processes within which transfer rates in and out of the recruit group are low as "closed" socialization. On the other hand, "open" socialization, according to Van Maanen, also involves collective socialization, but the mode is marked by changing personnel across time within the recruit group. An interesting study in this regard is reported by Torrance (1955), who examined the decision-making abilities of Air Force flight crews who had trained together for some ten weeks. After training, some crews were scrambled (open-collective socialization), whereas the remaining crews stayed intact (closed-collective socialization). To Torrance's surprise, the scrambled crews were far superior on the performance of various task-related problems than were the intact crews. Interpreting these results, he concluded that the relative lack of power differentials and social status among the scrambled groups allowed for a more open and honest consideration of alternative solutions to the problems facing the group than would be possible when power and status were established and relatively fixed as was the case for the intact crews. Janis (1972) has recently reported some very similar findings.

15. Part of the difficulty for recruits in this matter is that they normally have very little to offer experienced organizational members in exchange for being taught the norms of a particular role. It is not the case that veteran members dislike or distrust novices (though in some instances they may), but it is merely the case that recruits have nothing substantial to contribute to the matters at hand. Thus, newcomers in the informal mode must often first behaviorally demonstrate their value to their would-be teachers by, say, performing "gofer" duties such as fetching work materials, snacks, and coffee, running little necessary but inconsequential errands, doing the "dirty work" others on the scene wish to avoid, and displaying an "eager" or "good" attitude when engaged in such tasks. In exchange for this willingness, a teaching relationship may then emerge. See Lortie, 1975; Haas, 1972; and Rubenstein, 1973 for some good examples in this regard.

16. This suggests that many socialization programs begin with universalistic concerns in which standards are taught as well as the uniform application of these standards. However, perhaps almost as many programs end with very particularistic concerns where recruits are taught that there are shifting standards which are applied uniquely to individual cases. This certainly reflects the typical content of the two socialization phases (formal and informal) mentioned in the text. Consider too that in many organizations the strict adherence to the rules (such as what is usually taught in a formal socialization process) may well reflect a sort of cultural incompetence when the recruit actually "goes to work" rather than competence, since, as all "good" members of the organization know, it is necessary to know the operating *rules about the rules* to perform adequately on the job. A further consideration of this

popular and frequent formal-to-informal socialization sequence is presented on the following pages of the text.

17. Some illustrations are perhaps useful here. Consider the fact that in many organizations employees misrepresent their overtime statements or expense allowances; budget makers pad their budgets with either fictitious expenses or exaggerated amounts for a given item; and supervisors invariably overrate the performance of their subordinates. None of these practices are likely to be conveyed during the first wave of formal socialization. Moreover, a member who strictly adheres to the formal or correct practices (the proper) rather than the social practices currently in use within the work setting (the smart) is likely to be considered by others to be an "organizational dope" until the second wave of socialization provides the recruit with the necessary learning. In other words, the "organizational dope" is one who has not been fully socialized.

18. As Professor Barry Staw (personal communication) rightly suggests, the degree to which the substantive base of a socialization process can be presented in a sequential fashion depends, in part, upon the availability to those directing the process to call upon a fully developed and shared intellectual or disciplinary paradigm. Thus, when classifying socialization processes in educational institutions, mathematics or physics are far more likely to be presented sequentially to student-recruits in those fields than are, for example, history or sociology. In work organizations, the use of sequential processes leading to a given organizationally defined role will also vary according to the degree that agents have recourse to shared knowledge about and/or experience with the target role. From this standpoint, financial anslysts or production supervisors are perhaps more likely to be socialized in a sequential manner than are organizational development specialists or new product line managers. However, we can press this analogy too far, because in work organizations, as in educational ones, pedagogical disputes over the *proper sequence of learning* are indeed quite common even when there exists a widely accepted paradigm among socialization agents.

19. Fairy tales may sometimes come true but certainly not all disjunctive socialization processes have happy endings. An informative and perhaps limiting case is provided by Klineberg and Cottle (1973). They note that first-generation rural-to-city migrants suffer a serious break between their past and present experiences. So serious is this break, in fact, that the migrant's image of a better future usually lies unconnected to any concrete activities toward which the migrant can direct his present efforts. It would seem, therefore, that extremely disjunctive experiences risk demolishing that most delicate bridge between means and ends. If this occurs, anomie and alienation are sure to result (Van Maanen, 1977a).

20. We should note that in these summary propositions we do not take a position on all socialization tactics. When a particular tactic is not explicitly mentioned in the proposition, it is because we feel that the tactic could go either way depending on more specific circumstances. In the first proposition, for example, formal-informal and collective-individual socialization tactics are not mentioned, because we feel that their use, in any combination, neither adds to nor detracts from the prediction as stated. To include these tactics would require more information—information of the sort partially spelled out in the proposition itself. To wit, formal-individual processes are potentially the most powerful, but also the most expensive and capable of producing custodial as well as innovative responses. On the average, formal-collective processes are probably likely to produce custodial orientations, but they can also facilitate the development of group perspectives which are highly innovative. Informal-collective processes are not at all common and therefore are quite hard to predict. And, while informal-individual processes are relatively common, the results of such processes are at best ambiguous without first specifying both the individual's initial orientation toward the particular role he or she is being prepared to assume and the other tactics to be associated with the process.

REFERENCES

1. Argyris, C., and D. Schön (1974 *Theory in Practice: Increasing Professional Effectiveness*, San Francisco: Jossey-Bass, Inc.
2. Avery, R. W. (1968) "Enculturation in industrial research," in B. G. Glaser (ed.), *Organizational Careers: A Source Book for Theory*, Chicago: Aldine Publishing Company. pp. 175–181.
3. Barnard, C. (1938) *The Functions of the Executive*, Cambridge: Harvard University Press.
4. Becker, H. S. (1970) *Sociological Work*, Chicago: Aldine Publishing Company.
5. ———. (1964) "Personal change in adult life," *Sociometry 27*, 40–53.
6. ———, and A. Strauss (1956) "Careers, personality, and adult socialization," *American Journal of Sociology 62*, 404–413.
7. ———, Geer, B., and Hughes E. (1968) *Making the Grade: The Academic Side of College Life*, New York: John Wiley — Sons, Inc.
8. ———, B. Geer, E. C. Hughes, and A. Strauss (1961) *Boys in white: Student Culture in Medical School*. Chicago: University of Chicago Press.
9. Beigel, H., and A. Beigel (1977) *Beneath the Badge: A Story of Police Corruption*, New York: Harper & Row, Publishers.
10. Bell, C. G., and C. M. Price (1975) *The First Term: A Study of Legislative Socialization*, Beverly Hills, Calif.: Sage Publications, Inc.
11. Berlew, D. E., and D. T. Hall (1966) "The socialization of managers: Effects of expectations on performance," *Administrative Science Quarterly 11*, 207–223.
12. Bettleheim, B. (1976) *The Uses of Enchantment: The Meaning and Importance of Fairy Tales*, New York: Alfred A. Knopf., Inc.
13. Biddle, B. J., and E. J. Thomas (eds.). (1966) *Role Theory: Concepts and research*, New York: John Wiley & Sons, Inc.
14. Bidwell, C. W.)May, 1962) "Pre-adult socialization," paper read at the Social Science Research Council Conference on Socialization and Social Structure. New York.
15. Blankenship, R. (Ed.) (1977) *Colleagues in Organization: The Social Construction of Professional Work*. New York: John Wiley & Sons, Inc.
16. Balu, P. M. (1955) *The Dynamics of Bureaucracy*, Chicago: University of Chicao Press.
17. ———, and R. A. Schoenherr (1971) *The Structure of Organization*. New York: Basic Books, Inc., Publishers.
18. Blumer, H. (1969) *Symbolic Interactionism*, Englewood Cliffs, N.J. Prentice-Hall, Inc.
19. Brim, O. G., and S. Wheeler (1966) *Socialization After Childhood*, New York: John Wiley & Sons, Inc.
20. Burke, K. (1950) *A Rhetoric of Motives*, Englewood Cliffs, N.J.: Prentice-Hall, Inc.
21. Burns, T. (1955) "The reference of conduct in small groups," *Human Relations 8*, 467–486.
22. ———. (1958) "Forms of conduct," *American Journal of Sociology 64*, 137–151.
23. ———. (1961) "Micropolitics: Mechanisms of institutional change," *Administrative Science Quarterly 6*, 257–281.
24. Campbell, T. (1956) *The Hero With a Thousand Faces*, New York: Anchor Books.
25. Caplow, T. (1964) *Principles of Organization*, New York: Harcourt, Brace and World.
26. Chinoy, E. (1955) *Automobile Workers and the American Dream*, New York: Random House, Inc.
27. Crozier, M. (1964) *The Bureaucratic Phenomenon*, Chicago: University of Chicago Press.
28. Daley, R. (1973) *Target Blue: An Insider's View of the New York City Police Department*. New York: Delacorte Press.

29. Dornbush, S. M. (1955) "The mititary academy as an assimilating institution," *Social Forces 33*, 316–321.
30. Edelman, M. (1967) *The Symbolic Uses of Politics*, Urbana, Ill.: University of Illinois Press.
31. Erikson, E. H. (1959) "Identity and the life cycle," *Psychological Issues 1*, 1–171.
32. ———. (1968) *Identity: Youth and Crisis*, New York: W. W. Norton & Company, Inc.
33. Eshelman, B. (1962) *Death Row Chaplain*, Englewood Cliffs, N.J.: Prentice-Hall, Inc.
34. Evan, W. M. (1963) "Peer group interaction and organization," *American Sociological Review 28*, 436–440.
35. Faulkner, R. R. (1974) "Coming of age in organizations: A comparative study of career contingencies and adult socialization," *Sociology of Work and Occupations 1*, 173–191.
36. Feldman, D. C. (1976) "A contingency theory of socialization," *Administrative Science Quarterly 21*, 433–452.
37. Fishgrund, T. J. (1977) "Policy making on decentralization in a large urban police department," unpublished doctoral dissertation. MIT.
38. Glaser, B. G. (1964) *Organizational Scientists: Their Professional Careers*, Indianapolis: The Bobbs-Merrill Co., Inc.
39. ———. (Ed.) (1968) *Organizational Careers: A Source Book for Theory*, Chicago: Aldine Publishing Company.
40. Goffman, E. (1959) *The Presentation of Self in Everyday Life*, New York: Doubleday & Co., Inc.
41. ———. (1963) *Asylums*, New York: Random House, Inc.
42. Goode, W. J. (1969) "The theoretical limits of professionalization," in A. Etzioni (Ed.), *The Semi-Professions and Their Organization*, New York: The Free Press. pp. 226–314.
43. Gordon, J. C. (1977) "The congruence between the job orientation and job content of management school alumni," unpublished doctoral dissertation, MIT.
44. Gouldner, A. W. (1954) *Patterns of Industrial Bureaucracy*, New York: The Free Press.
45. Haas, J. B. (1972) "Educational control among high steel ironworkers," in B. Geer (ed.), *Learning to Work*, Beverly Hills, Calif.: Sage Publications, Inc. pp. 31–38.
46. Hall, D. T. (1976) *Career Development*, Santa Monica, Calif.: Goodyear Publishing Co. Inc.
47. Holland, J. L. (1966) *The Psychology of Vocational Choice: A Theory of Personality Types and Environmental Models*, London: Ginn.
48. Hughes, E. C. (1971) *The Sociological Eye*, Chicago: Aldine Publishing Co.
49. ———. (1958) *Men and Their Work*, Glencoe, Ill.: The Free Press.
50. Hulme, K. (1956) *The Nun's Story*, Boston: Little, Brown and Company.
51. Hyman, H.H. (1959) *Political Socialization*, Glencoe, Ill.: The Free Press.
52. Inkeles A. (1966) "Society, social structure and child socialization," in J. A. Clausen (Ed.), *Socialization and Society*, Boston: Little, Brown and Company: pp. 146–161.
53. Janis, I. (1972) *Victims of Groupthink*, Boston: Houghton Mifflin Company.
54. Kanter, R. M. (1968) "Commitment and social organization: A study of commitment mechanisms in utopian communities," *American Sociological Review 33*, 409–417.
55. Keen. P. G. W. (1977) "Cognitive style and career specialization," in J. Van Maanen (Ed.), *Organizational Careers: Some New Perspectives*, New York: John Wiley & Sons, Inc.: pp. 89–105.
56. Kimball, S. T., and J. G. Watson (1972) *Crossing Cultural Boundaries: The Anthropological Experience*, San Francisco: Chandler Publishing Company.

57. Klineberg, S., and T. J. Cottle (1973) *The Present of Things Past*, Boston: Little, Brown and Company.
58. Kroll, A. M., L. B. Dinklage, J. Lee, E. D. Morley, and E. H. Wilson (1970) *Career Development: Growth and Crisis*, New York: John Wiley & Sons, Inc.
59. Laing, R. D. (1960) *The Divided Self*, London: Tavistock.
60. LeVine, R. A. (1973) *Culture, Behavior, and Personality*, Chicago: Aldine Publishing Company.
61. Lieberman, S. (1956) "The effects of changes in roles on the attitudes of role occupants," *Human Relations 9*, 467–486.
62. Light, D. (1970) "The socialization of psychiatrists," unpublished doctoral dissertation. Northwestern University.
63. Lipsky, M. (1971) "Street level bureaucracy and the analysis of urban reform," *Urban Affairs Quarterly 6*, 122–159.
64. Lortie, D. C. (1975) *Schoolteacher*, Chicago: University of Chicago Press.
65. Lyman, L. M. and M. B. Scott (1970) *A Sociology of the Absurd*, New York: Meredith.
66. Manning, P. K. (1970) "Talking and becoming: A view of organizational socialization," in J. D. Douglas (ed.), *Understanding Everyday Life*, Chicago: Aldine Publishing Company. pp. 239–256.
67. ———. (1977) "Rules, colleagues and situationally justified actions," in R. Blankenship (Ed.), *Colleagues in Organizations: The Social Construction of Professional Work*, New York: John Wiley & Sons, Inc. pp. 263–289.
68. ———, and J. Van Maanen (Eds.) (1978) *A View From the Streets*, Santa Monica, Calif.: Goodyear Publishing Co. Inc.
69. Mead, G. H. (1930) *Mind, Self and Society*, Chicago: University of Chicago Press.
70. Mead, M. (1956) *New Lives for Old*, New York: William Morrow & Co.
71. Merton, R. K. (1957) *Social Theory and Social Structure*, New York: The Free Press.
72. Moore, W. E. (1969) "Occupational socialization," in D. A. Goslin (ed.), *Handbook of Socialization Theory and Research*, Chicago: Rand McNally & Company, pp. 1075–1088.
73. Newcombe, T. M. (1958) "Attitude development as a function of reference groups: The Bennington study," in E. E. Maccoby, T. M. Newcomb, and E. L. Hartley (eds.), *Readings in Social Psychology* (3rd ed.). New York: Holt, Rinehart, and Winston, pp. 117–129.
74. Olesen, V. L., and E. W. Whittaker (1968) *The Silent Dialogue: A Study in the Social Psychology of Professional Socialization*. San Francisco: Jossey-Bass, Inc., Publishers.
75. Parsons, T. (1951) *The Social System*, New York: The Free Press.
76. Perrow, C. (1972) *Complex Organizations: A Critical Essay*, New York: Scott, Foresman and Company.
77. Piaget, J. (1962) *The Moral Judgment of the Child*, New York: Collier Books.
78. ———. (1969) *The Child's Conception of Time*. London: Routledge and Kegan Paul.
79. Platt, E. C. (1972) "Social Traps," *Science 56*, 18–24.
80. Porter, L. W., E. E. Lawler, and J. R. Hackman (1975) *Behavior in Organizations*, New York: McGraw-Hill.
81. Prewitt, K., H. Enlou, and B. Zisk (1966) "Political socialization for political roles," *Public Opinion Quarterly 30*, 112–127.
82. Psathas, G. (ed.) (1973) *Phenomenological Sociology*, New York: John Wiley & Sons, Inc.
83. Roe, A. (1957) "Early determinants of vocational choice," *Journal of Counseling Psychology 4*, 212–217.
84. Rose, A. M. (1960) "Incomplete socialization," *Sociology and Research 44*, 241–253.

85. Rosenbaum, J. E. (1976) *Making Inequality: The Hidden Curriculum of High School Tracking*. New York: John Wiley & Sons, Inc.

86. Roth, J. (1963) *Timetables,* Indianapolis, Ind.: The Bobbs-Merrill Co. Inc.

87. Rubenstein, J. *City police.* New York: Farrar, Strauss, and Giroux, 1973. Community and occupation. London: Cambridge University Press,

88. Schein, E. H., Schneier, I. and Baruer, C. H. (1961a) *coercive Persuasion,* New York: W. W. Norton & Company, Inc.

89. ———. (1961b) "Management development as a process of influence," *Industrial Management Review 2,* 59–77.

90. ———. (1963) "Organizational socialization in the early career of industrial managers." Office of Naval Research, MIT, Contr. No. 1941(83).

91. ———. (1964) "How to break in the college graduate," *Harvard Business Review 42,* 68–76.

92. ———. (1968) "Organizational socialization and the profession of management," *Industrial Management Review 9,* 1–15.

93. ———. (1970) *Organizational Psychology,* 2nd ed., Englewood Cliffs, N.J.: Prentice-Hall, Inc.

94. ———. (1971a) "The individual, the organization, and the career: A conceptual scheme," *Journal of Applied Behavioral Science 7,* 401–426.

95. ———. (1971b) "Occupational socialization in the professions: The case of the role innovator," *Journal of Psychiatric Research 8,* 521–530.

96. ———. (1978) *Career Dynamics: Matching Individual and Organizational Needs,* Reading Mass.: Addison-Wesley.

97. ———, W. G. Bennis (1965) *Personal and Organizational Change Through Group Methods,* New York: John Wiley & Sons, Inc.

98. Schutz, A. (1970) *On Phenomenology and Social Relations,* Chicago: University of Chicago Press.

99. Shafer, "Selling "selling," unpublished Master's thesis, MIT 1975.

100. Shibutani, T. (1962) "Reference groups and social control," in A. Rose (ed.), *Human Behavior and Social Processes,* Boston: Houghton Mifflin Company, pp. 128–147.

101. Stanton, A. H., and Schwartz, M. S. (1954) *The Mental Hospital,* New York: Basic Books, Inc., Publishers.

102. Stonequist, E. V. (1937) *The Marginal Man,* New York: Charles Scribner's Sons.

103. Strauss, A. L. (1959) *Mirrors and Masks,* Glencoe, Ill.: The Free Press.

104. Super, D. E., R. Starishevsky, N. Matlin, and J. P. Jordaan (1963) *Career Development: Self-Concept Theory,* Princeton, N.J.: College Entrance Examination Board.

105. Taft, R. (1976) "Coping with unfamiliar cultures," in N. Wareer (ed.), *Studies in Cross Cultural Psychology* Vol. 1, London: Academic Press, 452–475.

106. Torrance, E. P. (1955) "Some consequences of power differences on decision making in permanent and temporary groups," in A. P. Hore, E. F. Borgatta, and R. F. Bales (eds.), *Small Groups,* New York: Alfred A. Knopf, Inc. pp. 179–196.

107. Turow, S. (1977) *One L: An Inside Account of Life in the First Year at Harvard Law School,* New York: G. P. Putnam's Sons.

108. Van Gennp, A. (1960) *The Rites of Passage,* Chicago: University of Chicago Press.

109. Van Maanen, J. (1973) "Observations on the making of policemen," *Human Organizations 32,* 407–418.

110. ———. (1974) "Working the streets: A developmental view of police behavior," in H. Jacob (ed.), *The Potential for Reform of Criminal Justice,* Beverly Hills, Calif.: Sage Publications, Inc., pp. 53–130.

111. ———. (1976) "Breaking-In: Socialization to work, in R. Dubin (ed.), *Handbook of Work, Organization, and Society,* Chicago: Rand McNally & Company, pp. 67–130.

112. ———. (1976) "Experiencing organization: Notes on the meaning of careers and socialization, in J. Van Maanen (ed.), *Organizational Careers: Some New Perspectives,* New York: John Wiley & Sons, Inc., pp. 15–45.

113. ———. (1977b) "Toward a theory of the career," in J. Van Maanen (ed.), *Organizational Careers: Some New Perspectives,* New York: John Wiley & Sons, Inc, pp. 161–179.

114. ———. (1978) "People processing: Major strategies of organizational socialization and their consequences," in J. Paap (ed.), *New Directions in Human Resource Management,* Englewood Cliffs, N.J.: Prentice-Hall, Inc.

115. ———, and E. H. Schein (1977) "Career development," in J. R. Hackman and J. L. Suttle (Eds.), *Improving life at work.* Santa Monica, Ca.: Goodyear Publishing Co. Inc. pp. 30–95.

116. Vollmer, H. M., and D. J. Mills (Eds.). (1966) *Professionalization,* Englewood Cliffs: N.J., Prentice-Hall, Inc.

117. Wamsley, G. L. (1972) "Contrasting institutions of Air Force socialization: Happenstance or bellweather?" *American Journal of Sociology, 78,* 399–417.

118. Westley, W. (1970) *Violence and the Police,* Cambridge, Mass.: MIT Press.

119. Wheeler, S. (1966) "The structure of formally organized socialization settings," in O. G. Brim and S. Wheeler (eds.), *Socialization After Childhood,* New York: John Wiley & Sons, Inc. pp. 51–116.

120. Wilensky, H. L. (1964) "The professionalization of everyone?" *American Journal of Sociology 70,* 137–158.

121. Zaner, R. M. (1970) *The Way of Phenomenology,* New York: Pegasus.

THE POLITICS OF UPWARD INFLUENCE IN ORGANIZATIONS

Lyman W. Porter, Robert W. Allen and
Harold L. Angle

ABSTRACT

Social influence processes are generally acknowledged to be a pervasive aspect of organizational life. The consensual importance of this topic has been reflected in an abundance of research on downward influence processes, under such general frameworks as leadership, and lateral influence processes, as treated in the literatures of group dynamics or socialization. Unfortunately, research on downward influence has not been balanced by a proportional concern for upward influence, especially those self-serving upward influence activities that occur within the context of another underresearched topic—organizational politics. This paper argues that political influence in organizations is directed, with only rare exceptions, hierarchically upward. The paper explores the present state of the art, regarding our understanding of some key relevant aspects of organizational politics and upward influence, at a "micro" level of analysis. Finally, an episodic model of upward political influence is presented, from the perspective of an individual political actor. Keyed to this model are several testable propositions intended to stimulate systematic research.

This paper jointly addresses two topics that have been generally ignored in the organizational behavior literature: political behavior and upward influence. The existence of political processes in organizations has been well recognized in the "popular" management press (e.g., Hegarty, 1976; Jay, 1967; Packard, 1962), yet has had less than its share of notice in the academic literature. A mid-1970's survey of more than 70 textbooks in industrial-organizational psychology, management and organizational behavior revealed only 70 pages in which the topic of organizational politics was addressed—about 2/10 of 1 percent of the textbook content! A review of eight of the most appropriate academic journals revealed less than a dozen articles on the topic, out of a total of more than 1,700 articles over a 16-year period (Porter, 1976). Furthermore, much of what has been written about organizational politics has addressed what might be termed the "macro" politics of organizations—the bargaining process among subunits, through which organizational goals are established (March, 1962). The "micro" processes, such as the management of personal upward influence, have been given shorter shrift. As with political behavior, the topic of upward influence has seldom received concerted attention from those in the OB field and, indeed, has always been in the shadow of its "big brothers," namely, downward influence (i.e., management and leadership), and lateral influence (i.e., group dynamics and socialization). It is our contention that a joint examination of organizational politics and upward influence may help point the way toward some important avenues for future research and for conceptualizations about behavior processes in organizations.

It is worth noting at the start of our consideration that the two topics are not unrelated. It appears reasonable to say that while not all (or even most) upward influence involves political behavior, most political behavior (in organizations) does involve upward influence. Taking the first part of this statement, much of upward influence involves, of course, the normal routine-reporting relationships that exist in all organizations. There is a substantial segment of upward influence, however, that we could contend involves what can be labeled as "political behavior" (to be defined later). What the ratio is of nonpolitical to political upward influence behavior in organizations is an empirical question. The answer would vary from organization to organization. (Some of the variables assumed to be critical to this cross-organizational variation are discussed later in our conceptual model presented.) The other part of the statement about the relationship between the two topics—that most political behavior in organizations involves upward influence—is based on the assumption that the typical object of influence will be someone or some group possessing more formal, legitimate power than the would-be political actor. While it is possible to cite clear exceptions to this proposition, we would, nevertheless, contend that the vast majority of *political* attempts at influence are in the upward direction. (Later parts of this paper will attempt to provide additional support for this assertion.)

The source of a political influence attempt can be an individual acting alone, an individual acting on behalf of a group, or a coalition of individuals acting as a group. In this paper, we intend to maintain a focus on political influence as an individual phenomenon. This is not because we consider coalitional political processes in organizations either uninteresting or unimportant. On the contrary, the many-on-one (or many-on-several) influence event is a fairly common fact of organizational life. However, we believe that the one-on-one political influence situation is a particularly prevalent, albeit little-understood, organizational reality. In the ensuing analysis, the focus will be on gaining a better understanding of the decision logic of the individual "politician," without the confounding effects of the dynamics of group decision making.

Before proceeding further, two definitional matters must be dealt with: (1) "upward influence"; and (2) "political behavior." The first is simple, the second complex. For our purposes, we will define upward influence as "attempts to influence someone higher in the formal hierarchy of authority in the organization." Thus, while the target person will typically have more total power (of all types) than the political actor attempting influence, that will not always be so—as in the case of someone with slightly greater formal authority but much less in the way of expertise. In that case, we would predict a relative absence of attempts at political influence. In any event, again, "upward influence" means influence attempts directed toward someone higher in the formal hierarchy. And when considering upward influence, it is critical to note that this salient feature—the fact that the person attempting to exercise influence cannot rely on formal authority—results in a situation that is distinctly different from that of downward influence. This feature alone makes the topic especially intriguing.

"Political behavior in organizations" or "organizational politics" is not an easy term to define. Despite this, a number of authors have recently offered definitions (e.g., Frost & Hayes, 1977; Mayes & Allen, 1977; Robbins, 1976), and our definitional framework will be consistent generally with the thrust of these definitions. However, any one of them may not include all four of the elements contained in our definition. For the purposes of the present paper, *organizational political behavior* is defined as:

1. Social influence attempts
2. that are discretionary (i.e., that are outside the behavioral zones prescribed or prohibited by the formal organization),

3. that are intended (designed) to promote or protect the self-interests of individuals and groups (units),
4. and that threaten the self-interests of others (individuals, units).

While we do not wish to go into a lengthy discourse here on all the subtleties of this or any other definition of organizational politics, a few brief comments are in order about each of the four components of the definition. First, we take it as a given that regardless of what else it is, political behavior is behavior aimed at influencing others; behavior carried out in such a way that there are no intended direct effects on others would fall into the category of nonpolitical behavior. Second, any behavior that the organization ordinarily requires and expects is nonpolitical; e.g., coming to work every day and carrying out the assignments and expectations of the formal role. Likewise, behavior forbidden by formal rules or commonly accepted standards of behavior (e.g., fighting, stealing, etc.) would be excluded. That leaves discretionary behavior relating to the work situation (and meeting the other definitional requirements) as that which would be labeled "political." Third, we believe that the intention of promoting or protecting self-interests is a necessary (though not sufficient) element of political behavior. Of course, as we point out later, attributions of intention often vary widely between those who are the source of the behavior and those who are observing or labeling the behavior. It is our contention that if the behavior is *seen* by organizational participants as intended to promote or protect self-interests then (meeting the other criteria) the label "political" is appropriate. Finally, we believe that unless the behavior threatens the self-interests of others, it is nonpolitical. This puts political behavior squarely in the camp of competitive as opposed to collaborative behavior, and focuses on the zero-sum aspect of organizational resource allocation. (It leads, as noted later, to the clear prediction that the scarcer the resources the higher the level of political activity.) In the words of Frost and Hayes (1977), this last part of the definition emphasizes that political behavior is "nonconsensus" behavior.

The remainder of this paper will consider the following: First, key elements relating to upward political influence, i.e., norms, situational factors, actor characteristics, target selection, and influence method selection. (Throughout this chapter, we will use a variety of terms, including "agent," "actor," and "source," to describe the person exerting political influence.) Here we will attempt to review relevant literature, suggest some of the key issues, and by implication highlight some of the more significant gaps in our knowledge. In the latter part of the article we will try to point the way to future research directions, first noting some research methodology considerations and then putting forth a rudimentary conceptual scheme for viewing upward influence attempts of a political nature. This section will offer some potentially testable propositions relating to this process. We will conclude with some (very) broad overview observations.

KEY CONSIDERATIONS

Certain considerations emerge as particularly salient when one considers the present state of knowledge (or gaps in our knowledge) of political influence in organizations. What (if any) political norms exist in organizations and how do organizational members learn about them? What situational factors influence the prevalence of political activity? Further, what kinds of individuals are prone to engage in organizational politics? Finally, what factors lead to selection of particular organizational members as political influence targets, and what methods are available, and preferred, for political influence?

Political Norms

Our definition of organizational politics has incorporated the notion that organizationally political behaviors fall outside the range of those either prescribed or prohibited by the organization. At first blush, the implication would seem to be that "political" behaviors in organizations take place outside the normative framework. No such conclusion, however, is intended. As will be brought out in the following discussion, it is very likely that strong norms do exist in organizations, relative to "political" activity. However, the basis for these norms will not be found in official prescriptions originated by the formal organization. Rather, the signals by which the organizational member pieces together a picture of "political reality" originate from the informal organization, and are apt to be sent in disguised format and against a noisy background.

Organizational norms, both political and nonpolitical, can be viewed two ways: as an objective aspect of the environment, i.e., an attribute of the organization; or as a set of personal perceptions, i.e., existing only in the eye of the beholder. Both views can be useful, depending on the purposes to which the concept is to be put. An analogy can be drawn to the study of organizational climate, in which the concept is drawn sometimes in "macro" terms and, at other times, as a "micro" variable (James & Jones, 1974). Here, we will take a relatively "macro" perspective, treating political norms as an aspect of "organizational reality" which members must endeavor to learn. In a later section, we will construct a model of upward political influence which incorporates political norms from the perspective of the individual's belief system.

The Learning of Organizational Norms. All interactive social systems develop sets of behavioral rules for their participants, and organizations—formal and informal—are no exception. These rules, or norms, act as constraints on participants' behavioral variation. In this context, norms are prescriptive rather than merely descriptive in nature. Instead of simply summarizing prevalent or modal behavior in a social system, norms carry an "ought to" connotation. Furthermore, for every norm there is a corresponding shared belief as to what should or will happen in the event of deviance, i.e., violation of normative behavior prescriptions (Clark and Gibbs, 1965).

Two basic issues, each subsuming several subissues, appear salient with respect to the micro-political norms of upward influence. First, what norms exist? Do norms ever permit or prescribe upward political influence attempts, or are all such attempts acts of deviance? Assuming that there are at least some circumstances under which upward political influence is condoned, what are the contingent factors? Do political norms differ in different parts of the organization? How does the goal or purpose behind an influence attempt bear upon its acceptability? Do norms prescribe or proscribe particular influence tactics?

A second general issue relates to the way political norms are learned in organizations. How clear are the "norm messages" regarding upward political influence? Are they transmitted "in the clear," or are they buried in subtlety and innuendo? This raises the parallel issue of norm consensus. Is there sufficient exchange of unambiguous norm information to permit consensual validation, or must each participant rely on a fallible attribution process? Assuming the latter, how accurate are attributions regarding the extent to which upward influence is attempted and the purpose or intent of the actor when such attempts are perceived?

Political Norm Structure. Norms are not either-or phenomena. Jackson (1966) proposed that, rather than attempting to deal with norms as "things," we should learn to think in terms of "degrees of normness." As with roles (Kahn, Wolfe, Quinn, Snoek & Rosenthal, 1964; Katz & Kahn, 1978), norms are "sent" by significant others; however the norm senders seldom all transmit identical messages. Jackson (1965) referred to the extent of members' norm consensus as "norm crystallization," and considered this to be a basic criterion regarding the extent to which a given norm exists.

There is ample reason to believe that informal "political" norms abound in organizations. Schein (1977) asserted that political processes ". . . may be as endemic to organizational life as planning, organizing, directing and controlling" (p. 64). Real-world reports of life in organizations (e.g., Frost, Mitchell & Nord, 1978; Kanter, 1977) are rich in anecdotal material of political processes at work. Tushman (1977) saw conflict, bargaining, and other political behaviors as ". . . a logical deduction of systems thinking" (p. 207).

While informal political norms probably exist in nearly all organizations, it is unlikely that such norms are invariant across all situations or in all parts of the organization. There is, for instance, reason to believe that political influence norms vary situationally. Frost and Hayes (1977) posit that there are two phases in the distribution of organizational resources; the *negotiation* phase and the *enactment* phase. In the negotiation phase, conflict is seen as institutionalized. Values, goals and priorities are not given, but are subject to establishment and clarification by a bargaining process. Thus, Frost and Hayes consider political behavior to be endemic (and appropriate) to the negotiation phase.

The enactment phase follows the negotiation phase. Here consensus, rather than conflict, becomes institutionalized, with values, goals and priorities seen as "given." Now, it is no longer openly acceptable to maneuver for one's own interests.

Thus, the norms of upward political influence may differ substantially, in a given organization, depending on whether the issue at hand is (in Frost and Hayes' terminology) in the negotiation or enactment phase. Influence attempts that are accepted (even expected) in the former phase may become taboo in the latter.

Political norms may also differ with location in the organization. Madison, Allen, Porter, Renwick and Mayes (1980) found that more than 90 percent of managers interviewed reported that organizational politics occurred more frequently at upper and middle levels of management than at lower managerial levels. A related study (Allen, Madison, Porter, Renwick & Mayes, 1979) found that lower-level managers describe the traits of political actors in more pejorative terms than do upper-level managers, indicating perhaps that political activity is more often considered counternormative at lower hierarchical levels.

In addition, managers in the Madison *et al.* study reported political activity as more prevalent in staff, as opposed to line positions, and relatively more endemic to certain organizational subunits. Departments in which organizational politics was seen as most prevalent were marketing and sales, while accounting/finance and production were seen as lowest in political activity.

It appears, then, that the "politically active" functional areas are those in which uncertainty is most prevalent. Organizational members in such roles may need to rely on political skill to deal with the conflicting demands of intra- and extra-organizational associates. Thus, norms that favor political influence as a means of conducting the day's business may arise, out of necessity, in such subunits.

In summary, searching for "the" organization's political norms might be far too simplistic a pursuit. Porter and Lawler's (1965) critical review, which was updated and supported by Berger and Cummings (1979), provided an early illustration of the heterogeneity of attitude-behavior relationships, across organizational subunits. As we are coming to recognize that organizations don't always have a single "structure" (cf. Hall, 1962; Jelinek, 1977), we should also be prepared to discover a mosaic of political-norm subsystems embedded in organizations.

Learning of Upward Political Influence Norms. Learning of political norms may pose special problems for the organizational initiate. The stimuli are immeasurably more complex, and entire configurations of cues must be learned as *gestalts* (Sarbin & Allen, 1968). While this difficulty pertains to all norm acquisition, there is a second problem that relates to the learning of political norms per se. Unlike many organizational norms, political norms are, within our definitional framework, exclusively the norms of the *informal* organization. Since the formal organization neither prescribes nor forbids political behaviors, political norms are not transmitted in the form of explicit organizational policy. So, unlike the cues provided for the norms that support formal organizational policies, political norm cues may often be implicit, requiring considerable sensitivity on the part of the receiver of a norm message.

Messages regarding the informal norms that *condone* political acts may be even more vague than norm messages that *condemn* such behavior. Thus, while a norm that condemns certain "political" acts (for example, disclosing organizational secrets to an outsider in order to gain support and leverage to obtain some personal end) might be explicitly communicated in the informal organization, norms that actually condone other self-serving actions might never be openly discussed, even via informal communication channels. Thus, many political norms must be learned through inference, by watching the "political" activities of others and noting the positive or negative reactions of persons in the observed actor's "norm set."

The organizational novice, attempting to learn the organization's political norms by observing the activities of other members, faces a series of attributional tasks (Shaver, 1975). The first task is *observation of action,* i.e., judging whether an act of social influence has occurred. It is probably safe to assume that a competent "organizational politician" will attempt to conceal *political* influence attempts from third-party observation and, if she/he is to survive in the organization, will probably be relatively successful at such concealment. Many, if not most, acts of political influence may therefore evade general detection. Yet, observation of action is a necessary condition before any further "political" attributions are possible.

Assuming that a social influence act (or attempt) has been observed, the second stage of the attribution process is *judgment of intention*. If the event is attributed to a chance occurrence, further attributions would be meaningless and the attribution sequence would, therefore, stop. Only if the observer attributes the episode as *intentional behavior* will a third attribution stage ensue—that of making either a "situational" or "dispositional" attribution, i.e., to get at the question "why?"

At this stage, there are two possibilities. On the one hand, the person might have acted because of forces in the situation that would compel any reasonable person to so behave (i.e., a result of "environmental coercion"). On the other hand, he or she might have behaved completely autonomously (i.e., because of the person's "disposition"). Although attribution theory usually treats such judgments as dichotomous (cf. Shaver, 1975), we consider it more reasonable to view the situational/ dispositional attribution as occurring along a continuum. Nearly all human behavior has both personal and environmental determinants. The task at this stage, therefore, may more correctly be one of judging the *extent* to which behavior is situationally vs. dispositionally mediated. In this respect, the nearer the attribution to the situational extreme, the less likely the behavior will be seen as "political," and vice versa.

Assuming that the third-stage attribution was that the behavior was *not entirely* environmentally coerced, then the door remains open for another attribution, critical to our definition of organizational politics—that of self-serving intent.

There are two subcategories of self-serving intent: (1) congruent with organizational goals; or (2) incongruent with organizational goals (Schein, 1977). While either is potentially "political," the latter may lead to further attribution problems. If individual and organizational goals are incongruent, the influence means employed will almost certainly be covert. Furthermore, the "politician" using a covert strategy may further complicate the picture by overtly displaying a fictitious set of intentions and means, in order to give the impression that personal and organizational objectives are actually aligned. Such a "cover story" can further complicate the attribution process, and thereby add to the observer's difficulties in attempting to learn the organization's political norms.

A key aspect of our definition of organizational politics is the idea that "political" behavior is self-serving while at the same time not intended to serve others (or intended, in fact, to misserve others). Such behavior, then, will be resisted, *if recognized* by others (Frost & Hayes, 1977). Again, the implication is that the actor will take pains to conceal attempts at political influence, adding to the ambiguity encountered by observers.

In discussing the acquisition of organizational power, a pursuit closely related to political influence, Moberg (1977) asserted that societal norms require unobtrusiveness. The "politician" must take care to avoid having his/her behavior attributed, by others, to a self-serving intent. Creation of the impression that behavior is legitimate (or nonexistent) may be accomplished by acting in ways that make reliable attributions difficult. Some of the "smokescreen" tactics aimed at manipulating observers' attributions might include making certain that there is a reasonably credible organizational rationale for one's actions, i.e., creating the impression that one's actions are situationally or environmentally mandated. The political actor can even create "attributional noise," by acting so enigmatically that observers lose confidence in their attributions, or by publicly advocating a "version" or interpretation of organizational goals that actually serves personal objectives.

Thus, the observer of upward influence activity is not only forced to rely on inference under ambiguous circumstances, but may become the target of active deception, as well. It would appear that the general consequence of this deception, assuming that at least some deception efforts are successful, would be an underestimate of the extent of political influence activity in one's organization.

However, there are biases in the attribution process, per se, that may lead to overestimates, as well. Heider (1958) first identified a consistent human propensity that Ross (1977, p. 183) later dubbed the "fundamental attribution error." Observers of the behavior of others tend to underestimate the impact of situational variables, while overestimating the impact of dispositional factors. Actors and observers appear to differ in susceptibility to this fundamental error. While actors tend to attribute their own behavior choices to situational constraints, external observers are apt to attribute the actor's choices to dispositional factors (Jones & Nisbett, 1971). However, the difference requires further qualification, i.e., the tendency to overattribute to dispositional determinants of others' behavior may depend, in part, on the observer's expectations, and on whether the result of the other's behavior is interpreted by the observer as a "positive" or "negative" outcome (Harvey, Arkin, Gleason & Johnston, 1974). In general, however, there frequently exists in organizations a tendency to attribute the influence activities of others to "political" intent, even though the same behavior in oneself may be seen as apolitical (i.e., the behavior is simply mandated by the situation).

One determinant of an individual's ability to behave appropriately in a social situation is the accuracy with which she or he perceives the existing system norms (Jackson, 1960). There is a common tendency to assume that social system members both share and are aware of each others' norms for the behavior of all members (Biddle, 1964). However, Schank (1932, cited in Biddle, 1964) observed that, when either communication or behavior observation is restricted, a state of "pluralistic ignorance" can exist. In effect, members of a social group might come to share a wholly mistaken view of the group's norms. Furthermore, the false consensus concerning these norms may become self-perpetuating. In view of the particular communication and attribution problems that surround political norm learning, it would appear that political-influence norms in organizations constitute a prime candidate for "pluralistic ignorance."

Thus, a misleading consensus may come to exist with respect to which "political" behaviors the informal organization condemns, and which such behaviors are condoned. This, in turn, may lead political actors to overestimate the extent of their own deviancy, resulting in their taking great pains to disguise their behavior. The vicious circle thus created can perpetuate a situation in which discovery of the "real" political norms in an organization may pose serious problems for researchers and organization members, alike.

As we have seen, informal political norms are a critical contextual factor in the politics of upward influence. There are also other contextual considerations surrounding any potential political act. The following section discusses several such situational factors.

Situational Factors

Whereas the political norms in an organization provide an ambient, steady-state political climate, other factors specific to the immediate situation may temporarily become even more influential, with respect to political activity, than are the norms themselves. There is some evidence that certain organizational situations tend to be intrinsically "political." Madison *et al.* (1980) reported that managers saw certain situations as characterized by relatively high levels of political activity. Examples of such situations included reorganization changes, personnel changes and budget allocation. On the other hand, such organizational situations as rule and procedure changes, establishment of individual performance standards and the purchase of major items were characterized as relatively low in prevalence of political activity. These differences were discussed by Madison *et al.* in terms of three variables: (1) uncertainty; (2) importance of the activity to the larger organization; and (3) salience of the issue to the individual.

While some might view uncertainty or situational ambiguity simply as the obverse of structuring of activities, this would be something of an oversimplification. Even in a relatively mechanistic organization possessing a characteristically "tight" control structure, certain specific occurrences might be ambiguous. For example, in the "political" situations identified by Madison *et al.* (1980), e.g., reorganization, great uncertainty is apt to exist regarding power allocation and assignment of responsibilities and tasks—even in those organizations that are ordinarily closely structured. In such instances, it may be the organization's structuring, itself, that is in doubt.

The other major relevant variables proposed by Madison *et al.* seem to relate to what is at stake, both for the individual and for the entire organization. In their research, some of the issues rated as low in political activity were those in which relatively low stakes were involved, even though they may have involved some uncertainty.

The situations in which political activity may be most prevalent seem to combine situational ambiguity with sufficient personal stake to activate the individual to consider actions that fall outside the boundaries of the formal organizational norm system. While lack of structure or situational ambiguity may provide recognition of *opportunity* to engage in upward political influence, it is personal stake that may provide the *incentive* to engage in political behavior, per se.

A fourth situational factor, not explicitly addressed by Madison *et al.*, but which appears particularly relevant to organizational politics, is resource scarcity. The essence of the political process is the struggle over the allocation of scarce resources, i.e., who gets what, where and when (Lasswell, 1951). The relative abundance of resources represented by various organizational issues may have a great deal of influence regarding the extent to which "political" means become employed in their resolution.

While the preceding discussion of norms and of situational factors has described some aspects of what the potential political actor *finds* in the way of contextual factors—factors that may influence his/her "political" activity in the organization—it is also necessary to consider what the individual *brings* to the situation. These actor characteristics will now be considered.

Actor Characteristics

The ambient political norms and the situational factors that have been discussed thus far, even if perfectly understood, would fall far short of enabling perfect prediction of political behavior. We have discussed only half of Lewin's (1935) famous equation, $B = f(P \cdot E)$. We now turn, therefore, from an analysis of the political environment to consideration of the focal person—the political actor.

Each potential agent of upward political influence brings to the scene a rich array of personal characteristics. Such individual factors could easily lead two different organizational members either to perceive an identical situation differently or, even if they share identical perceptions, to behave characteristically in different ways. This now leads us to consider some particular classes of individual differences that might help predict organizational members' relative propensities to engage in upward political influence.

Beliefs About Action–Outcome Relationships. The truism, "organizational behavior is a function of its perceived consequences," is certainly as applicable in the arena of organizational politics as it is in other spheres of organizational life. It is a basic psychological tenet that behavior that has been rewarded in the past becomes more probable in the future.

From the perspective of expectancy theory (Vroom, 1964), which is isomorphic with subjective expected utility (SEU) theory (Edwards, 1954, 1961), organizational members are believed to behave in a manner that maximizes their expected net value. This, in turn, suggests that organization members undertake a series of subjective cost-benefit analyses, using salient available information. Some of the more explicit information available is the political actor's knowledge of the results of past attempts at social influence. Thus, the individual's "expectancy set" regarding the efficacy of engaging in upward political influence will be at least in part determined by what has gone before.

Manifest Needs.   Most substantive or content theories of human motivation are based on the premise that individuals harbor a relatively stable set of needs, and that these needs incite action directed toward need satisfaction (Campbell, Dunnette, Lawler & Weick, 1970). While the assumption base underlying the need-satisfaction paradigm has not gone unchallenged (Salancik & Pfeffer, 1977; 1978), the concept of manifest needs, stemming from Murray's (1938) pioneering work, continues to influence research.

Although Murray's taxonomy included as many as twenty needs, recent focus, particularly in organizational settings, seems to have settled on need for achievement (nAch) and need for power (nPow) (Atkinson & Feather, 1966; McClelland, 1965; McClelland & Burnham, 1976). In particular, nPow appears to be a likely candidate for investigation as a correlate of political activity in organizations.

McClelland and Burnham (1976) found nPow to be widely distributed, particularly among successful managers, in organizations. While power motivation, according to McClelland, can often be "socialized" (i.e., oriented toward organizational, rather than personal objectives), nPow can also center on the desire to further one's own goals. Shostrom (1967) characterized man as a manipulator, and set forth the view that, for many, control of others can become its own reward apart from any extrinsic accomplishment that might be the ostensible object of the maneuver. Among the individual differences that might influence the accuracy of Shostrom's characterization, it would seem that nPow would be rather important.

Locus of Control.   Rotter's (1954, 1966) theory holds that people differ systematically in their beliefs that their personal successes and failures are the result either of uncontrollable external forces, or of their own actions. "Internals" tend to view their outcomes as the result of ability or effort, while "externals" would attribute personal consequences to the result of innate task difficulty or to luck (Weiner, 1974). Thus, when faced with a problem in which upward political influence might be within the feasible set of coping strategies, it might seem reasonable that an "internal" might arrive at a different SEU computation than would an "external." For the average outcome, an "internal" will probably assume a higher expectancy of effort leading to attainment. This might, in turn, lead "internals" to favor political activism, while "externals" might be more prone toward political apathy.

Machiavellianism. Christie and Geis (1970) developed this complex construct, based on the advice about the tactics of social influence and the views of human nature explicated by Niccolò Machiavelli in such writings as *The Prince* (originally published about 1532). A wide variety of studies reported by Christie and Geis (1970) indicate that Machiavellianism may be more an interpersonal style than a personality trait. Furthermore, the construct may contain considerable unique explanatory power. There have been few significant correlations reported between Machiavellianism and such variables as intelligence, racial attitudes, or such personality measures as nAch or authoritarianism (Shaver, 1977).

People who score high on Christie and Geis's Machiavellianism scale (High Machs) are characterized as manipulators of other people. They tend to initiate and control the structure of interpersonal interaction. While they are rational and can be persuaded by cogent argument, they are relatively unmoved by normative social pressure. Thus, the most advantageous situation for the High Mach would be face-to-face contact, for in such situations he/she can be ". . . an extremely successful agent of social influence even in the absence of any obvious source of social power" (Shaver, 1977, p. 479).

Risk-Seeking Propensity. Decision makers differ in their psychological reaction to risk. While some exhibit a conservative bias, eschewing risk when possible, others appear to place a positive value on risk, per se. In the language of decision theory, the former are termed risk averters while the latter are called risk seekers (Keeney & Raiffa, 1976). (There are also many people, of course, who are essentially "risk neutral".) To the extent that an organizational member is a risk seeker, it might be reasonable to expect that he/she would be tempted to engage in a political influence attempt (which can indeed be dangerous) that might be shunned by a risk averter.

While the foregoing list of individual factors does not purport to be an exhaustive taxonomy of the individual differences related to the propensity to engage in upward political influence, they do appear to comprise several of the more important factors.

Next, we turn to consideration of the other participant in the dyadic process of upward political influence—the influence target.

Target Selection

Importance of Power. Engaging in organizational politics necessitates the selection of a target of influence. An essential ingredient that a chosen target must possess is the control of scarce resources, or the ability to influence scarce resource controllers. This is basically a question of who has either the *power* to allocate desired resources or the ability to *influence* other desired resource powerholders. Power is considered to be the capacity to influence, while influence is viewed as a process of producing behavioral or psychological (e.g., values, beliefs, attitudes) effects in a target person. Power is frequently partitioned into ostensible sets of mutually exclusive and collectively exhaustive subtypes or bases (Baldridge, 1971; Bell, 1975; Bucher, 1970; Dahl, 1957; French & Raven, 1968; Marwell & Schmitt, 1967). The political actor is concerned with identifying and selecting as a target an individual(s) who possesses an appropriate base, or bases, of power that as indicated earlier is sufficiently high to do or get done what the political actor desires. This point was recognized by Tedeschi, Schlenker, and Lindskold (1972), when they indicated that individuals possessing relatively greater expertise, status or prestige than the source will be prime candidates as targets of influence.

Costs of Approaching Target. It seems clear that the potential risks or costs to the political actor are also an important consideration in choosing among various powerholders in the organization, as potential targets of political influence. The target must possess sufficient power to accomplish the outcome desired by the source *and* at a minimal, or acceptable, cost to the political actor. By costs to the agent, we are referring to possible negative outcomes that may be experienced by the agent as a result of the influence attempt. These negative outcomes range from the agent's failure to promote or protect self interests in the specific situation at hand, to loss of the ability to promote or protect self-interests in other future situations. Indeed, the ultimate cost could be loss of position within the organization.

Therefore, while especially powerful individuals may be able to do what the agent desires, these are the same individuals who can impose the greatest adverse effects (costs) upon the agent. The power that makes a person attractive as a target could be used, were the target so to choose, against the source. Tedeschi *et al.* (1972) clearly recognized this point when they proposed that the most probable influence target would be the weakest person who possesses sufficient power to enable the influencer to realize his or her goal. It was suggested that, with respect to target selection in organizations, ". . . people have a 'natural' tendency to go through the channels of authority" (p. 314), i.e., the most likely target of influence would be the immediate superior. Allen, Angle, and Porter (1979) found that the immediate superior is, in fact, the most frequent target of attempted influence. About two-thirds of their respondents (143) selected their immediate superior as a first-choice target of influence.

Agent–Target Relationship. An important consideration concerning the potential costs in selecting a target from among various powerholders in the organization may be the concept of interpersonal attraction between the agent and the potential target. Tedeschi (1974) discusses evidence that "liking relationships" tend to arouse the expectation that the liked person will "provide benefits or favors of various types and values across a number of situations over time" (p. 198). We would argue that this tends to place the cost of approaching a target in an inverse relationship with interpersonal attraction in the mind of the political actor, thereby reducing the felt risks of attempting to influence an interpersonally attractive target.

Ideally, the selected target will possess sufficient power to provide the outcomes desired by the political actor *and* sufficiently high interpersonal attraction to be willing to do so at minimal or acceptable costs to the agent. The evidence concerning the importance of relative power and interpersonal attraction in choosing a target of influence is scarce. Influence processes in general have received research attention mostly under the concepts of leadership and group and interpersonal dynamics. The principal concern in such investigations has been downward or lateral influence processes, i.e., between a leader and members of a group or between two or more co-equal group members. In these studies, the relative ability of the influence target to do what the influence agent desires—i.e., the power possessed by the target person—has not been an important variable. Thus, in downward and lateral influence studies, the target is either "given" (as in leadership studies) or selected from a rather restricted set (i.e., other immediate group members) on some basis other than ability to comply—e.g., because of deviancy from group norms, etc.

In upward influence, the political actor does not enjoy a given target, or even a "natural" set of targets. The appropriateness of a particular individual as an influence target is situationally determined, i.e., the target will vary according to the outcomes desired by the source. The common denominator of potential political targets is the possession of sufficient power to provide, or assist in providing, outcomes desired by the political actor. It is the political actor's task to identify, select, and influence these organizational influentials to comply, willingly or unwittingly, with the intent of the political actor.

The only research known to the writers concerned with the importance of relative power and interpersonal attraction in choosing a target of influence in a political situation was conducted by Allen (1978). In this study of 143 vice presidents and department managers in four electronics-oriented firms it was found, consistent with the earlier cited literature, that *both* perceived relative power and interpersonal attraction are important in the choice of a target for influence. Individuals possessing both high relative power and high interpersonal attraction were found to be the most frequent choices of influence attempts in two political situations (one dealing with a reorganization change and the other concerned with budgetary allocations). However, the results were also clear that perceived relative power was the predominant variable in choosing an influence target. The target, as indicated earlier, must be viewed by the political actor as able to do what the political actor desires. It seems reasonable to propose that, if the source believes that the target can do what is desired, the existence or absence of interpersonal attraction may play a more important role in the tactics used by the political actor in his or her influence attempt than in the selection of a target. For example, an open influence mode (as discussed in the next section) such as promises or persuasion may be selected if the political actor feels that there is high interpersonal attraction and, therefore, lower potential costs of approaching the target openly. On the other hand, a lack of sufficiently high interpersonal attraction with the selection target may cause the political actor to choose an influence tactic(s) that is more manipulative in nature. This point was well made by Wortman and Linsenmeier (1977) when they stated:

> An ingratiator may seek attraction because he is personally gratified by liking and approval from others, or he may value attraction or positive evaluation not as an end in itself, but because it is instrumental in achieving other goals (p. 134).

In this situation, ingratiation (a manipulative influence technique) may serve to increase the willingness of the target to provide desired outcomes though a process of increasing the target's interpersonal attraction for the political actor. There are many other manipulative tactics that may be chosen by the political actor that are not at all concerned with increasing interpersonal attraction, but may be viewed by the political actor as potentially as effective, or more effective, in gaining compliance of the target. This will be discussed in greater detail in the following section.

Methods of Upward Influence

The one inescapable fact about upward influence—that the agent of influence possesses less formal authority than the target of influence—colors any examination of the selection of methods of upward political influence. The fact that the political actor cannot rely on formal authority, and most likely has considerably less power (compared to a downward situation) to wield positive and negative sanctions, means that the search for an effective method or methods of upward influence will be different from the search that takes place in downward attempts.

Before discussing a classification of possible methods of upward political influence and the factors that will affect the choice of methods, it is important to keep in mind another aspect of the situation; the methods can be utilized (as Allen, *et al.*, 1979b, have pointed out) to promote self-interests (usually in a proactive manner) or protect those interests (usually in a reactive manner). The former use refers to upward influence attempts designed to advance self interests and move the agent from a current position (in terms of access to organizational resources and rewards) to a better position. Such upward influence attempts typically require *initiation* by the agent. In the latter mode, ordinarily requiring a *response* by the agent, attempts are made to reduce or minimize potential damage to self interests that would tend to move the agent from a current position to a less desirable position. It is clear that political attempts at upward influence can be exercised in either of these modes.

Classification of Methods. A number of writers (e.g., Cartwright, 1965; Mowday, 1975; Rosenberg & Pearlin, 1962; Steger & Tedeschi, 1971) have put forth classifications of methods of influence without regard to direction. Most of the analyses of these classification approaches generally have focused on downward influence, as in the typical managerial or leadership situation in organizations. However, except for the use of formal authority, these classification schemes can serve just as well as a basis for consideration of upward influence. The only—but important— distinction would be that the frequency of use of particular methods is assumed to be different for the two directions of influence.

The various sets or categories of methods of influence as provided by the writers mentioned above (as well as others) have a fair degree of overlap, and are succinctly summarized in a table from Mowday (1975). As can be seen from this summary table (Table 1), the major categories of methods are: negative sanctions, positive sanctions, informational, and (formal) authority. Since we are focusing in this chapter on upward influence, the latter category—formal authority—can be deleted from the list of available methods. (As discussed previously, upward influence is taken to mean that the influence agent possesses less formal authority than the influence target and cannot thereby "order" the target to comply based on the "legitimate right" of the agent to expect compliance.)

Building upon these previous classification efforts, a modified categorization scheme may be useful for the purposes of analyzing upward

Table 1. Summary of Methods of Influence (from Mowday, 1975)

Methods	Cartwright (1965)	Gilman (1962)	Harsanyi (1962)	Rosenberg & Pearlin (1962)	Russell (1938)	Steger & Tedeschi (1971)
Negative Sanctions	Physical Control Control over Costs	Coercion	Unconditional distribution of punishments Conditional distribution of punishments	Coercion	Physical power Punishments	Threats Mediation of punishments
Positive Sanctions	Control over Gains		Unconditional distribution of rewards Conditional distribution of rewards	Contractual power	Reward	Promises Mediation of rewards
Informational	Control over information	Persuasion Manipulation	Supply Information	Persuasion Manipulation	Influence on opinion	Persuasion Manipulation
Authority	Use of attitudes toward being influenced	Authority	Legitimate Authority		Legitimate Authority	Activation of commitments
Attraction						Interpersonal attraction
Miscellaneous						Probes Nondecisions

Table 2. Classification of Methods of Upward Political Influence

	Types of Methods	Predicted Relative Frequency of Use
I. Sanctions	A. Positive	Low
	B. Negative	Low
II. Informational	A. Persuasion	Low to Medium
	B. Manipulative Persuasion	High
	C. Manipulation	High

political influence. This revised scheme is shown in Table 2. As can be seen, types of methods have been classified into two major categories: sanctions and informational. In turn, we have further subdivided each of these two categories. Sanctions have been divided into the familiar sets, "positive" and "negative." Informational methods have been divided into three types: "persuasion" (both the actor's objective and the influence attempt are open); "manipulative persuasion" (the objective is concealed but the attempt is open); and "manipulation" (both the objective and the attempt are concealed). It should be noted that this latter three-way split of informational methods differs from the typical two-way (persuasion and manipulation) distinction made by most previous writers. We believe this tripartite distinction is crucial, because in some situations commonly labeled as "manipulative" it is the actor's objective that is hidden but not the attempt, while in other cases both the objective and the attempt are hidden.

Each of the five methods listed in Table 2 can be considered as a possible method for use by individual political actors. As will be discussed below, and as shown in Table 2, we have indicated what we think is the relative frequency of use: namely, positive and negative sanctions are not likely, persuasion is low to medium in likelihood, and manipulative persuasion and manipulation are (relatively) highly likely.

Considering each of the five methods in turn:

Positive Sanctions: In upward political influence situations, it is unlikely (though certainly by no means impossible) that positive sanctions, i.e., rewards and promises of rewards, will be a very widely utilized method by individuals. The apparent reason is that the individual vis-à-vis his/her upward target is unlikely to control a wide range of rewards. To put it simply, while the upward target can do a lot for the would-be political actor in the way of providing rewards, he/she is relatively limited in the rewards that can be administered upward. The source does have his/her own performance that can serve as a reward—it can, for example, help make the boss look good—but since relatively good performance is such an expected part of normal organizational behavior it is not likely to serve as a frequent reward in an upward direction unless it is truly exceptional performance. Other types of rewards (e.g., favors) can be promised by the lower-level individual attempting upward influence, but on balance they are likely to be of limited and circumscribed impact.

Negative Sanctions: Individuals (as Mechanic, 1962, pointed out many years ago) certainly have it within their repertoire of actions to be able to provide negative sanctions (punishments or threats of punishments) in an upward direction. As Mechanic noted, ". . . secretaries . . . accountants . . . attendants in mental hospitals, and even . . . inmates in prisons" (p. 350) can individually, if they wish, "gum up the works" by various tactics. Whether this is a very prevalent method, however, is a function of the possible costs or penalties for doing so. The use of coercion or negative sanctions presents a number of inherent problems for the influence agent: e.g., they may produce more resistance than other methods, they may require the influence agent to exercise surveillance to be effective, and the like (Schopler, 1965). In particular, when influence is being attempted hierarchically upward, there are normative restrictions on the use of negative sanctions. While both the superior and subordinate may fully understand that the subordinate is in a threatening posture, face-saving norms (Goffman, 1955) may require that neither party openly acknowledge the subordinate's threat. Were the threat to become overt, the superior would likely be compelled to retaliate. Thus, upward threats seldom will be explicit; rather, to the extent they exist at all, upward negative sanctions will tend to take the form of what Berne (1964) termed "covert transactions." In general, it is our view that negative sanctions will not be selected often as a viable upward influence method.

Persuasion: The term "persuasion" is usually substituted as a shorthand term for open informational methods. Persuasion can be defined as "the display of judgment in such a way that those exposed to it have an opportunity to become aware of the potential value of accepting it in place of their own" (Gilman, 1962, p. 107). As Mowday (1975, p. 40) notes, persuasion involves several key characteristics: "First, the locus of control concerning the decision to comply with the influence attempt resides with the influence target . . . Second, the influence target is generally aware of the intentions of the influence agent . . . (Third), the use of persuasion requires a base." Such bases for persuasion, as Mowday points out, could include expertise, source credibility, prestige, trustworthiness, and the like.

It seems obvious that persuasion, or the open utilization of an informational base, is a frequent and common method of *non*-political upward influence on the part of the individual agent. However, when the aim of such persuasion is the promotion or protection of the self interests of the influence agent, and where the self-interests of others are threatened, its use becomes far more problematical. Since the intentions of the influence agent are open as well as the method (i.e., a direct attempt to convince), the response will be based directly on the target's evaluation of the message and the source of the message. The "costs," therefore, may be greatly increased because of the possibility of a negative reaction on the part of the target—as opposed to perhaps mere indifference in nonpolitical situations. For this reason, we would argue that the likelihood of persuasion being utilized in upward political influence situations would be low to moderate.

It should be noted that the nature of the arguments in persuasion can take many forms, including pointing out probable consequences to the target for complying or failing to comply with the agent's wishes. Tedeschi *et al.* (1972) refer to this type of argument as the use of "warnings and mendations" (as contrasted with the direct sanctions of threats, punishments and promises of rewards). That is, warnings and mendations involve discussions of events where the influence agent can picture negative or positive consequences for the target (e.g., from the environment or third parties in the organization) but does not have control over them. As Tedeschi *et al.* note, for example, in discussing the use of warnings in persuasion attempts: "A warning . . . refers to environmental contingencies involving probable punishments for the target, which the source communicates to the target in an attempt to influence him. The important distinction between a threat and a warning is that the source controls the punishment in the first instance but not in the second" (p. 292). This distinction is equivalent to that made by Skinner (1969), in specifying the difference between *tact* and *mand,* as discriminative stimuli. Tacting consists of pointing out the environmental relationship between what a target person does and the consequences, while manding specifies that those consequences will be arranged by the sender of the "mand message."

Manipulative Persuasion: The essence of this method of upward influence involves the deliberate attempt of the agent to conceal or disguise his/her true objectives, *even though* the agent is *open* about the fact that an influence attempt is taking place—it is the objective, not the influence attempt, that is concealed. This is illustrated by the well-known "hidden agenda" phenomenon.

We contend that manipulative persuasion is a frequently utilized approach to upward influence of a political sort. The reason, of course, is the influence agent's belief that if the (higher level) target knew what the source was trying to accomplish, the target would reject or ignore the message and thus avoid being influenced, or might even penalize the source. The influence agent's calculus would go something like this:

"If I can convey my message in a way so that my own self-interests are disguised, I have more of a chance at successful influence." Thus, whether such an influence attempt is successful depends to a large extent on how the target characterizes the message, and the attributions the target makes about the agent's intentions or objectives. As with any attribution, the target's characterization may or may not coincide with the agent's attribution: i.e., the target may fail to attribute self-interest objectives on the part of the agent when in fact the agent knows they are there. In any event, in this method the agent is openly attempting to influence but is simultaneously attempting to disguise his/her intentions. The effectiveness of the influence method, therefore, depends on how effective is the disguise of objectives. There is probably no message so *in*effective as one that is labeled by the target: "He/she is *only* trying to get me to do that because it will advance his/her own self-interests."

Manipulation: This form of influence involves the concealment of *both* the intent of the political actor *and* the fact that an influence attempt is taking place. This obviously involves greater effort on the part of the influence agent, as both intentions and the attempt must be disguised. Despite the potential difficulties, this is a common method of upward political influence. For example, in a study of managerial perceptions of the utilization of political tactics, Allen *et al.* (1979b) found that "the instrumental use of information" was one of the three most commonly observed tactics mentioned by the managerial respondents from 30 small-to-medium-sized industrial firms. As these authors pointed out, this category of tactics involved withholding, or distorting information (short of outright lying), or overwhelming the target with too much information. All three specific uses of information could be regarded as a pure form of manipulation where the intent was to obscure or disguise the agent's intentions and where the target was not likely to be aware that an influence attempt was taking place. Thus, Allen *et al.* report that "most of the examples of information distortion mentioned by managers were related to creating desired impressions through selective disclosure, innuendo, or engaging in speculation concerning other individuals or events with an appearance of 'objectivity.'" Or, in the case of providing information overload to the target, an agent, when confronted with a possible threat, and acting in a reactive mode, may "bury or obscure an important detail the political actor believes could harm him [or her], when the risk of withholding the information is too great" (p. 79). The other two most frequently cited tactics by the respondents in the Allen *et al.* study could also be interpreted as the utilization of pure manipulation: namely, "attacking or blaming others" and "image building/impression management." Obviously, the success of these and similar tactics, including ingratiation, would appear to depend largely on how effectively the influence agent's intentions and the attempt at influence are concealed. Attacking others, for example, is likely to be dismissed if it is regarded as being only, or primarily, in the service of the attacker's self-interests and/or as an influence attempt.

Factors in the Choice of Method. If we assume that someone (individual or group) in an organization has made a decision to attempt upward influence for the purpose of promoting or protecting self-interests, then that person or group faces the choice of what method to use. Since we are focusing on *upward* influence, that choice will be greatly affected by the knowledge that the target has more formal authority than the agent. A choice that might be effective in downward influence might not, as noted earlier, be equally effective in the upward direction.

The motivation of an agent to exert influence has been classified by Cartwright (1965) into *intrinsic* motivation and *instrumental* motivation. The former motivation, involving as it does the satisfaction to the individual (or group) derived from the process of exercising influence, is more likely to affect the frequency or amount of influence attempts. The direction of such attempts, and therefore the choice of method, is more likely to be affected by instrumental motivation—the attempt to obtain particular outcomes (with satisfaction deriving from the attainment of the outcomes rather than from the process of attaining them). The agent is presumed to have some notion of what values he or she places on certain outcomes, and some idea of the probability that a given action will lead to various outcomes. It is this latter factor, the calculation of the probability that a particular method will lead to valued outcomes, that would seem to be the key ingredient in the choice of methods of influence. Alternatively, this could be thought of as a calculation of cost/benefit ratios for various possible methods. Those methods would be chosen which would bring the greatest benefits for the lowest cost.

Such calculations can be presumed to be dependent on the agent's assessment of: (1) agent (self) characteristics; (2) target characteristics; (3) characteristics of the situation; and (4) the characteristics of the method. Agent characteristics would include the agent's assessment of the various resources he/she possesses vis-à-vis the target: e.g., degree of expertise, potential to provide the target with positive or negative outcomes, possession of exclusive information, ability to disguise true intentions, general persuasive ability, risk-taking propensity, and the like. Target characteristics would include such variables as: perceived susceptibility to persuasion, likelihood of attributing self-interest motivation to the agent, power to provide the desired outcome, and so forth. Finally, some assessment would be made of the characteristics (costs and benefits) of the method itself. For example, in deciding whether to use some form of manipulation such as withholding information or attempting ingratiation, the *perceived* costs involved in detection may or may not be viewed as greater than the potential gains of straightforward persuasion. It would appear, then, that the choice of methods of influence, particularly in an upward situation, is a complex process. It is also one about which we know little, in organizational settings.

Thus far, we have presented a somewhat fragmented view of upward political influence, by considering separately several aspects of the individuals involved and the situations in which they find themselves. We have also portrayed the topics of upward influence and organizational politics as having been, so far, generally underresearched. The following section will highlight some methodological considerations and outline a conceptual model that might serve as a guide to future research.

FUTURE DIRECTIONS

Before presenting our conceptual model, we first need to note briefly several of the methodological difficulties that might have deterred researchers in the past from becoming deeply involved in the general area of organizational politics.

Methodological Considerations

It is well and good to say that organizational politics (or, in the case of our concerns here, the politics of upward influence) is both an intriguing and an underresearched topic in the field of organizational behavior. All manner of interesting hypotheses (see next section) present themselves, and would-be researchers are faced more with the problem of selecting a hypothesis to test than with the problem of formulating one in the first place. However, there is one other not-so-small problem: how to utilize an appropriate methodology to investigate the particular research questions in this area. This problem arises because research topics relating to organizational politics are fraught with more than the normal amount of sticky and methodological obstacles. This is particularly so, perhaps, if the researcher is inclined to approach the topic with a field type of study.

Issues related to political behavior in organizations are especially difficult to study in the field situation for some rather obvious reasons. The most fundamental problem is that the general topic (of organizational politics) tends to carry a negative connotation. It is one thing to go into an organization and say that the researcher is attempting to study some aspect of "motivation" or "leadership." By and large such topics are seen as either neutral or, more likely, even positive. After all, most organizations would like to think that they are at least concerned with, if not promoting, higher levels of motivation. Likewise, it seems logical to organizations or to individual respondents that leadership is something that is crucial to organizational functioning and is (from the point of view of the individual) something that is desirable to know something more about. Even a topic such as "conflict" is one that individuals or organizations may approach in a relatively "open" manner. That is, while many organizations or individuals might desire that there be less conflict or that it be better resolved, most will acknowledge that it exists (it would be difficult to deny in most instances) and that it is probably important to study.

Political aspects of behavior in organizations, on the other hand, are something that organizations (qua organizations) tend to deny exists in their *own* operations, or at least tend to deny that it affects any crucial decision making; likewise, individuals tend to deny that they themselves engage in it, even though they (just as organizations) may acknowledge— indeed, strongly aver—that it is practiced by others. It is a topic, then, that is highly sensitive, strongly hidden from public view insofar as the organization or individual is willing to attribute behavior to itself (him/ herself), generally socially "undesirable," and about which there is great defensiveness ("who, me?"). It is, in a phrase, the "dark side" of organizational behavior. For all of these reasons and more, any *direct* attempts to study the politics of upward influence in a field setting are virtually doomed from the start (except in certain situations where one might be focusing on the attributions that organizations or respondents make about "others' " political behavior; e.g., as in the Madison *et al.* [1980] study).

The normally hidden state of political behavior in organizations no doubt accounts for part of the reason why this has been a generally underresearched area. It also suggests that from a methodological standpoint researchers either will have to resort to laboratory investigations, or to field investigations that are designed to deal explicitly with this problem. Most likely, advances in our knowledge in this area over the next decade will come from some combination of both laboratory and field investigations. The relative advantages and disadvantages of each major type of approach have been thoroughly discussed elsewhere (e.g., Kerlinger, 1973; Weick, 1967) and are, in any event, beyond the scope of this paper. Suffice it to say that it is highly improbable that either laboratory investigations alone, or field investigations alone, will provide as much cumulative insight as the two approaches taken collectively (though not necessarily, of course, simultaneously by a given researcher).

The type of interplay of laboratory and field investigations that ideally would be desirable would be something like the "five-stage logical path for programmatic research" originally described some fifteen years ago by McGrath (1964, pp. 535–541).

In Stage 1, exploratory field studies are carried out "when little is known about the phenomena." This is followed by Stage 2, "follow-up studies for precise testing of key hypotheses," involving primarily experimental simulations or laboratory experiments. Stage 3 would be computer simulations for "elaboration and refinement of theoretical models." Stage 4 would again involve primarily laboratory experiments for the purpose of "validation of theoretical models in limited situation context(s)." Stage 5 would be a return to the field situation for "cross validation of theory in a real-life situation." As McGrath notes, "what is not specified here, and perhaps cannot be answered in the general case, is how to allocate time and effort among the various classes of methods . . . In any actual case . . . choice of methods must be determined on the basis of available resources, as well as on the basis of our present stage of knowledge about the problem." Since we know relatively little about the politics of upward influence in organizations, it suggests that the appropriate place to start is somewhere in the vicinity of Stages 1 and 2.

One particular methodological quandary should be noted for the record: political behavior, as stressed earlier, often involves covert objectives and/or covert methods. Thus, to the extent that self interest objectives are not acknowledged by the actor, the question of whether an upward influence behavior is *designed* to advance or protect self interests at the expense of others is one of attribution. Regardless of the "true" intent of the actor, if the observer characterizes the behavior as political, it *is* political to the observer. Likewise, if the actor acknowledges self interest intents, whether or not this is perceived or attributed by the observer or target, the behavior is political insofar as the actor is concerned. Thus, while all behavior is potentially observable, the actor's intent is solely one of attribution (by self or other).

We will now turn to an attempt to integrate the various relevant personal and situational variables into a conceptual model which encompasses several relational propositions, each proposition suggesting one or more testable hypotheses. In developing this model, we will adopt the upward political influence episode as the level of analysis. The episode is seen as an ordered series of cognitions and decisions, which comprise the core components of the model. Each component of the episode is impacted by one or more individual or situational variables which, in combination, render certain cognitions or actions more or less probable.

The model adopts the frame of reference of the potential political actor. Accordingly, all situational features—even those having objective referents—are framed in terms of the political actor's perceptions.

A Conceptual Model of Upward Political Influence
Figure 1 shows an episodic model of the upward political influence

Figure 1. Episodic Upward Political Influence Model

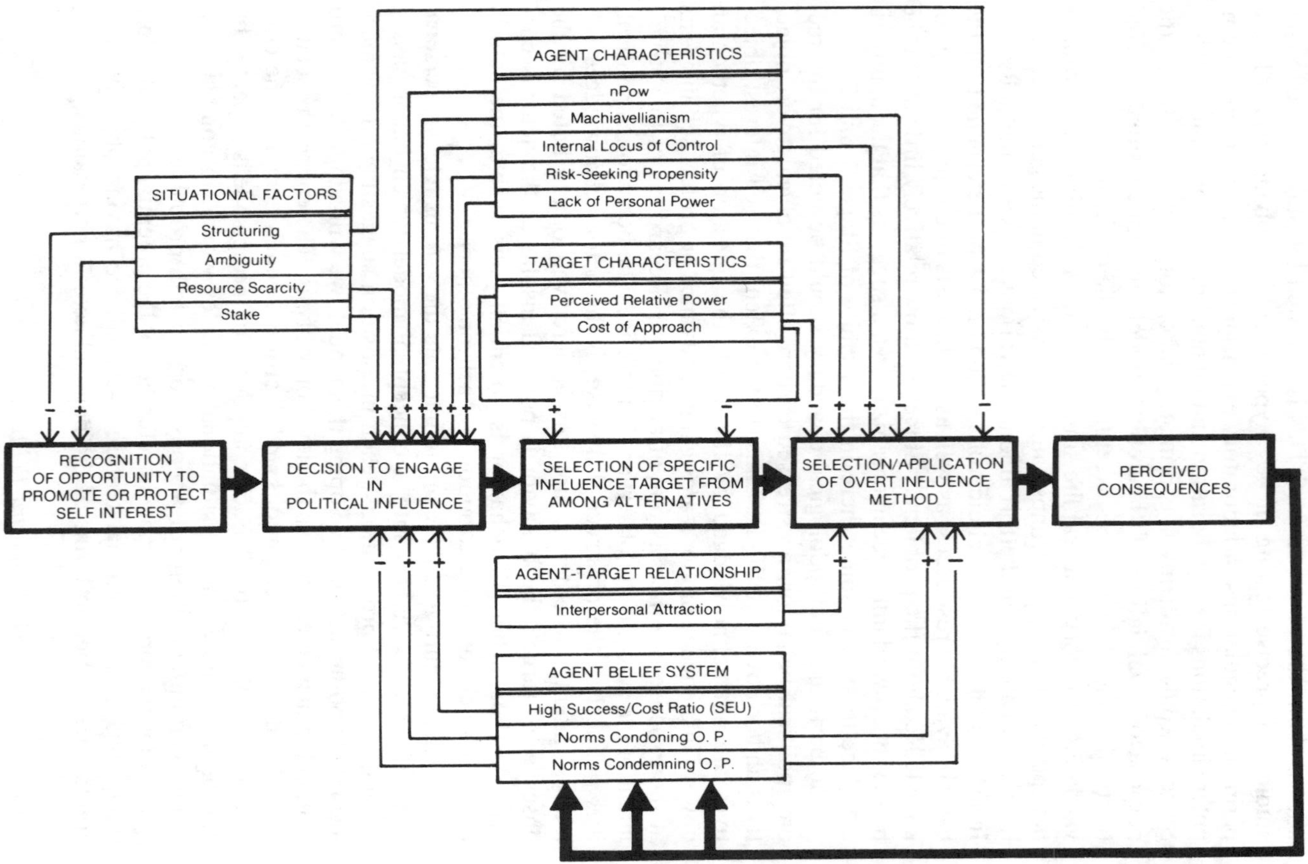

process. The model sets forth five major components, each of which comprises either a cognitive event or a concrete decision. The first component is cognitive; recognition by the focal person of an opportunity to promote or protect self-interest. Following are three discrete decisions. The decision to attempt political influence must precede the other two. We also believe that, in the vast majority of cases, the decision to select a particular influence target will precede the decision to use a particular influence method. We can envision reversals of this order, but would consider these rare. The final major component is the outcome of the attempt. More specifically, it is the actor's cognition of the outcome; that is, knowledge of results.

Each major component (with the exception of the outcome) is influenced by one or more situational factors or characteristics of the persons involved. Each influencing variable relates probabilistically to one or more the major components of the model; that is, the influencing variable is postulated to render the relevant decision or cognition either more or less probable. Thus, the probability of occurrence of each major component of the model depends on: (1) the occurrence of the preceding component, as a necessary condition; and (2) some weighted combination of all of the impacting variables.

The ensuing discussion will consider each major component of the model in turn, and will set forth a number of propositions regarding the influence of relevant personal or situational factors on specific cognitions or decisions. Although the model contains a relatively large number of elements, it is simple, in that each proposition addresses an essentially bivariate relationship and all propositions are stated on a ceteris paribus basis.

Recognition of an Opportunity to Promote or Protect Self-Interest. Sequencing in the model begins with the actor's recognition of an opportunity to promote or protect self-interest. This recognition is not simply an awareness of the existence of some organizational circumstance bearing on her/his self-interest, but a belief that an opportunity exists to do something about it.

Given that appropriate organizational circumstances exist (i.e., posing a potential threat to existing self-interest or an opportunity to promote new self-interest), two variables are proposed to affect the probability of the agent's recognition of an opportunity to act: (1) the amount of structuring in the organization; and (2) the level of ambiguity resident in the situation.

A highly structured organization will inhibit members' opportunities to act unilaterally, in their own self interest because of built-in controls. Although the case could be made that structuring can actually *increase* members' *motivation* to try to take matters into their own hands, individual differences may prevail. Over time, individuals tend to become self-selected into organizations (provided that interorganizational mobility is feasible). Accordingly, highly structured organizations should be expected to attract substantial proportions of members who are comfortable in such circumstances, and therefore not motivated to "react" (cf. Brehm, 1966) by individual political activity. Thus, we offer directional propositions with respect to perceived political *opportunity*, but not with respect to motivation.

Proposition 1:   *The more highly structured the organization, the lower the probability of recognition of an opportunity to promote or protect self-interest.*

Another factor that will impact the potential political actor's ability to recognize an opportunity to promote or protect self-interest is the ambiguity resident in the specific situation at hand.

Proposition 2:   *The more ambiguous the situation, the higher the probability of recognition of an opportunity to promote or protect self-interest.*

Although situational ambiguity will be less prevalent in highly structured or, to use Burns and Stalker's (1961) term, "mechanistic" organizations, Propositions 1 and 2 are not redundant. Even in mechanistic organizations, there will exist unprogrammed tasks (March & Simon, 1958), which will contain some degree of ambiguity. While unprogrammed areas will be more prevalent in "organic" organizations, they will exist to some degree in "mechanistic" organizations, as well. Regardless of organizational type, opportunistic recognition is most likely in the unprogrammed areas.

Decision to Engage in Upward Influence.   Once an opportunity to promote or protect self-interest has been recognized, the actor may consider three general options: (1) do nothing; (2) take direct action; or (3) influence someone else to take appropriate action.

Whether an individual chooses to take direct action toward protection or promotion of self-interest will depend, in part, on whether he/she possesses the wherewithal. Lacking such personal power (and assuming that the "inaction" option is not selected) the individual is apt to need the help of others who do possess adequate power.

Proposition 3: *The lower the relevant personal power possessed by the actor, the more probable either a political influence attempt or inaction.*

Resource scarcity is a prime component of political action. Even so, at a given level of resource scarcity, individuals may differ with respect to the urgency of their need to control a particular scarce resource, i.e., their "stake" in the matter.

Proposition 4: *The decision to engage in upward political influence will be affected by the salience of the issue at hand.*

Proposition 4.1: *The scarcer the resources at issue, the greater the likelihood of a political influence attempt.*

Proposition 4.2: *The greater the individual's personal stake in the issue, the greater the likelihood of a political influence attempt.*

Certain personal traits may predispose people toward influencing others: because of the tendency to find intrinsic satisfaction from the very act of acquiring and exercising power over others; because of a world view that one is captain of one's own fate; and/or because of a positive value placed on risk-taking.

Proposition 5: *Personal traits predispose certain individuals toward attempts to influence others.*

Proposition 5.1: *A high need for power (nPow) will increase the likelihood of a political influence attempt.*

Proposition 5.2: *A Machiavellian interpersonal style (High Mach) will increase the likelihood of a political influence attempt.*

Proposition 5.3: *An Internal Locus of Control will increase the likelihood of a political influence attempt.*

Proposition 5.4: *A preference for risk-taking will increase the likelihood of a political influence attempt.*

Two classes of political norms may exist, simultaneously, in organizations: those which condone (or even advocate) certain "political" behaviors; and those which condemn, or discourage, specific political behaviors. Whatever norms exist in an objective sense, only those norms that the focal person is aware of are operative in the model. Furthermore, at the point of deciding whether or not to engage in an influence attempt at all, only those norms that the focal person has internalized should have an impact on the decision.

Proposition 6: *The likelihood of an actor's engaging in a political influence attempt will be positively related to the extent of her/his internalization of local norms condoning such behavior, and negatively related to the extent of his/her internalization of local norms condemning such behavior.*

In addition to beliefs concerning the normative structure of relevant reference groups, the agent's belief system contains a set of expectations about certain action-outcome relationships, i.e., an expected costs-benefits ratio. In an expectancy or SEU framework this can be viewed as a ratio of the absolute value of the summed expectancy-valence products of all positively valued outcomes, to the summed expectancy-valence products of all the negatively valued outcomes:

$$SEU = \left| \frac{\Sigma\ E_i\ V_j}{\Sigma\ E_i\ V_j'} \right|$$

where: V = positive valence
        V′ = negative valence

It would be expected that the higher the SEU, as expressed by this ratio, the more likely a political influence attempt.

Proposition 7: *A high SEU will render a political influence attempt more likely.*

Selection of a Specific Influence Target from among Alternatives. Assuming that the decision has been made to attempt to exert political influence on another person, the actor must decide whom to select as a target. The prime consideration in this decision must necessarily be the potential targets' relative abilities to accomplish the actor's ultimate objective. At issue is the targets' relative power, relevant to the influence issue. All else being equal, the actor might be expected to approach that person in the feasible set who possesses the greatest power, i.e., "go directly to the top." However, all else is seldom equal. Possession of power to do something *for* the actor often implies possession of power to do something *to* the actor. Furthermore, there are often norms discouraging circumvention of the chain of authority, and there are persons ready to impose sanctions for norm violations. Thus, the most powerful figures in the organization may also be the most dangerous to approach directly. Accordingly, the political actor must weigh carefully the power of each potential target, against the possible costs of approach.

There are other "cost" factors to be considered by the potential influence agent. Targets may vary with respect to their susceptibility to influence, with some potential targets being more generally "hard-headed'' than others. Furthermore, specific circumstances might lead to a particular target's becoming susceptible, either because of some personal vulnerability (e.g., a situationally relevant ''political debt''), or because of a vested interest in the particular issue. In any event, whether because of dispositional or situational considerations, targets who are more willing to comply are therefore approachable at lower cost.

In general, the need to select an individual who possesses sufficient power to accomplish the actor's ultimate goal should result in *most* attempted political influence being directed hierarchically upward in the organization. If an actor does not possess sufficient power for direct action, he/she is more likely to find someone who does possess that power upward in the organization, than elsewhere.

Proposition 8:   *Agents' perceptions of relative power possessed by potential influence targets will result in the preponderance of political influence attempts being directed hierarchically upward.*

Proposition 8.1:   *The feasible set of potential influence targets will be limited to persons possessing higher relative power (relevant to the issue) than the actor.*

Proposition 8.2:   *With costs held constant, the person possessing the greatest perceived relative power will be selected, as an influence target, from among the feasible set.*

Proposition 8.3:   *With relative power held constant, the influence target selected will be that person for whom an influence attempt is expected to incur the lowest costs to the actor.*

Proposition 8.3.1:   *Influence targets who are judged to be amenable to influence will be seen by the influence agent as incurring lower costs of approach.*

Proposition 8.3.2:   *Influence targets who are judged to have a vested interest in achieving the influence agents' purpose will be seen by the agent as incurring lower costs of approach.*

Selection of an Overt Influence Method.   At this point in the model it is assumed that all preconditions have been met; that is, the decision has been made to attempt to influence some specific person in the organization. (While it is conceivable that some political actors may be so limited in repertoire that ''choice'' of a method effectively precedes target selection, we consider the normal situation to be one of selecting a method appropriate to a known target, rather than vice versa.)

In our discussion of methods of upward influence, we argued that positive sanctions would be an unlikely method of *upward* influence because of limitations on the range of rewards available, and that negative sanctions would also be unlikely, because of the target's potential for retaliation. Accordingly, upward influence will be pursued, for the most part, through informational means.

Within the informational subset, we specified three forms of influence: persuasion, manipulative persuasion, and manipulation. The first two methods can be considered *overt*, in that the agent discloses to the target that influence is being attempted (even though the ultimate purpose is obscured in manipulative persuasion). The third method is *covert*. The very existence of an influence attempt is hidden.

Several characteristics of the two persons involved (agent and target), as well as the social relationship between them, can be expected to influence method preference. Overt methods are more committing than covert methods, and should therefore be more attractive to persons who do not shun risk and who feel capable of following through and controlling the situation. On the other hand, certain behavioral styles might predispose individuals to prefer manipulation and subterfuge, whether or not tactically necessary.

> **Proposition 9:** *Individuals become predisposed to prefer either overt or covert influence methods, as a matter of behavioral style.*
> **Proposition 9.1:** *Risk-seekers tend to prefer overt methods, while risk-averters tend to prefer covert methods.*
> **Proposition 9.2:** *"Internals" tend to prefer overt influence methods; "externals" tend to prefer covert methods.*
> **Proposition 9.3:** *Machiavellians (High Mach) tend to prefer covert influence methods.*

Target characteristics may also influence the method chosen. There is inherently high risk in approaching certain targets.

> **Proposition 10:** *For a given influence target, the higher the expected cost of approach, the more likely the method selected by the agent will be covert.*

Since overt methods make the influence attempt public, the openness of the method selected should also be affected by the perceived normative climate.

> **Proposition 11:** *Overt influence methods are more probable when norms condoning political influence are perceived to exist, and less probable when norms condemning such influence are perceived to exist.*

In addition to the parties' individual characteristics, the quality of the relationship between them should bear on the choice of method. Interpersonal attraction is generally believed to be reciprocated (Berscheid & Walster, 1969). Therefore, high interpersonal attraction should facilitate the use of overt influence methods.

Proposition 12: *The use of overt influence methods is more likely under conditions of high interpersonal attraction, than low interpersonal attraction.*

Perceived Consequences. After the influence attempt has been performed, the actor perceives the consequences of the act. Knowledge of results feeds back to modify the actor's belief system regarding what leads to what. Two aspects of the belief system are affected. In the first place, the expectancy set might be revised, based on the experience, so that various action-outcome expectations are either raised or lowered. Secondly, some new norm learning may take place—particularly if the outcome included the imposition of sanctions for violation of norms, and/or the actor believes that the influence attempt was a matter of public knowledge.

Proposition 13: *Knowledge of results from a political influence attempt leads to a reevaluation of the actor's belief system.*

Proposition 13.1: *If an influence attempt has been successful, the actor's SEU for political influence is raised; if unsuccessful, the SEU is lowered.*

Proposition 13.2: *An unsuccessful overt political influence attempt leads to an increase in the saliency, to the actor, of norms condemning organizational politics; a successful overt attempt leads to an increase in the saliency, to the actor, of norms condoning organizational politics.*

Proposition 13.3: *An unsuccessful covert political influence attempt leads to an increase in the saliency, to the actor, of norms condemning organizational politics; a successful covert attempt does not change the actor's norm perceptions.*

The norm learning suggested by the above-listed propositions may be incremental. Because initial knowledge of the organization's informal political norms is apt to be incomplete, political actors may "experiment" with their behavior to test the political nature of the system, starting with less risky or extreme behaviors, and then escalate, gradually. Also, there might exist feedback loops not explicitly indicated in the Model (Figure 1). For example, the target's reaction to an influence episode could spur a revision of the source's perception of target characteristics. In an extreme case, an episode might trigger some organization-wide reaction aimed at preventing recurrence, such as a revision of the control structure. However, in the less dramatic cases, the feedback will probably be confined to the belief system, as depicted in Figure 1.

In Summary. The model depicts what might be considered a normal sequence of events in a complete upward political influence episode. While no attempt has been made to be exhaustive, either in selection of the relevant variables that impact the model's major components or in formulation of propositions suggested by the model's linkages, we believe the model suggests several research questions of the sort appropriate to McGrath's (1964) Stage 1 and Stage 2 research. While our penchant for open-systems thinking makes us all too aware of the shortcomings of a piecemeal approach such as suggested in this section, we are also aware that research in the micro-politics of organizations is in its infancy. We believe that the model presented is appropriate to the state of the art, and that more elaborate, interactive models should be built on the groundwork laid by the research suggested by the present model.

CONCLUDING OBSERVATIONS

Some years ago, Leavitt (1964) observed: "People perceive what they think will help satisfy needs; ignore what is disturbing; and again perceive disturbances that persist and increase" (p. 33). It is interesting to apply the selective-perception framework to the relative prominence given by the field of organizational behavior to downward and lateral influence processes, on the one hand, compared to the lack of attention given to upward influence processes and organizational politics, on the other. We believe there has been an overfocus on the former, and that the field needs to redress the imbalance by giving increased emphasis to the latter.

One can speculate as to why this imbalance has occurred. In part, at least, it has come about because those who run organizations traditionally have been interested in improving the performance of those being led or managed. Hence, they have pressed social and behavioral scientists to learn more about leadership and motivation. This has created a ready market for knowledge directed toward influencing subordinates to perform in a desired manner. Another factor shaping research, particularly with respect to both downward and lateral influence processes, has been the small group tradition in social psychology. When only small groups, as opposed to (large) formal organizations, are the object of study, it is likely that the focus will be strongly downward, or perhaps lateral—as in the case of group dynamics. Chains of authority exist only in organizations of some size, and thus if only groups are being researched it is difficult to investigate the intricacies of upward influence linkages—except for the limited case of the group's impact on the immediate leader (and, it should be stressed that even this circumscribed type of upward influence has only recently begun to be examined by organizational behavior researchers, e.g., Lowin & Craig, 1968). Our point is not that upward influence is more important than lateral or downward influence, only that it should be studied as much as the other two types. And, when one gets into the topic of upward influence in organizations, one is *inevitably* drawn into the realm of organizational politics. This, in turn, is a subject that has long been regarded as somewhat "taboo" by both organizations and researchers because of its mildly disturbing negative connotations—clandestine, self-serving, dysfunctional, etc.

While the three foregoing considerations do not, of course, comprise an exhaustive list of the reasons for a myopic focus on downward and lateral processes, they are certainly among the most telling. If attention is turned to upward influence and political behavior, our views of organizational behavior are necessarily broadened. As just one example, consider that a widely cited framework for classifying organizations according to the predominant method used in gaining compliance from organizational members (Etzioni, 1975), while very useful, neglects the fact that influence can operate upward as well as downward. If the framework were elaborated to include the possibility of upward influence, rather than *only* downward, the classification scheme might be altered considerably, with a corresponding change in some of the implications drawn from it.

Further, we feel that a broadened influence perspective—one that incorporates the concept of organizational politics—can contribute significantly to an understanding of many facets of organizational behavior. Tushman (1977) discussed implications of a political perspective for the fields of organizational development, management information systems and decision making, organizational design, leadership and reward and pay systems. Porter (1976) set forth additional implications of a political perspective for organizational communication, motivation and organizational development. We will not repeat these arguments, but do emphasize that our understanding of many topics within the field of organizational behavior would be enhanced, were we to take into account the possible existence of upward political influence processes.

If, as we believe, upward influence deserves equal billing with its mates, lateral and downward, then some sort of conceptual road map is needed to guide research in this area. Even though the politics of upward influence is an obviously complicated topic—there clearly are multiple system interactive features—it is necessary to begin somewhere. This we have attempted to do, insofar as the frame of reference of the political actor is concerned, by developing an episodic model of upward political influence. This model evolved out of the identification of key elements and relevant issues involved in the process. If nothing else, the abundance of research opportunities in this relatively unexplored area should be clear from viewing the propositions we have set forth.

In conclusion, we cite a statement made by March (1955) more than twenty years ago, regarding the necessity to broaden our understanding of influence processes:

> Failure to obtain generality in the study of influence has two major consequences. On the one hand, it has limited the comparability of studies of interpersonal influence (i.e., those studies that label a major variable as "influence"). On the other hand, it has concealed the potential relevance of studies in quite different areas of theory and research (p. 432).

As we enter the 1980's, our field still has not achieved "a generality in the study of influence." We hope that the present article has been a step toward redirecting the field to a widened perspective.

REFERENCES

Allen, R. W. (1978) "An Exploratory Study on the Choice of Targets to Influence in Organizational Settings." Ph.D. dissertation, University of California, Irvine.

Allen, R. W., H. L. Angle, and L. W. Porter (1979a) "A study of Upward Influence in Political Situations in Organizations." Unpublished manuscript, University of California, Irvine.

Allen, R. W., D. L. Madison, L. W. Porter, P. A. Renwick, and B. T. Mayes (1979b) "Organizational politics: Tactics and personal characteristics of political actors." *California Management Review* (in press).

Atkinson, J. W., and N. T. Feather (eds.) (1966) *A Theory of Achievement Motivation.* New York: Wiley.

Baldridge, J. V. (1971) *Power and Conflict in the University.* New York: Wiley.

Bell, D. V. J. (1975) *Power, Influence and Authority.* New York: Oxford University Press.

Berger, C. J., and Cummings, L. L. (1979) "Organizational Structure, Attitudes, and Behaviors." In B. M. Staw (ed.), *Research in Organizational Behavior,* Vol. 1. Greenwich, Conn.: JAI Press.

Berne, E. (1964) *Games People Play.* New York: Grove Press.

Berscheid, E., and E. H. Walster (1969) *Interpersonal Attraction.* Reading, Mass.: Addison-Wesley.

Biddle, B. J. (1964) "Roles, Goals, and Value Structures in Organizations." In W. W. Cooper. H. J. Leavitt, and M. W. Shelly II (eds.) *New Perspectives in Organization Research.* New York: Wiley.

Brehm, J. W. (1966) *A Theory of Psychological Reactance.* New York: Academic Press.

Bucher, R. (1970) "Social Process and Power in a Medical School." In M. N. Zald (ed.), *Power in Organizations.* Nashville, Tenn.: Vanderbilt Press.

Burns, T., and G. M. Stalker (1961) *The Management of Innovation.* London: Tavistock.

Campbell, J. P., M. D. Dunnette, E. E. Lawler III, and K. E. Weick, Jr. (1970) *Managerial Behavior, Performance and Effectiveness.* New York: McGraw-Hill.

Cartwright, D. (1965) "Influence, Leadership and Control." In J. G. March (ed.), *Handbook of Organizations.* Chicago: Rand McNally.

Christie, R., and F. L. Geis (1970) *Studies in Machiavellianism.* New York: Academic Press.

Clark, A. L., and J. P. Gibbs (1965) "Social Control: A Reformulation." *Social Problems*, 12: 398–415.

Dahl, R. A. (1957) "The Concept of Power." *Behavioral Science*, 2: 201–215.

Edwards, W. (1954) "The Theory of Decision Making." *Psychological Bulletin*, 51: 380–417.

—— (1961) "Behavioral Decision Making." *Annual Review of Psychology*, 12: 473–498.

Etzioni, A. (1975) *A Comparative Analysis of Complex Organizations* (revised). New York: Free Press.

French, J. R. P., and B. Raven (1968) "The Bases of Social Power." In D. Cartwright and A. Zander (eds.), *Group Dynamics*, 3rd ed. New York: Harper & Row.

Frost, P. J., and D. C. Hayes (1977) "An Exploration in Two Cultures of Political Behavior in Organizations." Paper presented at the Conference on Cross-Cultural Studies of Organizational Functioning, University of Hawaii, Honolulu, September.

Frost, P. J., V. F. Mitchell, and W. J. Nord (1978) *Organizational Reality: Reports from the Firing Line*. Santa Monica, Calif.: Goodyear.

Gilman, G. (1962) "An Inquiry into the Nature and Use of Authority." In M. Haire (ed.), *Organization Theory and Industrial Practice*. New York: Wiley.

Goffman, E. (1955) "On Facework." *Psychiatry*, 18: 213–231.

Hall, R. H. (1962) "Intraorganizational Structural Variation: Application of the Bureaucratic Model." *Administrative Science Quarterly*, 7: 295–308.

Harsanyi, J. C. (1962) "Measurement of Social Power, Opportunity Costs, and the Theory of Two-Person Bargaining Games." *Behavioral Science*, 7: 67–80.

Harvey, J. H., Arkin, R. M., Gleason, J. M., and Johnston, S. (1974) "Effect of Expected and Observed Outcome of an Action on the Differential Causal Attributions of Actor and Observer." *Journal of Personality*, 42: 62–77.

Hegarty, E. J. (1976) *How to Succeed in Company Politics*, 2nd ed. New York: McGraw-Hill.

Heider, F. (1958) *The Psychology of Interpersonal Relations*. New York: Wiley.

Jackson, J. (1965) "Structural Characteristics of Norms." In I. D. Steiner and M. Fishbein (eds.), *Current Studies in Social Psychology*. New York: Holt, Rinehart and Winston.

Jackson, J. (1966) "A Conceptual and Measurement Model for Norms and Roles." *Pacific Sociological Review*, 9: 35–47.

Jackson, J. M. (1960) "Structural Characteristics of Norms." In N. B. Henry (ed.), *The Dynamics of Instructional Groups: Sociopsychological Aspects of Teaching and Learning*. 59th Yearbook of the National Society for the Study of Education, Part II, Chicago: University of Chicago Press.

James, L. R., and A. P. Jones (1974) "Organizational Climate: A Review of Theory and Research." *Psychological Bulletin*, 81: 1096–1112.

Jay, A. (1967) *Management and Machiavelli*. New York: Holt, Rinehart and Winston.

Jelinek, M. (1977) "Technology, Organizations, and Contingency." *Academy of Management Review*, 2: 17–26.

Jones, E. E., and R. E. Nisbett (1971) "The Actor and Observer: Divergent Perceptions of the Causes of Behavior." In E. E. Jones, D. E. Kanouse, H. H. Kelley, R. E. Nisbett, S. Valins, and B. Weiner (eds.), *Attribution: Perceiving the Causes of Behavior*. Morristown, N.J.: General Learning Press.

Kahn, R. L., D. M. Wolfe, R. P. Quinn, J. D. Snoek, and R. P. Rosenthal (1964) *Organizational Stress: Studies in Role Conflict and Ambiguity*. New York: Wiley.

Kanter, R. M. (1977) *Men and Women of the Corporation*. New York: Basic Books.

Katz, D., and R. L. Kahn (1978) *The Social Psychology of Organizations*, 2nd ed., New York: Wiley.

Keeney, R. L., and H. Raiffa (1976) *Decisions and Multiple Objectives: Preferences and Value Tradeoffs*. New York: Wiley.

Kerlinger, F. N. (1973) *Foundations of Behavioral Research*, 2nd ed. New York: Holt, Rinehart and Winston.

Lasswell, H. D. (1951) "Who Gets What, When, How." In *The Political Writings of Harold D. Lasswell*. Glencoe, Ill.: Free Press.

Leavitt, H. J. (1964) *Managerial Psychology*, rev. ed. Chicago: University of Chicago Press.

Lewin, K. (1935) "Environmental Forces in Child Behavior and Development." In K. Lewin, *A Dynamic Theory of Personality: Selected Papers*, translated by D. K. Adams and K. E. Zener. New York: McGraw-Hill.

Lowin, A. and J. R. Craig (1968) "The Influence of Level of Performance on Managerial Style: An Experimental Object-Lesson in the Ambiguity of Correlational Data." *Organizational Behavior and Human Performance*, 3: 440–458.

Machiavelli, N. (c. 1532) *The Prince*, translated by W. K. Marriott, in R. M. Hutchins (ed.). *Great Books of the Western World*. Chicago: Encyclopaedia Britannica, Inc., 1952.

Madison, D. L., R. W. Allen, L. W. Porter, P. A. Renwick, and B. T. Mayes (1980) "Organizational politics: An Exploration of Managers' perceptions." *Human Relations*, 33: 79–100.

March, J. G. (1955) "An Introduction to the Theory and Measurement of Influence." *The American Political Science Review*, 46: 431–451.

——— (1962) "The Business Firm as a Political Coalition." *Journal of Politics*, 24: 662–678.

March, J. G., and H. A. Simon (1958) *Organizations*. New York: Wiley.

Marwell, G., and D. R. Schmitt (1967) "Dimensions of Compliance-Gaining Behavior: An Empirical Analysis." *Sociometry*, 30: 350–364.

Mayes, B. T., and R. W. Allen (1977) "Toward a Definition of Organizational Politics." *Academy of Management Review*, 2: 672–678.

McClelland, D. C. (1965) "Toward a Theory of Motive Acquisition." *American Psychologist*, 20: 321–333.

McClelland, D. C., and D. H. Burnham (1976) "Power Is the Great Motivator." *Harvard Business Review*, 54(2): 100–110.

McGrath, J. E. (1964) "Toward a 'Theory of Method' for Research on Organizations." In W. W. Cooper, H. J. Leavitt, and M. W. Shelley II (eds.), *New Perspectives in Organization Research*. New York: Wiley.

Mechanic, D. (1962) "Sources of Power of Lower Participants in Complex Organizations." *Administrative Science Quarterly*, 7: 349–364.

Moberg, D. J. (1977) "Organizational Politics: Perspectives from Attribution Theory." Paper presented to the 1977 Meeting of the American Institute for Decision Sciences, Chicago, Ill.

Mowday, R. T. (1975) "An Exploratory Study of the Exercise of Influence in Organizations." Ph.D. dissertation, University of California, Irvine.

Murray, H. A. (1938) *Explorations in Personality*. New York: Oxford University Press.

Packard, V. (1962) *The Pyramid Climbers*. New York: McGraw-Hill.

Porter, L. W. (1976) "Organizations as Political Animals." Presidential Address, Division of Industrial-Organizational Psychology, 84th Annual Meeting of the American Psychological Association, Washington, D.C.

Porter, L. W., and E. E. Lawler, III (1965) "Properties of Organization Structure in Relation to Job Attitudes and Job Behavior." *Psychological Bulletin*, 64: 23–51.

Robbins, S. P. (1976) *The Administrative Process: Integrating Theory and Practice*. Englewood Cliffs, N.J.: Prentice-Hall.

Rosenberg, M., and L. Pearlin (1962) "Power Orientation in the Mental Hospital." *Human Relations*, 15: 335–349.

Ross, L. (1977) "The Intuitive Psychologist and His Shortcomings: Distortions in the

Attribution Process." In L. Berkowitz (ed.), *Advances in Experimental Social Psychology*, Vol. 10. New York: Academic Press.

Rotter, J. B. (1954) *Social Learning and Clinical Psychology*. Englewood Cliffs, N.J.: Prentice-Hall.

Rotter, J. B. (1966) "Generalized Expectancies for Internal Versus External Locus of Control." *Psychological Monographs*, 80: 1–28.

Russell, B. (1938) *Power: A New Social Analysis*. New York: Norton.

Salancik, G. R., and J. Pfeffer (1977) "An Examination of Need-Satisfaction Models of Job Attitudes." *Administrative Science Quarterly*, 22: 427–456.

Salancik, G. R., and J. Pfeffer (1978) "A Social Information Processing Approach to Job Attitudes and Task Design." *Administrative Science Quarterly*, 23, 224–253.

Sarbin, T. R., and V. L. Allen (1968) "Role theory." In G. Lindzey and E. Aronson (eds.), *The Handbook of Social Psychology*, 2nd ed., Vol. 1. Reading, Mass.: Addison-Wesley.

Schanck, R. L. (1932) "A Study of a Community and Its Groups and Institutions Conceived of as Behaviors of Individuals." *Psychological Monographs*, 32: 1–133.

Schein, V. (1977) "Individual Power and Political Behaviors in Organizations: An Inadequately Explored Reality." *Academy of Management Review*, 2: 64–72.

Schopler, J. (1965) "Social Power." In L. Berkowitz (ed.), *Advances in Experimental Social Psychology*, Vol. 2. New York: Academic Press.

Shaver, K. G. (1975) *An Introduction to Attribution Processes*. Cambridge, Mass.: Winthrop.

——— (1977) *Principles of Social Psychology*, Cambridge, Mass.: Winthrop.

Shostrom, Everett L. (1967) *Man, the Manipulator*. Nashville, Tenn.: Abington Press.

Skinner, B. F. (1969) *Contingencies of Reinforcement: A Theoretical Analysis*. New York: Appleton-Century-Crofts.

Steger, J. A., and J. T. Tedeschi (1971) "Current and Future Trends in Organizational Development: Openness and Power Relations." Unpublished manuscript, Rensselaer Polytechnic Institute.

Tedeschi, J. T. (1974) "Attributions, Liking, and Power." In T. Huston (ed.), *Foundations of Interpersonal Attraction*. New York: Academic Press.

Tedeschi, J. T., B. R. Schlenker, and S. Lindskold (1972) "The Exercise of Power and Influence: The Source of Influence." In J. T. Tedeschi (ed.), *The Social Influence Process*. Chicago: Aldine-Atherton.

Tushman, M. E. (1977) "A Political Approach to Organization: A Review and Rationale." *Academy of Management Review*, 2: 206–216.

Vroom, V. H. (1964) *Work and Motivation*. New York: Wiley.

Weick, K. E. (1967) "Organizations in the Laboratory." In V. H. Vroom (ed.), *Methods of Organizational Research*. Pittsburgh: University of Pittsburgh Press.

Weiner, B. (1974) "An Attributional Interpretation of Expectancy-Value Theory." In B. Weiner (ed.), *Cognitive Views of Human Motivation*. New York: Academic Press.

Wortman, C. B., and J. A. W. Linsenmeier (1977) "Interpersonal Attraction and Techniques of Ingratiation in Organizational Settings." In B. M. Staw and G. R. Salancik (eds.), *New Directions in Organizational Behavior*. Chicago: St. Clair.

POWER AND PERSONALITY IN COMPLEX ORGANIZATIONS

Robert J. House

ABSTRACT

In this paper it is argued that there are several individual difference variables that are associated with power striving, power acquisition, and the exercise of power in complex organizations. Motivational personality traits that are associated with power acquisition are dominance, need for power, Machiavellianism, and Miner's (1978) motivation to manage. These motivational variables predispose individuals toward power striving and power acquisition. Interactions between these motivational variables and contextual variables relevant to the acquisition of power are specified. Four cognitive personal characteristics that facilitate power acquisition are self-confidence, expertise, cognitive complexity, and linguistic ability. These cognitive variables facilitate the acquisition of power. Organizational implications of the above personal characteristics are discussed with respect to several topics relevant to individual and organizational effectiveness and the distribution of power in complex organizations.

INTRODUCTION

Consider the role of individual differences in the establishment of dominance hierarchies. The effects of individual differences on the ascendence to dominant positions by some, and on the submission to the more dominant individuals by others, are well established for the animal kingdom, (Chase, 1982; Barchas & Fisek, 1984) for groups of children (Strayer & Strayer, 1976), and adolescents, (Savin-Williams, 1976) as well as adults (Megargee, Bogart, & Anderson, 1966).

Wilson (1975) defined dominance as "the assertion of one member of the group over another in acquiring access to a piece of food, a mate, a place to display, a sleeping site or any other requisite that adds to the genetic fitness of the dominant individual" (p. 257).

Chance (1967) ascribed to the dominance hierarchy in human groups the function of adding stability and predictibility to social living and thus contributing to group cohesiveness. He argued that dominance behavior is one mechanism for achieving these ends by reducing the amount of intragroup conflict.

According to Ray, (1981) human dominance is the outcome of both learned and unlearned (genetic) influence. Watson (1971) articulated the single major contextual variable that interacts with dominance, conceived as a stable personality characteristic, to predict or account for the emergence of dominating individuals in social situations. This variable is the opportunity to influence others.

Thus, it may be argued that dominance as a personality characteristic interacts with ecological variables and reflects evolutionary processes. These processes select and retain properties of the social system. These properties, in turn, contribute to the survival and fitness of the system. We will discuss evolutionary processes related to power-oriented behavior in a later section of this paper.

Current theories of power acquisition (Emerson, 1962; Hickson, Hinings, Lee, Schneck, & Pennings, 1971; Thompson, 1967; Pfeffer & Salancik, 1978; Bacharach & Lawler, 1980; Pfeffer, 1981) give little recognition to individual characteristics. These theories are structural in nature. They assert that in complex organizations the acquisition of power by individuals or subunits is a function of contextual variables such as the structure of the organization, scarcity of critical resources, and subunit and position attributes.

This chapter concerns the relative importance of individual characteristics for explaining and predicting power acquisition by individuals and subunits in complex organizations.

In this paper we argue that there are a number of individual difference variables that are relevant to theory and research concerned with the acquisition and exercise of power in complex organizations by individuals and subunits. Further, we argue that several of these individual difference variables interact with organizational contextual variables. Thus, the perspective taken here is a social psychological perspective dealing with interactions of individual differences and characteristics of social settings to explain power acquisition behavior in complex organizations.

In the first section of this paper we briefly review current theory and evidence concerning individual differences in the organizational behavior (OB) literature. In the second section we review current theory and evidence concerning the acquisition of power in complex organizations. In the third section we review research relevant to individual differences as predictors of power acquisition in organizations. Attention is focused on individual dominance, Machiavellianism, power motivation, expertise, self confidence and self-esteem, cognitive complexity, and linguistic ability. It is argued that these individual differences interact with contextual properties in organizations to account for individual and subunit acquisition of power. In the final section of this paper we engage in a speculative discussion of the implications of the first three sections for organization theory and practice.

INDIVIDUAL DIFFERENCES IN THE ORGANIZATIONAL BEHAVIOR LITERATURE: A BRIEF REVIEW

During the last several years a number of writers have called attention to the importance of individual differences in understanding behavior in organizations. House and Baetz (1979) cited a substantial number of studies that show that leader emergence, effectiveness, and success can be predicted from a knowledge of individual scores on personality traits measured by the dominance scale of the California Personality Inventory (Gough, 1968). Miner (1978) has shown, on the basis of 25 years of research including 33 predictive studies, that the personality construct entitled "Motivation to Manage" is predictive of managerial success in bureaucratic organizations. Kenny and Zacarro (1983) report an analysis of the degree to which variance in leadership rankings by group members can be accounted for by some stable personality characteristic. Each of 25 subjects worked with 4 fellow members in 6 group sessions. The sessions were structured so that no individual worked with another member in more than 1 session. Subjects worked on motor, artistic, mathematical, literary, social, and spatial problems. These authors found that the percent variance in leadership rankings due to stable characteristics of the leader was between 49% and 82%, representing lower- and upper-bound estimates.

Schneider (1983) also made a convincing argument for the need for an interactional approach to the study of organizational behavior. According to Schneider, researchers in the field of organizational behavior would be well advised to adopt an interactionist paradigm in which individual and situational variables are jointly taken into account.

More recently Weiss and Adler (1984) have discussed the role of personality characteristics as theoretical variables in organizational behavior and arrived at several conclusions.

First they concluded that

> both theoretical reasoning and prior research indicates that personality constructs have a legitimate logical status in Organizational Behavior Research (p. 43).

Second they concluded that

> It no longer makes any sense to discuss the usefulness of "personality" in global terms. Personality traits come in all sizes and shapes. Some relate to cognitive styles, some relate to motivational principles. Some constructs in use are well developed. Others are poorly conceptualized. Some have reasonable measurement procedures. Others do not. It is simply inappropriate to think in terms of the overall utility of "personality". We must instead recognize that usefulness relates to particular constructs, particular situations and particular issues (p. 43).

They further concluded that OB researchers have barely scratched the surface of the ways in which personality constructs may enter into theoretical systems (p. 43).

Weiss and Adler's (1984) review addresses a long standing issue in the organizational behavior literature. This issue concerns the relative importance of personality constructs in the prediction of individual behavior in complex organizations. Weiss and Adler note that there is a widely held opinion that personality traits are relatively unimportant.

For example, one rather predominant theory of task design asserts that individual needs are irrelevant to organizational members' adjustment to task characteristics (Salancik & Pfeffer, 1978). These authors view organizational members strictly as information processors, influenced by social sources of information as well as factual data. To these authors, expressions of needs and attitudes are epiphenomena—nothing more than rationalizations of prior events. As such, needs and attitudes are regarded as irrelevant to task performance or adjustment.

Weiss and Adler (1984) attribute the origins of this school of thought partially to misinterpretations of Stogdill's (1948) review of traits as predictors of leader effectiveness. In his famous 1948 article Stogdill concluded that leader traits alone were insufficient to predict accurately leader emergence or leader effectiveness. He argued that it is necessary to study personality traits in interaction with contextual variables. As Weiss and Adler note, Stogdill's conclusions were vastly misinterpreted. Stogdill *did not* conclude that personality traits were irrelevant to the understanding of leader behavior and effectiveness. Rather, he concluded that such traits interact with situational cues such that it is unlikely that many leader traits will be consistently associated with leader emergence or effectiveness across a variety of widely differing situations. As Weiss and Adler note, Stogdill himself later pointed out that reactions to his 1948 article "over-emphasized the situational, and under-emphasized the personal nature of leadership" (Stogdill, 1974, p. 72).

It is argued here that the evidence for the existence of individual needs as motivators of behavior is very strong. Staw, Bell and Clausen (1986), have shown that personality characteristics are stable and predictive of attitudes over a time span of nearly 50 years. McClelland and Boyatzis (1982) had shown that measures of individual needs predict managerial performance 16 years later. While we agree that organizational members are significantly affected by situational variables, we argue that theories of behavior within organizations that do not include individual differences are incomplete.

This argument suggests the need for cross-level research in which situational variables are measured at the subunit or organizational level of analysis and personality constructs are measured at the individual level of analysis.

EXTANT THEORIES OF POWER ACQUISITION

Extant theories of power acquisition assert that individuals or subunits attain power by causing others to be dependent on them for desired resources or other outcomes. (Thompson, 1967; Hinings, Hickson, Pennings, & Schneck, 1974; Pfeffer & Salancik, 1978; Pfeffer 1981; Mintzberg, 1983; Mackenzie, 1985). In these theories power is defined as the ability of an organizational member to obtain compliance from others even if such compliance requires the powerful person to overcome resistance. In this paper we will use this general definition of power.

Extant theories are in general agreement that the power of an individual or subunit is largely determined by the control of critical contingencies facing the organization. Critical contingencies are defined as "those events and activities both inside and outside the organization that are essential for attaining organizational goals" (Daft, 1983, p. 392). Critical contingencies are seen to arise from the organization's relevant environment (Hickson et al., 1971; Pfeffer, 1981), its strategy (Hambrick, 1981), from position functions and attributes (Pfeffer, 1981), from characteristics of the organization's technology (Crozier, 1964; Thompson, 1967; Comstock

& Scott, 1977), or from subunit functions and attributes (Hickson et al., 1971).

Control over critical contingencies, it is argued, can be derived from one's position in the organization. Positions that permit incumbents to control information, personnel, material resources or monetary rewards, or to cope with critical contingencies, are said to enable the incumbent to wield power over those who are dependent on her or him. Further, under conditions where an individual or a subunit has the expertise required to deal with critical demands imposed on the organization, and when other individuals or subunits do not have such expertise, it is predicted that power will accrue to those possessing nonsubstitutable expertise. The above predictions have been widely supported in a number of studies (Hinings et al., 1974; Pfeffer & Salancik, 1978; Bagozzi & Phillips, 1982; Hambrick, 1981; Salancik & Pfeffer, 1974; Hills & Mahoney, 1978; Pfeffer & Moore, 1980; Salancik, Pfeffer, & Kelly, 1978).

The theory advanced by Hickson et al. (1971) asserts that certain attributes of subunits enhance the power of these subunits relative to other subunits.

The particular variables that Hickson et al. (1971) hypothesized to be associated with the acquisition of subunit power are: (a) the degree to which a subunit copes with uncertainty for other subunits, (b) the extent to which a subunit's coping activities are nonsubstitutable or irreplaceable, (c) the degree to which subunit activities are interlinked with the system, and (d) the degree to which activities of the subunit are essential in the sense that their cessation would quickly and substantially impede the primary workflow of the organization. These variables were labeled uncertainty coping ability, nonsubstitutability, centrality (or persuasiveness) of workflows, and immediacy of workflows. These variables were hypothesized to increase the dependence of other subunits on the focal subunit and therefore increase the focal subunit's power.

In a test of this theory of subunit power, Hinings et al., (1974) found that the formal authority of organizational subunits was significantly correlated with the subunit characteristics specified above, holding hierarchical level constant. In this study, the correlations between various measures of formal authority and subunit characteristics ranged from .40 to l81. We speculate that these same attributes can be used to describe positions as well as subunits. Further, we expect these attributes to have homologous relationships to position power or subunit power. Thus, as Blackburn (1981) argues, the theory by Hickson et al. (1971) can be applied to at least two levels of analysis: subunits and positions.

Pfeffer (1981) argues that in addition to subunit or position attributes the degree of consensus within a subunit influences the amount of subunit power. Under conditions of subunit consensus, the potential for conflict and misunderstanding within the subunit will be less. Further, subunits with a high degree of consensus can form stronger and more effective coalitions than those with a high degree of dissensus. Pfeffer and Moore (1980) inferred the level of consensus within university departments on the basis of the level of paradigm development of the departments' discipline. In summarizing the results of the Pfeffer and Moore (1980) study, Pfeffer states:

> The results indicate that in addition to the power that comes from provision of critical resources, subunits can have power because of their degree of consensus and shared paradigm, which permits them to advocate their interest with more clarity and consistency (Pfeffer, 1981, p. 124).

From the above findings we speculate that subunit consensus may be viewed as a variable that determines the degree to which situational determinants of subunit power will be translated into actual power with other subunits. This member consensus can be viewed as a moderator of the effect of such situational variables. That is, under conditions where subunit membership is in consensus with respect to a particular issue, the full force of the structural determinants as bases of power can be exploited by the members. However, under conditions where there is a lack of consensus, energy will be devoted toward infighting and resolving intragroup conflict. Such internal dissensus distracts the organizational members' attention away from dealing with other subunits. It also interferes with the ability of the leadership of the subunit to speak convincingly on behalf of the subunit to representatives of other parts of the organization. Thus, under conditions where consensus is low, we would expect significantly lower correlations between structural determinants of subunit power and the amount of power the subunit actually possesses.

Pfeffer and Salancik (1978) also posit an adaptation model of power distribution within organizations. According to this model environmental contingencies affect the selection and removal of top managers to keep the organization in line with its environment. Organizational survival is thus seen as a function of "fit" or "congruence" or "alignment" of the power distribution within the organization with the distribution of critical resources on which the organization is dependent for survival. There is substantial evidence for this model (Virany, Tushman & Romanelli, unpublished manuscript, 1985; Allen, 1981a,b; Allen & Panian, 1982; McEachern, 1975; Salancik & Pfeffer, 1980; House & Singh, 1987).

Summary: Current Theories

Theories of this class have been useful in helping identify both position characteristics, subunit characteristics, and environmental variables that permit individuals or subunits to acquire power. The following propositions summarize the research findings concerned with the structured theories of power acquisition described above:

Proposition 1: Incumbency in a position, or membership in a subunit, will be associated with the acquisition of power by the position holder or subunit member to the extent that the position or subunit has control of information or resources on which other positions or subunits depend. (Hinings et al., 1974; Pfeffer & Salancik, 1974; Hills & Mahoney, 1978; Pfeffer & Moore, 1980).

Proposition 2: Individuals or subunits gain power to the extent that (a) the functions of the subunits are critical to the organization, (b) the leadership of the subunit engages in broad based environmental scanning, and (c) the subunit copes effectively with critical contingencies facing the organization (Hambrick, 1981).

Proposition 3: Positions or subunits will control and be in a position to cope with critical contingencies facing the organization to the extent such positions or subunits perform functions characterized by uncertainty coping, nonsubstitutability, centrality, and immediacy of workflow (Hinings et al., 1974).

Proposition 4: Individuals or subunits acquire power to the extent that their position or subunit membership allows them to influence decision premises, alternatives considered, evaluation of alternatives, or control of information about the alternatives (Salancik, et al., 1978).

Proposition 5: Membership in a particular subunit will result in the acquisition of power over other subunits or members of other subunits to the extent that subunit members are in consensus with respect to critical issues they face when interacting with either the environment or other subunits (Pfeffer & Moore, 1980).

Proposition 6: Subunit consensus will moderate the relationship between the subunit structural characteristics and the acquisition of subunit power. Specifically, under conditions where subunit consensus is low, the relationships between subunit structural characteristics and subunit power will also be low. However, under conditions where consensus is high, these relationships will be high (Pfeffer & Moore, 1980).

In addition to the above propositions which concern power acquisition, we advance four propositions that summarize the research findings concerned with Pfeffer and Salancik's (1978) adaptation model of power distribution.

Proposition 7: Nonvoluntary chief executive succession (except in the cases of illness or death of the executive) occurs predominantly in response to problematic organizational environments and declining organizational performance (Scwartz & Menon, 1985; Pfeffer & Leblebici, 1973; Helmich, 1978; Osborn, Jauch, Martin, & Glueck, 1981; Virany et al., 1985; Grusky, 1960, 1963; James & Soref, 1981; Eitzen & Yetman, 1972; Brown, 1982; Gamson & Scotch, 1964; Schendel, Patton, & Riggs, 1976; Lubatkin & Chung, 1985; McEachern, 1975).

Proposition 8: In the event of succession of chief executives, such succession is more likely to lead to organizational effectiveness when the CEO has the ability to cope with organizational uncertainty (Pfeffer & Salancik, 1977), has a history of competence (Smith, Carson, & Alexander, 1984), and possesses relevant knowledge and external influence (Shetty & Peary, 1976).

Proposition 9: In times of poor performance or problematic environments, outside successors are more likely to make strategic internal changes and to be more effective in implementing successful turnarounds than successors appointed from within the organization (Reinganum, 1985; Helmich & Brown, 1972; Helmich, 1974; Samuelson, Galbraith, & McGuire, 1985).

Proposition 10: The greater the external control of an organization's management the greater the frequency of executive succession (Virany et al., 1985; Allen, 1981; Allen & Panian, 1982; McEachern, 1975; Salancik & Pfeffer, 1980).

Notice that all of the above propositions involve multiple levels of analysis. These propositions assert relationships that hold for the position level and either the subunit or the organizational level of analysis. Further, with the exception of proposition five these propositions assert direct (noncontingent) relationships between organizational or subunit characteristics and the acquisition of individual or subunit power.

As Mintzberg (1983) has stressed, both the acquisition and the exercise of power requires will and skill. These individual difference variables, will and skill, have been given scant attention in the literature on power in complex organizations. We now turn to an extension of current theory in which we advance a set of propositions concerning how individual differences interact with contextual variables in the acquisition of power in complex organizations.

AN EXTENSION OF CURRENT THEORY

Conception of the Organization

We conceive of organizations as collectivities governed by formal rules, policies, standard operating procedures, role definitions, and by informal norms that arise out of the collective interactions of the members. Accordingly, the relationship between an organization and its members is based on a formal or informal employment contract that specifies the rewards (or inducements) for membership and for performance of their role requirements. Under conditions where members perceive the employment relationship to be fair, and where the roles of the members are relatively unchanging and unambiguous, we expect the normal day-to-day functioning of the members to be oriented predominantly toward the fulfillment of role expectations and contributions to the larger collectivity.

Accordingly, Astley argues that functional interdependence with others within the organization will be one of the primary determinants of power. Such power takes the form of what Olsen (1978) refers to as functional dominance.

> As actors perform their routine activity in roles within the organization, they often unintentionally influence or control the actions of other interdependent actors, as well as the functioning of the entire organization. To the extent that this occurs, functional dominance is being exerted. (Olsen, 1978, 41; cited in Astley, 1979)

Several studies have shown that position centrality in the network of organizational relationships is significantly associated with power acquisition (Crozier, 1964; Pettigrew, 1972; Hinings et al., 1974; Brass, 1984, 1985). These findings are consistent with Astley's argument.

We view organizations as relatively stable collectivities in which the distribution of power is primarily determined by the attributes of the roles of individuals or the attributes of subunits. However, there are also conditions that strain stable existing role relationships. These conditions make it both possible and *at times necessary* for power to be used to clarify and stabilize role relationships. Specifically, role relationships are expected to be unstable when the terms of membership are viewed as unfair by role incumbents, when critical contingencies facing role incumbents or the means to deal with such contingencies cannot be accurately specified in advance, or when existing role relationships are inappropriate due to changes in the organization's goals, strategy, environment, or technology. Under these conditions, we expect individual behavior to be guided by personal characteristics, preferences, expectations, and informal organizational requirements. The more the above conditions prevail, the greater will be the strain or force toward redefining and clarifying role relationships. Under such conditions we expect role incumbents to engage in power tactics to redefine their role requirements in a manner favorable to their self interest. In such circumstances, the choice of power tactics is expected to reflect the individuals' personal characteristics as well as situational pressures.

Thus, we conceive of organizations as generally stable collectivities, parts of which, under some conditions, become unstable. These instabilities give rise to the need to use power or social influence. However, most frequently the exercise of power results in marginal adjustments in the power distribution throughout the organization. Such marginal adjustments occur because roles are influenced by their occupants and created around particular people once they have occupied a position for some length of time. Less frequently, major shifts in the organizations' environment (Miller & Friesen, 1984), demography (Pfeffer, 1983), or technology (Tushman & Romanelli, 1985), require global reorganizations and thus result in fundamental power redistributions rather than incremental or marginal adjustments (Miller & Friesen, 1984; Tushman & Romanelli, 1985).

This conceptualization of organizations suggests that major shifts in the distribution of power within an organization will occur under conditions where existing power relationships are unstable.

Conception of Individual Differences

We argue that individuals have relatively stable personality characteristics and that such characteristics, in certain circumstances, are predictive of individual behavior. As pointed out by Weiss and Adler (1984), personality constructs can be grouped into two broad categories, although some constructs have components of both of these categories. The first category of personality constructs is *motivational*. Motivational personality constructs are those stable individual differences that are predictive of why, when, where, and how behavior is energized and maintained. *Dominance* and *need for power* fall into this category and are related to the acquisition and exercise of power in complex organizations. Throughout this paper we use the terms motivation, needs, or predispositions interchangeably to refer to motivational personality constructs.

The second category of personality construct is *cognitive*. Cognitive personality constructs refer to characteristic properties of the individual's perceptual and thought processes, how the individual processes information. Such individual difference variables as *expertise, cognitive complexity*, and *linguistic ability* fit into this category. As we shall show, these cognitive variables are also relevant to considerations of power acquisition. Two additional individual difference variables that are relevant to theories of power acquisition are self-esteem and Machiavellianism. These variables appear to include both cognitive and motivational components.

The central argument of this chapter is that individual differences are useful constructs in helping to explain power acquisition in complex organizations. It is argued that some individual difference variables have a main effect in accounting for power acquisition in complex organizations. Further, it is argued that some individual differences interact with contextual variables in accounting for the acquisition of power in such organizations.

Interaction of Personal and Contextual Variables

While the precise functional relationships between the acquisition of power and either contextual or personal variables have not been established there is both theory and evidence to suggest how these variables relate to the acquisition of power.

According to social learning theory (Mischel, 1973).

Psychological "situations" and (experimental) 'treatments' are powerful to the degree that they lead all persons to construe the particular events the same way, induce *uniform* expectations regarding the most appropriate response pattern, provide adequate incentives for the performance of that response pattern, and instill the skills necessary for its satisfactory construction and execution. Conversely, situations and (experimental) treatments are weak to the degree that they are not uniformly encoded, do not generate uniform expectancies concerning the desired behavior, do not offer sufficient incentives for its performance, or fail to provide the learning conditions required for successful construction of the behavior.

Individual differences can determine behavior in a given situation most strongly when the situation is ambiguously structured (as in projective testing) so that subjects are uncertain about how to categorize it and have no clear expectations about the behaviors most likely to be appropriate (normative, reinforced) in their situation. To the degree that the situation is 'unstructured,' the subject will expect that virtually any response from him is equally likely to be equally appropriate (i.e., will lead to similar consequences), and variance from individual differences will be greatest.

Mischel's argument was supported by research conducted by Monson, Hesley, and Chernick (1982). These authors conducted two studies in which the participants were placed in either of three experimental conditions: forced extroversion, forced introversion, or neutral. Subject's talkativeness was measured in each condition. As predicted, variance in talkativeness among subjects was significantly higher in the neutral condition than in the forced-introversion or the forced extroversion condition. Thus this study supports Mischel's (1973) argument that contextual variables are most predictive of individual behavior in unambiguous situations and least predictive in ambiguous situations.

In a second study, Monson et al. (1982) asked participants to indicate the probabilities that they would engage in various behaviors in each of four hypothetical situations. They also asked participants to estimate the probabilities that other individuals would exhibit the same behaviors. On average persons were perceived to be most likely to exhibit extroverted behaviors when there were perceived situational pressures to do so, and least likely when such situational pressures were lowest. Correlations were also calculated between the participants' self-ratings of extroversion and the likelihood of exhibiting extroverted behavior in each of the conditions. Again, the correlation was found to be an inverse function of the degree of situational pressure. That is, self-ratings of extroversion were most predictive of extroverted behavior in situations that offer little guidance to the individual concerning what kind of behavior was appropriate in that situation. These findings support Mischel's general argument that individual differences will be most predictive of behavior when environmental conditions are unstructured. While this evidence supports the general argument advanced by Mischel, there remains a need to demonstrate specifically how it applies to power related behavior in complex organizations.

Theoretical arguments by Mischel (1973) together with the findings by Monson et al. (1982) suggest the following proposition:

Proposition 11: In complex organizations there will be an interaction between individual power striving predispositions and contextual variables. Specifically, individuals with power striving predispositions will acquire power under conditions where organizational and technological constraints are weak. When organizational and technological constraints are strong and provide cues and guidance for individual behavior, such predispositions will have significantly lower relationships to the acquisition of power in complex organizations.

We now turn to a discussion of several individual difference variables that have specific relevance to the acquisition of power in complex organizations.

MOTIVATIONAL INDIVIDUAL DIFFERENCES

Dominance

The Dominance scale of the California Personality Inventory (CPI) (Gough, 1968) is a self-report measure of the degree to which individuals are socially outgoing and comfortable in social situations, and the frequency with which individuals have engaged in influence attempts in prior experiences. *Contrary to the implications of the label "dominance," this scale does not include items that measure an inclination of an individual to be domineering, authoritarian, punitive, or aggressive.*

The relationship between the CPI dominance scale and the acquisition of power has been impressively demonstrated in two experiments by Megargee et al. (1966). These studies clearly demonstrated that when high and low dominant subjects worked together, and when the task was emphasized and leadership and control are deemphasized, there was a weak association between dominance and the assumption of the leadership role. However, under experimental conditions in which leadership, control, and followership status in the dyad are emphasized, and the subjects were free to assume either a follower or leader role, the association between dominance and the assumption of leadership becomes extremely strong. Specifically, Megargee et al. found that under this set of conditions, the high dominance members of fourteen out of sixteen high and low dominance pairs assumed the leadership role when conducting the experimental task. The argument that dominance plays a significant role as a determinant of the acquisition and exercise of power is also supported by several studies in addition to those reviewed above (Barron & Egan, 1968; Berkowitz & Hawthorne, 1955, Borgatta, 1961; Brown, Grant, & Palton, 1981; Dyson, Fleitas, & Scoili, 1972; Gorecki, Dickson, & Ritzler, 1981; Gough, 1968; Johnson and Fraudson, 1962; Liddle, 1958; Mahoney, Sorenson, Jerdee, & Nash, 1963).

Thus, the above findings concerning the need for dominance inform us about one of the major situational cues that are likely to moderate the effect of individual predispositions to acquire power. Specifically, these findings suggest the following proposition:

Proposition 12: Under conditions where contextual variables make issues of leadership, control or power salient, but do not constrain power-striving behavior, individual predispositions to acquire power will be more highly predictive of power acquisition than under conditions where contextual variables do not make such issues salient.

We generalize the findings for dominance to the broader category of individual predispositions because, as will be shown, there are similar interactions between the other motivational personality traits and contextual variables as well.

The Power Motive

A second personal characteristic predictive of power striving and power acquisition is the power motive,[1] commonly referred to as need for power or N-pow. According to McClelland (1985), the need for power is a socially learned motive. McClelland argues that the exercise of power results in the release of catecholamines: adrenaline, epinephrine, norepinephrine, endorphins, and dopamine. These catecholamines, when released have been found to increase both anger and aggression as well as feelings of pleasure in humans (Berlyne, 1967). Catecholamine release has been shown to be correlated with arousal of the power motive and with the exercise of power. These findings indicate that the satisfaction one receives from exercising power is derived from catecholamine release. According to McClelland, when humans learn that the exercise of power results in the experience of positive affect, one is said to have learned the power motive or the need for power. Thus, according to McClelland, the need for power is a socially learned set of associations between the arousal or exercise of power and the experience of positive affect.

The need for power is most frequently measured by an individual's response to unstructured ambiguous stimuli. Typically, research subjects are asked to write an imaginative story about a picture or about a short written description of an event. Responses of this sort are assumed to be a projection of the subordinate's *unconscious* motive to attain and exercise power. McClelland argues that it is necessary to use such a projective test because individuals are largely incapable of expressing nonconscious motives. Therefore, objectively scored questions that ask respondents direct questions about their motives do not tap the unconscious component of one's motivation.

Construct validity. McClelland and his associates have conducted a substantial number of studies on the power motive construct, approaching 100 as of our last count. These studies provide convincing evidence of the validity of the need for power as a theoretical construct. Further, these findings demonstrate both construct and predictive validity of the power motive measure. For example, it has been shown that the power motive can be aroused by showing subjects inspirational speeches such as Churchill's speech at Dunkirk or Henry V's speeches in Shakespeare's *Life of Henvy V*. After the power motive is aroused there is a marked gain in norepinephrine excretion in the subjects' urine and in subjects' physiological activation (Steele, 1973; 1977). Further, the gain in norepinephrine is positively correlated ($r = .66$, $p < .01$) with the amount of power imagery in stories written after inspirational speeches were heard.

Subjects high on the need for power react more sensitively to power-related stimuli than to neutral stimuli, as evidenced by findings assessing the electrical responsitivity of the brain to various stimuli (McClelland, Davidson, & Saron, unpublished manuscript, 1979; Davidson, Saron, & McClelland, 1980). Individuals high in the need for power recall more "peak" experiences that are described in power terms (McAdams, 1982) and more power related facts relative to neutral facts, than do low or neutral power subjects (McAdams & McClelland, unpublished manuscript, 1983). Individuals high in the power motive also respond to several experimental treatments differently than individuals low in the power motive.

For example, Fodor and Farrow (1979) demonstrated experimentally that individuals high in the need for power show partiality towards ingratiating followers to a greater extent than those low on the need for power. In another study, high power–motivated individuals were found to inhibit group discussion more than low power–motivated individuals. As a consequence, the number of alternatives considered were fewer and the quality of decisions lower for groups led by high power–motivated individuals (Fodor & Smith, 1982). High power–motivated individuals become more highly activated when supervising others than low power individuals. Activation was found to be highest when high power–motivated individuals were in an experimental condition in which productivity was stressed and rewarded but attempts by the individuals to gain control of the situation and increase productivity were thwarted (Fodor, 1984). Finally, high power males report that they have more arguments, play competitive sports more, have less stable interpersonal relations, favor more assertive foreign policies, experience more emotional problems and are more impulsively aggressive than low power males (McClelland, 1985).

Females respond to power-arousing stimuli in a manner similar to males. Specifically, females have been found to respond to a hypnosis demonstration or to an inspirational speech, as evidenced by their responses to the Thematic Apperception Test, to approximately the same extent as men (Stewart & Winter, 1976; Steele, 1977).

However, in one study females high in power motivation were found to be less overtly assertive and competitive than men (McClelland, 1975). McClelland suggests that this finding is likely due to the fact that women may inhibit their impulses to be assertive due to stereotypic sex-role expectations. This speculation is consistent with findings of a prior study in which it was found that females who are "self-defining" behave in ways similar to males, whereas among "socially defining" females power motivation predicts behaviors that are congruent with the stereotypic female role (Winter & Stewart, 1978).

Managerial career advancement. The need for power, in combination with high achievement motivation, low need for affiliation and high power inhibition has been found to be predictive of managerial career progress (Winter, 1979; McClelland & Boyatzis, 1982; cf. House & Singh, 1987, for a more detailed review of these studies). The need for achievement and the need for affiliation are well known in the motivational literature (cf. McClelland, 1985, for an extensive review). However, the construct of power inhibition is less well known and therefore is described here.[2]

Power inhibition is, according to McClelland (1985), a personality trait that serves to psychologically constrain one from the exercise of power in socially undesirable or coercive ways such as manipulation, impulsive aggressiveness, authoritarian behavior or the use of violence. The research on this personality construct suggests that individuals with both high power motivation and high power inhibition are more likely to use socially desirable behaviors in the exercise of power. Individuals who are high in power motivation and low in power inhibition are more likely to use coercion or other socially undesirable means to exercise power.

Studies by McClelland and Boyatzis (1982) and by Stahl (1983) are of particular interest. McClelland and Boyatzis found that the need for power in combination with inhibition predicted higher levels of advancement after 8 and 16 years of experience. However, this finding held only for managers in nontechnical jobs. No such association between leader motivation and promotion was found for technical managers. Need for achievement was associated with managerial success for lower level technical jobs. It is suggested that at these levels, promotions are heavily dependent on individual contributions. At higher levels, need for achievement is not associated with success as was the inhibited power motive (the combination of high power motivation and high power inhibition). These findings confirm Winter's (1979) earlier findings that the inhibited power motive had low predictive power with respect to success of technical managers. Perhaps some combination of other motives might have higher predictive utility. Since technical supervisors constitute a substantial proportion of managers, research concerning the motivational determinants of success among technical managers is called for.

Stahl (1983) has also found managers' power motivation to be associated with a number of predicted dependent variables including ratings of managerial performance and managerial promotion rate. Further, no differences between males and females or between races was found on Stahl's measures of achievement and power motivation. Stahl's findings are based on a measure of motivation that is objectively scored and therefore not tied to the use of the Thematic Apperception Test generally used by McClelland and his associates. The measure is based on respondents' choices of hypothetical occupational positions. Choice of positions that hypothetically allow position incumbents to influence others is taken as an indication of the need for power. Since career progress is associated with progression up the line of authority, we take such progress to be an indication of the acquisition and maintenance of formal authority—institutionalized power.

A qualification is in order here. While Stahl's findings are impressive, it has been pointed out that they are correlational and not predictive (McClelland, personal communication, 1986). McClelland argues that responses to direct questions or choices among hypothetical job choices, are more cognitively than emotionally based and not likely to be a valid measure of motives. Clearly, this is an important issue that goes to the very nature of human motivation. Tests of the *predictive* validity of Stahl's measure are needed to resolve this issue.

Managerial effectiveness.   Three studies have also shown that the power motive, in combination with the achievement motive, is associated with managerial or organizational effectiveness (Cummin, 1967; Wainer & Rubin, 1969; Varga, 1975). If one assumes that managerial effectiveness is in turn associated with power acquisition, as resource dependency theory (Pfeffer & Salancik, 1978) would suggest (because effectiveness usually implies control of critical contingencies and resources) it would be expected that the need for power is associated with power acquisition in complex organizations.

The results of the studies of managers are consistent with the findings of Miner (1978) and his associates based on 25 years of research including 33 predictive studies. Like McClelland, Miner also uses a projective measure of motivation: the Miner Sentence Completion Scale (MSCS). This scale has been shown to have predictive validity in bureaucratic organizations. However, it does not predict success in small nonbureaucratic organizations, in positions requiring technical ability such as R & D organizations, or for lower level managerial jobs where managers are primarily concerned with the technical or physical operations of the organization. Thus, the findings by McClelland and Boyatzis (1982), by Winter (1979), and also by Miner and his associates (1978), suggest that the power motive is predictive of managerial success only under conditions in which the assertion of social influence is critical and technical expertise is less critical to performance.

The above findings suggest the following proposition:

Proposition 13:   In bureaucratic organizations and in positions that require administrative decision making rather than technical decision making, individuals with a high need for power will be more likely to acquire power than individuals with a low need for power.

Arousal of the power motive.   The need for power, like the trait of dominance, is most likely to be predictive of power acquisition under conditions that make issues of control, power, or leadership salient. Various techniques have been used in laboratory studies to arouse the power motive. These include giving individuals an opportunity to exercise power over others (Uleman, 1972), having subjects observe others engaged in the expression of power (Steele, 1977), or by causing the subject to have a loss of personal influence or control (Fodor, 1984).

We would expect that all three of the above arousal processes occur in complex organizations. That is, we believe that individuals in complex organizations are often given opportunities to exercise power, often observe the exercise of power by others, and are sometimes threatened with and experience loss of autonomy or control. Under such conditions of power arousal individuals high in the need for power are expected to become activated toward power striving and toward the exercise of power over others. Therefore, research on the need for power suggests the following propositions:

Proposition 14:   The acquisition and exercise of power will be experienced as more rewarding by individuals high in the need for power than the acquisition and exercise of power by individuals low in the need for power.

Proposition 15:   When significant others are observed as engaging in power oriented behavior, individuals high in the need for power will emulate that behavior and will be successful in gaining power to a greater extent than individuals low in the need for power.

Proposition 16:   When threatened with or when experiencing the loss of personal influence or control, individuals high in the need for power will assert more power oriented behaviors and will be successful in gaining power to a greater extent than individuals low in the need for power.

Measurement issues.   The need for influence measure developed by Uleman (1972), the measure of the need for power (n-pow) developed by McClelland and Watson (1973), the measure of hope for power (h-pow) developed by Winter (1973), and measures of need for socialized power and personalized power developed by McClelland (1975) have all been shown to be related to behavior of individuals in a manner that suggests that these measures are associated with a strong desire to acquire and exert power over others. Since all of these measures are based on different scoring responses to the TAT, it would be possible in future research efforts to compare the relative validity of these scoring systems by use of the same set of TAT responses. Further, it would be possible to determine the relationship between these measures and objectively scored measures as well as the amount of variance in power acquisition accounted for by each.

Further, the measure of power inhibition requires further validation, although the evidence reported thus far is promising (McClelland, 1985). This measure is simply the number of times the word "not" is expressed in responses to TAT stimulus materials. It would be helpful to determine whether this measure is predictive of altruistic and constructive power related behavior in experimental settings or in longitudinal field research.

Machiavellianism

Machiavellianism, as conceived by Christie and Geis (1970) refers to cognitive agreement with the prescriptions of Nicoli Machiavelli. Accordingly, individuals who score high on Machiavellianism, as measured by Mach IV or Mach V scales, (Christie & Geis, 1970) are described as exhibiting the "cool syndrome" and individuals who score low on Machiavellianism are described as being "a soft touch." The cool syndrome of the high Mach is characterized by resistance to social influence, orientation to task-related cognitions rather than to emotional or moral involvement with others, and a strong tendency to initiate and control interactions with others. In contrast, the soft touch syndrome of the low Machs is characterized by susceptibility to social influence, orientation to others that results in a tendency to be distracted by affective, nontask-related interpersonal considerations, and acceptance of control and structure initiated by others.

Empirical research has generally supported the description of high Machs as possessing the "cool" syndrome. High Machs are consistently found to be less influenced by social pressure and resist being controlled by others (Epstein, 1969; Geis, Krupat, Berger, 1965; Harris, 1966; Droy and Gluskinos, 1980). They have also been shown to be quicker to initiate control (Weinstein, Backhouse, Bromstein and Stein, 1968), to be more influential in group discussions (Rim, 1966) and to contribute more to group task performance and progress (Geis et al. 1966). Further, high Machs use deception more, bluff more, and generally engage in manipulative behavior more than others in competitive situations (Christie & Geis, 1970; Geis et al. 1965; Oksenberg, 1968; Droy & Gluskinos, 1980). The characteristic "cool" syndrome of the high Machs is exhibited under competitive conditions that (a) allow face to face interactions between high Machs and others, (b) allow latitude for improvision of both content and timing of her or his responses to the task to other people, and (c) are likely to induce "irrelevant affect," in situations that permit considerations that can interfere with manipulative behavior and effective bargaining (Christie & Geis, 1970). Low Machs experience affective arousal in such situations while high Machs remain cool.

These findings suggests the following proposition:

Proposition 17: Under competitive conditions that allow face to face interaction, latitude for improvisation and arousal of irrelevant affect, individuals who score high on the Machiavellian scale will exert power over others to a greater extent than individuals low on the Machiavellian scale.

Interpretation of Motivational Predispositions

We interpret an individual's scores on the above measures to be, in large part, a reflection of an individual's prior learning (Mischel, 1973). Thus, predispositions to acquire and assert power are seen here as primarily socially learned. This prior learning may be a function of the individuals' experience with the environment. These predispositions may also be a function of genetic make up that gives some individuals a proclivity to learn power-striving behavior more than other individuals (Bouchard, 1984). If this is the case power-striving predispositions are socially learned outcomes of the interaction between proclivities and experiences with one's environment. Research concerned with the origins of such predispositions is clearly indicated. Such predispositions are assumed to be relatively enduring but subject to modification through future learning. Further, such predispositions are arousable by certain discriminant stimuli, as evidenced by Megargee et al. (1966). Stimuli of this kind are situational cues that have been correlated with the individual's successful use of power in prior situations or stimuli that have been correlated with the observation of successful use of power by others in prior situations (Bandura, 1979).

Based on this interpretation of the above evidence we advance the following two propositions:

Proposition 18: Individuals will have a predisposition to acquire and exercise power to the extent that they have observed the successful exercise of power in prior similar situations, or to the extent that prior attempts at exercising power have been rewarded in similar situations in their past.

Proposition 19: The predisposition to acquire and assert power is arousable by situational cues which have been correlated with the individual's successful use of power in prior situations or with the individual's observation of successful use of power in prior situations.

Summary of Motivational Predispositions

Based on the above arguments and supporting evidence it can be concluded that individuals vary in the degree to which they are predisposed toward the acquisition and exercise of power. Such predispositions as need for power, dominance and Machiavellianism interact with situational cues in the acquisition of power. Individuals high on these predispositions acquire more power in situations where cues make leadership, control and power salient than do individuals low on these predispositions. Further, such individuals most likely learn skills in the application of power more than other individuals. As we shall argue later these predispositions and skills have implications for the distributions and redistributions of power in complex organizations.

Researchers concerned with individual differences as predictors of power-related behavior should be well advised to employ both the dominance scale and the Machiavellian scale, as well as the TAT, simultaneously. This would allow them to determine the correlation among the various measures, the degree to which they measure the same or different underlying characteristics of respondents, and the degree to which they predict the same or different behaviors under different circumstances.

COGNITIVE INDIVIDUAL DIFFERENCES

In addition to the above variables, which we view as motivational predispositions to acquire power, there are also a number of individual difference variables that are more cognitive than motivational in nature, although some of these have both cognitive and motivational components. These cognitive individual difference variables are viewed here as facilitators of power acquisition rather than predispositions toward power acquisition. Thus we speculate that individuals who are high on both predisposition toward power acquisition and the cognitive variables described below will be highly effective in acquiring and maintaining power in complex organizations. As such these variables are more like cognitive skills than motivational dispositions. We now turn to a discussion of these facilitative personal characteristics.

Self Confidence

Tedeschi, Schlenker, & Lindskold (1972) and Kipnis (1976) have argued that individuals choose to attempt to use power on the basis of their perceived subjective expected utility (SEU) of the outcomes of the power attempt. That is, individuals choose to use power based on their perception of the likelihood that the power attempt will be successful, their expectations of gains from the power attempt and the cost of using the power attempt. A study by Mowday (1978) provides support for this assertion, based on responses and observations of managers in complex organizations.

Mowday (1978) found that the perceived instrumentality of power attempts significantly predicted the frequency with which power was employed by managers. Thus, individual characteristics that increase one's perceived instrumentality of prospective power attempts will also increase one's propensity to assert power.

Self-confidence is one such personality variable. Generalized self-confidence leads to increased confidence in the exercise of power (Mowday, 1978; Instone, Major, & Bunker, 1983). Further, high or low self-confidence can be temporarily induced by various laboratory manipulations such as positive feedback with respect to task effectiveness. Marak (1964) found a positive relationship between induced task competence and confidence and frequency of power attempts. Moreover, when groups were offered a monetary bonus, the relationship was much stronger. Thus, individuals who perceived themselves as competent engaged in more power attempts than individuals who perceived themselves as less competent. This effect was further heightened when there was an incentive to do so. Individuals who make more influence attempts tend to acquire more influence than those who do not. This likely occurs for several reasons. First, the attempt may fill a vacuum. Group members may be groping for leadership and direction but remain too timid or unskilled to assert influence themselves. Second, willingness to exert influence may indicate to others willingness to compete for power and may intimidate them. Successful intimidation allows the influence agent to acquire influence without competition from others. Third, individuals who make many influence attempts are likely to be more skilled and have more confidence than others who do not. They may be more skilled at the particular tasks which they attempt to influence or more skilled at interpersonal influence processes. Finally, frequency of influence attempts may reflect confidence which in turn may be based on a realistic self assessment of one's resources and expertise. Thus:

Proposition 20:   The greater the self-confidence of an individual the more frequently that individual will attempt to assert power

and the more likely the assertion of power will be successful.

Expertise

Another variable that increases one's perceived likelihood of success
is task expertise. Tedeschi, et al. (1972) argue that a person's expertise
is proportional to his or her informational resources. They argue that the
greater the expertise of individuals, the more self-confident they would
be and the more often their help would be sought by others. Possession
of expertise should also result in enhancing one's self-confidence and thus
increase the subjective probability of success of contemplated future power
attempts. Thus, the possession of expertise on the part of an influence
agent viewed as credible should increase the probability that the agent
will be successful in her or his power attempts. In addition to the evidence
reviewed by Tedeschi et al. (1972), both laboratory studies (Julian, Hollander, & Regula, 1969; Hamblin, Miller, & Wiggins, 1961) and field studies
(Comery, High and Wilson, 1955a, 1955b; Kahn & Katz, 1960; Baumgartel,
1956; Goodacre, 1951) provide support for this argument. These findings
have been demonstrated in such diverse settings as manufacturing operations, forest ranger stations, railroad operations, research endeavors,
military combat operations and experimental laboratory conditions.

Thus, based on the above evidence:

Proposition 21: The greater the expertise possessed by an individual
with respect to outcomes of her or his power attempts,
the more frequently that individual will attempt to assert power, and the more likely the assertion of power
will be successful.

Cognitive Complexity

Another cognitive variable that is likely to facilitate the acquisition of
power is cognitive complexity. Cognitive complexity is expected to facilitate an individual's diagnosis of power relations.

Cognitively complex individuals seek out more information, use it more
effectively, and are less subject to preconceived biases than cognitively
simple individuals. Further, cognitively complex individuals have been
shown to be more tolerant of situational uncertainty, more persuasive,
more considerate of others and better able to predict future related events
(cf. Streufert & Streufert, 1978, for a review of this research). Consequently, in organizations where the distribution of power is subtle and
complex, the cause and effect relationships are unknown or the environ-

ment is uncertain, individuals with a high degree of cognitive complexity are more likely to be able to cope with the complexity of the power distributions.

We assume that the ability to gain power rests, in part, on an accurate diagnosis of extant power relationships and the ability to arrange coalitions with powerful others. As Pfeffer notes "the building of coalitions requires finding areas of common interest (1981, p. 30) . . . of course, by looking at similarities (correlations) among preferences across political actors, potential coalitions of interests can be identified" (p. 38).

We would expect individuals who have a high degree of cognitive complexity to be able to diagnose power relations in organizations more effectively than less cognitively complex individuals. Thus, such individuals are expected to be more successful in forming or joining strong coalitions. Further, we would expect that cognitively complex individuals are more able to take advantage of major shifts in the environment, technology, or structure in the organization to increase their political influence relative to others in the organization.

The above rationale and research findings thus suggest:

Proposition 22: There will be a positive relationship between the acquisition of power and the acquirer's level of cognitive complexity.

Linguistic Ability

Finally, linguistic ability is likely to be another cognitive personality characteristic that facilitates power striving. It is assumed that the ability to be articulate with respect to arguments and issues is also a characteristic associated with coalition formation, one tactic used to acquire political influence. Coalition formation, after all, involves the ability to persuade others that they share common interests with the influence seeker and that they will gain by entering into a coalition with her or him.

Thus:

Proposition 23: There will be a positive relationship between the acquisition of power and the acquirer's level of linguistic ability.

ORGANIZATIONAL IMPLICATIONS

It can be argued that the above propositions and supporting evidence have several practical and social implications for organizations as well as several implications for organizational theory. In this section we discuss these implications. We believe the above propositions, except for those explicitly labeled as speculative when presented, rest on solid empirical evidence. However, the discussion to follow is much more speculative. Further, this discussion goes beyond considerations of power acquisition per se and concerns power *arousal* and *the exercise of power* in complex organizations as well. We are open to alternative interpretations and implications of the above literature review. Where such alternative interpretations exist, they call for further empirical investigation to resolve controversial issues.

It would be a socially desirable organizational world, from a humanistic perspective, if those who attain power could be relied on to use their power in open and constructive ways in the interest of their organizations and others rather than their own interests primarily. An organizational world in which such coercive tactics as political manipulation, impulsive aggressiveness and authoritarian behavior is not permitted is often called for as a solution to conflicts between organizational requirements and the needs of organizational members and society members (Argyris, 1957; Bennis, 1966; Likert, 1961; Tannenbaum, 1968). While such a conception of an ideal organization may be extremely difficult to achieve, a knowledge of the dynamics of power striving and the exercise of power in complex organizations would be helpful.

If organizations could be designed to control and inhibit the use of coercive power tactics, and if the power strivers who rise to positions of power were also psychologically and organizationally constrained not to use coercive power tactics, we would be able to go a long way toward the development of this ideal of humanistic organizations. This ideal and the possibility of its attainment is a significant social issue because the way in which power is exercised has significant implications for the economic, physical, and mental welfare of targets of power holders.

Situational Factors that Foster Power Oriented Behavior

One organizational implication of the above literature review concerns the organizational conditions under which individual differences have their greatest effect. Based on the theoretical argument by Mischel (1973), and the supporting evidence reviewed above we would expect that the effects of individual characteristics will be strongest in those parts of organizations where there are few situational cues to constrain actions and decisions and yet issues of power and influence are made salient.

It is also likely that several of the very conditions that foster the exercise of power in organizations make it possible for individual characteristics to have their most potent effect. Consider the conditions which, according to Pfeffer (1981, Ch. 3), foster and *require* the exercise of power in complex organizations. These are resource scarcity, interdependence of social actors, heterogeneous goals or preferences, and heterogeneous beliefs about cause and effect relationships governing technology and decentralization of power throughout the organization. We agree with Pfeffer that these are the conditions under which power is required in order to resolve conflict. However, it is argued here that it is under these same conditions that individual differences give parties to the conflict a differential advantage.

Heterogeneous beliefs about technology and lack of structural constraints, such as decentralized authority, are in fact the very conditions under which there are few situational cues to guide behavior. Thus it is under these conditions which, according to Pfeffer (1981) foster the exercise of power, that we are likely to find the effect of personal characteristics on the acquisition of power to be greatest. Recent investigations by Allen, Madison, Porter, & Renwick (1979) and Madison, Allen, Porter, & Renwick (1980) are consistent with this argument. These investigators found that the use of political power (as opposed to institutionalized authority) was reported by managers to be most prominent under conditions of ambiguity, lack of structure, and technological uncertainty.

Given the above argument by Mischel (1973), the supporting evidence by Monson et al. (1982), the prior findings concerning the interaction of predispositions with situational variables, and more recent findings of Allen et al. (1979) and Madison et al. (1980), it seems clear that heterogeneous beliefs about technology and lack of structural constraints should lead to greater variance in behavior than when beliefs are homogeneous and structure is highly constraining. Further, it is these same conditions that permit those predisposed to acquire power to have a differential advantage in its acquisition.

Control of Machiavellian Behavior

Another implication of the above research concerns the organizational conditions under which Machiavellian behavior is likely to be aroused and to be effective. High Machs engage in power striving and manipulative behavior under certain select conditions: conditions that allow latitude for improvisation, that arouse affect in low Machs, and permit face-to-face interaction.

Notice that these conditions are also similar to some of the conditions that Pfeffer (1981) argued require the use of power for resolution of the conflict. Specifically, conditions of technological uncertainty, goal uncertainty, or heterogeneous beliefs concerning cause and effect relationships allow latitude for improvisation of one's response to the situation or to others. Further, critical or important decisions are more likely to have implications for subsequent interpersonal relations within the organization, for the value system by which the organization is governed and for equitable distribution of resources, power, and prestige throughout the organization. Thus, critical decisions are likely to arouse affect on the part of low Machs and give high Machs a bargaining advantage. Finally, almost all important decisions are arrived at through face to face interaction among organizational members (Mintzberg, 1973; Mintzberg, Theoret, & Raisiinghani, 1974). Thus, the conditions which, according to Pfeffer (1981), require the use of power to resolve conflicts also arouse and facilitate the Machiavellian behavior of high Machs.

Based on the evidence reviewed above, we would also expect high Machs to gain power and to use manipulative methods in situations where information can be distorted to their ends. Thus, situations in which there is a great deal of secrecy or restriction of information allow high Machs to twist meanings, deceive and bluff. A recent study by Coates (1984) is relevant here. Coates asked 79 managers to report the number of contacts they had with superiors and peers. Since this measure of communication frequency did not vary within departments, but did vary between departments, it was considered a structural (departmental) variable rather than a reflection of individual differences. Respondents also completed the Machiavellian scale. Finally, ratings of the amount of power possessed by each respondent were collected from the respondents' superiors. Hierarchical regression analyses were conducted to determine whether departmental communication activity and Machiavellianism interacted to account for variance in ratings of the respondents' influence. Significant interactions were found between communication activity and Machiavellianism. Specifically, it was found that Machiavellianism was more strongly related to the subjects' power ratings under conditions of low communication activity.

Thus, the findings by Coates together with the earlier experimental findings on Machiavellianism indicates that managerial practices that stress open communications and overtly intended rational practices are likely to inhibit the acquisition of power by high Machs and the exercise of Machiavellian behavior.

Position Self Selection

In complex organizations there are several kinds of positions that can be expected to attract power. First and most obvious are positions requiring direct supervision of others. Second, some position responsibilities require the incumbent to solve complex problems for which solutions are uncertain and that must be coordinated with others who are affected by the solutions. Solving and coordinating such problems usually requires lengthy discussions of differences in opinion and persuasion of those who will be affected. Further, some positions require incumbents to negotiate with others over the procurement or allocation of resources. Such negotiation is more likely to be satisfying to individuals with power oriented predispositions to be attracted to such positions.

Several studies have shown support for this expectation. High power–motivated males and females, as compared to others low in power motivation, report holding more offices (Winter, 1973). High power–motivated males and females with full-time careers pursue the same occupations, those that allow individuals to exert significant influence over others. High power–motivated individuals choose such occupations as teaching, psychology, business, journalism, or organizational positions of influence. Low power–motivated individuals choose positions in other occupations that allow less opportunities to influence others (Wilsnack, 1974; Stahl, 1983).

Mowday (1978) further argues that individuals with strong predispositions to assert power can be expected to take an active role with respect to the work environment. Thus, such individuals initiate influence attempts more frequently. Accordingly, for individuals with such predispositions, satisfaction is gained from the process of influencing others as well as from the outcomes of the process. We would expect such individuals to have gained considerable skill in influencing others through a history of prior influence attempts. Based on this rationale we would expect individuals with power-oriented predispositions to seek out positions in which they can assert power over others. This self-selection process is one tactic by which individuals acquire power in organizations.

Proposition 24: Individuals will acquire power to the extent that they have an enduring predisposition to exert power over others in interaction with the degree to which they perceive their positions as offering opportunities to exert such power over others.

Selection and Socialization

It is also necessary to consider the effects of selection and socialization processes on the distribution of personal characteristics in complex organizations. Pfeffer (1977) argues that through processes of self selection, selection by others, and socialization, individuals within organizations become highly homogeneous with respect to their attitudes, values, and predispositions. If this is indeed the case then we would expect very little variance in personal characteristics of individuals who have been with stable organizations through an extended period of socialization. Consequently, personal characteristics are likely to be less predictive of power acquisition in organizations that have enjoyed extended periods of environmental and technological stability. However, in times of expansion, or when major environmental or technological shifts occur there will also be shifts in critical contingencies with which the organization must cope. Under such conditions we would expect to find more variance in personal characteristics of organizational members. Consequently, under such conditions we would expect personal characteristics to be more predictive of power acquisition. Indeed it is through the importation of new executives that organizations adjust to environmental demands and redistribute power throughout organizations, as indicated by the studies supporting proposition nine above.

Power Motivation and Managerial Effectiveness

The research on the need for dominance reviewed above and the research by Miner (1978) and by McClelland (1985) and their associates strongly suggests that in hierarchical organizations, or in hierarchical parts of organizations, that managers with a high degree of power motivation are indeed necessary for such organizations to be managed effectively. If this inference is valid we have a dilemma of some importance. According to our current state of knowledge, high power–motivated managers may either exercise power openly and supportively in the interest of the organization and its members or alternatively, high power–motivated individuals may exercise power coercively in their own self-interest or that of their own subunits. There is now some research, reviewed above, to suggest that individuals who shun the exercise of coercive power and who favor the exercise of power in an intendedly rational and supportive manner may be identified at the time of selection into either the organization or into managerial ranks.

First, McClelland's findings strongly suggest that individuals high on power motivation and also high on power inhibition are generally likely to use power tactics that are open and rationally intended. These findings also suggest that individuals who are high on the power motive and low on activity inhibition are more likely to use covert and coercive power tactics. While the evidence for this finding is only suggestive at this time, it is indeed sufficient to warrant additional research.

Second, Kipnis (1976) and a number of other investigators (cf. Tedeschi et al., 1970) have shown empirically in a number of laboratory and field studies that the exercise of coercive power is inversely related to self-confidence and self-esteem. Kipnis (1976) has also shown in a number of laboratory and field studies that internal locus of control is inversely related to the use of coercive power tactics. That is, internally oriented individuals are more likely to use open and supportive means of influencing others and externally oriented individuals are more likely to use arbitrary and harsh means to influence others.

We speculate that it is possible to couple organizational policies, socialization practices, and norms that stimulate and reinforce the use of overt-noncoercive power tactics with selection of power striving managers with high self-esteem, internal locus of control, and high power inhibition. This combination of management practices, norms, and selection criteria would go a long way in achieving the idealized kind of organization described above. Further, we expect that the behavior of managers thus selected would be emulated throughout the organization. Thus, we believe that it is possible to design organizations and select managers to foster an organizational culture that favors the open, constructive, and intendedly rational exercise of power by the power holders.

An alternative perspective would argue that power striving predispositions on the part of managers are only required in certain kinds of positions. There is reason to believe from the above review of the literature (Proposition 13) that at lower levels where managerial work is largely technically based, power-striving predispositions may not be necessary for managerial or organizational effectiveness. It is also likely that power-striving behavior will be less aroused in organic organizations. Organic organizations make issues of control, influence, and leadership less salient. However, organic organizations are also less constraining. Thus, in organic organizations there are two competing forces at work. First, power-striving behavior is likely to be aroused less frequently. However, in those instances when such arousal does occur, power strivers will be less constrained in their pursuit of power. Even in organic organizations there will be some subunits that of necessity must be organized hierarchically and formalized bureaucratically, to some extent. As organic organizations become larger, there is an inevitable need for some division of authority and for hierarchical stratification and differentiation. Thus, even in organic organizations, there will be positions that confer on their incumbents significant power over others. We speculate that power-striving individuals are likely to gain such positions, even in organic organizations.

In contrast, bureaucratic organizations arouse power-striving behavior and at the same time constrain such behavior. Further, the hierarchical structure of bureaucratic organizations is likely to encourage the use of coercive power by those in positions of formal authority. This characteristic of bureaucratic organizations is discussed in more detail below in the section entitled "Power Arousing Properties of Formal Organizations."

The possibility that power-striving motivation may be required in some positions or some organizations and not in others is worthy of future research. Such research requires analysis of position requirements. Selection based on such research would be aimed at matching managerial motives and skills to position requirements, rather than selecting *all* managers on the basis of power motives and skills as well as other position requirements. Medcof (1985) has provided a theoretical framework that predicts appropriate power motivation profiles in different kinds of organizations and in different parts of the organization.

Leadership

Theory and evidence concerning predispositions to acquire and exercise power also have implications for leadership theory and practice. As shown earlier, individuals who are high in dominance or in power motivation are likely to be more successful and possibly more effective leaders. This should not come as a surprise given the nature of managerial work and the situations under which the exercise of leadership occurs. House and Baetz (1979) speculate that there are certain properties of *all* leadership situations that are present to a significant degree, and relatively invariant. Consequently, there are likely to be specific traits required in most, if not all, leadership situations. First, leadership always takes place with respect to others. Therefore, social skills are likely always to be needed if attempted influence acts are to be viewed as acceptable by followers. Second, leadership requires a predisposition to be influential. Therefore, such traits as dominance or the need for power are also hypothesized to be associated with leadership.

Recent research by House, Woycke, and Fodor (1986) illustrates the importance of power motivation as it relates to charismatic leadership of U.S. presidents. We asked eight political historians to classify U.S. presidents as charismatic or noncharismatic with respect to their cabinet members. A charismatic leader was defined as one who induces a high degree of loyalty, commitment, and devotion to the leader; identification with the leader and the leader's mission; emulation of the leader's values, goals and behavior; a sense of self-esteem from relationships with the leader and his mission; and, an exceptionally high degree of trust in the leader and the correctness of his beliefs.

Seven of the eight historians agreed on the classification of six charismatic and six noncharismatic U.S. Presidents. The charismatic presidents were Jefferson, Jackson, Lincoln, Theodore R. Roosevelt, Franklin D. Roosevelt, and Kennedy. The noncharismatic presidents were Tyler, Pierce, Buchanan, Arthur, Harding, and Coolidge. Biographies of these presidents and of their cabinet members were content analyzed to determine differences between charismatic leaders and noncharismatic leaders with respect to their effects on followers. The biographies of cabinet members reporting to charismatic presidents were found to have significantly more expressions of positive effect toward these presidents.

The inaugural addresses of the presidents were content analyzed to determine whether charismatic presidents evidenced different motives than noncharismatic presidents. The achievement, power, and affiliation motives were coded according to the major theme statements following Donley and Winter (1970). This coding clearly indicated that charismatic presidents have a consistent motive pattern that distinguishes them from noncharismatic presidents. Specifically, the charismatic leaders were, as a group, one half standard deviation higher on *both* the need for achievement and the need for power as reflected in the inaugural addresses (p < .001).

All six charismatic presidents were either reelected or assassinated during their first term. Only one of the six noncharismatics was reelected and none were assassinated. Thus this study clearly indicates that the power motive and the achievement motive are implicated in presidential reelection rate and the attribution of charisma.

Using previously collected opinions of political historians toward presidents (Maranell, 1970), it was found that charismatic presidents are viewed by political historians as engaging in significantly stronger actions, being more prestigious, more proactive, more flexible, and having accomplished more in their administrations.

Despite the rather substantial evidence reviewed above concerning dominance, managerial motivation (Miner, 1978) and inhibited power motivation as predictors of leader emergence and effectiveness, current theories do not include any of these variables as predictors of leader behavior or leader effectiveness.

Research concerning the inhibited power motive pattern, that is the combinations of high need for power together with high power inhibition, suggests that this motive pattern is predictive of the exercise of power that is open, constructive, and in the interest of the broader collectivity rather than in the power holder's self interest. Further, this research suggests that such exercise of power will be supportive rather than manipulative or coercive. While the research to date shows this motive pattern to be predictive of leader success and suggests it might also be predictive of leader effectiveness, additional research is required.

Research to date has not been concerned with the prediction of the specific kinds of leader behavior that are associated with the inhibited power motive. If indeed the prior research involving the inhibited power motive pattern is replicated in future research, it would be very useful to know the kinds of leader behavior implicated in this motive pattern. Such knowledge would be useful for both managerial selection and training purposes.

Managerial Training

A related practical issue concerns the efficacy of managerial training. Two issues are of concern here. First, whether individuals can be trained in power motivation, and second whether individuals high in power motivation can be trained to engage in the exercise of power in a positive manner and to avoid the exercise of power negatively. By positive exercise of power we mean power that is exercised in the interest of the broader collectivity as well as in the interest of power holders. Further, the positive exercise of power is characterized by being overt rather than covert, intendedly rational rather than political, and supportive rather than punitive. By negative exercise of power we mean power that is exercised covertly, politically, and/or coercively in the personal self-interest of the power holder rather than the interest of broader collectivity.

There is suggestive evidence that it is possible through training in power motivation to help individuals to be more effective in their personal lives (Fersch, 1971), to overcome problems of alcoholism (McClelland, 1977) and to increase managerial effectiveness (Miner, 1978). In prior research McClelland (1977) found that heavy drinking was a response to a strong impulsive need for power and that drinking was one means whereby alcoholics could satisfy their power needs. McClelland (1977) compared the effects of a standard alcoholic therapy program to a program that consisted of the standard treatment plus power motivation training. After the standard treatment, about one-quarter of the alcoholics were considered to have improved significantly a year later. In contrast, the standard treatment combined with power motivation training yielded a 50% improvement rate.

In another training program, McClelland, Rhines, Smith and Kristensen (1975) attempted to change the power motive of staff members or neighborhood workers associated with community action agencies. The objective of the program was to help participants to experience ways of strengthening their organization by making others feel strong, by cooperating rather than competing, by confronting and resolving conflicts and difficulties rather than denying them, and by stimulating others to take pro-active, strong action rather than be passive. Three types of inputs were included in the training—namely increasing power motive strength, improving perceived probability of success, and emphasizing the importance of becoming more effective influencers. The first of these inputs concerns the need for power, whereas the latter two inputs attempted to increase cognitions relevant to effective use of power. 52% of those who had been trained were judged to have improved in performance over how they had behaved previously. A baseline figure was estimated by calculating the percentage who improved from two agencies that began but did not complete the power motivation training. Only 25% of these latter staff members were judged by an interviewer to have improved their performance, although the interviewer had no way of knowing that the power motivation training in this instances had been incomplete.

McClelland and Burnham (1976) trained managers who were members of the same company and operated in 16 sales districts in different parts of the country. The effectiveness of the training was assessed by a comparison of how their subordinates perceived the organizational climate in their districts before and after their managers were trained. After the training program, the salesmen reported feeling a greater sense of responsibility, more organizational clarity, and greater team spirit. Further, post-training increases in sales were found to be associated with sales districts in which climate and morale scores improved significantly.

While these findings are suggestive, they must be viewed with caution since there were not adequate control groups in any of these studies.

Miner (1978) reviewed the results of 17 evaluations of training in managerial motivation. In 9 of these evaluations, comparisons were made with control groups. As Miner points out, managerial motivation, as measured by the Miner Sentence Completion Scale, measures positive emotions associated with various role prescriptions which have been identified as general characteristics of managerial positions in bureaucratic settings.

The evaluations of the training program designed to increase positive affect toward managerial role activity demonstrated positive motivational changes in 16 of 17 instances. Further, in all cases where control groups were utilized, change could be attributed to the training. The most consistent effect occurred with respect to assertiveness and power motivation. In addition, increased positive attitudes toward authority and desire to perform administrative duties appeared in over half of the studies. Significant changes occurred among female subjects as well as males.

Miner (1978) points out that McClelland's views on achievement and power motivation appear to be conceptually similar to his views with respect to managerial motivation. Thus, the findings by McClelland and his associates, together with the findings by Miner and his associates, strongly suggest that training can have an impact on motivation, as measured by projective tests.

The second issue, whether people high in power motivation can be trained to exercise power in socially positive ways, has not been systematically investigated. However, several managerial consulting firms offer seminars to train managers in the use of power in an open, noncoercive manner. One of the more prominent of these consulting firms is the McBer Corp. which was founded by David McClelland.

Decision Making

Another theoretical issue concerns organizational decision making. There is little research concerning the effects of power striving predispositions on the decision-making behavior of individuals. However, laboratory experimental evidence clearly indicates that high Machs are likely to attempt to manipulate decision making in their self-interest rather than the interest of the organizations or organizational members. Further, there are laboratory studies that demonstrate that individuals high in the need for power suppress open decision making (Fodor & Smith, 1982) and favor ingratiators—yes men and yes women (Fodor & Farrow, 1979). Thus, laboratory findings suggest that there are likely to be significant dysfunctional behaviors associated with Machiavellianism and with the need for power when it comes to decision making.

These laboratory experiments did not control for personality traits that are likely to serve as power inhibitors such as power inhibition, locus of control, or self-esteem. Further, these studies are based on university students and not mature and experienced managers. Nevertheless, these findings are suggestive of the decision making behavior we might expect from high Machs and uninhibited power-oriented managers.

There is some indirect evidence relevant to decision making based on the behavior of power-motivated U.S. presidents. Using TAT scores derived from twentieth century presidential inaugural addresses, Winter and Stewart (1977) found that the power motivation of twentieth century presidents was predictive of frequency of assassination attempts on the presidents ($r = .81$, $p < .01$), frequency of U.S. entry into war ($r = .62$, $p < .01$), and of selection of cabinet members who had previous legislative or cabinet experience ($p < .05$). In contrast, achievement motivation among presidents was inversely predictive of selection of such cabinet members ($-.85$, $p < .01$) and affiliative motivation among presidents was correlated .80 ($p < .01$) with frequency of entering into arms limitation agreements. These findings show that high power–motivated presidents attract more violent opposition to themselves, have more aggressive foreign policies, and favor cabinet members who are politically rather than academically or business oriented. We find these findings to be impressive for several reasons. First, they are based on objective indicators rather than sources that might reflect measurement error. Second they deal with extremely important socially relevant outcomes. Finally, they are predictive, not correlational, in nature.

Power Arousing Properties of Formal Organizations

Another implication of the above review of the literature is that organizational settings are likely to differ with respect to their power arousing properties. Bureaucratic organizations stress symbols of power, hierarchical differentiation, social stratification between hierarchical levels, identification with positions, organizational loyalty rather than loyalty to a professional or personal code of ethics, and reliance on formal authority rather than personal expertise and appeal to reason. We argue that these bureaucratic aspects of organizations arouse, facilitate and psychologically justify the acquisition and use of *coercive* power.

Some individuals are predisposed toward the exercise of coercion towards others. Preliminary findings concerning the power inhibition construct are relevant to the exercise of coercion. We speculate that highly bureaucratic organizations are likely to attract persons who are high in power motivation and low in power inhibition. In such organizations the motivation of individuals who have a predisposition to acquire and use power coercively will be aroused to do so. Further, the use of coercive power in the form of formal authority will be encouraged by the bureaucratic aspects of organizations for several reasons.

Legitimate authority has been used to justify the exercise of coercion and to induce targets to inflict pain on and coerce others whom they otherwise would not coerce. For example, Berkowitz (1983) describes the experiences of Adolf Eichmann, head of the Jewish office in the Gestapo. In a meeting in January, 1942, Eichmann and a group of top-level civil servants in the Nazi government met to coordinate efforts in the Final Solution, Hitler's plan to exterminate the Jews of Europe. Berkowitz quotes Arendt (1963) as follows:

> There was another reason that made the day . . . unforgettable for Eichmann. Although he had been doing his best right along to help the final solution, he had still harbored some doubts about 'such a bloody solution through violence' and these doubts had now been dispelled. 'Here now . . . the most prominent people had spoken. . . . Not only Hitler . . . not just the SS or the Party, but the elite of the good old Civil Service were vying and fighting with each other for the honor of taking a lead in these bloody matters. At that moment, I sensed a kind of Pontius Pilate feeling, for I felt free of all guilt.' (Arendt, 1963, p. 101, cited in Berkowitz, 1980)

Eichmann stated during his war crime trial that his conscience was soothed because "he could see no one, no one at all, who actually was against the Final Solution" (Arendt, 1963, p. 103, cited in Berkowitz, 1983).

Berkowitz argues that because of the legitimated authority of the Nazi government it was possible for Eichmann to rationalize his actions as being those of a law-abiding citizen. He was able to tell himself and others that he did as he was told, obeying not only orders but also the law. Thus, acting as a citizen and as a soldier in obeying the law provided Eichmann with a psychological justification for carrying out his ruthless activities and ordering millions of Jews to their death.

Similar reactions to legitimate authority have been demonstrated in a famous series of laboratory experiments by Milgram (1963). In these studies, it was shown that over 65% of experimental subjects could be quite readily induced to exercise extreme and severe coercion over targets. This occurred under conditions where the subjects believed the targets were suffering severe pain from repeated high voltage electric shocks. Subjects continued to shock their victims (the experimental confederate) while the victim was demanding to be released from the experimental electric-shock chair, was screaming of severe pain, proclaiming that he had a weak heart, and that he was in serious danger. This occurred when the experimenter appealed to the duty of the experimental subject to follow the legitimate directions of the experimenter.

There are several forces associated with the use of legitimate authority that makes the justification of coercion possible. First, when individuals respond to the directives of authorities, they are less likely to assume personal responsibility for the outcomes of their compliance and thus less likely to experience guilt for such consequences. Second, when coercing others in response to a legitimate authoritative direction, it is possible to justify the action in the name of one's position or one's duty, rather than action taken as a result of one's own volition. "I don't like to punish others, but as foreman it is my duty to enforce discipline." Third, clothing position holders in symbols of legitimate authority such as titles, badges, and uniforms differentiates them from their targets, and further, identifies the action of the position holder with the position rather than the person. This process of "deindividuation" has been shown in a number of studies to have the effect of reducing subjects' inhibition to use coercion toward others (cf. Diener, 1980 for a review of this literature). Fourth, the use of authority establishes a status differentiation between the target and the authority holder and thus permits the authority holder to view targets of lower status as inferior. Fifth, if the target is a member of a well defined group (the enemy, the union, the blue-collar workers) the authority holder can rationalize the effects of coercion as being justified because that coercion is directed toward a member of an impersonal group rather than toward an individual who has feelings and sensitivities. Thus, when targets are "dehumanized" or even "depersonalized" authority holders feel less inhibited in the use of coercion toward the targets.

Proposition 25: Under conditions where authority holders have strong identification with their roles and where authority holders and targets are socially stratified, there will be fewer inhibitions against the use of coercion by authority holders than when such conditions do not exist.

The need for power, coupled with low-power inhibition, is likely to predispose one to engage in authoritarian behavior in dealing with others and to be impulsively aggressive toward others. Such behavior is encouraged by bureaucratic features of organizations such as hierarchical differentiation and social stratification. This reasoning suggests the following propositions.

Proposition 26: The more bureaucratic the organization, the more individuals who have a high need for power coupled with low activity inhibition are likely to be authoritarian in dealing with followers and to be impulsively aggressive toward others.

This proposition has significant implications for understanding behavior in organizations. It suggests several corollary propositions:

Proposition 27: The greater the social stratification resulting from the division of authority throughout the hierarchy, the greater the use of coercion by higher level authority holders as a means of obtaining compliance from lower level targets.

Proposition 28: The more an authority holder has internalized the norms of egalitarian occupational reference groups (such as professional associations or unions) the less likely he or she will be to use coercion as a means of obtaining compliance from others who are members of the *same* group.

Proposition 29: The more an authority holder identifies with the organization the more he or she will use coercion as a means of obtaining the compliance of lower status targets.

These propositions suggests that we would find less use of coercion in organic than mechanistic-bureaucratic organizations, since organic organizations are less stratified socially and hierarchically and since formal positions in organic organizations are less well defined. These propositions further explain why labor unrest is more common in mechanistic organizations. In mechanistic organizations managers have clear symbols of authority and hierarchical stratification is enforced. Under such conditions the use of coercion is likely to be high. It is in response to coercion and feelings of powerlessness that much labor unrest occurs.

The above propositions also suggest that coercion is less likely to be used by employees referred to in the sociological literature as cosmopolitans or "cosmos" (Gouldner, 1957, 1958) since such employees identify less with their employing organizations than they do with their professional associations and other more egalitarian reference groups.

The above propositions suggest, by implication, the variables that can be managed to minimize the use of coercion. For example, symbols of authority and status separation are clearly amenable to management. Under conditions where the organizational technology and environment requires a high degree of formalization, stratification between hierarchial levels and strong identification with the organization on the part of managers, one can expect abuses of authority to occur more frequently. One prescriptive implication of this argument is that under these conditions jurisdictional rules and appeal procedures need to be established to prevent abuses of legitimate authority and to resolve conflicts between superiors and subordinates.

Resistance to Power Redistribution and Organizational Inertia

Individuals who possess expertise or who control critical resources or information, or individuals in positions of authority, are not only in a position to assert power successfully, but are also in a position to maintain and increase their current level of power. Individuals who have gained positions of power by virtue of the predisposition to attain and exercise power will strive to retain their power. Further, since they will already have acquired such power, these individuals are in a favored position to insure that their power continues.

As we have shown, individuals with strong predispositions to acquire power are more likely to be self-selected or promoted to positions of significant formal authority-institutionalized power. The combination of motives and skills possessed by such individuals, coupled with the institutionalization of power, provides those in power with significant resources to maintain the status quo and thus to maintain their own power.

As a result of the predisposition of power holders to retain power, we would expect power distributions within an organization to become stable over time and not to change unless there are major shifts in environmental or technological demands. Even then, because of the tendency for influential individuals to retain or enhance their power, we would expect power distributions within organizations to change slowly and we would expect such changes to favor the power holders rather than those with little power.

Major shifts in the balance of power are not likely to come about without replacing the power holders (Tushman & Romanelli, 1985). Such replacement is unlikely unless there are major shifts in the environment or technology. Environmental shifts involve what Miller and Friesen (1984) call quantum changes. Technological changes are what Tushman and Romanelli (1985) call technological discontinuities. As Tushman and Romanelli argue, such discontinuities can have competence enhancing or competence destroying effects on organizations.

When an environmental or technological shifts enhance the competence of those in power, the shift favors the maintenance of the status quo. Of course such shifts may bring about a marginal redistribution of power by permitting some lower or middle level managers (whose competence is enhanced by the environmental change) to gain power. However, competence-enhancing shifts are most likely to result in improved organizational performance. Such shifts are therefore not likely to bring about the replacement of top managers or redistribution of power because it is primarily as a result of problematic environments, not competence-enhancing environments, that major power redistribution at top levels of organizations occur (see Proposition 7).

When environmental discontinuities are competence destroying, those within the organizations whose competence has been destroyed or decreased are likely to lose power. However, such power redistribution is usually the result of prolonged debate, disagreement and conflict. Major redistributions of power are likely to be the outcome of long and hard fought battles among members of the organization's dominant coalitions (Narayan & Fahey, 1982). Those who are in possession of institutional power have the advantage of the will and skill of power strivers *plus* the advantage of being in positions of institutionalized power. Some of these advantages are connections with influential others within the organization and influential others in the organizations' environment, control of resources, control of strategic information, control of decision processes and decision premises and frequently the power that comes with consensus among the dominant coalition; normally the top management team.

Thus the dominant coalition is in a position to suppress dissent, eliminate dissenters, and divide (and conquer) potential rebels or critics. We recognize that such tactics cannot preserve the existing order indefinitely in the face of major discontinuities. However, in the short-term (that may be many years, cf. Miller & Friesen, 1984) the established order clearly has the advantage.

Further, because of barriers to entry into the competitive market place, the dominant coalition is in a position to alter organizational domains, diversify products and markets, and alter the organizational design in such a way that the organizational structure will be adjusted to the changed environment *without* a major distribution of power *at the top* of the organization. Reorganizations that involve major structural changes and do not involve replacement or reshuffling of the top management team would be one class of such adjustments. Reorganizations that involve major decentralization, centralization, divisionalization, the creation of new corporate staff groups and the redistribution of responsibilities to existing functional areas can also be examples of power maintenance tactics. Thus, in hierarchical organizations there are strong forces acting to preserve the status quo. Given other forces toward inertia, such as prior commitments, sunk costs, bureaucratization, and tendency for incremental decision making, the widely observed inertia in organizations can be understood (Hannan & Freeman, 1977). This reasoning suggests:

Proposition 30:   When there is a change in the critical contingencies facing an organization, the greater the institutionalization of power the longer the time lag in the redistribution of power to meet the new performance demands facing the organization.

Proposition 31:   Changes in the distribution of power will favor those with the greatest power and will disfavor those with the least power in the short term.

These propositions explain the tendency of many organizations to resist major changes and to perpetuate the status quo. There appear to be few well-known organizational practices or mechanisms to offset these forces toward the preservation of the status quo.

Pfeffer and Salancik (1977) suggest several ways of making the power structure more permeable. These are: broadly disseminate critical information throughout the organization with respect to organizational actions, outcomes, and alternatives; adjust the formal structure to informal patterns of behavior; rotate those in influential positions; create multiple centers of power and control; engage operating personnel in the planning process by use of task forces or planning groups; encourage cross sectional and cross level interaction by use of physical layout and organizational design; reward managers for environmental scanning and planning; and, differentiate and decouple parts of the organization with differing interests or constituencies when communication or technical demands are not tightly interconnected. As Pfeffer and Salancik (1977) point out, some organizations have adopted parts of the above solution but none have employed the whole design.

Conditions that Foster Empowerment and the Positive Use of Power

In addition to minimizing or removing the conditions that foster manipulative and coercive use of power, it is also theoretically possible to establish conditions that foster the exercise of power in a positive way. Kanter (1987), has argued that individuals in organizations use power negatively. Kipnis (1976) has argued theoretically and demonstrated empirically, that individuals who feel powerless are more likely to use power in a harsher and more assertive manner. His findings indicate that individuals with low self-esteem, low confidence in their ability to influence others, and low internality as measured by the Locus of Control (Rotter, 1966) are inclined to use power negatively. We take these findings to indicate that individuals who feel powerless or helpless in their situations are more likely to use harsher means of power than individuals who feel confident and in control of their environment—that is, individuals who feel empowered.

There are several management practices that can be employed to empower organizational members. First, appropriate selection is required. Individuals need to be selected who have the abilities to perform their task demands. Frequently, individuals need to assert social influence, or informal power, in order to accomplish their task objective. Clearly, linguistic and social influence skills should be considered in addition to the technical skills required to do particular tasks. We believe that it is possible to use the information in the literature reviewed above to guide the selection of individuals with requisite social influence predispositions and skills.

For positions that require the use of a significant amount of social influence, we would suggest the use of several measures of the power predispositions used above. First, we would recommend that individuals be selected who are high on the inhibited power motive, high on the California Personality Inventory dominance scale, and low on the Machiavellian scale. It is possible that these scales may not adequately measure or predict power predispositions when respondents know that their responses to these scales are being used for selection purposes. Further research is required to determine if this is indeed the case. If so, selection of people who would be strongly inclined to exercise power in a positive manner may require the development of tests specifically designed with the demand characteristics of the selection setting in mind.

The cultural values, or norms, stressed by management will also affect the degree to which organizational members feel empowered. A culture that stresses self-determination—a positive "can do" attitude, collaboration rather than competition or conflict, and high performance standards, is likely to cause organizational members to feel empowered and to reinforce self confidence, and internality.

Individual feelings of empowerment are likely determined to a very substantial degree by the leadership style of the individual's immediate superior. Superiors who employ leadership styles characterized by expression of confidence in subordinates and high performance expectations for subordinates would likely cause such subordinates to have high confidence in and expectations for themselves (Rosenthal & Jacobson, 1968; House, 1977; Eden & Ravid, 1982). There is substantial evidence to support this speculation (cf. House & Singh, 1987, for a review of this literature; Smith, 1984; Howell, 1985; Bass, 1985; Avolio & Bass, 1985). We further speculate that individuals will feel empowered partially to the extent that they have opportunities to influence decisions and job conditions that directly affect them. Further, autonomy from bureaucratic constraint and supervision, especially from authoritarian supervision, is likely to cause individuals to have increased feelings of empowerment.

Policies that stress nondiscrimination and meritocracy rather than policies that allocate opportunities and rewards on the basis of ascribed status characteristics such as gender, race, or religion, are likely to contribute generalized feelings of empowerment among organizational members.

Socialization into the values of such a culture would also likely enhance feelings of empowerment. Such socialization involves early training and opportunities for on the job development, supervision by leaders who by their own personal behavior enact the norms described above, and leaders who have high expectations for and confidence in their followers.

Finally, training can be provided to ensure that organizational members have the necessary expertise to perform both the technical and social skills required to accomplish their tasks. If such training were effective, it would likely result in increased task confidence. Further, if the above practices were applied simultaneously and consistently, we speculate that they would result in increased generalized self-esteem for organizational members.

Thus, selection, leadership, socialization, training, and the development of organizational culture are suggested here as means for fostering the positive use of power in organizations.

Power Acquisition and Distribution in an Evolutionary Context[3]

Finally, we present some observations on how our understanding of organizational behavior may be improved by an explicit and systematic examination of the processes that affect the evolution of power distributions in complex organizations. Historically, students of organizational behavior have usually tried to understand *why* specific empirical regularities relating to power acquisition and distributions are observed in organizations. Instead, we ask here *how* these empirical regularities developed? Such a view stresses a more historical and evolutionary view of organizational behavior than has traditionally been the case. These observations are somewhat speculative, since not much theoretical and empirical work has been done in this area. Specifically, we briefly examine processes of ecological selection and their impact on patterns of power distributions.

Ecological selection.   In recent years, the ecological selection perspective has emerged as a significant theoretical approach to the study of organizational change. March (1981) and Nelson and Winter (1982) argue that behavior in organizations reflects rule following, and a significant part of organizational behavior is governed by these rules and standard operating procedures (March, 1981; Nelson & Winter, 1982). Thus, the evolution of organizational behavior and of power distributions results from the changing mix of rules and procedures in an organization's repertoire, which may itself result from some adaptive responses to changing environmental and technological demands.

Such selection processes play quite an important role in how power distributions in organizations change over time. Extant theories of intraorganizational power reviewed above argue that power in organizations accrues to those individuals or subunits that successfully deal with the critical demands or contingencies facing the organization. As the environment changes, and with it the critical contingencies, the power distribution changes and this is an important mechanism by which organizations adapt to their environments. Such change in power distribution is also normatively appropriate, and organizations whose power distribution changes too little, or inappropriately, become misaligned with their environment and are eventually selected out. Such a selection process would lead to organizations with adapted power distributions outsurviving maladapted organizations. Further, such a selection process suggests that behavior within organizations will also be governed by ecological selection processes and that individuals who have certain skills and predispositions will also be selected into or out of critical positions that confer power on their incumbents. Thus, according to this view the power distribution and the acquisition of power by individuals is a function of selection pressures imposed by the changing critical contingencies confronting the organization. Unfortunately, the ecological argument leaves individual differences out of the equation. Yet, once one considers that selection pressures favor those individuals with predispositions to acquire and exercise power, it follows that the ecology of power is not often so adaptive. Environmental change and the uncertainty that comes with it may lead to the selection of power oriented managers as well as, and perhaps even in lieu of, managers who are most competent to lead. This may be another reason why adaptive and fundamental change is so difficult to achieve in organizations.

CONCLUSION

Extant theories of power acquisition and distribution in complex organizations are primarily structural in nature. These theories focus on attributes of subunits and positions and on organizational design as explanatory variables and pay scant attention to characteristics of individuals. Further, one rather prominent theory of task design (Salancik & Pfeffer, 1978) denies the utility of individual needs as variables that explain or predict individual motivation and behavior in complex organizations. We argue here that theories of power acquisition and motivation that do not include individual differences as explanatory variables are incomplete.

In this chapter we have argued that individuals vary in their motivation to acquire power and in cognitive characteristics that theoretically facilitate power acquisition. In so doing we have speculated about how such personal characteristics interact with organizational characteristics to acquire power in complex organizations. For many of the propositions advanced here, we assert relationships at two or more levels of analysis. These propositions serve to integrate constructs at the individual level with constructs at the position, subunit, or organizational level of analysis. Several theoretical, social, and practical implications are inferred from these propositions. We believe that incorporating individual difference variables into theories of power acquisition will improve the explanatory and predictive accuracy of such theories.

ACKNOWLEDGMENTS

I am indebted to Jitendra V. Singh, Alan Saks, and Barry M. Staw for their helpful comments on an earlier draft of this paper. I am also indebted to Blake Ashforth, Joel Baum, Tina Madan, and John Usher for their helpful assistance in conducting a literature review.
This paper was made possible by Grant number 410-84-0095-R2 from the Social Sciences Humanities Research Council of Canada.

NOTES

1. A lengthier review of the literature concerned with the power motive is presented in "Organizational Behavior: Some New Directions for I/O Psychology," by R.J. House and J.V. Singh, to appear in the *Annual Review of Psychology,* L. Porter and M. Rosenzweig, (Eds.), 1987.

2. There have been a number of methods by which TAT protocals have been operationalized and interpreted. Veroff and Veroff (1972) have interpreted their original measure of need for power as a reflection of individuals' fear of being powerless—fear of power. Uleman scored TAT protocols differently and labled his measure need for influence which he interpreted as reflecting a predisposition to use power in a nondomineering manner. Winter (1973) distinguished between the need for power, fear of and hope for power. McClelland and Burnham (1976) distinguish socialized power (high need for power and high power inhibition) from personalized power (high need for power and low inhibition). Finally, McClelland (1985) and McClelland and Boyatzis (1982) have developed an independent measure of inhibition to use power in a domineering and self-aggrandizing way. Individuals high on this measure, which they label as activity inhibition, and high on need for power using Winter's (1973) scoring system are referred to here as having an inhibited power motive in this paper. The research reviewed here is based on studies employing measures which are inferred by the writer to reflect the uninhibited versus the inhibited power motive (e.g., Medcof, 1981) for a critical review of the above scoring system and their construct validity.

   Medcof (1985) has described a typology of organizational situations and a typology of personality profiles and argues that there are organizational situations that call for, or require, particular personality profiles for effective managerial performance. He further argues that situational-personality mismatches will result in individual maladjustment and ineffective managerial performance.

3. This section draws heavily on House and Singh (1987).

REFERENCES

Allen, M.P. (1981a). Power and privilege in the large corporation: Corporate control and managerial compensation. *American Journal of Sociology, 86,* 1112–1123.

Allen, M.P. (1981b). Managerial power and tenure in the large corporation, *Social Forces,* *60,* 482–94.

Allen, M.P., & Panian, S.K. (1982). Power, performance and succession in the large corporation. *Administrative Science Quarterly, 27,* 538–547.

Allen, R.W., Madison, D.L., Porter, L.W., Renwick, P.A., & Mayes, B.T. (1979) Organizational politics: Tactics and characteristics of its actors. *California Management Review, 22,* 77–83.

Arendt, H. (1963). *Eichmann in Jerusalem.* New York: Viking.

Argyris, C. (1957). *Personality and Organization.* New York: Harper and Row.

Astley, W.G. (1979). *Political and apolitical faces of organizational power,* Paper presented at the Annual Meeting of the Academy of Management, Atlanta, GA.

Avoloi, B.J., & Bass, B.M. (1985). *Charisma and beyond.* Presented at Biannual Symposium, Lead. Lubbock, TX.

Bacharach, S.B., & Lawler, E.J. (1980). *Power and politics in organizations,* Washington: Jossey-Bass Publishers.

Bagozzi, R.P., & Phillips, L.W. (1982). Representing and testing organizational theories: A holistic construal. *Administrative Science Quarterly, 77,* 459–489.

Bandura, A. (1979). *Social learning theory.* Englewood Cliffs, NJ: Prentice-Hall.

Barchas, P.R., & Fisek, M.H. (1984). Hierarchical differentiation in newly formed groups of rachus and humans. In N.R. Barchus (Ed.), 22–100. *Social Hierarchies: Essays towards a socio-psychological perspective.* Freeport, CT: Greenwood Press.

Barron, F., & Egan, D. (1968). Leaders and innovators in Irish management. *Journal of Management Studies* (Dublin), *5,* 41–60.

Bass, B.M. (1985). *Leadership and performance beyond expectations.* New York: Free Press.

Baumgartel, H. (1956). Leadership, motivations, and attitudes in research laboratories. *Journal of Social Issues, 12,* 24–321.

Bennis, W. (1966). *Changing Organizations.* New York: McGraw-Hill.

Berkowitz, L., & Haythorn W. (1955). *The relationship of dominance to leadership choice.* Research Laboratory, AF Personnel and Training Reserve Center, Randolf AF Base, CRL-LN-55-58.

Berkowitz, L. (1983). Imitation, conformity and compliance. In B.M. Staw (Ed.), *Psychological Foundations of Organizational Behavior,* second edition, Glenview, IL: Scott, Foresman & Company.

Berlyne, D.E. (1967). Arousal and reinforcement. In D. Levine (Ed.), *Nebraska symposium on motivation.* Lincoln: University of Nebraska Press.

Blackburn, R.S. (1981). Lower participant power: Toward a conceptual integration. *Academy of Management Review, 6,* 127–132.

Borgatta, E.F. (1961). Role-playing specifications, personality and performance. *Sociometry, 24,* 3, 218–233.

Bouchard, T. (1984). Twins reared together and apart: What they tell us about human diversity, in *Individuality and Determinism,* S.W. Fox (Ed.), Plenum Publishing, 147–184.

Brass, D.J. (1984). Being in the right place: A structural analysis of individual influence in an organization. *Administrative Science Quarterly, 29,* 518–539.

Brass, D.J. (1985). Technology and the structuring of jobs: Employee satisfaction, performance, and influence. *Organizational Behavior and Human Decision Processes, 35,* 216–240.

Brown, M.C. (1982). Administrative succession and organizational performance: The succession effect. *Administrative Science Quarterly, 29,* 245–273.

Brown, J.S., Grant, C.W., & Patton, M.J. (1981). A CPI comparison of engineers and managers. *Journal of Vocational Behavior, 4,* 145–153.

Buss, D.M., & Craik, K.H. (1983). Act prediction and the conceptual analysis of personality scales: Indices of act density, bipolarity, and extensity. *Journal of Personality and Social Psychology, 45,* 1081–1095.

Chance, M.R.A. (1967). Attention structure as the basis of primate rank orders. *Man, 2,* 503–518.

Chase, I.D. (1984). Social process and hierarchy formation in small groups: A comparative perspective. *American Sociological Review, 45,* 905–924.

Christie, R., & Geis, F.L. (1970). *Studies in Machieavellianism.* New York: Academic Press.

Chursmir, L.H. (1986). Personalized versus socialized power needs among working women and men. *Human Relations, 39,* 149–160.

Chursmir, L.H., & Parker, B. (1984). Dimensions of need for power: Personalized versus socialized power in female and male managers. *Sex Roles, 11,* 759–769.

Coates, J. (1984). *Personality and situational variables as determinants of the distribution of power in a company organization.* Ph.D. dissertation. Toronto: University of Toronto.

Comrey, A.L., High, W.S. and Wilson, R.D. (1955). Factors influencing organizational effectiveness, VI. A survey of aircraft supervisor. *Personnel Psychology, 8,* 245–257.

Comstock, D.E., & Scott, W.R. (1977). Technology and the structure of subunits: Distinguished individual and workgroup effects. *Administrative Science Quarterly, 22,* 177–202.

Crozier, M. (1964). *The bureaucratic phenomenon.* Chicago: University of Chicago Press.

Cummin, P. (1967). TAT correlates of executive performance. *Journal of Applied Psychology, 51,* 78–81.

Daft, R.L. (1983). *Organization theory and design.* St. Paul, MN: West Publishing Company.

Davidson, R.J., Saron, C., & McClelland, D.C. (1980). Effects of personality and semantic content of stimuli on augmenting and reducing in the event-related potential. *Biological Psychology, 11,* 249–255.

Diener, E. (1980). Deindividuation: The absence of self awareness and self regulation in group members. In P. Paulus (Ed.), *The Psychology of group influence.* Hillsdale, NJ: Lawrence Erlbaum.

Donley, R.E., & Winter, D.G. (1970). Measuring the motives of public officials at distance: An exploratory study of American Presidents. *Behavioral Science, 15,* 227–236.

Droy, J.W., & V.M. Gluskinos, (1980). Machiavellianism and leadership. *Journal of Applied Psychology, 65,* 81–86.

Dyson, J.W., Fleitas, D.W., & Scioli, F.P. (1972). The interaction of leadership personality and decisional environments. *Journal of Social Psychology, 86,* 29–33.

Eden, D., & Ravid, G. (1982). Pygmalion versus self-expectancy: Effects of instructor—and self-expectancy on training performance. *Organizational behavior and human performance. 3,* 312–329.

Eitzen, D.S., & Yetman, N.R. (1972). Managerial change, *Science Quarterly, 17,* 110–116.

Emerson, R.M. (1962). Power-dependence relations. *American Sociological Review, 27,* 31–41.

Epstein, G.F. (1969). Machiavelli and the devil's advocate. *Journal of Personality and Social Psychology, 11,* 38–41.

Fersch, E.A., Jr. (1971). Inward bound: The motivational impact of a combined outword bound-upward bound program on adolescents from poverty families. Unpublished doctoral dissertation. Harvard University.

Fodor, E.M. (1984). The power motive and reactivity to power stresses. *Journal of Personality and Social Psychology, 47,* 853–859.

Fodor, E.M., & Farrow, D.L. (1979). The power motive as an influence on the use of power. *Journal of Personality and Social Psychology, 37,* 2091–2097.

Fodor, E.M., & Smith, T. (1982). The power motive as an influence on group decision making. *Journal of Personality and Social Psychology, 42,* 178–185.

Gamson, W.A., & Scotch, N.A. (1964). Scapegoating in baseball. *American Journal of Sociology, 70,* 69–72.

Geis, F.L., Krupat, E., & Berger, D. (1965). *Taking over in group discussion.* Unpublished manuscript. New York: New York University.

Goodacre, D.M. (1951). The use of a sociometric test and a predictor of combat unit effectiveness. *Sociometry, 14,* 148–152.

Gorecki, P.R., Dickson, A.L., & Ritzler, B.A. (1981). Convergent and concurrent validation of four measures of assertion. *Journal of Behavior Assessment, 3,* 85–91.

Gough, H.G. (1985). A work orientation scale for the California Psychological Inventory. *Journal of Applied Psychology, 70,* 505–513.

Gough, H.G. (1968). California Psychology Inventory: An Interpreter's Syllabus, Consulting Psychologists Press.

Gouldner, A.W. (1957–58). Cosmopolitans and locals: toward an analysis of latent social roles—I and II. *Administrative Science Quarterly, 2,* 281–306, 444–480.

Greer, F.L., Galanter, E.H., & Nordi, P.G. (1954). Interpersonal knowledge an individual and group effectiveness. *Journal of Abnormal and Social Psychology, 49,* 411–414.

Grusky, O. (1963). Managerial succession and organizational effectiveness. *American Journal of Sociology, 69,* 21–31.

Grusky, O. (1960). Administrative succession in formal organizations. *Social Forces, 39,* 105–115.

Hamblin, R.L., Miller, K., & Wiggins, J.A. (1961). Group morale and competence of the leader. *Sociometry, 24,* 295–311.

Hambrick, D.C. (1981). Environment, strategy, and power within top management teams. *Administrative Science Quarterly, 26,* 253–276.

Hannan, M.T., & Freeman, J. (1977). The population ecology of organizations. *American Journal of Sociology, 22,* 929–964.

Harris, T.M. (1966). Machiavellianism, judgement, independence and attitudes toward teammate in a cooperative judgement task. Unpublished doctoral dissertation, Columbia University.

Helmich, D.L. (1974). Organizational growth and succession patterns. *Academy of Management Journal, 4,* 771–775.

Helmich, D.L. (1978). Leader flows and organizational process. *Academy of Management Journal, 21,* 463–478.

Helmich, D.L., & Brown, W.E. (1972). Successor type and organizational change in the corporate enterprise. *Administrative Science Quarterly, 17,* 371–381.

Hickson, D.J., Hinings, C.R., Lee, C.A., Schneck, R.J., & Pennings, J.M. (1971). A strategic contingencies' theory of intraorganizational power. *Administrative Science Quarterly, 30,* 61–71.

Hills, F.S., & Mahoney, T.A. (1978). University budgets and organizational decision making. *Administrative Science Quarterly, 23,* 454–465.

Hinings, C.R., Hickson, D.J., Pennings, J.M., & Schneck, R.E. (1974). Structural conditions of intraorganizational power. *Administrative Science Quarterly, 19,* 22–44.

House, R.J. (1977). A 1976 theory of charismatic leadership. In J.G. Hunt & L.L. Larson (Eds.), *Leadership: The cutting edge.* Carbondale, IL: Southern Illinois University Press, 189–107.

House, R.J., Woycke, J., & Fodor, E.M. (1986). Charismatic Leadership in U.S. Presidential Office. *Academy of Management,* San Diego, CA.

House, R.J., & Baetz, M.L. (1979) Leadership: Some empirical generalizations and new research directions. *Research in Organizational Behavior, 1,* 341–423.

House, R.J., & Singh, J.V. (1987). Organizational Behavior: Some New Directions for I/O Psychology. *Annual Review of Psychology,* M.R. Rosenweig and L. Porter (Eds.), Vol. *38,* 669–718.

Howell, J.M. (1985). *A laboratory study of charismatic leadership*. Presented at Annual Meeting of Academy of Management, San Diego, CA.

Instone, D., Major, B., & Bunker, B.B. (1983). Gender, self confidence, and social influence strategies: An organizational simulation. *Journal of Personality and Social Psychology, 44*, 322–333.

James, D.R., & Soref, M. (1981). Profit constraints on managerial autonomy: Managerial theory and the unmaking of the corporation president. *American Sociological Review, 46*, 1–18.

Johnson, R.T., & Fraudson, A.N. (1962). The California psychological inventory profile of student leaders. *Personnel Guidance Journal, 41*, 343–345.

Julian, J.W., Hollander, E.P., & Regula, C.R. (1969). Endorsement of the group spokesman as a function of his source of authority, competence, and success. *Journal of Personality and Social Psychology, 11*, 42–49.

Kahn, R., & Katz, D. (1960). Leadership practices in relations to productivity and morale. In D. Cartwright and A. Zander (Eds.), *Group Dynamics Research Theory*. New York: Harper and Row.

Kanter, R.M. (1987). *Men and women of corporation*. New York: Basic books, Inc.

Kenny, D.A., & Zacarro, S.J. (1983). An estimate of variance due to traits in leadership. *Journal of Applied Psychology, 68*, 678–685.

Kipnis, D. (1976). *The Powerholders*. Chicago: The University of Chicago Press.

Kipnis, D. (1984). Technology, power and control. In *Research in the Sociology of Organizations, 3*, 125–256.

Liddle, G. (1958). The California psychological inventory and certain social and personality factors. *Journal of Educational Psychology, 6*, 291–296.

Likert, R. (1961). *New patterns of management*. New York: McGraw-Hill.

Lubatkin, M., & Chung, K. (1985). Leadership origin and organizational performance in prosperous and declining firms. *Academy of Management Proceedings*.

Mackenzie, L., (1986). Power and Virtual Positions, *Management Science*, October.

Madison, D.L., Allen, R.W., Porter, L.W., Renwick, P.A., & Mayes, B.T. (1980). Organizational politics: A exploration of manager's perceptions. *Human Relations, 33*, 79–100.

Mahoney, T.A., Sorenson, W.W., Jerdee, T.H., & Nash, A.N. (1963). Identification and prediction of management effectiveness. *Personnel Administration, 26*(4), 12–22.

Marak, G.E., Jr. (1964). The evaluation of leadership structure. *Sociometry, 27*, 164–182.

Maranell, G.M. (1970). The evaluations of presidents: An extension of Schlesinger-Poll. *Journal of History, 57*, 104–113.

March, J.G. (1981). Decisions in organizations and theories of choice. In A.H. Van de Ven & W. Joyce (Eds.), *Perspectives on Organization Design and Behavior*, New York: Wiley Interscience.

March, J.G., & Olsen, J.P. (1976). *Ambiguity and Choice in Organizations*. Bergen, Norway: Universitetsforlaget.

McAdams, D.P. (1982). Experiences of intimacy and power: Relationships between social motives and autobiographical memory. *Journal of Personality and Social Psychology, 42*, 292–302.

McAdams, D.P., and McClelland, D.C. (1983). Social motives and memory. Unpublished manuscript, Harvard University Department of Psychology and Social Relations.

McClelland, D.C. (1975). *Power: The inner experience*. New York: Irvington Press.

McClelland, D.C. (1977b). The impact of power motivation training on alcoholics. *Journal of Studies on Alcohol, 38*(1).

McClelland, D.C. (1985). *Human motivation*. Glenview, IL: Scott, Foresman.

McClelland, D.C., & Burnham, D.H. (1976). Power is the great motivator. *Harvard Business Review*, March-April, 100–110; 159–166.

McClelland, D.C., & Boyatzis, R.E. (1982). Leadership motive pattern and long term success in management. *Journal of Applied Psychology, 67*, 737–743.

McClelland, D.C., Davidson, R.J., & Saron, C. (1979). *Evoked potential indicators of the impact of the need for power on perception and learning.* Unpublished manuscript, Harvard University.

McClelland, D.C., Rhinesmith, S., and Kristensen, R. (1975). The effects of power training on community action agencies. *Journal of Applied Behavioral Science, 11*, 92–115.

McClelland, D.C., and Watson, R.I., Jr. (1973). Power motivation and risk-taking behavior *Journal of Personality, 41*, 121–139.

McEachern, W.A. (1975). *Managerial control and performance.* Lexington, MA: Heath.

Medcof, J.W. (1985). The power motive and organizational structure: A micro-macro connection, *The Canadian Journal of Administration,* Studies 2, 1, 95–113.

Megargee, E.I., Bogart, P., & Anderson, B.J. (1966). Prediction of leadership in a simulated industrial task. *Journal of Applied Psychology, 50*, 292–295.

Meyer, J.W., & Rowan, B. (1977). Institutionalized organizations: Formal structure as myth and ceremony. *American Journal of Sociology, 83*, 340–363.

Milgram, S. (1963). Behavioral studies of obedience. *Journal of Abnormal and Social Psychology, 67*, 371–78.

Miller, G., & Friesen, P.H. (1984). *Organizations: A quantum view.* Englewood Cliffs, NJ: Prentice-Hall.

Miner, J.B. (1978). Twenty years of research on role-motivation theory of managerial effectiveness. *Personnel Psychology, 31*, 739–760.

Mintzberg, H. (1973). *The nature of managerial work.* New York: Harper and Row.

Mintzberg, H. (1983). *Power in and around organizations.* Englewood Cliffs, NJ: Prentice-Hall.

Mintzberg, H., Theoret, A., & Raisinghani, D. (1974). The structure of "unstructured" decision processes. *Administrative Science Quarterly, 21*, 246–275.

Mischel, W. (1973). Toward a cognitive social learning reconceptualization of personality. *Psychological Review, 80*, 252–283.

Monson, T.C., Hesley, J.W., & Chernick, L. (1982). Specifying when personality traits can and cannot predict behavior: An alternative to abandoning the attempt to predict single-act criteria. *Journal of Personality and Social Psychology, 3*, 385–499.

Mowday, R. (1978). The exercise of upward influence in organizations. *Administrative Science Quarterly, 23*, 137–156.

Narayan, V.K., & Fahey, L. (1982). The micro politics of strategy formulation, Academy of Management Review, 7, 25–34.

Nelson, R.R., & Winter, S.G. (1982). *An Evolutionary Theory of Economic Change.* Cambridge, MA: Belknap Press of Harvard University Press.

Olsen, M.E. (1978). The process of social organization. *Power and Social Systems.* New York: Holt, Rinehart, & Winston.

Osborn, R.N., Jauch, L.R., Martin, T.N., & Glueck, W.F. (1981). The event of CEO succession, performance, and environmental conditions. *Academy of Management Journal, 24*, 183–191.

Oksenberg, L. (1968). *Machiavellianism and organization in five-man task-oriented groups.* Unpublished doctoral dissertation, Columbia University.

Pettigrew, A. (1972). Information control as a power resource. *Sociology, 6*, 187–204.

Pfeffer, J. (1981). *Power in organizations.* Marshfield, MA: Pitman Publishing Inc.

Pfeffer, J. (1983). Organizational demography. In L.L. Cummings and B. Staw (Eds.) *Research in Organizational Behavior.* Greenwich, CT: JAI Press, Inc.

Pfeffer, J., & Leblebici, H. (1973). Executive recruitment and the development of interfirm organizations. *Administrative Science Quarterly, 18*, 449–461.

Pfeffer, J., & Moore, W.L. (1980). Power and politics in university budgeting: A replication and extension. *Administrative Science Quarterly, 25,* 387–406.

Pfeffer, J., & Salancik, G.R. (1974). Organizational decision making as a political process: The case of a university budget. *Administrative Science Quarterly, 19,* 135–151.

Pfeffer, J., & Salancik, G.R. (1977). Organization design: The case for a coalition model of organizations. *Organizational Dynamics, 6,* 15–29.

Pfeffer, J., & Salancik, G.R. (1978). *The external control of organizations: A resource dependence perspective.* New York: Harper & Row.

Ray, J.J. (1981). Authoritarianism, Dominance and Assertiveness. *Journal of Personality Assessment, 45(4),* 390–397.

Reinganum, M.R. (1985). The effect of executive succession on stockholder wealth. *Administrative Science Quarterly, 30,* 46–60.

Rim, Y. (1966). Machiavellianism and decisions involving risks. *British Journal of Social and Clinical Psychology, 5,* 5–36.

Rosenthal, R., & Jacobson, I. (1968) Pygmalion in the classroom: Teacher expectations and pupils' intellectual development. New York: Holt, Rinehart, and Winston.

Rotter, J.B. (1966). Generalized expectancies for internal versus external locust of control. *Psychological Monographs,* A.D. 1–28.

Salancik, G.R., & Pfeffer, J. (1980). Effects of ownership and performance on executive "tenure" in U.S. Corporations. *Academy of Management Journal, 23,* 653–664.

Salancik, G.R., Pfeffer, J., & Kelly, J.P. (1978). A contingency model of influence in organizational decision making. *Pacific Sociological Review, 21,* 239–256.

Salancik, G.R., & Pfeffer, J. (1974). The bases and use of power in organization decision making: The case of a university budget. *Administrative Science Quarterly, 19,* 453–473.

Salancik, G.R., & Pfeffer, J. (1978). A social information processing approach to job attitudes and task design. *Administrative Science Quarterly, 23,* 224–253.

Samuelson, B.A., Galbraith, C.S., & McGuire, J.W. (1985). Organizational performance and top management turnover. *Organizational Studies, 6,* 275–291.

Savin-Williams, R.C. (1976). An ethological study of dominance formation and maintenance in a group of human adolescents. *Child Development,* 976–978.

Schendel, D., Patton, G.R., & Riggs, J. 1976. Corporate turnaround strategies: A study of profit decline and recovery. *J. General Manage.* 3(3):3–11.

Schneider, B. (1983). In L. Cummings and B. Staw (Eds.), *Interactional psychology and organizational behavior.* (1–31). Greenwich, CT: JAI Press.

Schwartz, K.B., & Menon, K. (1985). Executive succession in failing firms. *Academy of Management Journal, 28,* 680–686.

Shetty, Y.K., & Peary, N.S. (1976). Are top executives transferable across companies? *Business Horizon, 19,* 23–28.

Smith, J.E., Carson, K.P., & Alexander, R.A. (1984). Leadership: It can make a difference. *Academy of Management Journal, 27,* 765–776.

Stahl, M.J. (1983). Achievement, power and managerial motivation: Selecting managerial talent with the job choice exercise. *Personnel Psychology, 36,* 775–789.

Staw, B.M., Bell, N.E., & Clausen, J.A., (1986). The dispositional approach to job attitudes: A lifetime longitudinal test. *Administrative Science Quarterly, 31,* 56–77.

Steele, R.S. (1973). The psychological concomitants of psychogenic motive arousal in college males. Unpublished Ph. D., Harvard University.

Steele, R.S. (1977). Power motivation, activation, and inspirational speeches. *Journal of Personality.*

Stewart, A.J., & Winter, D.G. (1976). Arousal of the power motive in women. Journal of Consultation Clinical Psychology, 44, 495–496.

Stogdill, R.M. (1948). Personal factors associated with leadership: A Survey of the literature. *Journal of Psychology, 25,* 35–71.

Stogdill, R.M. (1974). *Handbook of leadership.* New York: Free Press.

Strayer, F.F., & Strayer, J. (1976). An ethological analysis of social agonism and dominance relations among preschool children. *Child Development, 47,* 980–989.

Streufert S., & Streufert, S.C. (1978). *Behavior in the complex environment.* New York: Halsted Press.

Tannenbaum, A.S. (1968). *Control in organizations.* New York: McGraw-Hill.

Tedeschi, J.T., Schlenker, B.R., & Lindskold, S. (1972). The exercise of power and influence: The source of influence. In James T. Tedeschi (Ed.), *Social Influence Processes.* Chicago: Aldine.

Thompson, J.D. (1967). *Organizations in action.* New York: McGraw-Hill.

Tolbert, P.S., & Zucker, L.G. (1983). Institutional sources of change in the formal structure of organizations: The diffusion of civil service reform, 1880–1935. *Administrative Science Quarterly, 28,* 22–39.

Tushman, M.L., & Romanelli, E. (1985). Organizational Evolution: A metamorphosis model of convergence and reorientation. In L. Cummings & B. Staw (Eds.), *Research in Organizational Behavior.* Greenwich, CT: JAI Press.

Uleman, J.S. (1972). The need for influence: Development and validation of a measure, and comparison of the need for power. *Genetic Psychology Monographs, 85,* 157–214.

Varga, K. (1975). N Achievement, n power and effectiveness of research development. *Human Relations, 28,* 571–590.

Virany, B., Tushman, M. & Romanelli, E. (1985). A longitudinal study on determinants of executive succession, Unpublished Working Paper. Columbia University.

Wainer, H.A., & Rubin, I.M. (1969). Motivation of research and development entrepreneurs: Determinants of company success. *Journal of Applied Psychology, 53,* 178–184.

Watson, D. (1971). Reinforcement theory of personality and social system: Dominance and position in a group power structure. *Journal of Personality and Social Psychology, 20,* 180–185.

Weinstein, E.A., Beckhouse, L.S., Blumstein, P.W., & Stein, R.B. (1968). Interpersonal strategies under conditions of gain or loss. *Journal of Personality, 36,* 616–634.

Weiss, H.M., & Adler, S. (1984). Personality and organizational behavior. In B.M. Staw & L.L. Cummings (Eds.), *Research in Organizational Behavior* (1–50). Greenwich, CT: JAI Press Inc.

Wilsnack, S. (1974). The effects of social drinking on women's fantasy. *Journal of Personality, 42,* 43–61.

Wilson, E.O. (1975). *Sociology: The new synthesis.* The Belknap Press of Harvard University Press, Cambridge, MA.

Winter, D.G. (1973). The need for power. In D.C. McClelland & R.S. Steels (Eds.), *Human motivation.* Morristown, NJ: General Learning Press.

Winter, D.G. (1979). *Navy leadership and management competencies: Convergence among tests, interviews and performance ratings.* Boston: McBer and Company.

Winter, D.G. (1982). *The power motive in women.* Unpublished manuscript, Wesleyan University, Department of Psychology.

Winter, D.G., & Stewart, A.J. (1978). Power motivation. In H. London & J. Exner (Eds.), *Dimensions of personality.* New York: Wiley.

Winter, D.G., & Stewart, A.J. (1977). Content analysis as a technique for assessing political leaders. In M.G. Hermann (Ed.), *A Psychological Examination of Political Leaders.* New York: Free Press.

PRINCIPLED ORGANIZATIONAL DISSENT:

A THEORETICAL ESSAY

Jill W. Graham

ABSTRACT

Organizational members sometimes utilize moral criteria to assess issues in the workplace. An organizational policy may be described as "unethical," the quality of a product as "an unwarranted threat to public safety," the conduct of another organizational member as "corrupt." One possible response to the perception by an employee of moral wrongs within the workplace is *principled organizational dissent,* a protest and/or effort to change the organizational status quo because of a conscientious objection to current policy or practice. This paper develops a theoretical model of principled organizational dissent on the basis of a review of related literatures in the social sciences, humanities, law, and journalism. Propositions are derived from the model in contemplation of a program of research which will estimate the magnitude of principled organizational dissent as a form of individual behavior in the workplace; identify and analyze factors which affect the causes and consequences of principled organizational dissent; and suggest, to both individuals and organizations, what might be done to make principled organizational dissent more effective as a stimulus for constructive organizational change.

INTRODUCTION

Principled organizational dissent is the effort by individuals in the work-place to protest and/or to change the organizational status quo because of their conscientious objection to current policy or practice. It can arise when an organizational member evaluates behavior in or by the organization in terms of some impersonal system of value, and finds it wanting. The term *principled* applies to the issue at stake, e.g., one which violates a standard of justice, honesty, or economy: it does not necessarily describe the ultimate motive of the person who raises it.

An assumption of the current research is that understanding the process of principled organizational dissent may be useful in converting dissidents' moral sensitivity, analytical skills, and energy for action into resources for organizational improvement. The change process in organizations ultimately begins with one person's analysis of how things might be better (variously defined) if organizational policies and practices were altered. Whether and how that person's ideas are communicated and received by others, and what impact they have, are issues central to the study of principled organizational dissent.

The following paper utilizes an interdisciplinary approach to study principled organizational dissent. The unit of analysis is the individual, but organizational, political, and sociocultural factors are examined, in addition to individual-level variables. In the first section, internal dissent is positioned relative to the other economic and political forces which might stimulate organizational reform. The second section introduces an analytical framework to describe a variety of responses individual organizational members might make in response to the perception of low or declining organizational performance. The third and longest section of the paper reviews literature in the wide range of fields which have considered topics related to principled organizational dissent. In the fourth section a theoretical model of principled organizational dissent is developed, and research questions related to its components are proposed.

MECHANISMS FOR REGULATING ORGANIZATIONAL PERFORMANCE

It is crucial to long-term organizational well-being (as indicated by social legitimacy as well as economic prosperity) that mechanisms exist to counteract instances of low and/or deteriorating organizational performance. Although the discipline of the free market is one such mechanism, there are a number of reasons why markets alone may not be enough to regulate performance quality. One is the assumption of classical economic models that both individual and organizational actors are rational. Research at all levels of analysis—organizational, group, and individual—indicates that, especially under conditions of environmental change and uncertainty, rational information processing is severely restricted (see Staw, Sandelands, & Dutton, 1981, for a summary of research on this topic). A second assumption of free market economics is the inability of any single economic actor to influence the equilibrium price, i.e., to tamper with market forces. While large organizational size by itself does not necessarily indicate domination of an industry, it does represent potential political power, and as such can be used to encourage the state to regulate the market in such a way as to buffer existing large organizations from market discipline (McNeil, 1978). Finally, the magnitude of the threat from some forms of organizational misfeasance (or malfeasance) may be so large that after-the-fact market discipline is simply too little and too late. The possibility of bankruptcy for General Public Utilities, the electric company responsible for the nuclear plants at Three Mile Island, is no guarantee against accidents such as the near-disaster that occurred there in 1979.

The alternative to market discipline as a regulator of organizational performance is political action (Hirschman, 1970, 1974). The source of political action can be either internal or external to the organization. Externally applied political constraints generally result from a cumbersome process of legislative and regulatory action, which by definition is general in application and thus insensitive to specific times and places. As indicated in the previous paragraph, moreover, the external political environment is corruptible by concentrations of economic power, thereby lowering the probability that powerful economic institutions can be effectively regulated by external constraints. The remaining option for regulating the quality of organizational performance is internal political action by members of the organization—i.e., organizational dissent. Where dissent concerns issues of principle such as justice, honesty, or economy, it is *principled organizational dissent.*

FORMS OF PRINCIPLED ORGANIZATIONAL DISSENT

Principled organizational dissent can take a variety of forms. Examples include constructive criticism or protest expressed to others within the organization; reports to interested audiences outside the organization; blocking actions, such as working to rule or even sabotage; and resigning in protest. One way to conceptualize different types of principled organizational dissent is by reference to Hirschman's (1970, 1974) analysis of exit and voice as two prototypical forms of response to the perception

by their members of unsatisfactory (or declining) organizational performance. The exit dimension concerns the decision to retain or surrender
membership in the organization. Hirschman describes it as a market response in that the choice between options is assumed to turn on their
relative costs and benefits without regard to sentimental ties. Hirschman's
voice dimension concerns the level of effort "to change, rather than to
escape from, an objectionable state of affairs" (Hirschman, 1970, p. 30).
If exit is a market response, voice is a political one. Exit and voice conceptually are independent of one another (although as a practical matter
a high level of voice may often lead to involuntary exit). As a result, a
typology of forms of principled organizational dissent can be derived by
crossing exit and voice as two independent dimensions (see Figure 1).

In Figure 1, the no-exit and no-voice cell (Cell 1: "stay in silence") is
the form of behavior that traditionally is described as representing loyalty
(the"Love it" part of "Love it or leave it"; or see Farrell, 1983). The
kind of loyalty Hirschman (1970) describes, by contrast, is "Stay with
voice" (Cells 2a and 2b). He defines as loyal those for whom the exit
alternative is a viable option (e.g., those who are in an advantageous labor
market situation), but who choose instead to respond to perceived organizational decline by remaining and trying to improve things from within,
i.e., to engage in principled organizational dissent. In Figure 1 the "stay
with voice" cell is divided into two parts, depending on whether voice is
exercised entirely within the organization or reaches outside organizational
boundaries (whistleblowing). The "exit with no voice" cell (Cell 3 "go
in silence"—the "Leave it" part of "Love it or leave it"), although perhaps implying opposition grounded in principle, reflects the absence of
organizational loyalty.

Voice and exit can be combined in two ways, both of which are examples
of principled organizational dissent (Cells 4a and 4b). In one case, an employee resigns because of an objection to organizational (tolerance of)
wrongdoing, and explains his/her reasons for leaving to others in the organization in private conversation or correspondence. Cabinet officers in
the United States typically take that course of action when resigning for
reasons of conscience; public announcements invariably attribute such
resignations to unspecified "personal reasons" (Weisband & Franck,
1975). In the British parliamentary system, by contrast, another combination of exit and voice predominates: the "public protest resignation."
In that case the resigning critic explains his/her reasons for quitting to an
audience beyond the organization itself, often through the news media.
The nuclear safety engineer who resigned from the Nuclear Regulatory
Commission and chose to announce his resignation and the reasons for
it in an interview on "60 Minutes" provides a domestic illustration (Weil,
1977).

| | | Exit Dimension | |
		Stay	Go
Voice Dimension	Silence	1. No action; traditional (blind) loyalty	3. Quiet departure
	Internal criticism	2a. Protest or internal change effort using only internal channels	4a. Explain reasons for resignation in exit interview
	External reporting (whistleblowing)	2b. Protest or internal change effort using external pressure	4b. Exit-with-voice, public protest, resignation

Figure 1. Typology of responses to organizational decline.

PRIOR WORK RELATED TO PRINCIPLED ORGANIZATIONAL DISSENT

Principled organizational dissent is a topic that does not have a long history of study in the discipline of organizational behavior. As a result the terminology and perspective taken here are original. It is not true, however, that no one anywhere has ever thought or written about related topics (see Bowman, Elliston & Lockhart, 1984, for a review). There exist in the popular press, for instance, several collections of case histories of whistleblowers, and those provide a rich resource for tracing the typical pattern of that particular form of principled organizational dissent. Moral philosophers have written about professional responsibility, the ethics of whistleblowing, multiple loyalties, and freedom of expression in the workplace. Scholars in the field of labor law have studied legal protection of employee dissent, as compared with the employer's right to discharge "at will."

Research in several of the behavioral sciences suggests factors which may influence the process of principled organizational dissent. In psychology, study of moral development suggests processes by which individuals acquire and practice the capacity to pass moral judgment. The study by social psychologists of interpersonal helping (or "prosocial") behavior can be used as a paradigm for considering prosocial behavior within organizations. The psychology and sociology of resistance to malevolent authority, to group norms, or to social conditions also give insight into the process of organizational dissent. The phenomenon of attempted upward influence in organizations has been studied by scholars in organizational behavior, although research in that area typically assumes that influence attempts concern personal rather than principled issues. A variety of organizational mechanisms for the expression and consideration of employee dissent have been identified and analyzed. Also within the field of organizational behavior, topics such as organizational culture and climate, reward systems, and organizational prosperity all speak to various aspects of the topic of dissent.

In this section of the paper each of those areas will be reviewed with the intent of building toward a conceptual model which describes and explains the process of principled organizational dissent.

Case Studies of Whistleblowing

A review of whistleblower case studies (Ewing, 1983; Mitchell, 1982; Nader, Petkas, & Blackwell, 1972; Perrucci, Anderson, Schendel, & Trachtman, 1980; Peters & Branch, 1972; Westin, 1981) suggests that principled organizational dissent is a process that exists through time, and that the development of that process depends to a large extent on the organization's response to employee reporting of (what the employee perceives to be) wrongdoing. The typical episode of principled organizational dissent begins when an employee becomes aware of a situation in the workplace which violates some general standard of value to which the person subscribes (see Figure 2).

A recent example is Frank Spinney, a management analyst in the Department of Defense, who discovered that basic cost assumptions in use at the Pentagon systematically underestimate the cost of new weapons systems, thereby misleading those who need accurate information to decide on authorization of the systems (Isaacson, 1983). A private sector example is David Edwards, a foreign exchange trader in Citibank's Paris office, who was concerned when he discovered that illegal financial transactions were being made in the bank's name by a colleague (Rowen, 1983). A third example is Dr. Grace Pierce, the only physician member of a drug research team at Ortho Pharmaceuticals, who was concerned about doing human testing of a drug containing high levels of a possible carcinogen (Westin, 1981). Finally, Hugh Kaufman, who works at the EPA as a toxic-wastes scientist, felt that the Congressionally mandated Superfund program

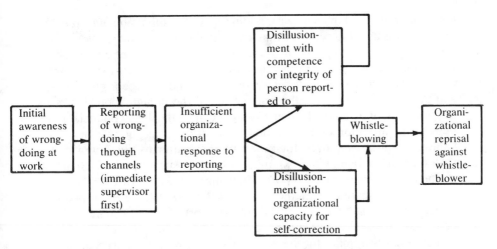

Figure 2. Descriptive Model of a Whistleblowing Episode

was being abused and underutilized under the direction of his supervisor, Rita Lavelle (Beck, 1983).

After initial awareness of an issue which the employee feels involves (or threatens to involve) some form of wrongdoing (i.e., an issue of principle), often the response of the employee is to report the issue to his or her immediate superior. Doing that much rarely constitutes principled organizational dissent by itself, because such reporting usually is done under the assumption that the superior is unaware of the problem. It is also assumed that, once made aware, the superior will either take corrective action directly or shepherd the matter up the chain of command to a level where corrective action can be taken. Such assumptions were made in three of the examples cited above—Spinney, Edwards, and Pierce (Kaufman's case is the exception, and is discussed subsequently). What actually happened when those individuals reported their concerns to their respective superiors, however, was not at all what they expected. Instead of initiating corrective action, their superiors instructed them to proceed with their work without raising further objections about it (in the case of Spinney and Pierce) or about the conduct of others (in the case of Edwards).

At that point the eventual whistleblower typically undergoes a transformation, a consciousness-raising experience about the character of the superior, or even about the nature of the employing organization as a whole. Previous assumptions about good faith and benign motives are called into question. A sense of disillusionment, even betrayal, often pushes the person into cynicism. Such a general reaction is prevented (or at least delayed) if the employee feels it is *only* the person of his/her supervisor who countenances wrongdoing, and that others higher up in the organization are different. In that case, the employee may try to bring the matter to the attention of those higher in the chain of command. If the employee suspects that the superior is merely following orders from above, however, he/she may decide to abandon normal reporting channels and take the issue outside the boundaries of the organization. Edwards (the banker) followed the former strategy, calling the illegal financial practices to the attention of ever-higher levels of Citibank; he was unable to believe, until he was fired for reporting the matter to the Board of Directors, that the bank would knowingly tolerate such practices. Spinney, on the other hand, wrote a report criticizing Pentagon cost-estimation assumptions and shared it with the staff of the Senate Defense Appropriations Subcommittee. Dr. Pierce enlisted the support of the other members of her research team, and together they took their case up the chain of command. Hugh Kaufman, the EPA scientist, felt from the start that his superior (Lavelle), Lavelle's superior (EPA Director Ann Gorsuch-Burford), and the next level up as well (the White House) supported the policy he felt was illegal, so he did not require the shock of unmet expectations to prompt him to move from routine reporting to whistleblowing. He was inclined from the outset to pursue channels of communication which led outside the normal chain of command.

Once an employee has ignored instructions to continue doing assigned tasks without raising objections, the dissident may receive some sort of reprisal from his or her superiors. Transfer to other (usually lesser) duties (Spinney and Pierce), low performance ratings and denial of pay increases (Kaufman), or termination of employment (Edwards) are common outcomes (see Ewing, 1980, for a list of "How Bureaucrats Deal with Dissidents"; Ewing's list is similar to "Management's Recourse: Ad Hominem Defined," which is a chapter in a 1978 U.S. Senate report on whistleblowing).

The first published studies of whistleblowers to involve the systematic collection of data across multiple respondents (as opposed to telling the stories of one or two) are based on a survey of women who filed Equal Employment Opportunity (EEO) complaints against their employers with the Wisconsin Equal Rights Division (Near & Jensen, 1983; Parmerlee, Near, & Jensen, 1982; Parmerlee, White, Near, & Jensen, 1980). In those studies the issue was one involving personal benefits to the whistleblowers, so the cases do not qualify as principled organizational dissent. Nevertheless the issue of organizational response to whistleblowing receives its first systematic analysis in that series of studies. Two opposing theories are suggested. One is that organizational retaliation against whistleblowers varies in direct proportion to the threat the whistleblower poses to the organization. Near and Jensen (1983) call that response *rationalistic*. The alternative they propose is called *strategic*: organizations retaliate most against whistleblowers representing the least threat. The Wisconsin data support the strategic rather than the rationalistic organizational response: "Organizations are most likely to retaliate against whistleblowers who are relatively vulnerable [rather than] whistleblowers who present the greatest threat" (Near & Jensen, 1983, p. 23).

The case studies of whistleblowers provide a primitive descriptive model of what an episode of principled organizational dissent usually involves (as shown in Figure 2), but there are serious limitations to their use in building a model of dissent that can stimulate constructive organizational change. First, the whistleblower stories, by definition, describe the experiences only of those employees who complete the whole process, i.e., those who decide to pursue a principled issue to higher levels in their organizations or even outside of it, as a result of not being listened to at lower levels. Other employees in the organization may have had access to the same information as did the whistleblowers but chose not to follow up on the information in the same way. What made the difference? To answer that question, comparative information about whistleblowers and non-whistleblowers is needed which, in turn, requires a theory to suggest what information to collect about people and their work environments. A second limitation of whistleblower case studies concerns the nature of the organizational response to reporters of wrongdoing. Whistleblowers whose stories are widely reported are the ones who encounter a hostile organizational response and respond by telling the story to outsiders. The experience of those who identify problems in the workplace and are rewarded (or at least not punished) for bringing problems to the attention of the appropriate authorities cannot be studied by focusing only on famous whistleblowers. If the Wisconsin survey of EEO whistleblowers is any guide, three fifths of whistleblowers report experiencing no organizational retaliation at all. Third, there are other possible forms of dissidence than whistleblowing (see Figure 1). Dissent which is voiced only within organizational boundaries does not get written up in the popular press. As a result, whistleblower case studies describe the experiences of only one type of principled organizational dissident.

To understand the role dissent can play in stimulating constructive organizational change, it is necessary to study those who are aware of principled issues and take a different route than whistleblowers; and to know what to study, it is necessary to be guided by a theory of behavior in response to the perception of wrongdoing. In the following sections of this paper, scholarship in a number of disciplines is reviewed, to lay the groundwork for such a theory. The first two—moral philosophy and law—concern the normative and legal environments in which principled organizational dissent occurs.

Moral Philosophy

Moral philosophy in recent years has taken up a number of issues related to principled organizational dissent. Four will be addressed in this section: social responsibility of professional employees, the ethics of whistleblowing, multiple loyalties, and justification for freedom of expression in the workplace. Philosophical analysis of such issues, although normative rather than descriptive in approach, suggests the moral principles which reflect prevailing social standards of conduct. Those standards are important to the process of principled organizational dissent, insofar as they influence individual behavior, either directly or through intervening social institutions (e.g., support groups, the legal system).

Social responsibility. Definitions of what it means to be a "professional" typically include reference to a social service ethic, a heightened sense of social responsibility. Weil (1979), for example, argues that because of their relative expertise, professional engineers and scientists are uniquely situated to foresee potential effects of projects on public health and safety, and that such insights should be shared even when unsolicited by management.

The view that professionals ought to be more socially responsible than nonprofessionals is not universally shared among philosophers. Ladenson (1979b), using *rational contractor theory* to distinguish between "morally required" behavior and "morally creditable but not required" behavior, puts professional social responsibility in the latter category. Ladenson rejects the idea that professionals have a special responsibility to prevent evil and promote good: instead they are called, as is everyone else, simply to refrain from doing evil themselves. The doing of evil can be punished; the failure to promote good cannot. Ladenson reasons that because enforcement of social responsibility is impractical, an obligation to uphold it cannot realistically be said to exist. He nonetheless supports the idea of professional associations having codes of ethics to serve as ideals for their members; he also supports what Nader et al. (1972) calls the *whistleblowing ethic*.

The dispute about the nature of professional responsibility is to some extent a disagreement over what is "right" and what is merely "good," that is, an absolute rather than a relativistic assessment. A related pair of concepts of responsibility—*assigned responsibility* and *assumed responsibility*—has emerged in the behavioral sciences. Culbert (1974) describes a sense of responsibility as including both "after-the-fact accountability" (assigned responsibility) and "before-the-fact consciousness" (assumed responsibility). Wynn (1982), citing Elbing (1970), suggests reserving the term *responsibility* for the future-oriented concept, and calling all retrospective uses *accountability*. He goes on to emphasize that, in organizations, although accountability may be demanded (assigned) by one's superiors, responsibility can only be accepted voluntarily (assumed). Milgram (1975), in describing the "agentic state" of those who submit to authority, notes that agents feel responsible *to* authority figures, but do not feel responsible *for* the outcomes of their behavior if they are following orders. In all those discussions of responsibility, two alternative usages are highlighted. The narrower, more concrete concept refers to those things for which one will be held accountable by an immediate authority; the other concept concerns outcomes to others, short- and long-term, which the decision maker deems important on his/her own initiative.

In Ladenson's (1979b) terms, assigned responsibility is akin to that which is "morally required," and assumed responsibility to that which is "morally creditable but not required." The debate over professionals' social responsibility suggests that occupational status (professional or non-professional) may influence a person's sensitivity to issues of principle, and also motivate the person to feel responsible for doing something about such issues when they arise, but that such inclinations may be controversial. The philosophical analysis of professional social responsibility also suggests that professional associations may be a potential source of social support for principled dissidents.

Whistleblowing ethics. The *ethics of whistleblowing* refers to the moral appropriateness of both choosing whistleblowing as a strategy and selecting whistleblowing tactics. It includes such issues as anonymity, exhaustion of normal remedies before going public, and interference with normal workplace operations and group morale. Elliston's (1982a) analysis of the issue of anonymous versus self-revelatory whistleblowing presumes that open dissent generally is favored on grounds of consistency of ends and means: the paradox of the anonymous whistleblower is that "he uses ignorance to promote knowledge, identifies others while hiding himself" (Elliston, 1982a, p. 49). Elliston offers four reasons, however, to support anonymous whistleblowing in certain circumstances. The first is the seriousness of the issue. If an issue poses a substantial danger, then anonymous whistleblowing, while not ideal, is still preferable to no whistleblowing at all. Similarly, if the probability of unfair retaliation against a whistleblower is high, then anonymity allows public knowledge of conditions that otherwise would pose unknown dangers. Third, group cohesiveness can generate strong pressures on members not to raise objections (Janis, 1972); if a principled issue exists, then the possibility of anonymous reporting may be the only way issues will be reported at all in a cohesive group setting. Elliston (1982a) analyzes all three of these situations in utilitarian terms: although open dissent may be preferred over anonymous dissent, anonymous dissent is preferred over no dissent, and, in certain situations, the social benefit of having some dissent is worth the cost of it being anonymous.

The fourth defense of anonymous whistleblowing is of a different type. It concerns the possibility that anonymity may sometimes increase the effectiveness of whistleblowing as an organizational change strategy, due to its motivating effect on others. Elliston (1982a) uses the Watergate-era character of Deep Throat to illustrate the point. Because Deep Throat gave leads about potential news stories without revealing either his/her own identity or the source of her/his information, the reporters Woodward and Bernstein (and, later, many others) were motivated to track down the details on their own. They were hooked on the story, certainly because of its inherent interest, but also, Elliston argues, because they had to work so hard to piece it together. A full statement read in public by a whistle-blower would not have kept the reporters' and the public's interest as well, so the fact that whistleblowing was anonymous enhanced the effec-tiveness of dissent.

In addition to the issue of anonymity, the ethics of whistleblowing also concern when and where whistleblowing is appropriate. As summarized by Westin (1981):

> Almost all the writing on whistleblowing—by courts, arbitrators, business executives, public-interest group leaders, and civil liberties advocates—stresses that employees have a general obligation to raise their protest inside the company before taking it to government bodies or the public. This is to ensure that management has a chance to correct any mistakes that may be the result of inadvertence, bad judgment by subordinates, or a failure to recognize that a problem existed. (p. 149)

Several exceptions to that general rule have been suggested (Elliston, 1982b; Westin, 1981). These include (paraphrasing Westin, 1981, p. 150)

- the absence of an accessible organizational dissent procedure;
- misconduct by those in charge of the dissent procedure;
- a history of organizational retaliation against those using dissent pro-cedures;
- suspicion that internal dissent will lead to destruction of evidence; and
- a high probability that using internal channels will unreasonably delay action to protect public safety.

Loyalty.   Another issue philosophers have considered concerns the moral claim of loyalty. Loyalties in the workplace are multiple and fre-quently conflict. As a result, the question in most instances is not whether to be loyal, but how to resolve conflicts of loyalty. There can be loyalty as a member of one or more organizations, loyalty to co-workers and/or a profession, loyalty to civic, ethical, and religious values, loyalty to friends and family. Moral philosphers and policy makers have proposed normative rules for resolving conflicts of loyalty. Elliston (1982a), for example, argues that loyalty freely given has a greater moral claim than loyalty which is demanded by the more powerful party in a relationship (e.g., the employer in most employment relations). Malin (1983) likewise cautions that loyalty does not involve blind obedience, and that an employer's claim to the contrary is both "illegitimate" and "has no moral value" (pp. 310). The U.S. Senate's Code of Ethics for United States Government Service (1978) is a legislated hierarchy to guide federal employees. It begins: "Any Person In Government Service Should: Put loyalty to the highest moral principles and to country above loyalty to person, party, or Government department." It also enjoins government employees to "expose corruption wherever discovered" (p. ix).

Insofar as beliefs about loyalty prioritization influence individual decision making, either directly or mediated by social support mechanisms, they are important to a model of principled organizational dissent. Such beliefs, however, are changeable and sometimes contradictory. Social philosophers identify two opposing cultural traditions for choosing among conflicting loyalties. Weisband and Franck (1975), citing Whyte (1957), portray this debate as between the Judeo-Christian ethic of personal moral responsibility for all one's behavior (which sometimes requires standing alone against popular opinion), and the organizational ethic of team loyalty. Those authors conclude that team loyalty (the "organization ethic") largely overshadows conscientious individualism (the "Puritan ethic") in the United States today, with the result that individual analysis of ethical issues, and action following up such analysis, is not as highly valued as it once was. Opinion on the effects of social change, however, is not unanimous. In a 1971 law review article, "The Employee's Duty of Loyalty and Obedience," Blumberg (1971) reports finding signs of "a new view of responsibility—a view that the employee's duty as a citizen transcends his duties as an employee" (p. 283). Even in the case where cultural norms favor team loyalty over rugged individualism, moreover, the possibility of conflict among loyalties to different teams still remains. Which loyalty exerts the strongest influence in a given instance depends on individual circumstances.

Malin (1983) takes the analysis of multiple loyalties further by distinguishing between two types of loyalty conflicts in the workplace: loyalty to subunit or supervisor conflicting with loyalty to top management, on the one hand, and loyalty to organizational interests conflicting with loyalty to individual conscience, on the other. He sees internal dissent as the appropriate resolution to the first conflict, and notes that:

> accusations that the employee who blows the whistle internally on employer mis-
> conduct is disloyal come from the perspective of the subgoal pursuits of a lower level
> manager. Where the employee reports activity which furthers the interests of a subunit
> but conflicts with the general interests of the firm the only disloyalty exhibited by
> the employee is to the subunit. The employee's actions exhibit loyalty of a high degree
> to the firm as a whole. (Malin, 1983, p. 308–309)

The distinction between types of loyalty conflicts is helpful in analyzing principled dissent as a developmental process. The first conflict experienced by employees aware of a principled issue is usually between loyalties to different units or levels within the organization (i.e., different "team loyalties"). It is only when reporting low-level misconduct to higher ups does *not* improve performance that reporters of wrongdoing experience the second conflict, i.e., the one between loyalty to organization (as a whole) and loyalty to conscience. It is at that point that external reporting (whistleblowing) becomes a viable option (see Figure 2).

Freedom of expression in the workplace. The final philosophical issue considered here is individual freedom at work. Ladenson's (1979a) discussion of freedom of expression in the workplace proposes two rationales for its defense. The first is what Ladenson call the *volunteer public guardian* approach: Because an individual employee is well situated to know what organizationally tolerated (or encouraged) wrongdoing is occurring, he or she may be the only one able to prevent irreparable harm being done to the public interest due to organizational corruption, waste, and negligence. Ladenson cautions, however, that there are costs as well as benefits to be considered. The employee who plays the role of volunteer public guardian may sometimes be in error, may exaggerate a minor problem (in error or to disguise an ulterior motive), or may sound an alarm in an unduly disruptive manner. Balancing costs and benefits to calculate a "net benefit" implies that the volunteer public guardian defense of freedom of expression in the workplace is successful only where the frequency and magnitude of organizational wrongdoing is high relative to costs such as disruption of the workplace and potentially false charges.

Ladenson (1979a) finds that a second rationale for freedom of expression in the workplace, the *fundamental liberty* approach, offers a stronger defense. From that perspective, individuality has ultimate value in itself, as a defining characteristic of the human condition, and not merely as a means to guard the public interest. Ladenson interprets John Stuart Mill's argument (in Chapter 3 of Mills's *On Liberty*) as claiming that individual freedom is not possible without the critical ability to examine alternatives and freely choose among them in an informed manner. Forbidding the use of critical analytical skills in those places where most adults spend the better part of their waking hours—the workplace—threatens the development and/or maintenance of the skills that are essential to the existence of fundamental liberty. Ladenson (1979a) submits that limits on freedom of expression that are "content based. . . are never justifiable . . . [although]. . .restrictions which go to time, place, and manner, rather than content, will be upheld so long as they are reasonable" (pp. 13–14).

Donaldson (1982) echoes Ladenson's remarks about "reasonable" restrictions on freedom of expression, but he uses a third rationale in addition to the public guardian and fundamental liberty approaches; "without criticism, corporations would plow ahead, blind to their worst faults, firing and penalizing the very employees who might cure their blindness. The real question is how *much* criticism to allow, and *when*" (p. 148). That formulation comes closest to the approach of the current study, which links principled dissent not only to individual conscience and social welfare, but also to organizational change and well-being.

Philosophical perspectives on conscientious dissent concern systems of social value that currently are or historically have been influential in our culture. One way for such systems of value to be manifested concretely is through legislation and judicial interpretation. These matters are considered in the next section.

Legal Perspectives on Employee Dissent

The availability of legal protection for principled dissent in the workplace is likely to be a factor in employees' decisions to risk the displeasure of their superiors by pursuing a principled issue after being advised to drop it. Historically, the legal environment for such dissent has been hostile, but there have been significant changes in the last 20 years. This section of the paper reviews recent court rulings on the common law "at-will" doctrine, arbitration decisions concerning employee grievances of "dismissal without just cause," and statutory protection of employee whistleblowing.

Common law. The *at-will doctrine* of employer–employee relations, which assumes that both parties enter the relationship freely and, hence, can both terminate it at will, is the traditional standard in common law:

> The source of common law protection of the employment relationship appears to be the Ordinance and Statute of Labourours, 23 Edw. III. St.1 (1349). . .[which was] enacted after the Black Death had reduced the labor force in England by almost one half. (Blades, 1967, p. 1424)

The classic American case is from a Tennessee court in 1884 (*Payne v. Western & A.R.R. Co.*, 81 Tenn. 507 (1884)):

> All may dismiss their employee(s) at-will, be they many or few, for good cause, for no cause, or even for cause morally wrong, without thereby being guilty of a legal wrong. (pp. 519–520)

Under the at-will doctrine employers are free from liability for unjust dismissal, at least in the absence of a contractual obligation to the contrary.

The position of would-be employee dissenters is further weakened by reliance on agency law rather than tort law regarding duties implied in an employment agreement. Under agency law the employee has a duty of loyalty to the economic interests of the employer. Aiding a competitor, even after hours, is disloyal; so is making any statements (even true ones) which damage the reputation of the employer (Blumberg, 1971; Malin, 1983; Michalos, 1979). The law of agency assumes human motivation to be driven only by personal economic well-being. Principled organizational dissent is not definable under agency law because no principle but self-interest is conceivable. Its closest relative is insubordination on the grounds of avoiding personal legal liability: an employee is protected from discharge for insubordination if compliance with a directive would have caused harm for which the employee could later be held legally accountable.

Until 1959, the law of agency and the at-will doctrine effectively prohibited legal support for principled dissent under common law. In that year a landmark case involving a Teamsters Union business agent introduced the *public policy exception* to the at-will doctrine. The union official had been fired from his job for refusing to commit perjury on the union's behalf. The official sued the union for unjust dismissal. A California state court wrote:

> The right to discharge an employee . . .may be limited. . . by considerations of public policy. . . . Public policy is the principles under which freedom of contract or private dealing is restricted by law for the good of the community. . . . Whatever contravenes good morals or any established interests of society is against public policy. (*Petermann v. Teamsters Local 396*, 174 Cal. App. 2d 184, 344 P.2d 27 (1959)).

Since 1959, courts in 20 states have relied on the public policy exception to the at-will doctrine in making decisions, and courts in 5 other states (plus the District of Columbia) have indicated they would use the public policy exception if a qualified case were to come before them (Bureau of National Affairs, 1982). Employee suits alleging "abusive discharge" (i.e., based on the public policy exception to the at-will doctrine) are argued under tort law. The law of torts, unlike agency law, allows an employee's concern for the public welfare as a defense against an employer's countercharge of breach of contract (insubordination), even in the absence of a threat of personal liability (Blumberg, 1971).

Another exception to the at-will doctrine applies only to public-sector employees. The U.S. Supreme Court has ruled that because public employers are governmental units, they are bound by the Constitutional prohibition against governmental infringement of free speech (*Pickering v. Board of Education*, 391 U.S. 563, 88 S.Ct. 1731, 20 L.Ed.2d 811 (1968)). As a result, public employees who feel they have been dismissed or disciplined because they engaged in principled dissent have legal standing to sue under the First Amendment.

Grievance arbitration. The at-will doctrine refers only to employment relationships under common law, not under contracts. Where a collective bargaining agreement or civil service law regulates employer–employee relations, wording protecting employees from dismissal or discipline without "cause" or "just cause" is almost universally included. A recent survey of "basic patterns in union contracts" finds that 90% of negotiated labor agreements contain such language (Bureau of National Affairs, 1979). Although such constraints limit arbitrary employer action, they do not automatically protect dissidents. Malin's (1983) review of arbitration decisions in whistleblower discharge cases reveals several contextual factors which are commonly considered by arbitrators, including

the employee's bad faith or malicious motive, his failure to resort first to internal channels, the tone and visibility of the employee's statements, the falsity of the employee's statements, the significance of the activity exposed . . . the harm done to the employer, and the employee's right of free expression. (pp. 290, 291)

Balancing such a diverse set of factors makes it difficult to predict the outcome of grievance arbitration. Nevertheless, about one fourth of all private-sector employees work under the protection of collective bargaining agreements, and the possibility that a whistleblower might, with union support, utilize the grievance process to protest management reprisal, and might eventually win, may act as a constraint on employer response to dissent (Westin, 1982).

Statutory protection. Antiretaliation provisions protecting complainants are included in several federal employment statutes, including Title VII of the Civil Rights Act, the Age Discrimination in Employment Act, the National Labor Relations Act, the Fair Labor Standards Act, and the Occupational Safety and Health Act. Employees seeking the protection of the provisions of any of those statutes can file a grievance with an appropriate government agency if they feel their employer retaliates against them for so doing. This protection is useful primarily to organizational dissidents pursuing suborganizational interests (e.g., personal grievances); principled dissidents benefit from the antiretaliation provisions in employment statutes only if they suffer reprisals as a result of helping others to claim their legal rights. The National Labor Relations Board ruled, for example, that the discharge of a supervisor who helped a group of subordinates to file an unfair labor practice charge at a regional National Labor Relations Board (NLRB) office was illegal (Malin, 1983, p. 296).

There are several other federal statutes which also contain antiretaliation provisions. This group of laws concerns issues affecting public health and safety (e.g., Safe Drinking Water Act, Toxic Substances Control Act, Clean Air Act, etc.). In these cases, the role of the employee as "volunteer public guardian" (Ladenson, 1979a) is built into the enforcement plan of the laws.

Finally, the states of Michigan and Connecticut enacted legislation (in 1981 and 1982, respectively) that encourages whistleblowing by prohibiting private-sector employers from retaliating against whistleblowing employees. Similar whistleblowing protection statutes have been introduced in four other states: Colorado, Massachusetts, Pennsylvania, and Wisconsin. Legislation at the federal level is not expected to be enacted any time soon (Bureau of National Affairs, 1982; Malin, 1983).

In summary, on certain topics in certain states, at certain times and with certain employers, there may be legal protection for principled dissent. The existence of such protection is likely to increase the probability

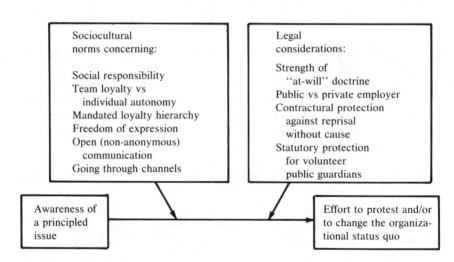

Figure 3. Environmental moderators of principled organizational dissent.

that someone who is aware of a principled issue will report it, and, if action is not taken at one level, will persevere in reporting it elsewhere. There are so many variables, however, that the net effect on dissent of the existence of legal protection is difficult to gauge.

Together with other sociocultural variables, legal considerations contribute to the extraorganizational environment surrounding individual dissent in the workplace. These variables act as moderators of the link between individual awareness and action, as shown in Figure 3.

The next two sections of the paper focus on individual-level characteristics and behavior. Research on the psychology of moral development, as well as on bystander intervention in response to another's need, is suggestive of who is likely to recognize principled issues at work, and how a decision to respond to such awareness might be made.

Psychology of Moral Judgment

Weisband and Franck (1975) define *ethical autonomy* as "the willingness to assert one's own principled judgment, even if that entails violating the rules, values, or perceptions of the organization, peer group, or team" (p. 3). Zald and Berger (1978) cite the possession of strong normative beliefs as one of the prerequisites for engaging in what they term *principled insurrection*. A capacity for critical evaluation of organizational practices is assumed in the current research to be tied both to initial awareness of issues of principle and to the inclination to act on such awareness. Psychological perspectives on the origin and practice of ethical judgment will be discussed in this section.

Cognitive theorists suggest that the ability to exercise ethical judgment is related to an individual's level of moral development. A two-stage cognitive theory of moral development was first proposed by Piaget (1932); it focused on the distinction between relying on older authority figures for absolute definitions of right and wrong, on the one hand, and on situational relativism, on the other. Kohlberg's (1969; 1976) six-stage theory expanded on Piaget's work; each of the first two stages was divided into an early and late phase, and a third major stage (moral autonomy) was added. Andrews (1981) summarizes the three basic stages as (1) *dualism,* where everything is divided neatly into "good" and "bad" according to the dictates of a trusted authority (e.g., parent, teacher, boss); (2) *multiplicity,* where multiple criteria for assessing "goodness" are all acknowledged as equally legitimate, and are used, if at all, according to convenience (e.g., to achieve peer acceptance); and (3) *commitment,* where the individual engages in moral reasoning by using definitions of *good* and *bad* that he or she has created and to which he or she commits her/himself. People at the first or third stages are more likely to hold strong normative beliefs than those at the second stage (moral relativists). Those at the first stage (dualism) are unlikely to challenge the morality of authority figures, although they might report the ethical misconduct (e.g., bribe-taking) of other employees to their boss. Those most likely to challenge the authority structure itself are at the third stage of ethical development (autonomous commitment). Rest (1979) has recently developed the Defining Issues Test, which measures the importance a person places on "principled moral" considerations, i.e., stages five and six of Kohlberg's theory, or what Andrews terms *commitment*.

The psychology of moral judgment in practice has been studied from two perspectives—feelings of injustice and impression formation. Unfortunately, the literature on the psychology of injustice focuses on the perceptions and cognitions of victims only. In his review article on causal inference, for instance, Hastie (1983) includes *moral inference* as a special type of causal reasoning. In discussing assessments of distributive justice and judgments of deservingness, however, Hastie considers only the perspective of an interested party (e.g., a victim of injustice) rather than that of a bystander. Such a perspective leaves unexamined the process of moral inference used by organizational members aware of organizational activities which threaten public (as opposed to personal) welfare.

Bystander assessment of the morality of individual persons is part of the literature on impression formation. Hamilton and Sanders' (1983) study finds that both the "deeds of an actor being judged and role-related social obligations governing what the actor should have done" (p. 199) affect judgment of morality (although the relative weight of deed vs. role effects varies across cultures). The dependent variable in such research is the judged morality of the target person. As such, the analysis stops with the act of judgment; the behavior of the judge after making a morality assessment is not examined. The study of prosocial behavior, however, considers both evaluation and subsequent action.

Prosocial Behavior

Studies of bystander helping behavior (see Latane & Nida, 1981; Staub, 1978 for recent reviews) focus attention on both individual and situational variables. Some of the individual-level variables were discussed in the previous section on the psychology of moral development. Very general situational variables, such as sociocultural norms, were discussed in the section on moral philosophy. The distinctive contribution of the helping-behavior literature is its attention to transient situational features, most notably the number and behavior of other bystanders. As summarized by Latane and Nida (1981), a consistent finding is that the larger the number of bystanders, the less likely it is that any one of them will offer assistance to someone in need, or attend to a general danger (e.g., report a fire). The leading theoretical explanation which accounts for "social inhibition of helping" (Darley & Latane, 1968; Latane & Darley, 1968, 1970) highlights three intervening stages between initial awareness of an event and choice of a behavioral response. These stages are assessment of the seriousness of the need, acceptance of personal responsibility for a response, and judgment about what behavior is possible and appropriate (see Figure 4).

In the first case, if the evidence for need is ambiguous, a bystander looks for cues in the environment to help make an assessment of its seriousness. An important source of information is the reaction of other bystanders; if none of them appears concerned about the situation, then the need may not be very serious. The larger the audience of unconcerned bystanders, the more reliable the evidence is taken to be. Group size, then, given an ambiguous stimulus, depresses assessment of seriousness because each bystander seeks in vain for signs of concern in others. Latane and Darley (1970) term that response *pluralistic ignorance*. Latane and Nida (1981) suggest that the fear of appearing an alarmist by overrating problem seriousness also depresses individual assessment of emergencies. The risk of embarrassment increases with the number of people who are in a position to observe another bystander's error, so again group size has an effect. Latane and Nida term that effect *audience inhibition*. The combined effect of pluralistic ignorance and audience inhibition is to minimize estimation of situation seriousness.

The second intervening stage between problem awareness and behavioral choice—responsibility assignment—is also affected by group size. If the responsibility for responding to a person in need is distributed equally among all bystanders, then the share attributable to any single bystander declines as their total number increases, responsibility being the reciprocal of group size (*diffusion of responsibility,* Darley & Latane, 1968). Such a condition applies only when all bystanders can be presumed to be equally responsible, i.e., it does not apply to the bystander who knows she or he has a distinctive ability to be helpful (e.g., a medical professional).

In the decision model of helping behavior proposed by Latane and Darley (1968, 1970), the final step between noticing an event, assessing its seriousness, accepting responsibility for a response, and actual behavior,

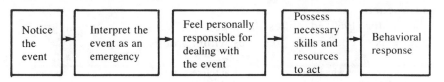

Figure 4. Model of bystander intervention in emergencies

is a judgment about what behavior is possible and appropriate. Latane and Darley describe that stage as a choice between attempting to render direct assistance or going to seek help from others (e.g., to call an ambulance or the police). The work of others in the helping-behavior area (Bar-Tal, 1976; Piliavin & Piliavin, 1972; Piliavin, Rodin, & Piliavin, 1969) suggests that stage includes a cost-benefit analysis of all possible responses to the situation.

The theoretical and empirical work available on the topic of interpersonal helping behavior suggests components of a model for prosocial behavior which may have application in other contexts as well. Specific variables which are highlighted as affecting stages of the model include the ambiguity of the stimulus, the number of other bystanders, and the relative capabilities of the bystanders to respond. Because bystander intervention in organizational settings, however, often involves not only initiative (i.e., being the first to intervene) but also opposition to the status quo, research about various types of opposition behavior is relevant to principled organizational dissent.

Resistance and Revolt

Research on topics ranging from group conformity and deviance, to civil unrest and revolution, suggest situational factors relevant to opposition behavior by individual members of organizations. Internal group dynamics, external social support for change, and conditions leading to social conflict are reviewed in this section.

Internal group dynamics. The empirical work of Asch (1951), Schachter (1960), and Milgram (1975) on conformity to group pressure and obedience to authority suggests specific situational variables which inhibit autonomous moral behavior (e.g., disobedience to malevolent authority). Milgram (1975) identifies four antecedent conditions for what he terms an *agentic state:* voluntary self-placement in an authority system, clear perception of who the authority figure is, perception that instructions given by the authority figure are plausibly related to the task situation, and acceptance of the social legitimacy of the entire enterprise. Employment in workplace organizations is generally thought to meet all four of those conditions. The reality status of that belief, however, is sometimes a matter of social construction.

Schachter (1960) identifies the urge to define social reality as one of the origins of conformity pressures within groups:

> On any issue for which there is no empirical referent, the reality of one's own opinion is established by the fact that other people hold similar opinions. Forces exist to establish uniformity and thus to create "reality" for the opinion. (p. 260)

In Milgram's (1975) obedience experiments, the "empirical referents" included the impressive-appearing teaching machine and the experimenter's lab coat, and the "other people" were all actors playing assigned parts. As a result, the definition of social reality which was presented to experimental subjects was well supported. Asch's (1951) experiments, however, indicate that the presence of a single ally decreases the effectiveness of group pressures toward conformity. Unanimity (staged or otherwise) in a group setting facilitates maintenance of a definition of social reality which encourages members to remain in an agentic state. Diversity in the group, however, allows challenges to the prevailing definition of the situation, thereby making dissent more likely.

Intragroup diversity can sometimes be supported or even stimulated from outside the group. Formal legal protection of dissent, as discussed earlier in the paper, is one concrete manifestation of social support for the expression of diverse points of view within the organization. Dissent may also be facilitated by (or inhibited by the lack of) other social institutions. The existence and aggressiveness of interested audiences (i.e., groups with which a dissident could share his/her views) are a crucial resource for internal change agents. Examples include the news media, congressional committees or government regulatory agencies, and organized interest groups (Gordon, Heinz, Gordon, & Divorski, 1973).

Social support for self-appointed change agents has consistently been found to be a major factor in successful reform efforts in natural settings (Broholm, 1982; Culbert, 1974; Kerr, Von Glinow, & Schreisheim, 1977; Moore, 1978; Perrucci et al., 1980; Schein, 1971; Zald & Berger, 1978). Examples include peers, professional associations, family support, political interest groups, unions, and religious organizations. Insofar as a support group can command loyalty to a set of principles or to itself as a "team," its advocacy of organizational change efforts can influence its members to decide on dissent in their places of employment. Although currently they are not widespread, small, religiouly grounded support groups, organized to allow their members to help one another work for the realization of religious or ethical values in their respective workplaces, have a powerful influence on their participants (Andover Newton Laity Project, 1981; Broholm; 1982).

Another form of support, suggested by Janis and Mann (1977), is sources for information and advice for dissidents qua dissidents (i.e., without regard to the substance of the issue). Examples they offer include legal counselors, the American Civil Liberties Union, and Nader's Raiders. Schein (1971) suggests several mechanisms by which principled dissent can not only be supported after it occurs, but stimulated in the first place. He discusses components of professional training and socialization, professional half-way houses, continuing education programs, and alumni activities to reinforce professional norms of role innovation and social responsibility. Weil (1979) adds to Schein's list the idea of portable pensions for professional employees, and mechanisms within professional associations to support members engaging in principled dissent. An example of such support is the *amicus curiae* brief, filed with a California court by the Institute of Electrical and Electronics Engineers, on behalf of three whistleblowing engineers who had worked on the San Francisco rapid transit system (Institute of Electrical and Electronics Engineers, 1975).

Social conflict. Social conflict, be it civil unrest or political revolution, is generally studied as a form of collective rather than individual action (Goldstone, 1982; Gurr, 1970, 1980; Tilly, 1978; Toch, 1965; Zald & Berger, 1978). As a result, the insights of that literature for individual dissent are limited. Nevertheless, two of the approaches to the study of social conflict highlight situational factors which may affect principled dissent in organizational settings. One approach describes social conflict as a consequence of system disequilibrium (e.g., economic collapse). With regard to principled dissent, it is possible that organizational chaos, whatever its cause, allows traditional definitions of reality to be challenged and conventional norms of behavior to be relaxed, so that previous constraints on criticism lose their force. Organizational disarray is thus an important contextual variable affecting the likelihood of dissent.

Another approach to the study of social conflict identifies historically grounded conflict processes (e.g., class conflict) as the ultimate cause of systemic collapse. As analyzed by Antonio (1979), historically grounded conflict at the organizational level involves the systematic displacement of the goal of "efficiency of production" by the goal of "efficiency of domination" as an organization ages. Those at the top become increasingly concerned with (and proficient at maintaining) their positions of privilege, even at the expense of organizational goal achievement. In her book on "bureaucratic opposition" (criticism in terms of ideal criteria), Weinstein (1979) offers as one of the grounds for opposition the violation of ideal bureaucratic norms. If Antonio's analysis is correct about the systematic sacrifice of productive efficiency to the goal of efficient domination, then "stage of bureaucratic development" would be a situational variable related to principled organizational dissent. The relationship would be a complex one, for in organizations which are well advanced (in Antonio's terms) there would be, because of management's violation of the bureaucratic ideal, more grounds for opposition; but because of the increased efficiency of domination, it would at the same time be more difficult to organize internal opposition.

So far, perspectives on dissent—especially principled dissent—have been reviewed from the disciplines of philosophy, law, individual and social psychology, sociology, and political science. A descriptive model of a typical whistleblowing episode was proposed, and a developmental model of prosocial behavior was reported. Before combining those models into one which focuses on principled organizational dissent, however, it is useful to examine the work of scholars whose major interest is organizations and behavior within organizations. In the following two sections, research on upward influence in organizations and on an array of formal mechanisms to allow (or even stimulate) organizational dissent is reviewed.

Upward Influence in Organizations

There is a growing literature, both conceptual and empirical, which suggests that subordinates influence leaders as well as vice versa. Mechanic (1971) suggests that attributes such as commitment, interest, willingness to use power, skill, attractiveness, time, centrality, and replaceability all are potential sources of power which can be utilized without regard to organizational level. Farris and Lim (1969), Greene (1975, 1979), Herold (1977), and Lowen and Craig (1968) all report empirical results indicating that leader behavior is at least to some extent a function of subordinate performance. In general, high levels of subordinate task performance result in (perceived) increases in supportive leader behavior and decreases in directive leader behavior. Crowe, Bochner, and Clark (1972) find that "leaders become more democratic when followers exercise initiative, offer ideas and set goals, and become more autocratic when followers are passive, request instructions and are unquestioning."

There seems to be a variety of ways for subordinates to exercise influence on their superiors, some wittingly and some not, but the leadership literature does not examine the reasons why followers might want to attempt upward influence. The literature on the politics of upward influence is more explicit. Porter, Allen, and Angle (1981, pp. 111–112) define *political upward influence* as

1.   a social influence attempt,
2.   which is discretionary,
3.   intended to promote or to protect self-interest, and
4.   threatens the self–interests of others.

They acknowledge that "much of upward influence involves, of course, the normal routine-reporting relationships that exist in all organizations" (Porter et al., 1981, p. 110). By restricting the purpose of "political" upward influence to suborganizational interests (see Item 3 in the preceding list), however, Porter et al. appear to define out of existence upward influence which *begins* as routine reporting but, because of management's unresponsiveness to a report of a principled issue, later develops into "a social influence attempt which is discretionary . . .and threatens the self-interests of others" (see items 1, 2, and 4 in the preceding list) (e.g., principled organizational dissent). Porter et al.'s omission leaves unexplored the possible organizational benefits of such upward influence attempts.

While not intended to apply to principled organizational dissent, the developmental stages of Porter et al.'s (1981) model of upward political influence (see Figure 5) nevertheless offers an important addition to the models of whistleblowing (Figure 2) and prosocial behavior (Figure 4) presented earlier.

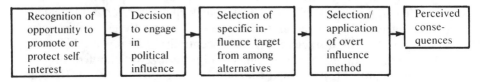

Figure 5. Model of upward political influence

Like the models shown in Figures 2 and 4, the political influence model begins with perception. The middle stages of the political influence model, however, concern the choice of what action to take to follow up on initial perception. These components of Porter et al.'s (1981) model are informed by the earlier work of Cartwright (1965), Kipnis, Schmidt, and Wilkinson, (1980), and Mowday (1978). Mowday (1978), following Cartwright's (1965) landmark article on influence and control, highlights "choice of influence target" and "method of influence employed" as two variables of particular importance to the empirical study of upward organizational influence. Mowday's measures of target characteristics are whether the target is in or out of the organization's chain of command and, if in, whether it is more than one level above the agent of influence. Porter et al. (1981) propose that the selection of an influence target is a function of the relative power of the target, and the costs of approaching it. The influence methods Mowday (1978) identifies include threats, legitimate authority, persuasive argument, rewards or exchange of favors, and covert manipulation. Kipnis et al. (1980) report on the frequency of use of eight methods of attempted upward influence among a diverse group of employed persons. Ingratiation and rational persuasion were the most commonly used techniques, followed by exchange, assertiveness, upward appeal, sanctions, blocking, and coalitions. Porter et al. (1981) order influence methods in terms of overtness: manipulation, manipulative persuasion, or open persuasion.

Nearly all the forms of behavior which are considered in the upward political influence literature are types of organizational communication, i.e., voice taken literally (Hirschman, 1970). Weinstein (1979) identifies a second category of bureaucratic opposition—direct action—which includes such behaviors as work slow-downs and strikes, working to rule, and sabotage. Recalling the typology of forms of principled organizational dissent pictured in Figure 1, even the cell of "quiet departure" conceivably is an example of direct action. Whether direct action is perceived by officials in positions of authority as bureaucratic oppostion, or is effective in stimulating organizational change, is a matter of empirical investigation. If an action (even quiet departure) is undertaken as a form of conscientious response to the perception of an issue of principle, however, it qualifies as principled organizational dissent.

Organizational Dissent Mechanisms

The existence of effective internal channels for the expression and consideration of employee criticism is likely to affect the choice of method and target for the expression of dissent. If a dissident never experiences the disillusioning discovery that the organization sanctions what she or he perceives as wrongdoing, for instance, then the decision point where internal criticism escalates into external reporting (whistleblowing) will not be reached (see Figure 2). Conscientious reporting of problems which are perceived to involve matters of principle may occur, and curiosity about what corrective action is taken in response to such reports may be high, but principled dissent to communication targets outside organizational boundaries should be rare. This section of the paper describes various proposals and actual practices regarding organizational dissent mechanisms.

Decision-making procedures. The utilization of formal dissent and other assumption-surfacing devices in organizational decision making is one mechanism for increasing consideration of basic value questions. A variety of techniques have been proposed and discussed, including use of a "corporate devil's advocate" (Herbert & Estes, 1977; Stanley, 1981), structured debate in the Hegelian tradition (Mason, 1969), strategic assumption analysis (Mitroff & Emshoff, 1979), and intentional resistance to concurrence-seeking norms (Smart & Vertinsky, 1977). One particularly engaging proposal (Kegan, 1981, pp. 80, 91) urges that:

> The wise fool shoud be welcomed back as a valued member of design and management groups . . . . A fool is needed to puncture the hubris of the planner, that prideful presumption that his/her perspective is correct. A fool's playfulness can also increase the variation that facilitates Darwinian selection and survival.

Formal dissent procedures.   Many organizations, especially those with unionized personnel or which operate within a civil service system, have formal grievance procedures to deal with employee complaints. Many nonunionized private-sector organizations also have instituted grievance procedures (Foulkes, 1980; Scott, 1965). In addition, myriad federal and state laws provide mechanisms for employees to complain about specific issues (such as coal mine safety, pension rights, illegal discrimination, etc.). To use these procedures and mechanisms, a grievant must demonstrate his or her "standing" to grieve, that is, must state how he or she was personally injured by the organizational action being protested.

The kind of dissent procedure of interest here, however, is not the sort which deals with personal employee grievances. The subject matter instead concerns an organizational policy or practice that violates, in the organizational member's view, a general normative principle such as justice, honesty, or economy. Early examples of appeal mechanisms of this latter type include the Office of the Inspector General in the U.S. Army, recourses and visitations in the Catholic Church, and the Public Review Board of the United Auto Workers Union (Scott, 1965). These three appeal systems specifically allow for "allegations of deficiencies, irregularities, waste, or fraud which may *or may not* affect the complainant" (Scott, 1965, p. 37, emphasis added). Other appeal procedures which have been proposed for that purpose include an ethics appeal board; an organizational "hot line" for entering complaints, asking questions, and making suggestions and criticisms (Gillespie, 1979); and an "open door policy" (Ewing, 1977; Foulkes, 1980). The importance of norms of due process in the use of appeal procedures is emphasized by Evan (1961) and Walters (1975) as a guarantee against reprisals for their use. Summers (1980) argues that appeal procedures which utilize outside arbitrators (Summers cites TWA, Lockheed, and Michael Reese Hospital as examples) provide more credible protection of employee rights than procedures which are internal to the organization.

IBM Corporation is a leader in devising various mechanisms for facilitating organizational dissent through formal procedures (Short, 1983). It was one of the first organizations to adopt an "open door policy" whereby employees may voice their concerns to anyone in the chain of command. To be sure opportunities for reporting problems are provided regularly, "skip level interviews" are conducted several times a year in some IBM divisions, wherein managers meet individually with all subordinates two levels below them in the chain of command. The purpose of the interviews is to provide a channel for the upward flow of information and concerns, and it is totally separate from the personnel evaluation and feedback process. A third procedure available at IBM is the "speak-up" program, which allows employees to submit criticisms and concerns in writing to upper management, and to do so in strict confidence. Finally, the adequacy of all those procedures is regularly reviewed by means of employee-attitude surveys.

Procedures that are similar, if not as far-reaching, were adopted by various federal agencies in the 1960s and 1970s (Nuclear Regulatory Commission, 1978). The State Department has a "dissent channel" and an "open forum," the Food and Drug Administration a procedure called "the critical pathway"; in the Federal Aviation Administration, "unsatisfactory condition reports" can be filed, and at the Nuclear Regulatory Commission a variety of less-formal mechanisms were replaced in 1980 by a formal system for consideration of "differing professional opinions."

Perhaps the largest-scale effort to provide organizational mechanisms for principled dissent was established with the passage of the federal Civil Service Reform Act of 1978. The old Civil Service Commission was separated into two different agencies—the Office of Personnel Management to administer the federal personnel system, and the Merit Systems Protection Board to hear cases alleging prohibited personnel practices and (through the Office of Special Counsel) to hear from government employees concerned about wrongdoing in their agencies. This system was designed for the express purpose of providing a mechanism for hearing, evaluating, referring, and following up on the substance of a employee reports of wrongdoing (e.g., fraud, waste, abuse, danger to public safety), *and* to provide a channel for appeal if an employee reporter of wrongdoing feels he or she has suffered reprisals for his or her action. To assess the adequacy of the new system, periodic surveys of federal employees have been conducted (Palguta, 1984; U.S. Merit Systems Protection Board, 1981).

Boards of directors. The role of the board of directors in facilitating normal dissent has been explored by Perrucci et al. (1980), Stone (1975), and Aram and Salipante (1981). Perrucci and his colleagues (1980) argue that a board of directors lacking "outside" members who are there to represent the public interest will be unlikely to hear or promote dissent. They also note that a board which lacks an independent staff will have no way to oversee management in any but the most cursory manner. Stone (1975) suggests a possible role for boards of directors as the repository of an organization's superego: legal and ethical audits might be sponsored by the board, and members of the organization with ethical concerns would be encouraged to present them directly to members of the board. Aram and Salipante (1981) endorse using boards of directors as the appropriate organizational unit for considering internal conflicts which involve social values (i.e., superorganizational interests). They note that an organization's board of directors is "responsible for integrating the organization with society and may be able to assume explicit responsibility for resolving conflicts that have external, ethical, social, or legal ramifications" (Aram & Salipante, 1981, p. 203).

Designated officer.   Another suggestion for institutionalizing the capacity for normal dissent is the creation of an ombudsman office, one which would hear concerns about issues of principle in the organization, as well as more traditional grievances. Waters (1980) recommends that ombudsmen not only hear from dissenters, but also that they (the ombudsmen) launch internal investigations to uncover what he terms "organizational blocks," that is, "those aspects of organizations which may get in the way of the natural tendency of people to react against illegal and unethical practices" (p. 373).

An historical example of particularly enterprising ombudsmen is provided by Berger's (1963) interpretation of Israelite prophecy. Berger argues that the Old Testament prophets occupied a traditionally defined role (office) within the organizational structure of their socioreligious community. One of the duties of the prophet was to remind others in the organization of their covenant with Yahweh (i.e., their values and commitments). Organizationally sanctioned prophesying (or "wise foolishness" in Kegan's [1981] terms) can be expected to increase the likelihood that organizational members will be sensitive to issues of principle.

Protection of dissidents.   Although many procedures have been proposed or adopted to institutionalize internal dissent, a major concern has been the risk of reprisal from others in the organization against those engaging in dissent. Westin (1982, p. 7) identifies four elements of effective complaint and dissent procedures:

1. They define an employee's right to complain and appeal, with guarantees against reprisal for doing so.
2. They supply some kind of assistance or advocacy element to help the employee, whether it is a designated aide from the personnel office, a fellow employee, or other device.
3. They provide a high-level investigative inquiry, conducted by a staff person with authority from top management, to examine the facts without fear or favor, often under instructions to assume that the complaining (or dissenting) employee is right until the facts prove otherwise.
4. They offer a final appeal process that tries to supply high credibility for its impartiality and fairness. This may take the form of an enlightened chief executive or special top management committee or a joint employee-management committee.

The procedures for "differing professional opinions" (DPOs) developed by the Nuclear Regulatory Commission, first as a policy proposal (NRC, 1979), and then in final form (NRC, 1980), add an additional requirement to Westin's list: periodic review of the adequacy of the dissent procedures qua dissent procedures. Following its own advice, NRC convened the first Special Review Panel in September 1982 to evaluate how the procedures had worked in the 10 cases for which they were used in their first 18 months of existence. The panel was composed of two representatives of management, two from labor (the National Treasury Employees Union), and, as stipulated in the regulations, was chaired by an outsider, in this case the Executive Officer of the American Association for the Advancement of Science. The panel recommended several changes in the original procedures, but concluded overall that "the procedures have been working well and have provided an opportunity for employees to express differing professional opinions and to have those opinions heard and considered by management" (Singer, 1982, p. 1).

In summary, organizational mechanisms for allowing and protecting principled dissent are of many sorts. Were they to be evaluated in terms of their relative effectiveness, some might be found to facilitate dissent better than others, and/or contextual factors might be discovered which define conditions when some mechanisms work better than others. Although no such comparative studies have yet been done, it is assumed here that dissent mechanisms which are effective encourage dissenters to utilize internal procedures rather than to become whistleblowers to persons or agencies outside the organization. As such, an individual's knowledge of and confidence in the effectiveness of dissent procedures is likely to influence his or her choice of method for expressing dissent. Organizational factors which might contribute to such knowledge and confidence are reviewed in the next section.

Organizational Characteristics which Encourage Principled Dissent

Organizational culture and climate, informed by organizational goals and perpetuated by characteristics of the reward system, provide the intraorganizational environment for dissent. That environment influences the process of principled dissent at two points: (1) the potential dissenter's choice of behavior, and (2) the organization's response to dissent. The relative prosperity of the organization also contributes to the environment for dissent. In this section of the paper organizational culture and climate, reward systems, and relative prosperity will be examined.

Organizational culture and climate. Dyer (1982) defines the essence of culture as the "taken for granted" beliefs about self, others, and the environment. Included in such beliefs are assumptions about the nature of truth and knowledge. Mitroff and Turoff (1973) provide examples of various epistemological beliefs which can be culturally favored. Some stress the legitimacy of knowledge pronounced by authority, or arrived at by a consensual process; some describe knowledge as a perpetual state of controversy which, at any given point in time, can be summarized only in probabilistic terms. The cultural legitimacy of dissent would be greater in the latter than in the former systems. An organizational culture which values the process of continuous learning fosters normal dissent as a necessary and desirable part of organizational life (Argyris, 1973, 1982; Campbell, 1971; Schilit & Locke, 1982; Staw, 1977).

An organizational climate which respects individual conscience and fosters interpersonal trust encourages reporting of issues of principle (Ewing, 1977; Walters, 1975). Sgro, Worchel, Pence, and Orban (1980) find leader interpersonal trust to be highly correlated with tolerance of freedom. Gaines (1980) reports empirical results indicating that employee trust in supervisors increases the proportion of upward communication which is related to problem identification, and decreases the proportion dealing only with routine activities. Van Maanen and Schein (Schein, 1971; Van Maanen, 1976; Van Maanen & Schein, 1979) have developed a model of organizational socialization for which the major outcome variable is custodial vs. innovative response to one's work role. An organization which socializes its employees in ways which encourage innovative responses is likely to have more internal diversity than an organization which fosters custodial role performance.

Diversity within the organization also is increased by leader promotion of independent thought and action among subordinates—what House and Baetz (1979) term *participatory supervision*. Maier (1970) makes a similar point, describing participatory leadership as that which encourages and facilitates the airing of all points of view. Cole (1981) emphasizes the importance of actually adopting creative suggestions offered by employees, if an organization is serious about encouraging widespread participation in organizational learning. In 1979, General Motors (GM) adopted 23% of its workers' suggestions, while Nissan Motors' adoption rate was 86%. At the same time, GM received less than one suggestion per worker per year, whereas Nissan averaged nine suggestions per worker per year (Cole, 1981, p. 38). The suggestions involved in these comparisons related mainly to production issues, but the same kind of relationship may exist between organizational utilization of criticism and the likelihood that employees will engage in constructive efforts to maintain or improve organizational well-being.

Reward systems. Job performance standards can be either objective or subjective in character. Both types of standards can affect principled organizational dissent, although in different ways. Objective performance standards can be applied either to a series of specific work activities or to the accomplishment of a complete task. Ouchi and Maguire (1975) refer to those alternatives as *behavior control* and *output control,* respectively. Perrucci et al. (1980) found that the work roles of dissident employees tend to have little daily supervision, and positions with low surveillance are cited by Zald and Berger (1978) as one of three preconditions of "principled insurgency." Assuming that behavior control is maintained by close supervision, employees subject to behavior control would be less likely than those subject to output control to engage in dissident activity.

The application of subjective rather than objective performance standards also may affect the dissent process. Evan (1961) notes that, where performance evaluation is based on purely subjective factors, a subordinate tends to define his or her job as pleasing the boss, not as exercising independent judgment. The implication of Evan's analysis is that workers constrained by the need to ingratiate themselves with their superiors are unlikely to engage in an activity (e.g., open opposition) which risks incurring the boss's displeasure. The existence of subjective performance standards, then, may either deter dissent altogether or influence the dissenter's choice of tactics (e.g., the overtness of the tactics).

Systematic rule breaking (such as evasion of established shop routines, or appropriation of company materials for personal use) is sometimes allowed by an organization as an informal political compromise, or as a form of reward for extra performance (Dalton, 1959; Roy, 1952, 1954). A similar dynamic may exist wherein employees are given enough discretion in complying with specific rules and procedures that they can design and implement ways of performing their jobs which avoid raising ethical questions. Such an opportunity can provide an outlet for the worker who feels that organizationally acceptable quality standards are too low. Lipsky (1980) describes "street level bureaucrats" whose job autonomy allows pursuit of personal service ideals which exceed official standards. Craftspeople who create products exceeding organizational or customer requirements are another example.

Organizational prosperity. The degree to which an organization's environment can be characterized as one of scarcity has been shown to have an effect on internal organizational dynamics (Staw & Szwajkowski, 1975; Staw et al., 1981). One possible outcome is an increased tendency to engage in illegals acts (Staw & Szwajkowski, 1975), an effect which could lead to the generation or enlargement of principled issues. Other possible outcomes of scarcity in an organization's environment include restriction of information-processing capabilities, and tightening of organizational control (Staw et al., 1981). Both of those outcomes make an organization's response to internal dissent more hostile and, in time, make an organization's mechanisms for normal dissent less operative.

A benefit of environmental munificence (above and beyond avoiding the problems just described) is the organizational slack which is allowed. Slack translated into time can set the stage for reflective activity. Reconsideration of questions long forgotten, recognition of issues which had gone unnoticed, identification of opportunities on the horizon, the generation of genuinely new ideas—all these are possible given the opportunity for reflection.

DEVELOPMENT OF A THEORETICAL MODEL

A framework for the origin of the process of principled organizational dissent is suggested by empirical investigations of issue perception, especially those concerning moral judgment and bystander intervention in emergencies. The outcomes of the process, on the other hand, have been examined in case studies and surveys of organizational response to whistleblowers. Research on other topics (reviewed earlier) suggest factors which might influence interpretation and evaluation of perceived events, as well as the choice and design of a response to issue awareness. What does not yet exist is a conceptual model which ties the beginning of the process together with the end, locating all the theoretically important factors in between. The function of this section of the paper is to propose such a model. This will be done in two parts: first, the stages of a model of principled organizational dissent will be described, and then a causal analysis of the predictors of each stage will be proposed.

Stages of Principled Organizational Dissent

The sequential stages of the process of principled organizational dissent shown in Figure 6 are adapted from the models of whistleblowing, prosocial behavior, and upward political influence presented earlier in this paper (Figures 2, 4, and 5, respectively). The focal unit chosen for this analysis is the individual. It is an individual's perceptions, beliefs, and behavior which are used to define the stages in an episode of principled organizational dissent.

The process of principled organizational dissent pictured in Figure 6 begins when the potential dissident becomes aware of an "issue of principle," an organizationally relevant situation which she/he interprets as involving wrongdoing (e.g., activities deemed corrupt, unjust, grossly inefficient, socially harmful, unlawful, or otherwise unethical). In order for the person to make any response to her or his observation, the problem or issue must be assessed as nontrivial, some sense of personal respon-

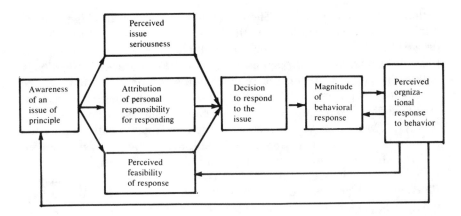

Figure 6. Model of principled organizational dissent.

sibility for responding to the situation must be felt (n.b., this does *not* imply claiming responsibility for the problem's existence), and some form of response must appear to be feasible. These three conditions are based on the intermediary stages between perception and behavior in the decision-making model of bystander helping behavior: (1) interpret the event as an emergency, (2) feel personally responsible for dealing with the event, and (3) possess the necessary skills and resources to act (see Figure 4). Although Latane and his colleagues (1968, 1970, 1981) describe these three evaluation tasks sequentially, other researchers have comingled them in a single cost-benefit matrix (Bar-Tal, 1976; Piliavin et al., 1969; Piliavin & Piliavin, 1972). The latter approach is followed here in order to allow for plausible reciprocal relationships. Very serious issues (for example, an imminent threat to public health) may generate feelings of responsibility to respond, and/or the belief that a solution *must* be feasible. Felt helplessness, on the other hand, may depress felt responsibility, and lead to belittling of situational seriousness.

Once the three evaluation tasks are completed, the person decides whether or not to respond to the situation. If the answer is yes, then the person must select a type and magnitude of response. For example, she or he can report the matter to a superior, use some other channel available in the workplace for reporting observations of wrongdoing (e.g., the Office of Inspector General in federal agencies, or the "open door" at IBM), go outside the organization (i.e., become a whistleblower), or engage in some form of direct action (e.g., working to rule, or quitting).

The organization's response to principled dissent is on two levels: response to the issue itself, and response to the person of the dissident. The issue can be attended to or not, possibly leading to a change in organizational practices or policy. The dissident can be rewarded, ignored, or punished for pursuing an issue in the face of resistance from others in the organization. Because there may be multiple observers of dissent, it is possible that a variety of responses will exist. For purposes of feedback within the process model, the organization's response is whatever the dissident perceives to be the organizational result of his/her initial dissent, and, as such, is taken into account when choosing his/her follow-up action (if any). "Awareness of a principled issue" at Time 2 is affected by the organization's response to dissent at Time 1: the problem may be resolved and therefore no longer exist, and/or the dissident's sensitivity to such issues may be enhanced or diminished as a result of organizational action. Change in the "perceived feasibility of response" also is possible as a function of prior experience as a dissenter. Two feedback arrows are included in the model to accommodate these possibilities. In addition, both dissidence and organizational response to dissidence may take on a life of their own, ricocheting back and forth until some resolution of the issue (or change in one of the parties) calls a halt.

The basic elements of the process of principled organizational dissent are identified in Figure 6, but (except for the initial step) they are portrayed as a string of dependent or endogenous variables. The independent or exogenous variables which affect the model still require specification. In the next section of the paper, a model for each of the variables in Figure 6 is proposed, drawing on the theory and research reviewed earlier in the paper.

Questions for Research

The discussion of research questions in this section parallels the seven variables pictured in Figure 6: awareness of a principled issue, perceived issue seriousness, attribution of personal responsibility for a response, perceived feasibility of response, decision to respond, magnitude of behavioral response, and perceived organizational response to behavior.

Awareness of a principled issue. The likelihood that any particular organizational member will be aware of an issue of principle in the workplace is a function of the existence and seriousness of such issues in the organization, plus individual attention, ability, and motivation to attend to them.

The first question raises a figure–ground issue. Where the social legitimacy of organizations is secure, principled issues are likely to be rare occurrences, thereby reducing the opportunity for issue perception (Milgram, 1975; Moore, 1978; Simon, 1976). Chronic issue seriousness in an organization, on the other hand, as indicated by the magnitude of the threat or the frequency of its occurrence, provides many opportunities for issue perception, thereby increasing the probability that organizational members will be aware of principled issues at work. Alternatively, in an environment where few issues exist, those that do may be more visible than in an organization where principled issues are commonplace. Issue visibility increases the probability that an issue of principle will be noticed, and issue visibility may be greatest where issues are rare.

A second figure–ground issue concerns the relationship between job tenure and awareness of principled issues. In general, the longer a person works in a given position, the more accustomed she or he becomes to things as they are. The definition of *normal* is based increasingly on how things typically are, rather than on how they might be ideally, i.e., if they conformed to some ideal norm. As a result, job tenure is likely to reduce awareness of principled issues.

Access to information about a wide variety of organizational activities increases the possibility that issues of principle will come to a person's attention. Exposure to information about many aspects of organizational life increases with organizational level. As a result, job level may increase the likelihood of awareness of issues of principle.

Sensitivity to wrongdoing in the workplace can be either an assigned or an assumed responsibility (Culbert, 1974; Elbing, 1970; Milgram, 1975; Wynn, 1982). If responsibility is assigned (e.g., to an internal auditor), then the person's work performance is assessed partly in terms of how well problems are detected. If responsibility is assumed voluntarily (e.g., by someone with a high level of social responsibility), then the motivation is intrinsic rather than extrinsic, but sensitivity to issues is maintained all the same. In either case awareness of principled issues is made more likely.

Attention to issues of principle also varies with the amount of time the person has to observe and consider things outside his or her narrow duties. People's everyday lives vary as to their fullness. Some have considerable leisure time, others are so full of activity that opportunities for quiet reflection are rare. This measure of activity level refers to the total of a person's obligations, including those at work. Full-time employment, routine work, and close supervision on the job may decrease the likelihood of issue awareness, by encouraging concentration only on the narrow confines of normal routine (Perrucci et al., 1980; Zald & Berger, 1978).

The intellectual ability to disengage oneself from the details of an immediate situation and to evaluate that situation in terms of an abstract normative standard increases the likelihood of issue awareness (Moore, 1978). That ability is one component of a high level of moral reasoning. The other component—possessing strong normative beliefs—also enhances the ability to evaluate specific situations in terms of normative standards, thereby facilitating awareness of issues of principle (Moore, 1978; Zald & Berger, 1978).

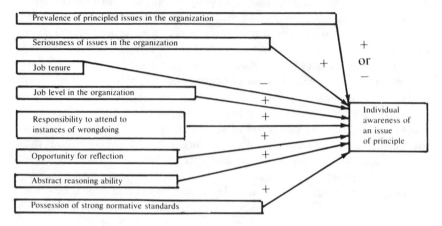

Figure 7.   Determinants of issue awareness.

Perceived issue seriousness.   The degree to which an issue is perceived as being serious (by the person who is already aware that an issue exists) is a function of the objective characteristics of the situation, the apparent assessment of others concerning issue seriousness, and any individual tendency to exaggerate or minimize the severity of perceptual stimuli.

Issue seriousness as an objective characteristic can be measured in a number of ways, depending on the nature of the issue. Where an issue is assessable in terms of its monetary impact, issue seriousness increases with cost. The seriousness of an issue which threatens to harm people increases both by harming more rather than fewer people, and by causing major rather than minor harm to each victim. Issue seriousness is also a function of the certainty of negative outcomes, and their timing (Elliston, 1982a). Where issue seriousness can be measured quantitatively, the greater the issue's likely negative impact, the greater perceived issue seriousness will be.

Another measure of seriousness is the frequency with which some form of wrongdoing occurs. Frequency can influence the perception of seriousness in two conflicting ways. Objectively, a problem which happens frequently is a more serious overall threat than a single instance of the same event. On the other hand, especially under conditions of situational ambiguity, a problem which occurs frequently may be perceived as less serious, due to the operation of pluralistic ignorance and audience inhibition (Latane & Darley, 1968, 1970; Latane & Nida, 1981). The observer might assume that a chronic problem must be familiar to many others, and, sensing no feeling of general concern, and not wanting to risk creating unnecessary alarm, the observer might conclude that the problem must be trivial. Empirical evidence is needed to ascertain whether the effects of problem frequency increase or decrease the perception of issue seriousness in a given situation. The number of others presumed to be knowledgeable about the issue, however, is likely to reduce perceived issue seriousness due to the effects of pluralistic ignorance (Latane & Darley, 1968).

The effect of social inhibition notwithstanding, individual differences exist with respect to issue evaluation in general. Some people systematically exaggerate objective evidence as compared to other observers. Such a tendency can be termed *alarmism,* and its effect is likely to increase perceived issue seriousness.

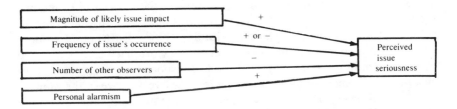

Figure 8. Determinants of perceived issue seriousness.

Attribution of personal responsibility for a response. The psychological state of feeling personally responsible for responding to an issue of principle is related to job assignment, personal sense of social responsibility, and extent of issue exposure. The types of assigned job responsibilities that are relevant to issues of principle include responsibility for reporting information (e.g., an auditing assignment), and responsibility for overseeing operations (e.g., supervisors and managers). If the person's assignment is to do reporting, then issue awareness should lead to an attribution of personal responsibility to respond to the issue by reporting it. If the person's assigment is supervisory or managerial, on the other hand, issue awareness may sometimes stimulate denial of responsibility. Two kinds of responsibility—responsibility for the existence of a problem and responsibility for providing a solution (Brickman et al., 1979)—are involved here, and it is important to distinguish between them, even though the presence of one may lead to a denial of the other. Insofar as the observer of a principled issue fears he/she might be blamed for the existence of the problem (because of assigned responsibility), his or her response to issue awareness may depend on the feasibility of taking direct action to correct the situation. If direct action is not feasible, and problem solution requires reporting the situation to someone else, then attribution of personal responsibility for a response may be denied, as part of an avoidance strategy with respect to admitting responsibility for the problem's existence.

A sense of personal responsibility for social welfare is a result of cognitive moral development (Kohlberg, 1969, 1976; Piaget, 1932; Rest, 1979), and social learning. It can be sustained by internalization of a professional ethic of social responsibility (Ladenson, 1979b; Weil, 1979). The personal characteristic of having a strong sense of social responsibility inclines a person to accept responsibility even where others do not (Schwartz, 1977). Such a characteristic increases the likelihood of attributing personal responsibility for a response to an issue of principle.

The presence of others who are presumed to share awareness of an emergency situation affects attribution of responsibility by diffusing responsibility among all those present. The greater the number of observers, the greater the diffusion, and the less responsibility any single person attributes to him- or herself (Darley & Latane, 1968). Diffusion of responsibility with respect to principled issues in the workplace can be affected by group size in the same way. Diffusion of responsibility might also occur as a person's exposure to problems increases. Irrespective of the number of other observers, the more issues a person is aware of, the less likely she or he is to feel personal responsibility for responding to any single one of them.

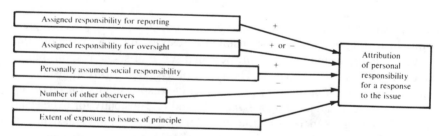

Figure 9. Determinants of personal responsibility attribution.

Perceived feasibility of response. The perception that a response to an issue of principle is feasible depends on two major factors: knowledge of one or more response options likely to be effective in correcting the problem, and confidence that the personal cost of employing such options will not be prohibitive (Porter et al., 1981).

Channels of communication or formal dissent procedures provide options for someone seeking a way to respond to issues of principle. Such mechanisms can be both internal to the organization (e.g., an open door, hotlines, labor–management committees, special investigatory units) and external (interested audiences such as the news media, public interest lobbies, or government regulatory agencies). The mere existence of such options is not sufficient by itself, however; the observer of an issue of principle must (1) be knowledgeable about the available options, and (2) must have enough self-esteem to imagine that his or her action might stimulate organizational change (Goodman, Bazerman, & Conlon, 1980; Howard & Somers, 1971; Hunsaker, 1982). Porter et al. (1981) suggest using internal locus of control as a measure of self-confidence as a potential change agent.

In addition to the existence of corrective mechanisms, the likely personal cost of using them is a factor in assessing response feasibility. The primary cost is the risk of reprisal from those in the organization who oppose disruption of the status quo (Ewing, 1980; Harshbarger, 1973; O'Day, 1974; U.S. Senate, 1978). The risk of reprisal is less where organizational culture encourages role innovation (Van Maanen & Schein, 1979), independent thought and action (House & Baetz, 1979), widespread participation (Maier, 1970), and includes epistemological assumptions favoring experimentation and continuous learning (Argyris, 1973, 1982; Campbell, 1971; Mitroff & Turoff, 1973; Staw, 1977). More concretely, personal costs are reduced where assistance in the preparation and presentation of critical arguments is provided within a formal dissent mechanism (Westin, 1982), and where guarantees against reprisal also exist (Nuclear Regulatory Commissions, 1978). The existence of allies (co-dissenters) and/or supporters (e.g., professional associations) may reduce the likelihood of reprisal. Specific legal protection for freedom of expression (e.g., free speech for public employees), volunteer public guardians (e.g., under the public policy exception to the at-will doctrine, statutory antiretaliation protection, and the Michigan or Connecticut whistleblower protection acts), or par-

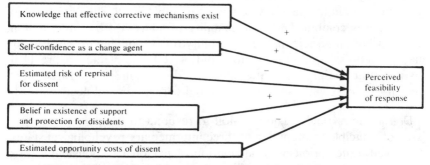

Figure 10. Determinants of perceived feasibility of response.

ticipatory decision making (e.g., as stipulated in a formal labor agreement), also reduce the risk of retaliation for utilizing dissent mechanisms (Malin, 1983). An agent–target relationship of mutual respect affects perceived "costs of approach" (Porter et al., 1981) by reducing the risk of reprisal. Another cost is a form of capital depletion. Hawley and Nichols (1982) report that no one in their study "approached the decision to participate in one issue as though it were independent of their ability to participate and be effective in other issues" (p. 116).

Reciprocal relationships.   The perception of issue seriousness, attribution of personal responsibility for a response, and perceived feasibility of response may be reciprocally related. Equity theory (Adams, 1965; Walster, Bersheid, & Walster, 1973), for example, suggests a relationship between perceived issue seriousness and attribution of personal responsibility for a response. According to equity theory, the magnitude of the inequity (which is a measure of issue seriousness for one type of principled issue) determines the motivational force to correct the inequity. It follows that issue seriousness in general may stimulate attribution of personal responsibility to respond to principled issues. Going the other way, attribution of responsibility can be bolstered by exaggerating issue seriousness (Janis & Mann, 1977); by the same token, denial of responsibility can be bolstered by diminishing the seriousness of the issue.

The relationship between perceived issue seriousness and perceived feasibility of response is very similar to that between seriousness and responsibility attribution. In both cases the estimate of seriousness may be adjusted to justify the levels of responsibility and feasibility which are chosen. Very high levels of need, moreover, may serve as both moral and practical imperatives to spur a response. Imminent disaster in and of itself may generate an attribution of personal responsibility to respond, and stimulate creation or enlargement of the set of feasible responses.

Attribution of personal responsibility and perceived feasibility of response may also interact reciprocally. If the cost of responding is likely to be high, as in the case where personal culpability for the existence of a problem is combined with an inability to address it by direct action, then attribution of personal responsibility for responding to the situation may be depressed in an effort to avoid or shift the blame. Figure 11 illustrates the reciprocal relationships predicted among the three intermediary process variables between initial perception and decision.

Decision to respond.   The decision to respond to the perception of an issue of principle is a function of three intermediary psychological states: perceived issue seriousness, attribution of personal responsibility for a response, and perceived feasibility of response. The incidence of a re-

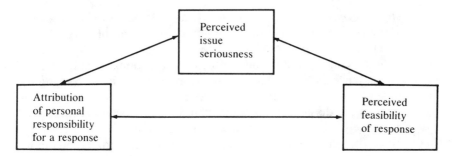

Figure 11. Reciprocal Relationships Among mediating processes.

sponse, such as reporting the issue to those in authority, is therefore hypothesized to depend on all the factors discussed so far, mediated by the three psychological states.

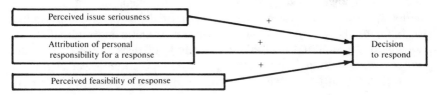

Figure 12. Determinants of decision to respond.

Magnitude of behavioral response. The magnitude of response to the perception of issues of principle is a function of the same variable set as is the decision to respond, with one modification. The operational definition of *perceived feasibility of response* needs to be expanded in order to avoid ceiling effects. A single feasible response option is sufficient to allow the initial choice of whether to respond. For magnitude of response to vary, however, the person must know about more than one response option, (e.g., those beyond the local work group, be they in other parts of the organization, or outside the organization altogether). Magnitude of response can then be gauged in terms of the highest target chosen, or the number of targets approached.

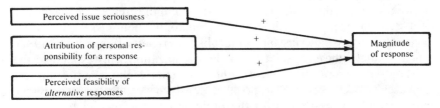

Figure 13. Determinants of response magnitude.

Perceived organizational response to behavior. The consequences of principled organizational dissent, for the dissenter and for problem resolution, are a function of the person of the dissenter, the dissent itself, various organizational characteristics, and immediate situational conditions.

Near and Jensen (1983) oppose two theoretical rationales relating the magnitude of a dissenter's threat to the organization to the latter's retaliation against the dissident: the organization may be deterred from retaliating because of the personal power of the dissident (a "strategic" response), or the organization might retaliate most when threatened most, i.e., by someone who might be able to force organizational change (a "rationalistic" response). Near and Jensen (1983) assume that the rationales are mutually exclusive. An alternative approach is to separate the independent variable into two parts: the dissenter and the dissent. Dissenters vary in terms of personal power (i.e., ability to threaten the organization). However, the threat posed by dissent is also a function of the *behavior* engaged in by the dissenter. The magnitude of dissent behavior can vary independently of the personal power of the dissenter. Recognizing that distinction allows both the strategic and rationalistic rationales to be supported. Holding magnitude of dissent constant, a dissenter who is personally weak (e.g., with low position power or low expertise) may suffer reprisals even though the threat posed to the organization is small. Holding vulnerability of dissenter constant, greater magnitude of dissent may elicit greater retaliation because the organization is more threatened.

The identity of the dissenter and the nature of dissent behavior may also affect organizational responsiveness to the substance of the principled issue. Successful social influence, according to McGuire (1969), requires that the agent of influence receive from the target of influence three things: attention, understanding, and yielding. High personal credibility for a dissenter (the agent of influence) is likely to enhance both attention and yielding from organizational listeners (targets of influence). Repetition of a message (which is one measure of dissent magnitude), on the other hand, may facilitate understanding of message content. In both cases, organizational responsiveness to the issue would be increased.

Magnitude of dissent, however, may also operate in other ways. Dissent may be seen as a threat to the organization, and the greater the magnitude of dissent the greater the threat. The common response to threat, by individuals, groups, and organizations alike, is rigidity (Staw et al., 1981), which reduces the probability that the organization will respond to the substantive issue raised by the dissenter. Whether high-magnitude dissent increases or decreases organizational responsiveness to the principled issue may depend on the reason for the problem's persistence in the organization. If the reason is ignorance or misunderstanding, then perseverent dissent might help to bring about change by increasing understanding. If the reason is informed advocacy of the status quo, then dissent of increasing magnitude is likely to elicit only rigidity and reactance. An exception to that may be when dissent reaches very high levels (e.g., whistleblowing). In that case, problem resolution may occur because outside intervention overcomes the organization's rigidity response to threat.

Enduring organizational characteristics may also affect the organization's response to dissent. The same set of organizational variables that contributed to "perceived feasibility of response"—organizational climate and reward systems that encourage role innovation, independent thought and action, widespread participation, and epistemological assumptions favoring experimentation and continuous learning—decreases organizational hostility toward dissidents, and increases the probability of problem resolution.

Situational factors which might affect organizational response to dissent include the seriousness of the issue, and the economic prosperity of the organization as a whole. The effects of issue seriousness on the probability of problem resolution are complex. On the one hand, issue seriousness should increase the likelihood of problem-solving effort because of the potential liability to the organization of leaving a severe problem unattended. On the other hand, issue seriousness may be directly related to problem difficulty. Such a relationship implies that issue seriousness decreases the likelihood of problem resolution. Empirical studies are needed to untangle these countervailing effects.

The relationship between organizational prosperity and problem solving is likely to be more straightforward. By providing the resources for problem correction, organizational prosperity increases the likelihood of problem resolution. Resource scarcity, on the other hand, not only limits the feasibility of problem resolution, but creates a "bunker mentality" wherein dissent is especially unwelcome (Janis, 1972; Smart & Vertinsky, 1977). As a result, organizational hostility toward dissidents would increase in times of scarcity.

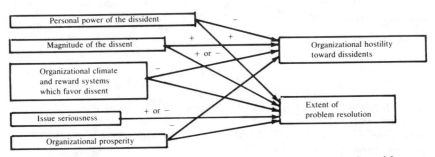

Figure 14. Determinants of organizational Nostility and of problem resolution.

CONCLUSION

This paper is an effort to set the stage for a program of research on a topic that is related to scholarly work in a wide range of disciplines. The variety and complexity of conceptual research which has been done on topics closely related to principled organizational dissent is impressive. Given that fact, it is intriguing to speculate why more empirical research has not yet taken place.

One possible explanation is that principled organizational dissent is a low base rate phenomenon, a product of journalistic hyperbole. What evidence exists on the subject, however, indicates otherwise. A recent U.S. government study revealed that nearly half the civilian government workforce was aware of principled issues during a 12-month period, and that almost 30% of them reported their observations to others (Graham, 1983; U.S. Merit Systems Protection Board, 1981).

A second explanation for the paucity of empirical research concerns access to research sites. It is easy to find individual dissidents who want to share their case histories, but very difficult to find sites for cross-sectional or longitudinal studies of whole organizations. It has been my experience that managers initially find the possibility of capitalizing on principled dissent to be full of promise. On reflection, however, and after checking with others in the organization, they estimate the risk of allowing research on principled dissent to be too great. That experience is supported by Porter et al.'s (1981) observation that researchers interested in studying the "dark" side of organizational life, such as political behavior in the workplace, are not generally welcomed by organizational gatekeepers.

Principled organizational dissent is a topic which allows both the study and the exercise of some very human characteristics: fallibility and fear, confession and a capacity to learn, virtue and a vision of a better world. The substantive issues which are the focus of principled organizational dissent, the organizational behavior of both individuals and collectivities, the sociocultural and legal environment where it all takes place—all these and more are appropriate subjects for future research.

REFERENCES

Adams, J. S. (1965). Inequality in social exchange. In L. Berkowitz (Ed.), *Advances in experimental social psychology* (Vol. 2) (pp. 267–299). New York: Academic Press.

Andover Newton Laity Project. (1981). *Covenanted support for ministry: A guide for beginning groups.* Newton Centre, MA.

Andrews, J. D. W. (1981). Student development and the goals of higher education: A conceptual framework for selecting teaching strategies. *Exchange, 6*(2), 5–14.

Antonio, R. J. (1979). The contradiction of domination and production in bureaucracy: The contribution of organizational efficiency to the decline of the Roman Empire. *American Sociological Review, 44,* 895–912.

Aram, J. D., & Salipante, P. F. (1981). An evaluation of organizational due process in the resolution of employee/employer conflict. *Academy of Management Review, 6*(2),197–204.

Argyris, C. (1973). *Intervention theory and method: A behavioral science view.* Reading, MA: Addison-Wesley.

Argyris, C. (1982). *Reasoning, learning, and action: Individual and organizational.* San Francisco: Jossey-Bass.

Asch, S. E. (1951). Effects of group pressure on the modification and distortion of judgments. In H. Geutzkow (Ed.), *Groups, leadership and men* (pp. 117–190). Pittsburgh: Carnegie Institute of Technology Press.

Bar-Tal, D. (1976). *Prosocial behavior: Theory and research.* New York: Wiley.

Beck, M. (1983, February 28). The toxic tar baby at Reagan's EPA. *Newsweek,* 14–15.

Berger, P. L. (1963). Charisma and religious innovation: The social location of Israelite prophecy. *American Sociological Review, 28*(6), 940–950.

Blades, L. E. (1967). Employment at will vs. individual freedom: On limiting the abusive exercise of employer power. *Columbia Law Review, 67,* 1404–1435.

Blumberg, P. I. (1971, August). Corporate responsibility and the employee's duty of loyalty and obedience. *Oklahoma Law Review,* 279–318.

Bowman, J. S., Elliston, F. A., & Lockhart, P. (1984). *Professional dissent: An annotated bibliography and research guide.* New York: Garland.

Brickman, P., Rabinowitz, V. C., Coates, D., Cohn, E., Kidder, L., & Karuza, J. (1979, July). *Helping.* Unpublished manuscript.

Broholm, R. (1982, May). *How can you believe you are a minister when the church keeps telling you you're not!* Study conducted for the Leadership Training Task Force, Board of Global Ministries, United Methodist Church (Preliminary report).

Bureau of National Affairs. (1979). *Basic patterns in union contracts* (9th ed.). Washington, D.C.: BNA, Inc.

Bureau of National Affairs, Labor Special Projects Unit. (1981). *The employment-at-will issue.* Washington, D.C.: BNA, Inc.

Campbell, D. T. (1971). *Methods for the experimenting society.* Draft of a paper delivered extemporaneously to the American Psychological Association, Washington, D.C.

Cartwright, D. (1965). Influence, leadership and control. In J. G. March (Ed.), *Handbook of organizations* (pp. 1–47). Chicago: Rand McNally.

Cole, R. E. (1981, July). The Japanese lesson in quality. *Technology Review,* 29–40.

Crowe, B. J., Bochner, S., & Clark, A. W. (1972). The effect of subordinates' behavior on managerial style. *Human Relations, 25,* 215–237.

Culbert, S. A. (1974). *The organization trap and how to get out of it.* New York: Basic Books.

Dalton, M. (1959). *Men who manage fusions of feeling and theory in administration.* New York: Wiley.

Darley, J. M., & Latane, B. (1968). Bystander intervention in emergencies: Diffusion of responsibility. *Journal of Personality and Social Psychology, 8,* 377–383.

Donaldson T. (1982). Employee rights. In T. Donaldson (Ed.), *Corporations and morality* (pp. 129–157). Englewood Cliffs, NJ: Prentice-Hall.

Dyer, W. G. (1982, June). *Patterns and assumptions: The keys to understanding organizational cultures* (TR–ONR–7). Cambridge, MA: Massachusetts Institute of Technology.

Elbing, A. O. (1970). *Behavioral decisions in organizations.* Chicago: Scott Foresman.

Elliston, F.A. (1982a, Winter). Anonymous whistleblowing: An ethical analysis. *Business and Professional Ethics Journal,* 39–58.

Elliston, F. A. (1982b). Civil disobedience and whistleblowing: A comparative appraisal of two forms of dissent. *Journal of Business Ethics, 1,* 23–28.

Evan, W. M. (1961, August). Organization man and due process of law. *American Sociological Review, 26*(4), 540–547.

Ewing, D. W. (1977). *Freedom inside the organization: Bringing civil liberties to the workplace.* New York: E.P. Dutton.

Ewing, D. W. (1980). How bureaucrats deal with dissidents. In W. C. Hamner (Ed.), *Organization shock* (pp. 328–331). New York: Wiley.

Ewing, E. W. (1983). *Do it my way or you're fired!* New York: Wiley.

Farrell, D. (1983). Exit, voice, loyalty, and neglect as responses to job dissatisfaction: A multidimensional scaling study. *Academy of Management Review, 26*(4), 596–607.

Farris, G. F., & Lim, F. G. (1969). Effects of performance on leadership cohesiveness, influence, satisfaction, and subsequent performance. *Journal of Applied Psychology, 53,* 490–497.

Foulkes, F. K. (1980). *Personnel policies in large nonunion companies.* Englewood Cliffs, NJ: Prentice-Hall.

Gaines, J. (1980). Upward communication in industry: An experiment. *Human Relations, 33,* 929–942.

Gillespie, N. C. (1979). Corporate structures and individual freedom. In T. L. Beauchamp & N. E. Bowie (Eds.), *Ethical theory and business* (pp. 348–352). Englewood Cliffs, NJ: Prentice-Hall.

Goldstone, J. A. (1982). The comparative and historical study of revolutions. *Annual Review of Sociology, 8,* 187–207.

Goodman, P. S., Bazerman, M., & Conlon, E. (1980). Institutionalization of planned organizational change. In B. M. Staw & L. L. Cummings (Eds.), *Research in organizational behavior* (Vol. 2) (pp. 215–246). Greenwich, CT: JAI Press.

Gordon, A. C., Heinz, J. P., Gordon, M. T., & Divorski, S. W. (1973). Public information and public access: A sociological interpretation. *Northwestern University Law Review, 68*(2), 280–308.

Graham, J. W. (1983, August). *Principled organizational dissent.* Unpublished doctoral dissertation, Northwestern University, Department of Organization Behavior.

Greene, C. N. (1975). The reciprocal nature of influence between leader and subordinate. *Journal of Applied Psychology, 60,* 187–193.

Greene, C. N. (1979). Questions of causation in the path-goal theory of leadership. *Academy of Management Journal, 22,* 22–41.

Gurr, T. R. (1970). *Why men rebel.* Princeton, NJ: Princeton University Press.

Gurr, T. R. (Ed.). *Handbook of political conflict: Theory and research.* Glencoe, IL: The Free Press.

Hamilton, V. L., & Sanders, J. (1983). Universals in judging wrongdoing: Japanese and Americans compared. *American Sociological Review, 48*(2), 199–211.

Harshbarger, D. (1973, April). The individual and the social order: Notes on the management of heresy and deviance in complex organizations. *Human Relations, 26,* 251–269.

Hastie, R. (1983). Social influence. *Annual Review of Psychology, 34,* 511–542.

Hawley, K. E., & Nichols, M. L. (1982). A contextual approach to modeling the decision to participate in a "political" issue. *Administrative Science Quarterly, 27*(1), 105–119.

Herbert, T. T., & Estes, R. W. (1977). Improving executive decisions by formalizing dissent: The corporate devil's advocate. *Academy of Management Review, 2*(4), 662–667.

Herold, D. M. (1977). Two-way influence processes in leader-follower dyads. *Academy of Management Journal, 20,* 224–237.

Hirschman, A. O. (1970). *Exit, voice, and loyalty: Responses to decline in firms, organizations, and states.* Cambridge, MA: Harvard University Press.

Hirschman, A. O. (1974). 'Exit, voice, and loyalty': Further reflections and a survey of recent contributions. *Social Science Information, 13*(1), 7–26.

House, R. B., & Baetz, M. L. (1979). Leadership: Some empirical generalizations and new research directions. In B. M. Staw (Ed.), *Research in organizational behavior* (Vol. 1) (pp. 341–423). Greenwich, CT: JAI Press.

Howard, J. M., & Somers, R. H. (1971). Resisting institutional evil from within. In N. Sanford & C. Comstock (Eds.), *Sanctions for evil* (pp. 264–289, 353–356). San Francisco: Jossey-Bass.

Hunsaker, P. L. (1982, April). *Strategies for organizational change: The role of the inside change agent.* Paper presented at the Western Academy of Management Meeting, Colorado Springs, Col.

Institute of Electrical and Electronics Engineers. (1975, January 9). *Engineering ethics.* Amicus curiae brief filed with the Superior Court of California.

Isaacson, W. (1983, March 7). The winds of reform: Runaway weapons costs prompt a new look at military planning. *Time,* 12–30.

Janis, I. L. (1972). *Victims of groupthink: A psychological study of foreign-policy decisions and fiascos.* Boston: Houghton Mifflin.

Janis, I. L., & Mann, L. (1977). *Decision making.* New York: The Free Press.

Kegan, D. L. (1981). Contradictions in the design and practice of an alternative organization: The case of Hampshire College. *Journal of Applied Behavioral Science, 17*(1), 79–97.

Kerr, S., Von Glinow, M. A., & Schreisheim, J. (1977). Issues in the study of 'professionals' in organizations: The case of scientists and engineers. *Organizational Behavior and Human Performance, 18,* 329–345.

Kipnis, D., Schmidt, S. M., & Wilkinson, I. (1980). Intraorganizational influence tactics: Explorations in getting one's way. *Journal of Applied Psychology, 65*(4), 440–452.

Kohlberg, L. (1969). Stage and sequence: The cognitive developmental approach to socialization. In D. Goslin (Ed.), *Handbook of socialization theory and research* (pp. 357–480). Chicago: Rand McNally.

Kohlberg, L. (1976). Moral stages and moralization: The cognitive-developmental approach. In T. Lichona (Ed.), *Moral development and behavior* (pp. 31–53). New York: Holt.

Ladenson, R. F. (1979a, November). *Freedom of expression in the corporate workplace: A philosophical inquiry.* Paper presented at the Conference on Business Ethics, Western Michigan University.

Ladenson, R. F. (1979b, April). *The social responsibilities of engineers and scientists: A philosophical approach.* Center for the Study of Ethics in the Professions, Occasional Papers No. 1.

Latane, B., & Darley, J. M. (1968). Group inhibition of bystander intervention in emergencies. *Journal of Personality and Social Psychology, 10*(3), 215–221.

Latane, B., & Darley, J. M. (1970). The influences of social models on helping. In J. Macaulay & L. Berkowitz (Eds.), *Altruism and helping behavior* (pp. 13–28). New York: Academic Press.

Latane, B., & Nida, S. (1981). Ten years of research on group size and helping. *Psychological Bulletin, 89*(2), 308–324.

Lipsky, M. (1980). *Street-level bureaucracy: Dilemmas of the individual in public services.* New York: Russell Sage Foundation.

Lowen, A., & Craig, J. R. (1968). The influence of level of performance on managerial style: An object lesson in the ambiguity of correlational data. *Organizational Behavior and Human Performance, 3,* 490–497.

Maier, N. R. F. (1970). *Problem solving and creativity in individuals and groups.* Belmont, CA: Brooks-Cole.

Malin, M. H. (1983). Protecting the whistleblower from retaliatory discharge. *University of Michigan Journal of Law Reform, 16*(2), 277–318.

Mason, R. O. (1969). A dialectical approach to strategic planning. *Management Science*, *15*(8), 403–414.

McGuire, W. J. (1969). The nature of attitudes and attitude change. In G. Lindzey & E. Aronson (Eds.), *The handbook of social psychology* (2nd ed.) (Vol. 3) (pp. 136–314). Reading, MA: Addison-Wesley.

McNeil, K. (1978). Understanding organizational power: Building on the Weberian legacy. *Administrative Science Quarterly, 23*(1), 65–90.

Mechanic, D. (1971). Sources of power of lower participants in complex organizations. In B. L. Hinton & J. J. Reitz (Eds.), *Groups and organizations* (pp. 489–496). Belmont, CA: Wadsworth.

Michalos, A. C. (1979). The loyal agent's argument. In T. L. Beauchamp & N. B. Bowie (Eds.), *Ethical theory and business* (pp. 338–348). Englewood Cliffs, NJ: Prentice-Hall.

Milgram, S. (1975). *Obedience to authority*. New York: Harper & Row.

Mitchell, G. (1982). *Truth . . . and consequences: Seven who would not be silenced.* New York: Dembner Books.

Mitroff, I. I., & Emshoff, J. R. (1979). On strategic assumption making: A dialectical approach to policy and planning. *Academy of Management Review, 4*(1), 1–12.

Mitroff, I. I., & Turoff, M. (1973, March). The whys behind the hows: Effective application of the many forecasting methods requires a grasp of their underlying philosophies. *IEEE Spectrum*.

Moore, B. (1978). *Injustice: The social bases of obedience and revolt*. White Plains, NY: M. E. Sharpe.

Mowday, R. T. (1978). The exercise of upward influence in organizations. *Administrative Science Quarterly, 23*, 137–156.

Nader, R., Petkas, P. J., & Blackwell, K. (1972). *Whistle blowing*. New York: Grossman.

Near, J. P., & Jensen, T. C. (1983). The whistleblowing process: Retaliation and perceived effectiveness. *Work and Occupations, 10*(1), 3–28.

Nuclear Regulatory Commission. (1978). *A survey of policies and procedures applicable to the expression of differing professional opinions*. Washington, D.C.

Nuclear Regulatory Commission. (1979). *Proposed policy and procedures for differing professional opinions for comment*. Washington, D.C.

Nuclear Regulatory Commission. (1980). *Chapter 4125: Differing professional opinions*. Washington, D.C.

O'Day, R. (1974). Intimidation Rituals: Reactions to Reform. *Journal of Applied Behavioral Science, 10*(3), 373–386.

Ouchi, W. G., & Maguire, M. A. (1975). Organizational control: Two functions. *Administrative Science Quarterly, 20*(4), 559–569.

Payne v. Western & A.R.R. Co., 81 Tenn. 507 (1884).

Palguta, J. M. (1984, May). *Federal agency mechanisms that encourage dissent.* Paper presented to the American Association for the Advancement of Science, New York City.

Parmerlee, M. A., Near, J. P., & Jensen, T. C. (1982). Correlates of whistle-blowers perceptions of organizational retaliation. *Administrative Science Quarterly, 27*(1), 17–34.

Parmerlee, M. A., White, R. W., Near, J. P., & Jensen, T. C. (1980, August). *Correlates of the severity of organizational reprisal against whistle-blowers.* Paper presented at the Academy of Management Annual Meeting.

Perrucci, R., Anderson, R. M., Schendel, D. E., & Trachtman, L. E. (1980). Whistle-blowing: Professionals' resistance to organizational authority. *Social Problems, 28*(2), 149–164.

Petermann v. Teamsters Local 396, 174 Cal. App. 184, 344 P.2d 25 (1959).

Peters, C., & Branch, T. (1972). *Blowing the whistle: Dissent in the public interest*. New York: Praeger.

Piaget, J. (1932). *The moral development of the child*. London: Kegan Paul.

Pickering v. Board of Education, 391 U.S. 563, 88 S.Ct. 1731, 20 L.Ed.2d 811 (1968).

Piliavin, I. M., Rodin, J., & Piliavin, J. A. (1969). Good samaritanism: An underground phenomenon. *Journal of Personality and Social Psychology, 13,* 289–299.

Piliavin, J. A., & Piliavin, I. M. (1972). Effect of blood on reactions to a victim. *Journal of Personality and Social Psychology, 23,* 353–362.

Porter, L. W., Allen, R. W., & Angle, H. L. (1981). The politics of upward influence in organizations. In L. L. Cummings & B. M. Staw (Eds.), *Research in organizational behavior* (Vol. 3) (pp. 109–149). Greenwich, CT: JAI Press.

Rest, J. (1979). *Development in judging moral issues.* Minneapolis: University of Minnesota Press.

Rowen, R. (1983, January). The maverick who yelled foul at Citibank. *Fortune, 10,* 46-56.

Roy, D. (1952, March). Quota restriction and goldbricking in a machine shop. *American Journal of Sociology, LVII,* 427–442.

Roy, D. (1954, November). Efficiency and 'the fix': Informal intergroup relations in a piece-work machine shop. *American Journal of Sociology, LX,* 255–266.

Schachter, S. (1960). Deviation, rejection, and communication. In D. Cartwright & A. Zander (Eds.), *Group dynamics: Research and theory* (2nd ed.) (pp. 260–285). Evanston, IL: Row, Peterson.

Schein, E. H. (1971). Occupational socialization in the professions: The case of the role innovator. *Journal of Psychiatric Research, 8,* 521–530.

Schilit, W. K., & Locke, E. A. (1982). A study of upward influence in organizations. *Administrative Science Quarterly, 27*(2), 304–316.

Schwartz, S. H. (1977). Normative influence in altruism. In L. Berkowitz (Ed.), *Advances in experimental social psychology* (Vol. 10) (pp. 221–279). New York: Academic Press.

Scott, W. G. (1965). *The management of conflict appeal systems in organizations.* Homewood, IL: Irwin.

Sgro, J. A., Worchel, P., Pence, E. C., & Orban, J. A. (1980). Perceived leader behavior as a function of the leader's interpersonal trust orientation. *Academy of Management Journal, 23*(1), 161–165.

Short, A. E. (1983, March 21). IBM Corporation personal communication.

Simon, H. A. (1976). *Administrative behavior* (3rd ed.). New York: The Free Press. (Orig. 1945).

Singer, K. (1982, September 22). *Minutes of the special review panel for differing professional opinions.* Washington, D.C.: Nuclear Regulatory Commission.

Smart, C., & Vertinsky, I. (1977). Designs for crisis decision units. *Administrative Science Quarterly, 22*(4), 640–657.

Stanley, J. D. (1981). Dissent in organizations. *Academy of Management Review,* 6(1), 13–19.

Staub, E. (1978). *Positive social behavior and morality* (Vols. 1 & 2). New York: Academic Press.

Staw, B. M. (1977). The experimenting organization: Problems and prospects. In B. M. Staw (Ed.), *Psychological foundations of organizational behavior* (pp. 466–486). Santa Monica, CA: Goodyear.

Staw, B. M., Sandelands, L. E., & Dutton, J. E. (1981). Threat-rigidity in organizational behavior: A multilevel analysis. *Administrative Science Quarterly, 26*(4), 501–524.

Staw, B. M., & Szwajkowski, E. (1975). The scarcity-munificence component of organizational environments and the commission of illegal acts. *Administrative Science Quarterly, 20*(3), 345–354.

Stone, C. D. (1975). *Where the law ends: The social control of corporate behavior.* New York: Harper & Row.

Summers, C. W. (1980, January–February). Protecting all employees against unjust dismissal. *Harvard Business Review,* 132–139.

Tilly, C. (1978). *From mobilization to revolution.* Reading, MA: Addison-Wesley.

Toch, H. (1965). *The social psychology of social movements.* Indianapolis: Bobbs-Merrill.

U.S. Merit Systems Protection Board, Office of Merit Systems Review and Studies. (1981, October). *Whistleblowing and the federal employee: Blowing the whistle on fraud, waste, and mismanagement—Who does it and what happens.* Washington, D.C.: U. S. Government Printing Office.

U.S. Senate Committee on Governmental Affairs. (1978, February). *The whistleblowers: A report on federal employees who disclose acts of governmental waste, abuse and corruption.* Washington, D.C.: U.S. Government Printing Office.

Van Maanen, J. (1976). Breaking in: Socialization to work. In R. Dubin (Ed.), *Handbook of work, organization and society* (pp. 67–130). Chicago: Rand McNally.

Van Maanen, J. & Schein, E. H. (1979). Toward a theory of organizational socialization. In B. M. Staw (Ed.), *Research in organizational behavior* (Vol. 1) (pp. 209–264). Greenwich, CT: JAI Press.

Walster, E., Bersheid, E., & Walster, G. W. (1973). New directions in equity research. *Journal of Personality and Social Psychology, 25*(2), 151–176.

Walters, K. D. (1975). Your employee's right to blow the whistle. *Harvard Business Review, 53*(4), 26–34, 161–162.

Waters, J. A. (1980). Catch 20.5: Corporate morality as an organizational phenomenon. In W. C. Hamner (Ed.), *Organizational shock* (pp. 372–386). New York: Wiley.

Weil, V. M. (1977). *The Brown's Ferry case.* Center for the Study of Ethics in the Professions.

Weil, V. M. (1979, August). *Action and responsibility in the engineering profession.* Center for the Study of Ethics in the Professions, Occasional Paper No. 2.

Weinstein, D. (1979). *Bureaucratic opposition.* New York: Pergamon Press.

Weisband, E., & Franck, T. M. (1975). *Resignation in protest.* New York: Grossman.

Westin, A. (Ed.). (1981). *Whistle blowing! Loyalty and dissent in the corporation.* New York: McGraw Hill.

Westin, A. (1982, Fall). Individual rights and fair procedure systems. *ILR Report, 20*(1), 5–8.

Whyte, W. H. (1957). *The organization man.* Garden City, NY: Doubleday.

Wynn, C. T. (1982, April). *Responsibility: A potential keystone to effective organizational behavior.* Paper presented to the Western Academy of Management Meeting.

Zald, M. N., & Berger, M. A. (1978). Social movements in organizations: Coup d'etat, insurgency, and mass movements. *American Journal of Sociology, 83*(4), 823–861.

ORGANIZATIONAL STRUCTURE, ATTITUDES, AND BEHAVIORS[1]

Chris J. Berger and L.L. Cummings

ABSTRACT

This paper reviews and evaluates the research published since 1965 that examines the relation between organizational structural characteristics and participant attitudes and behaviors. The effects of organizational level have received the widest attention, with particular emphasis being given to the relation of level to participant satisfaction. Other structural characteristics examined include line-staff function, size, span of control, complexity, and shape. An explicit attempt is made to evaluate progress since the last major review of this literature (Porter and Lawler, 1965). Progress continues to be constrained by the lack of clearly formulated, sophisticated conceptual networks,

by limited methodological designs, and by inappropriate analyses. Suggestions for
improvements are offered along with cautious conclusions concerning present knowledge.

This paper represents what might be called a pretheoretical analysis of the
relation of organizational structure to attitudes and behavior. As such it
aims toward a "cleaning-up" and interpretation of the relevant literature.
It distinguishes between the relevant and irrelevant studies, given a priori
standards of relevancy, and critiques and interprets the relevant ones.

A decade ago, Porter and Lawler (1965) published a review of the
literature concerning the relationship of organizational structural characteristics to job attitudes and job behaviors. Drawing the distinction between variables which were appropriate for intra- and total organizational
analysis, Porter and Lawler focused on the following seven structural
characteristics.

Organizational levels
Line and staff hierarchies
Span of control
Subunit size
Total organization size
Tall or flat shape
Centralized or decentralized shape

The dependent variables examined were job attitudes (broadly defined as
an opinion concerning some job aspect) and job behavior (performance,
turnover, absenteeism, and employee-grievance rates). After reviewing
research published through 1964, they concluded that "at least 5 of these
7 structural variables (with possible exceptions being span of control and
centralized/decentralized shape) were found to be significantly related to
one or more attitude or behavioral variables" (p. 23).

Since the Porter and Lawler review, more than forty empirical studies
investigating the relationship between some aspect(s) of organization
structure and members' attitudes and/or behavior have been reported.
While James and Jones (1976) have recently reviewed the *conceptual*
literature that theorizes about the relation between structural characteristics and individual attitudes and behaviors, the *empirical* literature of the
past ten years has not been reviewed, integrated, and critiqued. The purposes of the present paper are to: (1) review this literature of the past
decade, (2) indicate empirical generalizations which may be drawn from
the literature and compare these with the generalizations derived by Porter and Lawler, and (3) discuss a number of conceptual and methodological problems in this literature.

The scope of this review has been affected by several considerations.
First, the time period covered is 1964 to the present. Second, unpublished

studies have been omitted. Third, only empirical studies which measured more than one level of a given structural variable have been included, thus focusing on comparative research. Fourth, in contrast to the Porter and Lawler review, studies which sampled individuals in organizations other than business and industry have been included. Fifth, studies which focused on dependent variables at the organizational level of analysis have been excluded. Thus, for example, a study which related organization size to performance was included if individual members' performance was measured, but was excluded if performance was measured across an entire department, plant, or organization. This was done for two reasons: Our primary interest centers on the behavior of persons within organizations, and we wish our review to be cumulative with the earlier review by Porter and Lawler (1965).

A final category of studies excluded from this review is that focusing on organizational climate. Only those studies researching climate in which the authors specifically addressed the relationship of organizational structure (as distinct from climate) to members' attitudes and/or behaviors have been included. Three reviews of the organizational climate literature have appeared recently (Hellriegel and Slocum, 1974; James and Jones, 1974; Schneider, 1975).

The paper is broadly organized into two sections. The first of these examines the empirical evidence. Here, an attempt is made to create a review which is cumulative with the Porter and Lawler (1965) review and thus utilizes a similar categorization scheme wherever possible. Within the seven structural categories, studies are separated by attitudinal and behavioral dependent variables. Important studies are described and examined in detail, and analytical comments appropriate only to a particular study are included. Brief summary statements appear at the end of each of these sections.

The second major section of the paper attempts to provide a broader critique and perspective on the methodology of the studies reviewed, with the explicit purpose of detailing major methodological flaws which continue to plague us and severely limit our ability to generate useful cumulative evidence in this area.

REVIEW OF EMPIRICAL LITERATURE

SUBORGANIZATIONAL: ORGANIZATIONAL LEVELS

Organizational level refers to an individual's position in the vertical hierarchy of authority and ranges from nonsupervisory workers at the lower end of the scale to the chief executive at the upper extreme.

While the definition of organizational level would appear straightforward, most researchers have not explicitly defined this variable at a conceptual level and none have discussed its theoretical relationship with other organizational and/or individual variables. Operationally, most studies have simple asked respondents for a self-report of their position within their organization's hierarchy of authority. A few studies have categorized individuals according to their position in a hierarchy relative to the total number of levels in their particular organization, thus facilitating comparison between equivalent positions in organizations with differing numbers of levels.

Relation to Attitudes

Need and job satisfaction   After reviewing more than a dozen studies relating two or more orgnaizational levels to individuals' job satisfactions, Porter and Lawler (1965) concluded that the literature as of 1964 showed increasing job satisfaction across increasing hierarchical levels. While many of the early studies they reviewed sampled blue-collar workers, Porter (1962, 1964) reported the results of a survey of nearly 2,000 managerial personnel at various organizational levels in different business and industrial organizations. These two reports combined with Porter and Lawler's review apparently set the stage for subsequent researchers' attempts to broaden our knowledge with respect to the organizational levels/job satisfaction relationship in different types of organizations. One alternative sample employed by researchers since 1965 has been the military. Porter and Mitchell (1967), for example, surveyed 1,279 commissioned and noncommissioned U.S. Air Force officers. The Porter Need Satisfaction Questionnaire (PNSQ: Porter, 1962) was used to measure individual's perceived need fulfillment and need satisfaction. The thirteen scales comprising the PNSQ were designed to measure the need fulfillment and need satisfaction of five basic needs (security, social, esteem, autonomy, and self-actualization), following Maslow (1954). With respect to need fulfillment, each higher level of commissioner officers reported significantly higher need fulfillment. However, noncommissioned officers did *not* show a consistent increase in need fulfillment with increasing rank.

Concerning need satisfaction, in the noncommissioned officer group there was a positive and consistent relationship between organizational level and satisfaction, while the commissioned officers did not show this pattern. Thus, over all organization levels, the hypothesis of consistently increasing need fulfillment and/or satisfaction was not supported.

Johnson and Marcum (1968) related organizational level to need satisfaction in a sample of career U.S. Army officers. Officers were divided into three groups according to their miltiary rank. Need satisfaction was measured by a nine-item questionnaire similar in format to the PNSQ. The data was analyzed with Kruskal-Wallis one-way analysis of variance by ranks. In all, thirteen pair-wise comparisons were made, less than half of which showed significant differences across all three military ranks. Of those which were significantly different across ranks, need satisfaction did not consistently increase with increasing organizational level.

A third study exploring the need satisfaction/organization level relationship within the military was reported by Mitchell (1970), who surveyed 675 commissioned U.S. Air Force officers. The variables included in this study were need fulfillment and need satisfaction (PNSQ), organizational level (three military ranks), and line or staff assignment. Within the six line and staff assignment categories, data were analyzed by signed-rank tests. With differences between line and staff assignments controlled, there were fairly consistent increases in need fulfillment with increases in military rank, but inconsistent changes in need satisfaction with increases in military rank.

A second group of studies relating to the need satisfaction/organizational level hypothesis focuses upon samples drawn from public sector organizations. Rhinehart, Barrell, DeWolfe, Griffin, and Spaner (1969) for example, reported survey results of 2,026 employees of the federal Veterans Administration. Respondents were medical, professional, and nonprofessional supervisory personnel, who were classified into four managerial levels. Need satisfaction was measured by the PNSQ. Data were analyzed with signed-rank tests and indicated that need satisfaction increased consistently with organizational level.

A second study using a sample of government employees to examine the organizational level/job satisfaction relationship has been reported by Lichtman (1970). In a sample of ninety-four middle managers, first-level supervisors and "working-level technical employees" from two offices of the Internal Revenue Service, organizational level was related to job satisfaction, need achievement, organizational knowledge, job-related tension, internal control, and productivity (the latter five of which will be discussed subsequently). Global job satisfaction was measured with an instrument developed by Harris (1949). Overall differences in mean job satisfaction across the three organizational levels were statistically significant ($p < .01$) with job satisfaction increasing with organizational level.

Miller (1966a) studied the organizational level/job satisfaction relationship in a randomly selected sample of national-level officials of large craft and industrial unions. Organizational level was dichotomized into "higher"- and "lower"- level positions based on the individual's job title.

Need satisfaction was measured by the PNSQ. In craft unions, higher-level officials were more satisfied than lower-level officials. Within industrial unions, no significant differences in satisfaction were found.

Slocum (1971) utilized the PNSQ to study the need satisfaction of 210 managers of a Pennsylvania steel plant. He found higher satisfaction among middle and top managers (versus first-line supervisors) across esteem, autonomy, and self-actualization needs. Similar trends, though not statistically significant, were noted for security and social needs.

The seven studies reviewed above researching the organizational level/job satisfaction hypothesis in predominantly nonbusiness samples show mixed results. Studies sampling military personnel failed to show strong support for a positive relationship between level and satisfaction. While two studies (Porter and Mitchell, 1967; Johnson and Marcum, 1968) showed mixed support, a third (Mitchell, 1970) reported no significant increases in need satisfaction across organizational levels. Clearly, none of these three military studies provides support for the statement that need satisfaction increases consistently with organizational level.

On the other hand, two studies which sampled federal government employees (Rhinehart et al., 1969; Lichtman, 1970) did support the hypothesis of consistent and significant increases in need and job satisfaction with increases in organizational level. Finally, a study sampling national union officials (Miller, 1966a) and one study of business managers (Slocum, 1971) were not inconsistent with the hypothesis.

More complex studies   The following studies, while examining the impact of organizational level, differ from the preceding studies in terms of their design and/or analytical procedures. They include one or more of the following characteristics: *(a)* additional predictors of job or need satisfaction in terms of additional organizational and/or individual variables, *(b)* multivariate statistical analysis, and *(c)* multiple instruments used to measure job satisfaction.

None of the studies reviewed above related individual differences to differences in job or need satisfaction. Moreover, there were no estimates of the net relationship of organizational level and the individual level variables to satisfaction. In contrast, several studies have attempted to answer these questions within appropriate multivariate frameworks.

Lawler and Porter (1966) for example, examined the relationship between several organizational and individual variables and managerial pay satisfaction. Reporting data from Porter's (1962) survey of 1,916 managers, organizational level, line/staff position, organization size, tenure, age, education, and actual salary were used to predict managers' satisfaction with their pay. Multiple correlation indicated that organizational level showed a small but significant negative net relationship to pay satisfaction. Except for tenure, the demographic variables were not significantly related to pay satisfaction.

A more recent study considering the relationship of organizational level and pay satisfaction in a multivariate framework has been reported by Schwab and Wallace (1974). The sample consisted of 273 randomly selected employees (stratified by pay system) from one large firm. Individuals' age, sex, tenure with firm, type of pay system, pay level, and organizational level were used to predict satisfaction with pay using zero-order and partial correlational analyses.[2] Pay satisfaction was measured by appropriate items from the Minnesota Satisfaction Questionnaire (MSQ; Weiss, Dawis, England, and Lofquist, 1967) and the Cornell Job Descriptive Index (JDI; Smith, Kendall, and Hulin, 1969). When multiple correlation was used to control for the linear effects of other variables, all predictors except age and tenure in the case of the MSQ, and age in the case of the JDI were significantly related to satisfaction with pay. Organizational level showed small but significant negative net relationships with pay satisfaction as measured by both the JDI and the MSQ.

In a national random sample of 911 solid-waste management employees, Locke and Whiting (1974) found white-collar employees to be more satisfied with their jobs than blue-collar employees. In addition, the white-collar employees were more likely to associate variations in satisfaction with intrinsic rewards than with extrinsic sources and exhibited a greater tendency toward this distinction than the blue-collar employees.

MacEachron (1977) has recently reported findings indicating an interaction between field independence [as measured by Oltman's (1968) portable rod-and-frame test] and organizational level in relation to the JDI on a sample of seventy female nurses. Organizational level was indexed at three levels: nursing supervisors and RNs, licensed practical nurses, and nursing aides. While there was not a significant correlation between level and four of five JDI dimensions for the total sample, field independence did moderate the relation. Field-independent nurses exhibited a positive correlation between level and satisfaction on each of the five JDI dimensions while field dependents exhibited only one significant, negative correlation between level and satisfaction (co-workers). In addition, it is interesting to note that field independence was positively correlated with organizational level ($r = .38$).

A second group of studies using multivariate techniques has focused on job or need satisfaction in relation to organizational level and one or more additional structural variables. Two associated articles (El Salmi and Cummings, 1968; Cummings and El Salmi, 1970), for example, related several structural properties to various need measures. The sample consisted of 425 managers from a number of organizations. Need fulfillment, need importance, and need satisfaction were measured with the PNSQ.

Subjects also responded to an item concerning their "perceived chance of attaining the level of need fulfillment—for each item—they thought should exist in their present jobs" (Cummings and El Salmi, 1970, p. 2). Structural variables were organizational level, line or staff position, total organization size, and subunit size. All of the organizational variables were trichotomized, with organizational level and tall/flat shape being standardized across organizations.

Cummings and El Salmi (1970) found organizational level to be significantly related to need fulfillment and perceived possibility of need fulfillment. While need fulfillment increased consistently across all three organizational levels, the possibility of need fulfillment appeared to decrease with increasing level. Organizational level was not significantly related to either need importance or need satisfaction. Further, none of the six organizational variables measured were reported to be significantly related to need importance or need satisfaction in the univariate analysis.

El Salmi and Cummings (1968) reported the effects of three interactions (organizational level by line/staff position; organizational level by total organization size; and organization level by tall/flat shape) on several of the four need variables. The organizational level by total size interaction was significantly related both to need fulfillment and perceived possibility of need fulfillment. In the case of the former relationship, the highest-level managers reported more need fulfillment in small than in large organizations. However, middle and lower-middle managers in larger organizations reported more need fulfillment than did their counterparts in small companies. The organizational level by tall/flat shape interaction was significantly related to need satisfaction. A final interaction term (organizational level by line/staff position) was not significantly related to need fulfillment. Overall, then, these two reports (El Salmi and Cummings, 1968; Cummings and El Salmi, 1970) show no support for the univariate effect of organizational level on need satisfaction, although need fulfillment did increase with organizational level.

A third category of multivariate studies has used multiple measures of job satisfaction. One such study has been reported by Waters and Roach (1973). Their sample consisted of 101 managerial personnel in a national insurance company. Organizational levels ranged across all managerial ranks. Need satisfaction was measured by the PNSQ. In addition to the thirteen items contained in the PNSQ, three items concerning satisfaction with pay, being informed, and "pressure" experienced in the management position were measured using the PNSQ format. Also included was a measure of overall job satisfaction which was rated on a 12-point bipolar scale. These seventeen satisfaction items and the subjects' organizational level were then factor analyzed, from which four factors were identified: higher- and lower-order need satisfaction, esteem-prestige, and participation in the management process. Organizational level, which showed no relationship to the first three factors, loaded positively on the participation in management processes factor. Thus, in this sample at least, organizational level was positively associated with only a subset of satisfaction (with participation) and was not associated with any other satisfaction items or with overall job satisfaction.

Herman and Hulin (1973) measured job satisfaction with both the PNSQ and the JDI. Subjects were four levels of managerial personnel from one large organization. The organizational level/job satisfaction hypothesis was examined via discriminant analysis on the JDI and the PNSQ separately. Analysis of the JDI resulted in a significant overall solution and two significant linear functions discriminating between the four organizational levels. Scale loadings in this analysis indicated that group differences were based primarily on satisfaction with work and pay. In these functions, satisfaction generally tended to increase with each organizational level. The results of the discriminant analysis of the PNSQ, however, did not result in a significant overall solution.

A final group of studies to be reviewed in this section has many or all of the multivariate characteristics described above, and to varying degrees may be seen as partial replicates of one another in terms of methodology and/or variables studied.

Herman and Hulin (1972) utilized a number of aspects of the multivariate studies reviewed above in examining the organizational level/job satisfaction hypothesis. They measured multiple individual characteristics, organizational structural variables, and job attitudes on 307 salaried supervisory and nonsupervisory personnel in one plant of a large industrial organization. The individual variables consisted of respondents' age, education, and plant tenure. The structural variables were functional division, organizational level, and department. The attitudinal variables measured included general job attitudes, job satisfaction, and attitudes toward line/staff relations and leadership. Component analysis (Eckert and Young, 1936) was used to reduce this set of items to seventeen attitude variables. Discriminant analysis was then performed on these dependent variables for each of the three structural variables and the three personal variables. In addition, a multivariate analog of omega squared was used to estimate the power of the solutions and to compare the six independent variables. This analysis indicated that the three structural variables accounted for more attitude variance (department = .82; function = .60; level = .43) than did the individual variables (tenure = .40; age = .39; education level = .37). With respect to organizational level, the four classifications of respondents were first-level supervisors, second- and third-level supervisors, nonsupervisory personnel, and staff assistants who were not engaged in supervision. Herman and Hulin reported that differences between hierarchical groups related primarily to line/staff relation and co-worker satisfaction, and to evaluation of both superior/ subordinate relationships and supportive services. Thus, changes in organizational level were related to only a subset of total job satisfaction. While finding an overall increase in satisfaction with increasing organizational level, Herman and Hulin (1972) did not find a consistent increase in satisfaction at each higher level. Even disregarding the nonsupervisory staff group, respondents at the middle organizational level were more satisfied than their higher- or lower-level counterparts.

Herman, Dunham, and Hulin (1975) investigated both structural properties and participant demographic characteristics as these related to a number of attitudinal dependent variables. Herman et al. studied 392 employees in a printing plant. Organizational level and position (i.e., membership in an organizationally defined department and work shift) were examined. Using canonical and part canonical analysis, it was found that: (1) 22 percent of the total response variance across all dependent variables was accounted for by the total set of demographic and structural varibles, (2) the demographic variables accounted for 9 percent of the response variance, (3) the structural variables accounted for 19 percent of the response variance, (4) controlling for the covariation of demographic and structural variables, structural indices accounted for 13 percent of the response variance while demographic indices accounted for only 3 percent of the response variance. In terms of specific structural relations, persons in higher job levels expressed greater satisfaction with work and pay and experienced greater work-related motivation. In general, persons in nonproduction departments (primarily office and maintenance) expressed greater satisfaction and motivation than those in production departments.

In a related study, Adams, Laker, and Hulin (1977) have found a significant main effect ($p < .01$) of job level (three levels) and functional specialty (five classifications) on four of the JDI dimensions (excluding satisfaction with promotional opportunities) on a sample of 1,313 employees of a printing company. In addition, the job level × functional specialty interaction was significant ($p \leq .01$) and was due to the univariate F for satisfaction with work. Job level was determined by ratings of jobs done by the investigators across factors like training time or education required, responsibility, and authority. The ratings were done on 20-point scales applied to fifteen job categories. The resulting rating distribution was trichotomized into unskilled, skilled, and professional-supervisory categories. Job satisfaction increased on each of the four JDI dimensions across the unskilled, skilled, and professional-supervisory categories respectively.

In a sample of 710 employees from all levels and departments of one insurance company, Newman (1975) related personal characteristics (age, sex, education, tenure, and number of dependents) and organizational structure variables (hierarchical level, functional division, department, and work group) to job attitudes. The latter included job satisfaction (JDI) and a measure of personal work involvement (Lodahl and Kejner, 1965). Analysis was carried out via discriminant analysis separately on each personal and organizational characteristic and included the multivariate analogue of omega squared.

Results indicated that the greatest amount of attitude variance was associated with the personal variables of age (.30) and tenure (.28) and the structural variables hierarchical level (.31), department (.22), and work group (.34). Hierarchical level was positively related to satisfaction with the work itself, pay, supervision, co-workers, and to job involvement.

O'Reilly and Roberts (1975) also related individual characteristics (ability, personality traits, and motivational traits all measured by Ghiselli's [1971] Self-Description Inventory) and structural variables (organizational level, organizational tenure, and job tenure) to job satisfaction as measured by the JDI. The sample consisted of 578 officers and enlisted men in one "high technology" naval aviation unit. Analysis was conducted with canonical correlation. With structural variables partialed out, there were no significant relationships between personality variables and job satisfaction. However, with personality variables controlled, there were significant relationships between structure and job satisfaction. While the authors do not present specific data, they suggest that organizational level is positively related to satisfaction with pay and promotion.

Szilagyi, Sims, and Keller (1976) found satisfaction with work, supervision, and co-workers as measured by the JDI to increase with occupational level. They sampled 931 hospital employees at five occupational levels. In the hospital studies, occupational and organizational level appear to be highly and positively related. In addition, role ambiguity (versus role conflict) was more highly related to satisfaction at higher occupational levels while role conflict was more highly related to satisfaction at lower occupational levels. Thus, occupational level was both directly related to satisfaction indices and also moderated the relationship between two role dynamics variables and these satisfaction indices. In a related study, Sims and Szilagyi (1976) found that occupational level moderated the relation between perceptions of *task* characteristics (measured via the *JDS*) and satisfaction with work (measured via the *JDI*). For example, feedback and satisfaction with work were more highly related at higher than lower occupational levels while variety and satisfaction with work were more highly related at lower than higher occupational levels. Thus, occupational and organizational level may not only impact satisfaction directly, but may also influence the relation between the nature of the immediate work and affective reactions to that work.

While these studies are to be lauded for their analytical techniques and inclusion of personal variables, there are several weaknesses which should be pointed out. First, Herman and Hulin (1972), Herman et al. (1975), Newman (1975), and Szilagyi, Sims, and Keller (1976) all include department, work group, and/or occupational group as structural variables. These variables were measured by the organization's designation of department or work group. Thus, these are nominal variables which have meaning only within the context of the *particular* organization. Failure to specify what this variable means in terms of a more generic structural definition precludes generalization to other organizations and situations, and in several cases raises the danger of confounding several generic structural variables (e.g., line/staff position, specialization) and/or individual level variables (e.g., selection, supervision) encompassed within the department variable. The conclusion that structural variables account for more attitude variance than do personal variables must be regarded with caution, at least at this stage of the analysis.[3]

A second problem involves the classification of variables concerning the interface of the individual and the organization. For example, Herman et al. (1975) grouped tenure, participation in an apprentice program, and work shift as structural variables. O'Reilly and Roberts also classified organizational tenure and job tenure as structural variables. On the other hand, Herman and Hulin (1972) and Newman (1975) include tenure as a personal variable. Given that these variables are in fact meaningful only with respect to a specific organization-individual interface, attempting to proportion variance in attitudes between structural variables and personal or demographic variables is inappropriate.

To summarize, studies relating organizational level to one or more aspects of job satisfaction have been presented. These studies are summarized in Table 1. As can be seen from this table, samples, measures, and analytical techniques have varied widely, as have the results. Military samples have provided only limited support for the organizational level/job satisfaction hypothesis as stated in the Porter and Lawler (1965) review. Samples of government workers (Rhinehart et al., 1969; Lichtman, 1970) and national union officials (Miller, 1966a) did show support for the hypothesis.

Eleven studies have tested the hypothesis in business or industrial samples. While there is considerable method variance across the studies, and while job satisfaction does not appear to increase *consistently* with each organizational level, there is a relatively stable pattern between studies which indicates an overall positive association of organization level and job satisfaction.

Summary of Studies of the Job Satisfaction-Organizational Level Hypothesis

Study	Sample (n)	Number levels	Satisfaction measure	Multivariate aspects	Statistical procedure	Significant overall relationship	Direction of relationship	Consistent with each level
Miller, 1966	Union officials (171)	2	PNSQ	Craft/industrial	Signed-rank tests	Yes	Positive	Yes
Porter and Mitchell, 1967	Military (1,297)	6	PNSQ	None	Signed-rank tests	Yes	Positive	No
Johnson and Marcum, 1968	Military (504)	3	PNSQ	None	Kruskal-Wallis	Yes	Positive	No
Mitchell, 1970	Military (675)	3	PNSQ	Line-staff controlled	Signed-rank tests	No	Zero	No
Rhinehart et al., 1969	Government (2,026)	4	PNSQ	None	Signed-rank tests	Yes	Positive	Yes
Lichtman, 1970	Government (94)	3	Harris (1949)	None	ANOVA	Yes	Positive	Yes
Slocum, 1971	Business (210)	2	PNSQ	None	t-tests	Yes	Positive	Yes
Locke and Whiting, 1974	Business (911)	5	Locke and Whiting (1974)	Occupation controlled demographic	F-tests	Yes	Positive	No
Lawler and Porter, 1966	Business (1,916)	4	PNSQ (pay)	Structural individual	Multiple correlation	Yes	Negative	Yes
Schwab and Wallace, 1974	Business (273)	Not identified	MSQ; JDI (pay)	Individual	Multiple correlation	Yes	Negative	Yes
Cummings and El Salmi, 1970 / El Salmi and Cummings, 1968	Business (425)	3	PNSQ	None Structural	Signed-rank tests (see text) Chi-square (see text)	No Yes	Zero Interactive	No
Waters and Roach, 1973	Business (101)	4	PNSQ (and 4 other items)	Analysis	Factor analysis	Yes (one of 4 factors)	Positive	Yes
Herman and Hulin, 1973	Business (121) (158)	4	PNSQ JDI	Analysis Analysis	Discriminant analysis	No Yes	Zero Positive	No Yes
Herman and Hulin, 1972	Business (307)	4	Multiple items (see text)	Structural; individual; analysis	Component analysis; discriminant analysis	Yes	Positive	No
Herman, Dunham, and Hulin, 1975	Business (392)	Not identified	JDI	Structural; individual; analysis	Component analysis; canonical correlation	Yes	Positive	See text

Summary of Studies of the Job Satisfaction-Organizational Level Hypothesis (*continued*)

Study	Sample (n)	Number levels	Satisfaction measure	Multivariate aspects	Statistical procedure	Significant overall relationship	Direction of relationship	Consistent with each level
Newman, 1975	Business (710)	All levels	JDI	Structural; individual; analysis	Discriminant analysis	Yes	Positive	See text
O'Reilly and Roberts, 1975	U.S. Navy (578)	Not identified	JDI	Structural; individual; analysis	Canonical correlation	Yes	Positive	See text
Szilagyi, Sims, and Keller, 1976	Hospital (931) Business (192)	5 3	JDI	Analysis	Zero- and first-order correlations and nonparametric procedures	Yes	Positive	No
MacEachron, 1977	Hospital Nurses (70)	3	JDI	Structural; individual	Pearson product moment correlation; moderator analysis via subgrouping	No for 4 JDI dimensions; yes for 1 dimension	Positive for pay satisfaction	Not tested
Adams, Laker, and Hulin, 1977	Business (1,313)	3	JDI	Structural; analysis	MANOVA and discriminant analysis	Yes	Positive	Yes

300

Sources of job satisfaction   Three studies have examined the components and sources of job satisfaction as a function of the organizational level and context of the subjects. Starcevich (1972) examined the importance of eighteen job components in contributing to job satisfaction and dissatisfaction across three organizational levels. He found that organizational level (first-line managers, middle managers, and professional employees) did not affect the judged importance of the job components in determining satisfaction or dissatisfaction. Satisfaction means by organizational level were not reported. In general, however, job content factors (versus job context factors) were judged to be more important for both job satisfaction and dissatisfaction.

Harris and Locke (1974) found that white-collar employees (generally in higher-level positions) tended to derive satisfaction and dissatisfaction from "motivator" factors while blue-collar employees tended to derive satisfaction from "hygiene" factors. Most of the difference was attributable to the white-collar employees mentioning achievement-related events while blue-collar employees attributed satisfaction-dissatisfaction to monetary events.

Locke and Whiting (1974) have examined both environmental events and agents as sources of satisfaction and dissatisfaction in a sample of blue- and white-collar male employees in the solid waste management industry from both the private and public sectors. Events identified as sources of satisfaction for white-collar employees were promotions, feelings of achievement, and smoothness of work flow while for blue-collar employees sources of satisfaction included money, amount of work, working conditions, and interpersonal atmosphere. The pattern for sources of dissatisfaction was parallel. Agents serving as sources of satisfaction for white-collar employees were self and subordinates while blue-collars attributed satisfaction primarily to the organization. Dissatisfaction was attributed to subordinates and the union by the white-collars while blue-collars blamed supervisors and co-workers.

Other attitudes   Several studies have related organizational level to job attitudes other than satisfaction. For example, Mitchell and Porter (1967) found that commissioned Air Force officers ranked inner-directed traits as increasingly more important, and other-directed traits as increasingly less important with increasing organizational level. A similar trend was reported for noncommissioned officers, although these two groups did not form a consistent pattern over the six organizational level surveyed.

Miller (1966b) also examined differences in the perceived importance of inner- versus other-directed traits of national union officials Within the industrial union hierarchy, higher-level officials placed significantly more emphasis on inner-directed traits than did lower-level officials. Lower-level industrial union officials placed somewhat greater, but insignificant, emphasis on other-directed traits than did higher-level officials. Within the craft unions, the differences were in the same direction, but were not statistically significant.

Lichtman (1970) related organizational level to other job attitudes and individual characteristics. He reported differences in internal and external control (Rotter, 1966), job-related tension or role strain (Indik, Seashore, and Slesinger, 1964) and need achievement (French, 1948) as a function of organizational level. Analysis of variance indicated no significant differences in need achievement or internal control across organizational level. Job-related tension or role strain was inversely and significantly related to organizational level.

In an experimental study, Dierterly and Schneider (1974) examined the effects of three heirarchical levels (two supervisory and one clerical in a single chain of command) on subjects' perceptions of personal power within a simulated organization and on perceptions of the organization's climate. Position level exerted no main effects on either dependent variable. Bedrosian (1964) found top-level managers (presidents, vice presidents, general managers, department managers) to exhibit higher socioeconomic vocational interests than middle level managers (section heads, second-level supervisors). No differences were found between line and staff managers in level or patterning of vocational interests.

Bernardin and Alvares (1975) found the organization level of employees to be related to ratings of the perceived effectiveness of three methods of conflict resolution. Higher-level employees (versus lower-level employees) rated forcing behaviors to be more effective methods. Conversely, lower-level employees (versus higher-level employees) rated confrontation behaviors to be more effective. These differences in the perceived effectiveness of conflict-resolution methods were found to be related to differences in rated leadership effectiveness by level.

Finally, Downey, Hellriegel, Phelps, and Slocum (1974) reported that the organizational level of their respondents (104 management personnel of a specialty steel firm in central Pennsylvania) moderated the correlations between five satisfactions and six perceived organizational climate measures.

These seven studies, then, indicate that (as in the earlier Porter and Lawler review) organizational level is related to differences in work attitudes other than job satisfaction and to other individual characteristics.

Summary

Taken superficially, the research as reviewed might lead one to believe that organizational level is indeed related to job attitudes as Porter and Lawler (1965) concluded. It appears that most higher-level personnel are more satisfied with most job aspects. However, research since the Porter and Lawler review also suggests that simple univariate conceptualizations and analyses are inadequate. The relationships between organizational level and job attitudes and behavior appear to vary by sample, and to some degree by method. Moreover, a number of studies have explicated differences in job attitudes by individual characteristics as well as by hierarchical level. It also appears that many of the structural variables are interrelated, and that their effects are interactive. When this is the case, univariate analyses are clearly not appropriate, and one's confidence in the results based on that type of analysis is necessarily lessened.

SUBORGANIZATIONAL: LINE AND STAFF POSITIONS

The distinction between line and staff personnel has typically been drawn on the basis of task function. Those individuals involved in the primary output of the organization are termed line, while those whose function only indirectly involve primary output are staff. The latter are often involved in coordination, control, and support of line positions (Price, 1972).

Following a similar definition, the Porter and Lawler (1965) review concluded that:

> Staff managers derive less satisfaction from their jobs, feel they have to be more other-directed, and exhibit different patterns of behavior [than line managers] (p. 33).

However, Porter and Lawler (1965) also suggested that line and staff each form separate hierarchies of authority, and thus an individual could vary by function as well as organizational level. While most research to be reviewed below has controlled for this in some manner, few have considered this problem to the extent of estimating net and joint effects of level and function in the same analysis.

Relation to Attitudes

Two of the studies involving the organizational level/job satisfaction hypothesis in military samples also included line/staff distinctions. In the Johnson and Marcum (1968) study, officers alternated between line and staff positions during their career. Respondents were asked to indicate their need satisfaction concerning recognition or "credit for accomplishment" in line and staff positions they had occupied. No significant differences were found.

Mitchell (1970) reported need satisfaction separately for command and staff personnel within each military rank. Among the highest-ranking officers, commanders were significantly more satisfied over all need categories than were staff commanders in four of five possible comparisons. No significant differences in need satisfaction were found in any other intralevel line/staff comparisons.

Turning now to studies sampling individuals in business and industrial organizations, Lawler and Porter (1966) found essentially no relationship between managers' satisfaction with their pay and line, staff, or combined line/staff position in either zero-order or partial correlational analyses. A finding of no relationship between line, staff, or combined line/staff positions and several need-related variables (fulfillment, importance, satisfaction, and possibility of fulfillment) was reported by Cummings and El Salmi (1970) using univariate analysis, and by El Salmi and Cummings (1968) using multivariate analysis.

Herman and Hulin (1972) also examined the relation of line/staff position to job satisfaction. This multivariate study (described in more detail in the preceding section) related line/staff position to seventeen attitude variables using discriminant function analysis. The multivariate analog of the omega squared measure of association indicated that the function of line/staff position was the second most powerful predictor of job attitudes ($\omega^2 = .60$).

One additional study pertaining to attitudes other than job satisfaction as a function of line/staff position has been reported by Lifter, Bass, and Nussbaum (1971). This study sought to relate the line and staff position of 122 first-line supervisors to differential levels of the perceived importance of effort expenditure in determining salary increases. The results indicated that neither supervisors' perceived actual importance of effort nor their perceptions of normative importance of effort differed significantly as a function of line or staff position. Unfortunately, the line and staff supervisor's average span of control also differed significantly (line managers supervised an average of 8.8 more subordinates than did staff managers; $p < .001$). This confounding was not controlled for, and hence the results are totally ambiguous.

Summary

The seven studies reviewed above have not provided strong support for the existence of differential need satisfaction associated with line and staff positions. While Johnson and Marcum (1968) found no differences in recognition or accomplishment, Mitchell's (1970) military data suggests the possibility of an organizational level by line/staff function interaction. The Lawler and Porter (1966), El Salmi and Cummings (1968), and Cummings and El Salmi (1970) studies, although designed to test this hypothesis, did not find evidence of an interactive relationship. It is important to note that these studies (although varied in several respects) all had the common feature of measuring need satisfaction as a dependent variable. The Herman and Hulin (1972) study not only used instruments of different format, but of more specificity, which might be expected to yield specific attitudes affected by line/staff differences. Their data suggest, however, that such functional differences may relate to attitudinal differences concerned with *specific* interrelationships between line and staff groups, rather than need satisfactions in general.[4]

SUBORGANIZATIONAL: SPAN OF CONTROL

Porter and Lawler (1965) after noting that there had been considerable prescriptive debate on the subject, concluded that little research had been published on the effects of span of control, making it impossible to draw conclusions concerning span's impact on attitudes and behavior. They also noted that the effects of span of control may covary with other organizational variables such as hierarchical level and technology. This lack of empirical support and/or the proposed complexity of the phenomena may have bewildered, but not motivated, future researchers, inasmuch as only two studies pertaining to span of control have been reported during the period of this review.[5]

McDonald and Gunderson (1974) found a positive relation between number of persons supervised and superior job satisfaction in a sample of 5,851 Navy enlisted men. Span of control significantly and positively entered a multiple-regression equation in a cross-validation sample. In a longitudinal study of 151 engineers, Farris (1969) found that each of four performance measures (number of patents, number of technical reports, and two supervisory ratings) were positively related to span of control in two time periods. While these relationships were generally statistically significant, their magnitudes were generally small to moderate.

SUBORGANIZATIONAL: SUBUNIT SIZE

Subunit size, defined as any clearly delineated intraorganizational work unit, also has been decreasingly studied since 1965. Porter and Steers (1973) note that no post-1965 studies were found relating subunit size to absenteeism and turnover, and the present review found only one study relating subunit size to individual attitudes and one relating it to individual behavior.

Cummings and El Salmi (1970) found that subunit size was not significantly related to need fulfillment or need importance. Need satisfaction and the possibility of need fulfillment both increased with subunit size, although the former did not reach traditionally accepted significance levels. These results stand in contradiction to research reviewed by Porter and Lawler (1965), who found that need and job satisfaction *decreased* with increasing subunit size. Cummings and El Salmi suggest that differences between their results and previous research may be due to sample characteristics (managerial versus nonmanagerial). Unfortunately, with the paucity of other studies since 1965 on either blue-collar or managerial samples, this is difficult to evaluate.

Cummins and King (1973) examined the interaction between group (subunit) size and task structure as they impact group member performance in a large manufacturing plant. Subunit size was found to be positively related to productivity ratings only for highly structured, routine tasks. In subunits working on unstructured, ambiguous tasks, size and productivity were negatively, though not significantly, related.

TOTAL ORGANIZATION: SIZE

Total organization size is one area in which previous research was not particularly abundant. Much of the pre-1965 research had focused on subunit size to the neglect of total size, an outcome which led Porter and Lawler to conclude in a very tentative manner that job satisfaction tended to decrease with organization size. They also noted the possibility that organization size and hierarchical position might interact as evidenced by differential effects of size on the job satisfaction of blue-collar workers versus executives.

Relation to Attitudes

Several studies relating organization size to aspects of job and/or need satisfaction have been reported in the last decade. Lawler and Porter (1966) found that organization size had a small but statistically significant zero-order and partial correlational relationship to managerial pay satisfaction. Cummings and El Salmi (1970) found that while total size was not related to need satisfaction or need importance, need fulfillment was greater in medium-sized companies than in either large or small firms. In a multivariate analysis of this data, El Salmi and Cummings (1968) found significant interaction effects of organization level and total size on need fulfillment. In small organizations, the highest-level executives experienced more need fulfillment than did their counterparts in large organizations. However, lower levels of managers in large firms reported more fulfillment than did those in small firms.

In a sample of sixty chapters of an undergraduate business fraternity, Osborn and Hunt (1975) found a significant, positive correlation between organizational size and satisfaction with work as well as with overall satisfaction as measured by the JDI. In addition, they found that size interacted with leader consideration and initiating structure in relation to several JDI satisfaction dimensions. Multiple linear regression analysis indicated that size contributed little explained variance to satisfaction beyond that contributed by leader behaviors.

One study relating attitudes other than need or job satisfaction to total organization size has been reported by England and Lee (1973). Organization size and perceived organizational goals were examined in an international sample (U.S.A., Japan, Korea). Perceptions of organizational goals were measured by eight dimensions of England's Personal Value Questionnaire (England, 1967). In general, the concern with organizational goals increased with size of the organization, and in particular three specific goals (concern with high productivity, profit maximization, and organizational growth) showed significant linear increases with organization size. There were no cross-cultural differences.

Relation to Behavior

Only one study relating total organization size to job behaviors at the individual level of analysis has been found.[6] Ingham (1970) related organizational size (as measured by number of employees) to turnover and absenteeism of industrial workers in England. While there was no relationship between size and turnover, absenteeism showed a significant positive linear relationship with total organization size.

Summary

While the number of researchers studying attitudinal and behavioral differences associated with varying organization size has increased since Porter and Lawler's (1965) review, there has not been enough data reported to justify strong conclusions. Available evidence suggests that size may interact with other structural variables (such as hierarchical level and subunit size) in determining such differences. It also may be that the effects of total organization size operate through intervening constructs at the group and individual levels of analysis. Certainly, organizational size can be expected to influence information processing, communication systems, and control systems. These, in turn, may exert direct impacts on individual attitudes and behaviors as well as indirect impacts through intra- and intergroup processes.

TOTAL ORGANIZATION: VERTICAL AND HORIZONTAL COMPLEXITY

Tall versus Flat Shape and Specialization

Price (1972) has defined complexity as "the degree of structural differentiation within a social system" (p. 70). Encompassed within this definition are two subdimensions. The first of these is vertical complexity or tall versus flat shape. This dimension is generally defined and measured as the number of hierarchical levels relative to the organization's size. The second subdimension is horizontal complexity, and focuses on specialization or "role differentiation." Research relating to both of these dimensions will be reviewed.

Relation to Attitudes

Five studies have related vertical complexity and job attitudes. El Salmi and Cummings (1968) found that vertical complexity interacted with hierarchical level in its effect on need satisfaction. At the highest managerial levels, complex (tall) structures were associated with more need satisfaction than were intermediate or flat structures. At lower managerial levels, the relationship was reversed, with flat and intermediate structures being associated with more need satisfaction.

Ghiselli and Johnson (1970) found that tall or flat shape moderated the relationship between managerial need satisfaction and organizational success. Tall or flat shape was measured by the total number of hierarchical levels in the organization within a given total size category. Using a "slightly shortened version" of the PNSQ and Ghiselli's (1964) index of managerial success, the correlation between need satisfaction and success was determined for 413 managers from a diverse group of organizations. These relationships were then compared between tall and flat organizations over each need category. Only for higher-order needs (esteem, autonomy, and self-actualization) was need satisfaction significantly more positively related to managerial success in tall than in flat organizations.

In a similar study, Ghiselli and Siegel (1972) investigated the relationship between managerial success and attitudes toward authoritarian-democratic leadership styles as moderated by tall or flat shape. Four dimensions of managers' leadership attitudes were measured by an instrument developed by Haire, Ghiselli, and Porter (1966) and each of these was correlated with managerial success. These correlations, which were generally quite low (range, $-.14$ to $.29$), re then compared between tall and flat organizations. There were no ___ferences in the leadership attitude-success relationship on the "faith in others" or "participation" dimensions. The "sharing information" (with subordinates) dimension was negatively related to success in flat organizations ($r = -.14$)

while this relationship was positive ($r = .10$) in tall organizations. With respect to "internal group control," managers holding authoritarian views were more successful in flat organizations ($r = .29$) than in tall organizations ($r = .02$).

Gannon and Paine (1974) related the vertical complexity measure of unity of command to several attitudinal dependent variables in a sample of 304 General Services Administration employees, 181 of whom reported only to one superior while 123 reported to two or more superiors. Those reporting to a single boss reported that (1) personnel selections were more likely to be based on ability, (2) they experienced less role conflict and job pressure, (3) they experienced less need for coordination, and (4) that the responsibility and autonomy associated with their jobs were more adequate.

In a study of 295 trade salesmen in three organizations, Ivancevich and Donnelly (1975) found that salesmen in flat (versus tall and medium) organizations expressed greater satisfaction of self-actualization and autonomy needs and expressed less anxiety and psychological stress. Unfortunately, the three organizations differed on characteristics other than organizational shape, making it risky to attribute any of the differences to shape.

Relation to Behavior and Performance

A study relating vertical complexity to behavior was reported by Carzo and Yanouzas (1969), who tested the effects of tall and flat structures on performance (as measured by decision time, profits, and rate of return) in a laboratory experiment. Results indicated that decision time was not affected by the structural variable, while profits and rates of return were somewhat greater in tall than in flat structures. However, the main effects of the structural variable were not statistically significant for any of the three dependent variables.

Ivancevich and Donnelly (1975) reported that while salesmen in flat, medium, and tall structures did not differ on absenteeism and a route-coverage index, the salesmen from the flat organization were rated by their superiors as more efficient (total orders received by a salesman divided by the total number of retail outlets visited).

Horizontal Complexity and Behavior

Hage, Aiken, and Marrett (1971) related horizontal complexity (as measured by the "number of occupational specialties and degree of professional activity;" p. 866) to work-related verbal communications in sixteen health and welfare organizations. Communications were measured both as scheduled and unscheduled exchanges. The frequency of meetings and proportion of staff members involved also were measured. The occupational specialty measure was significantly related to three of eleven communication measures. The degree of professional activities measure was significantly associated with two of the eleven communication measures.

Summary

The studies grouped under the general category of organizational complexity have been diverse in subject population, design, analysis, and dependent variable measured. Clearly, it appears that complexity (particularly in the vertical dimension) affects organizational members' attitudes and behaviors. Results must be interpreted with caution, however, since few replications have been attempted.

TOTAL ORGANIZATION: CENTRALIZED OR DECENTRALIZED SHAPE

Noting that the literature through 1964 focused on a variety of definitions and a plenum of prescriptive formulations as well as an absence of confirmatory empirical evidence, Porter and Lawler (1965) concluded that:

> The studies reviewed offer no clear-cut support for the proposition that decentralization can produce either improved job attitudes or performance (p. 46).

Research on individual attitudinal and/or behavioral correlates of centralization *since* 1964 has not been abundant. The four studies to be reviewed in this section all focus on aspects of member participation in decision making as the operationalization of decentralization.

Relation to Attitudes

Aiken and Hage (1966) focused on alienation from work and from expressive relationships as a function of centralization in health and welfare organizations. Six interview questions concerning satisfaction with respondents' work and two questions concerning satisfaction with co-workers constituted the measures of alienation from work and expressive relationship respectively. Centralization was measured by indices of hierarchy of authority and participation in decision making. Formalization, as indicated by rule observation and job codification, also was measured. Participation in decision making was negatively related, while job codification and rule observation were positively related to alienation from work.

Bachman, Smith, and Slesinger (1966) measured centralization in terms of interpersonal and task control, and five bases of superiors' power or influence (referrent, expert, reward, coercive, and legitimate power) over their subordinates. These, in turn, were related to respondents' satisfaction with their office manager. Data analysis was based on zero-order correlations. Satisfaction was referenced to ". . . the way your office manager is doing his job" (p. 130). The results indicated a positive relationship with several task and interpersonal control measures. With respect to power, satisfaction was negatively related to reward, coercive, and legitimate power, and positively related to referrent and expert power.

In an experimental study, O'Connell, Cummings, and Huber (1976) found that male student subjects experienced less of three types of tension when making decisions within centralized, hierarchically structured groups. This was particularly the case when the subjects were required to assimilate highly specific information about their decision environment.

Relation to Behavior

The Bachman et al. (1966) study also related the power and control indices of centralization to a standardized measure of the salesmen's performance. Although generally of lesser magnitude, the pattern of results was the same for performance as it was for satisfaction.

In a study related to the one reported by Aiken and Hage (1966) and described above, Hage, Aiken, and Marrett (1971) related the participation in decision-making index of centralization to various measures of scheduled and unscheduled verbal work-related communication. Five of eleven types of scheduled and unscheduled communications were significantly and positively associated with decentralization in zero-order correlational analyses.

Summary

It appears, then, that there is some limited evidence that positive job attitudes increase, and the frequency of verbal communciations increase, as decentralization increases. However, as Porter and Lawler (1965) cautioned, there are likely to be many other variables affecting the desirability of decentralized decision making. Other structural, personal, and task-related variables are likely to be of considerable importance. Aiken and Hage's data suggest that satisfaction with work is affected only by one index of centralization (i.e., participation). Further, the data analyzed by Aiken and Hage (1966) and by Hage et al. (1971) is directly relevant only to professionals and semiprofessionals in service organizations. Generalization beyond these samples requires further evidence.

TENTATIVE CONCLUSIONS

It is tempting to conclude that the research reviewed here has established consistent relationships between structural properties of organizations and members' attitudes and behaviors. One could make such conclusions, particularly in areas such as organizational level where much research has been reported. However, for a number of reasons such conclusions are unwarranted, or warranted only in very limited terms. Problems such as interrelated structural variables, inappropriate designs and analyses, breaches in levels of analysis, variance between measurement techniques, and the lack of coherent conceptual and theoretical frameworks all plague our ability to draw conclusions concerning the research reviewed above.

METHODOLOGICAL CONSIDERATIONS

In order to interpret the observed relationships between organizational and individual variables which have been reviewed above, one must be able to eliminate competing hypotheses concerning research methods as sources of variance. Such hypotheses may derive from the definition and measurement of variables, research designs, and/or analytic procedures. In this section, these methodological problems are considered, and existing alternatives are noted where appropriate.

DEFINITION AND MEASUREMENT OF VARIABLES

Structural Variables

A fundamental prerequisite for comparing studies purportedly dealing with the same topic is agreement on the conceptual definitions of the variables involved. As one author has pointed out, however, ". . . agreement on naming of variables does not necessarily imply conceptual and/or operational agreement" (Pennings, 1973, p. 688). And, as noted in the review section above, such agreement often does not exist.

While lack of comparability is a serious drawback in itself, the problem is compounded in a number of ways when the measures are operationalized. First, as Freeman and Kronenfeld (1973) and Meyer (1971) have pointed out, the unintended redundancy in conceptual definitions leads to biased empirical estimation in the form of tautologies. Such self-fulfilling prophecies stem from "definitional dependencies" at the conceptual level, and lead to positive empirical results in which the observed relationship may be more illusory than real (Freeman and Kronenfeld, 1973).

A second problem involving the interface of conceptual and operational procedures involves the method of gathering information from the organization. The "institutional" or "objective" approach relies on the organization's records and information gathered from a few "key informants" who are generally near the top of the organizational hierarchy and thus are assumed to possess broad knowledge of the organization. An alternative is the "survey" or "subjective" approach, which relies on questionnaires and interviews in attempting to sample a broader spectrum of organizational members. Even when applied to the same construct, in the same sample, these techniques may lead to differing estimates of a given variable. Pennings (1973) and Azumi and McMillan (1973) found very little convergent and discriminant validity between the subjective and objective approaches concerning centralization and formalization. Similar problems may exist with other measures of structural variables. For example, such a "clean" variable as organization size may present difficulties. In the literature reviewed above, size has typically been measured by the number of employees in the organization. However, as Price (1972) points out, this measure confounds differing degrees of labor intensity, and he suggests that "scale of operations" may be a more meaningful construct.

A third problem with the operational measures used in many of the studies reviewed above concerns categorization of potentially continuous variables. For example, studies which trichotomized size (large, medium, or small) or dichotomized vertical complexity (tall versus flat shape) or centralization all lost considerable empirical information. Statistical analyses (to be discussed below) appropriate to categorical variables typically have less power than their counterparts involving continuous variables. Furthermore, estimates of the magnitude and form of main effects and estimation of both the direction and magnitude of interaction effects are less efficient when potentially continuous variables are categorized.

A final problem concerns the control of empirically related structural variables. As many of the studies reviewed here have noted, the dimensions of organization structure are interrelated and may interact in their effects on members' attitudes and behaviors. Multivariate statistical techniques designed to estimate main and interactive effects of nonorthogonal variables are available (e.g., Harris, 1975; Morrison, 1967; Tatsuoka, 1971). However, since survey designs cannot dictate independence of the explanatory variables, one *must* rely on conceptual analysis to assure the appropriateness of the empirical technique and to guide interpretation results (Draper and Smith, 1966, Chapter 8; Gordon, 1968).

Thus theoretical/conceptual analysis is necessary at all stages of the research process, and *particularly* at the stage of definition and measurement of variables if we are to have structural measures that (1) are valid, (2) can serve as the basis for choosing appropriate methods of analysis, and (3) provide a meaningful interpretation of results.

Dependent Variables

In comparison to the structural variables discussed above, some of the individual level dependent variables are less prone to measurement ambiguity. In particular, the DJI (Smith et al., 1969) and the MSQ (Weiss et al., 1967) as measures of job satisfaction are well developed and documented. On the other hand, measures of job behaviors have been almost nonexistent while attitudinal measures other than job satisfaction (e.g., "inner-other directedness") are less well understood. While these shortcomings are regrettable in that they lead to the same problems as noted above concerning structural variables, they will not be discussed explicitly here. Rather, one attitudinal measure which has been widely used in the research reviewed above and which poses some particular methodological problems will be discussed in detail.

PNSQ purports to measure need satisfaction as based on Maslow's need hierarchy theory of motivation. Five need categories (security, social, esteem, autonomy, and self-actualization) are measured by a total of thirteen items. The format of each of these items consists of asking the respondent *(a)* how much of an opportunity there "is now" to satisfy a particular need, *(b)* how much of an opportunity there "should be," and *(c)* how important the need is to the individual. Need fulfillment is measured by the subject's response to the "is now" question while need fulfillment deficiencies are measured as the differences between the "should be" and "is now" responses.

Recently, there have been a number of investigations concerning the characteristics of this instrument. Three studies have been designed to interpret the factor structure of the PNSQ. The results of studies by Herman and Hulin (1973), Roberts, Walter, and Miles (1971), and Waters and Roach (1973) have all shown that the PNSQ does not factor into the five a priori Maslow need categories. Further, the results of the factor analysis do not show a consistent pattern of factors. At best, there seems to be two semi-independent factors representing, perhaps, higher- and lower-order needs.

Two other studies have examined the measurement characteristics of need fulfillment deficiency scores ("d-scores") generated by the PNSQ. Wallace and Berger (1973) found that the d-scores did not meet accepted standards of reliability in any of two managerial and two nonmanagerial samples. Imparato (1972) investigated the scale characteristics of the PNSQ as a function of the size and location of d-scores. In his sample of professional and technical workers, Imparato found that while the size of the d-score was not related to job satisfaction (as measured by the JDI) the location of the d-scores (above and below the midpoint) was positively related to JDI measures of satisfaction.

Finally, Herman and Hulin (1973) and Imparato (1972) investigated the construct validity of the PNSQ via convergent and discriminant validity with the JDI. Both studies failed to find evidence of convergent or discriminant validity.

The results of these studies suggest that:

1. The PNSQ does not represent the five Maslow need categories and does not factor into any consistent pattern.

2. The scale scores (in either the form of the thirteen individual items or the aggregation of these items into the five need categories) are not independent.

3. The PNSQ does not show construct validity with well developed and validated measures of job satisfaction such as the JDI.

4. The d-scores (representing need satisfaction) generated by the PNSQ do not appear to be reliable or to represent interval scales.

Unfortunately, these problems with the PNSQ affect many of the studies reviewed above. In fact, well over one-third of the studies reviewed have used the PNSQ to measure need fulfillment and need satisfaction. In the most heavily researched area (hierarchical level), over half of the studies reviewed have used the PNSQ. The general lack of reliability and validity evidence on the PNSQ, combined with the more consistent results found with better-developed measures of satisfaction (e.g., Herman and Hulin, 1973) suggest that the most parsimonious explanation of the inconsistencies between structural variables and need satisfaction may simply be measurement error.

Recent research has suggested that alternative formulations and operationalizations of a need category concept may provide a firmer base for relating structural constructs to need importance and satisfaction (Alderfer, 1969; Hall and Nougaim, 1968; Lawler and Suttle, 1972; Mitchell and Moudgill, 1976; Schneider and Alderfer, 1973; Wahba and Bridwell, 1974).

RESEARCH DESIGNS

A second general area of methodological concern in interpreting the studies reviewed above focuses on research designs. The first problem here is the lack of longitudinal designs and almost a *complete* reliance on cross-sectional surveys. This approach leaves a number of important questions unanswered. Obviously, no estimates of change or causality can be made with single point-in-time survey designs. Even more important than the potential for oversimplification is the danger of erroneous conclusions based on cross-sectional data. Holdaway and Blowers (1971), for example, have shown that while larger organizational size tended to be associated with small administrative ratios in cross-sectional data, the relationship did not hold up in longitudinal analysis. Farris (1969), on the other hand, did find considerable stability between organizational factors and individual performance over a 6-year period. However, his research also indicated that the assumption of simultaneous measurement (i.e., zero time lag) implicitly made in cross-sectional research may be tenuous.

A second major problem with cross-sectional designs (as used in the research reviewed here) is that they highlight the relationship between structural variables and only a very limited set of variables describing organizational members. While job satisfaction and job performance are clearly of major importance as organizational outcomes, they may be an inadequate sample of the range of the phenomena to be explained.

This problem is compounded by research designs which jump directly from the macro (organizational) level of analysis to the micro (individual) level with simple bivariate and cross-sectional survey designs. For example, in the data reviewed above suggesting that job satisfaction and job performance are positive functions of organizational level, it may be that individuals further up in the hierarchy consistently are more satisfied and/or perform better partially because (1) of personal attributes (such as ability or education), (2) they are selectively promoted to higher positions based on their performance, (3) they have higher expectations concerning salient job outcomes, and/or (4) they receive more organizational rewards.

The use of longitudinal designs, combined with a richer sampling of personal attributes, may well be one method of increasing our understanding of the relationships between structural variables and members' attitudes and behaviors. In fact, a more inclusive model of individual attitudes and behavior may be a first step toward bridging the gap between macro and micro levels of analysis.

A second design consideration involves the use of survey versus experimental or quasi-experimental techniques. The vast majority of the studies reviewed above did not involve manipulation of any structural variable. Such reliance on survey data, while perhaps justifiable on the grounds of access or cost considerations, highlights our inability to make causal arguments. The conclusions of the present review in this respect are the same as Porter and Lawler who, in 1965, warned that:

... experimental "proof" of cause-effect relationships between structure and employee attitudes and behavior is elusive and almost nonexistent (p. 47).

The inability to delineate the effects of organizational variables through experimental procedures, combined with problems of interrelated structural variables highlights again the need for sound conceptual analysis, rigorous definition, measurement and control procedures as well as the need for longitudinal designs and a more complete description of organization members' attitudes, behaviors, and personal attributes.

STATISTICAL ANALYSIS

The problems outlined above concerning measurement and design have important bearing on the appropriateness of analytical techniques, and the conclusions derivable from those analyses. With respect to the literature reviewed above, there are two pressing problems: the first centers on the use of inappropriate analytical techniques; the second concerns the evaluation of research using inappropriate analyses. Comments on the second issue are offered in the next section.

In deciding on an appropriate technique for an analysis, one must consider the nature of the phenomena under investigation. It should be clear from numerous studies of organizations, and from much of the literature reviewed above, that organizational structure variables are likely to be interrelated, are often interactive in their effects on members' attitudes and behaviors, and that these effects occur over time. Indeed, Porter and Lawler warned of this 10 years ago.

Organizations appear to be much too complex for a given variable to have a consistent unidirectional effect across a wide variety of types of conditions. . . . there has been a tendency to oversimplify vastly the effects of particular structural variables (Porter and Lawler, 1965, p. 48).

What, then, are the appropriate techniques for dealing with this problem? Clearly, method variance due to definitional dependencies, measurement problems, etc., must be eliminated. But even with these problems resolved, the multivariate nature of the phenomena requires multivariate design and analysis. The need is compounded by an inability to beable to disentangle the effects of structural variables experimentally. What is needed are clear a priori conceptual frameworks matched by appropriate multivariate analyses.

A number of problems arise when univariate or inadequate multivariate models are applied to such complex phenomena as the effects of organizational structure on individual attitudes and behavior. In terms of the general linear regression model (which underlies many of the statistical techniques employed in the research reviewed above) when a relevant explanatory variable which is correlated with the included explanatory variables is omitted, the estimated effects of the included explanatory variables will be biased and inconsistent (Kmenta, 1971; Theil, 1971).

An additional problem arises when multiple univariate statistical tests are used to test correlated hypotheses. Such is the case, for example, when the PNSQ is used to measure need fulfillment and need satisfaction across each of several levels of an organizational hierarchy. As has been pointed out by Herman and Hulin:

> Whenever multiple comparisons are made on correlated dependent variables, the [type-I error rate] for each hypothesis is unknown. Trend analysis on the means of the hierarchical groups, first on the 13 Porter need deficiency items, then on the five derived scale scores . . . [is typically performed]. To the extent that the dependent variables covary, the significance of mean differences will be highly overstated by the assumption of independence made in multiple significance tests (Herman and Hulin, 1973, pp. 118–119).

This is of particular importance when a large number of hypotheses are tested, as has been done in the vast majority of studies using the PNSQ. Further, the tendency for nonsignificant results to be hidden and/or not reported (Dunnette, 1966; Bakan, 1966) leads to an overemphasis of what may be chance results relative to nonsignificant results and/or failures to replicate (Walster and Cleary, 1970).

A final problem arises in the use of the PNSQ, the scales of which ·apparently are not interval. Statistical techniques, then, must be nonparametric, and the use of these techniques limits the testing of interaction hypotheses (although, see El Salmi and Cummings, 1968, as an exception). A final limitation with nonparametric techniques is the lack of measures of the magnitude of effects.

DISCUSSION AND CONCLUSIONS

The limiting factors discussed above clearly must qualify and attenuate the conclusions which may be drawn from the research reviewed. Yet, with those limitations in mind, the following summary statements may be made.

1. The bulk of the research has focused on attitudinal rather than on behavioral differences associated with structural variations. Future research clearly should be directed toward behavioral as well as attitudinal variables. There is little evidence that we will learn much about behavior in organizations by studying attitudinal dependent variables. Furthermore, it is likely that a broader sampling of organizational members' attitudes, behaviors, and personal attributes will increase our understanding.

2. In terms of specific attitudes investigated, job and need satisfaction clearly have attracted the most attention. Need fulfillment and need importance (as measured by the PNSQ) have not shown consistent results. This may, as noted above, be an artifact of that particular instrument. Further use of the PNSQ should be preceded by additional investigation and modification of the instrument.

3. In terms of the structural variables investigated, the most frequently investigated characteristic has been hierarchical level. Given the large number of studies reviewed on this topic, it seems clear that organizational level is positively related to job and need satisfaction. However, it is not clear that this relationship is linear or even that need satisfaction *consistently* increases over ascending organizational levels. Results of level variations also appear to be modified by the type of social system studied (e.g., military versus business) and by interactions with other structural variables. Further, the relationship between organizational level and satisfaction may have been overestimated by a number of univariate studies testing multiple correlated hypotheses. Finally, to the extent that longitudinal and/or field-experimental studies have been absent, we know only that the relationship is associative. Future research should be directed at these questions, and should include more extensive conceptualizations involving other organizational and personal variables.

4. Other structural variables have been researched less than hierarchical level. Only two studies investigating the effects of span of control and two studies concerning subunit size have been found within the time perspective of this review. With respect to line-staff differences, attitudinal measures focusing on specific line-staff outcomes found significant differences while studies using more general measures of need satisfaction found mixed results. Research on total organization properties (total size, complexity, centralization) has been sparse and difficult to compare. While there appear to be some relationships with individuals' attitudes, the available evidence is mixed and suggests that these variables may interact with other structural variables in their effect on organizational members.

It is distressing to note the many problems plaguing our ability to draw strong conclusions from the literature reviewed above. Even more distressing is the fact that Porter and Lawler (1965) pointed out many of the problems (e.g., interactive effects of structural variables and the need for longitudinal and experimental designs) well before most of the present research was done. If, however, we are to benefit by this past research, then we should become aware of and *act on* the problems and potentials facing future researchers.

As a minimal first step, then, we need to focus upon the recurrent problems of measurement, design, hypothesis testing, and analysis. Solutions for these methodological problems are available and should be applied. If this is done, the difficulties of interpreting future results should be lessened. However, even if methodological problems were to be lightened, there would still be difficulty in interpreting results. It appears that we are at a point at which inductive empiricism cannot advance the state of our knowledge much further without the accompaniment of sound conceptual analysis. Simply the explicit awareness that many studies leap from the aggregate macro-organizational level (as independent variables) directly to the individual level of analysis (as dependent variables) should warn us that causality cannot be direct and simple cross-sectional, bivariate relationships between these two discrepant levels of analysis will not provide adequate explanation.

Surely, organizational processes such as selection and promotion of individuals within organizational ranks, the use of valued skills and abilities of individuals in various positions, and organizational controls on individual behavior, to name only a few, must intervene between structural and individual variables. In addition, the psychological processes through which structural characteristics impact individual attitudes and behavior are largely ignored in the studies reviewed. Inductive empiricism alone cannot solve these problems for several reasons. First, the sheer volume of research needed to obtain the empirical information necessary to eliminate rival hypotheses involving such a large set of variables would be overwhelming. Second, and perhaps more important, the interpretation of large amounts of empirical data without sound conceptual analysis is extremely inefficient, if not meaningless. This is not to argue that we should focus solely on theoretical analyses. Rather, rigorous conceptual *and* empirical approaches should be combined to complement one another if this area of inquiry is to progress further.

FOOTNOTES

1. The authors wish to acknowledge helpful comments on this manuscript by Randall Dunham, Alan Filley, Jeanne Herman, and Donald Schwab.
2. Organizational level was operationalized through a company-developed point system

of job evaluation. The most significant input into this system was the skill level required by the job (personal communication, D. P. Schwab).

3. Additional analyses of this variable are being performed by several of the authors concerned with this problem (personal communications, C. L. Hulin, June, 1975; R. B. Dunham, January, 1976).

4. See footnote 3 and associated discussion in the text.

5. As noted in the previous section, the Lifter, Bass, and Nussbaum (1971) study could be construed as pertaining to span of control equally as well as line-staff function, since these two variables were uncontrolled covariates.

6. A number of studies have been found which relate subunit size and/or total size to aggregated behavioral data (e.g., department or plant) beyond the individual level of analysis (e.g., Mahoney, Frost, Crandall, and Weitzel, 1972; Hrebiniak and Alutto, 1973; Ronan and Prien, 1973). These studies have been excluded as being beyond the scope of the present review in that they do not deal with behaviors at the *individual* level of analysis.

REFERENCES

1. Adams, E. F., D. R. Laker, and C. L. Hulin (1977) "An investigation of the influence of job level and functional specialty on job attitudes and perceptions," *Journal of Applied Psychology 62*, 335–343.

2. Aiken, M., and J. Hage (1966) "Organizational alienation: A comparative analysis," *American Sociological Review 31*, 497–507.

3. Alderfer, C. P. (1969) "An empirical test of a new theory of human needs," *Organizational Behavior and Human Performance 4*, 142–175.

4. Azumi, K., and C. J. McMillan (1973) "Subjective and objective measures of organization structure: A preliminary analysis," paper presented at the American Sociological Association meetings, New York.

5. Bachman, J. G., C. G. Smith, and J. A. Slesinger (1966) "Control, performance, and satisfaction: An analysis of structural and individual effects," *Journal of Personality and Social Psychology 4*, 127–136.

6. Bakan, D. (1966) "The test of significance in psychological research," *Psychological Bulletin 66*, 423–437.

7. Bedrosian, H. (1964) "An analysis of vocational interests at two levels of management," *Journal of Applied Psychology 48*, 325–328.

8. Bernardin, H. J., and K. M. Alvares (1975) "The effects of organizational level on perceptions of role conflict resolution strategy," *Organizational Behavior and Human Performance 14*, 1–9.

9. Bidwell, C. E., and J. D. Kasarda (1975) "School district organization and student achievement," *American Sociological Review 40*, 55–70.

10. Campbell, D. T., and J. C. Stanley (1966) *Experimental and Quasi-Experimental Designs for Research*, Chicago: Rand McNally & Company.

11. Carrell, M. R., and N. F. Elberg (1974) "Some personal and organizational determinants of job satisfaction of postal clerks," *Academy of Management Jounral 17*, 368–373.

12. Carzo, R., Jr., and J. N. Yanouzas (1969) "Effects of flat and tall organization structure," *Administrative Science Quarterly 14*, 178–191.

13. Crozier, M. (1972) "The relationship between micro and macrosociology," *Human Relations 25*, 239–251.

14. Cummings, L. L., and A. M. El Salmi (1968) "Empirical research on the bases and correlates of managerial motivation: A review of the literature," *Psychological Bulletin 70*, 127–144.

15. ——, and ——. (1970) "The impact of role diversity, job level, and organizational size on managerial satisfaction," *Administrative Science Quarterly 15*, 1–12.

16. Cummins, R. C., and D. C. King (1973) "The interaction of group size and task structure in an industrial organization," *Personnel Psychology 26*, 87–94.

17. Dieterly, D. L., and B. Schneider (1974) "The effect of organizational environment on perceived power and climate: A laboratory study," *Organizational Behavior and Human Performance 11*, 316–337.

18. Downey, H. K., D. Hellriegel, M. Phelps, and J. W. Slocum, Jr. (1974) "Organizational climate and job satisfaction: A comparative analysis," *Journal of Business Research 2*, 233–248.

19. Draper, N. R., and H. Smith (1966) *Applied Regression Analysis*, New York: John Wiley & Sons, Inc.

20. Dunnette, M. D. (1966) "Fads, fashion, and folderol in psychology," *American Psychologist 21*, 343–352.

21. Eckert, C., and G. Young (1936) "The approximation of one matrix by another of a lower rank," *Psychometrika 1*, 211–218.

22. El Salmi, A. M., and L. L. Cummings (1968) "Managers' perceptions of needs and need satisfactions as a function of interactions among organizational variables," *Personnel Psychology 21*, 465–477.

23. England, G. W. (1967) "Organizational goals and expected behavior of American managers," *Academy of Management Journal 10*, 107–117.

24. ——, and R. Lee (1973) "Organizational size as an influence on perceived organizational goals: A comparative study among American, Japanese, and Korean managers," *Organizational Behavior and Human Performance 9*, 48–58.

25. Farris, G. H. (1969) "Organizational factors and individual performance: A longitudinal study," *Journal of Applied Psychology 53*, 87–92.

26. Freeman, J. H., and J. E. Kronenfeld (1973) "Problems of definitional dependency: The case of administrative intensity," *Social Forces 52*, 108–121.

27. French, E. (1958) "Development of a measure of complex motivation," in J. W. Atkinson (ed.), *Motives in Fantasy, Action, and Society*, Princeton: D. Van Nostrnad.

28. Gannon, M. J., and F. T. Paine (1974) "Unity of command and job attitudes of managers in a bureaucratic organization," *Journal of Applied Psychology 59*, 392–394.

29. Gavin, J. F. (1975) "Organizational climate as a function of personal and organizational variables," *Journal of Applied Psychology 60*, 135–139.

30. Ghiselli, E. E. (1964) *Theory of Psychological Measurement*, New York: McGraw-Hill.

31. ——. (1971) *Explorations in Management Talent*, Pacific Palisades, Calif.: Goodyear.

32. ——, and D. A. Johnson, (1970) "Need satisfaction, managerial success, and organizational structure," *Personnel Psychology 23*, 569–576.

33. ——, and J. Siegel, (1972) "Leadership and managerial success in tall and flat organization structures," *Personnel Psychology 25*, 617–624.

34. Goldberger, A. S., and O. D. Duncan (1973) *Structural Equation Models in the Social Sciences*, New York: Seminar Press, Inc.

35. Gordon, R. A. (1968) "Issues in multiple regression," *American Journal of Sociology 74*, 592–616.

36. Hage, J., M. Aiken, and C. B. Marrett (1971) "Organization structure and communications," *American Sociological Review 36*, 860–871.

37. Haire, M., E. E. Ghiselli, and L. W. Porter (1966) *Managerial Thinking*, New York: John Wiley & Sons, Inc.

38. Hall, D. T., and K. E. Nougaim (1968) "An examination of Maslow's need hierarchy in an organizational setting," *Organizational Behavior and Human Performance 3*, 12–35.

39. Harris, C. W. (1963) *Problems in Measuring Change*, Madison, Wis.: University of Wisconsin Press.
40. Harris, F. J. (1949) "The quantification of an industrial employee survey. I. Method," *Journal of Applied Psychology 33*, 103–111.
41. Harris, R. J. (1975) *A Primer of Multivariate Statistics*, New York: Academic Press, Inc.
42. Harris, T. C., and E. A. Locke (1974) "Replication of white-collar, blue-collar differences in sources of satisfaction and dissatisfaction," *Journal of Applied Psychology 59*, 369–370.
43. Hellriegel, D., and J. W. Slocum, Jr. (1974) "Organizational climate: Measures, research, and contingencies," *Academy of Management Journal 17*, 225–280.
44. Herman, J. B., R. B. Dunham, and C. L. Hulin (1975) "Organizational structure, demographic characteristics, and employee responses," *Organizational Behavior and Human Performance 13*, 206–232.
45. ———, and C. L. Hulin (1972) "Studying organizational attitudes from individual and organizational frames of reference," *Organizational Behavior and Human Performance 8*, 84–108.
46. ———, and ———. (1973) "Managerial satisfactions and organizational roles: An investigation of Porter's need deficiency scales," *Journal of Applied Psychology 57*, 118–124.
47. Holdaway, E. A., and T. A. Blowers, (1971) "Administrative ratios and organization size: A longitudinal analysis," *American Sociological Review 36*, 278–286.
48. Hrebiniak, L. G., and J. A. Alutto (1973) "A comparative organizational study of performance and size correlates in inpatient psychiatric departments," *Administrative Science Quarterly 18*, 365–382.
49. Imparato, N. (1972) "Relationship between Porter's need satisfaction questionnaire and the Job Descriptive Index," *Journal of Applied Psychology 56*, 397–405.
50. Indik, B., S. E. Seashore, and J. Slesinger (1964) "Demographic correlates of psychological strain," *Journal of Abnormal and Social Psychology 69*, 26–38.
51. Ingham, G. (1970) *Size of Industrial Organization and Worker Behavior*, Cambridge, England: Cambridge University Press.
52. Ivancevich, J. M., and J. H. Donnelly, Jr. (1975) "Relation of organizational structure to job satisfaction, anxiety-stress, and performance," *Administrative Science Quarterly 20*, 272–280.
53. James, L. R., and A. P. Jones (1974) "Organizational climate: A review of theory and research," *Psychological Bulletin 81*, 1096–1112.
54. ———, and ———. (1976) "Organizational Structure: A review of structural dimensions and their conceptual relationships with individual attitudes and behavior," *Organizational Behavior and Human Performance 16*, 74–113.
55. Johannesson, R. E. (1973) "Some problems in the measurement of organizational climate," *Organizational Behavior and Human Performance 10*, 118–144.
56. Johnson, P. V., and R. H. Marcum (1968) "Perceived deficiencies in individual need fulfillment of career army officers," *Journal of Applied Psychology 52*, 457–461.
57. Kmenta, J. (1971) *Elements of Econometrics*, New York: Macmillan, Inc.
58. Krichner, W. K., and N. B. Mousley (1963) "A note on job performance: Differences between respondent and nonrespondent salesmen in an attitude survey," *Journal of Applied Psychology 47*, 223–224.
59. Lawler, E. E., III, D. T. Hall, and G. R. Oldham (1974) "Organizational climate: Relationship to organizational structure, process, and performance," *Organizational Behavior and Human Performance 11*, 139–155.

60. ———, and L. W. Porter (1966) "Predicting managers' pay and their satisfaction with their pay," *Personnel Psychology 19*, 363–373.
61. ———, and J. L. Suttle (1972) "A causal correlational test of the need hierarchy concept," *Organizational Behavior and Human Performance 7*, 265–287.
62. Lichtman, C. M. (1970) "Some intrapersonal response correlates of organizational rank," *Journal of Applied Psychology 54*, 77–80.
63. Lifter, M. L., H. R. Bass, and H. Nussbaum (1971) "Effort expenditure and job performance of line and staff personnel," *Organizational Behaivor and Human Performance 6*, 501–515.
64. Locke, E. A., and R. J. Whiting (1974) "Sources of satisfaction and dissatisfaction among solid waste management employees," *Journal of Applied Psychology 59*, 145–156.
65. Lodahl. T., and M. Kejner (1965) "The definition and measurement of job involvement," *Journal of Applied Psychology 49*, 24–33.
66. MacEachron, A. E. (1977) "Two interactive perspectives on the relationship between job level and job satisfaction," *Organizational Behavior and Human Performance 19*, 226–246.
67. Mahoney, T. A., P. Frost, N. F. Crandall, and W. Weitzel (1972) "The conditioning influence of organizational size upon managerial practice," *Organizational Behavior and Human Performance 8*, 230–241.
68. Maslow, A. H. (1954) *Motivation and Personality*, New York: Harper & Row, Publishers.
69. McDonald, B. W., and E. E. E. Gunderson (1974) "Correlates of job satisfaction in naval environments," *Journal of Applied Psychology 59*, 371–373.
70. Meyer, M. W. (1971) "Some constraints in analyzing data on organizational structures: A comment on Blau's paper," *American Sociological Review 36*, 294–297.
71. ———. (1972) "Size and the structure of organizations: A causal analysis," *American Sociological Review 37*, 434–440.
72. Miller, E. L. (1966a) "Job satisfaction of national union officials," *Personnel Psychology 19*, 261–274.
73. ———. (1966b) "Job attitudes of national union officials: Perceptions of the importance of certain personality traits as a function of job level and union organization structure," *Personnel Psychology 19*, 395–410.
74. Mitchell, V. F. (1970) "Need satisfactions of military commanders and staff," *Journal of Applied Psychology 54*, 282–287.
75. ———, and P. Moudgill (1976) "Measurement of Maslow's need hierarchy," *Organizational Behavior and Human Performance 16*, 334–349.
76. ———, and L. W. Porter (1967) "Comparative managerial role perceptions in military and business hierarchies," *Journal of Applied Psychology 51*, 449–452.
77. Morrison, D. F. (1967) *Multivariate Statistical Methods*, New York: McGraw-Hill.
78. Newman, J. E. (1975) "Understanding the organizational structure-job attitude relationship through perceptions of the work environment," *Organizational Behavior and Human Performance 14*, 371–397.
79. O'Connell, M. J., L. L. Cummings, and G. P. Huber (1976) "The effects of environmental information and decision unit structure on felt tension," *Journal of Applied Psychology 61*, 493–500.
80. Oltman, P. K. (1968) "A portable rod-and-frame test," *Perceptual Motor Skills 26*, 503–506.
81. O'Reilly, C. A., and K. H. Roberts (1975) "Individual differences in personality, position in the organization, and job satisfaction," *Organizational Behavior and Human Performance 14*, 144–150.

82. Osborn, R. N., and J. B. Hunt (1975) "Relations between leadership, size, and subordinate satisfaction in a voluntary organization," *Journal of Applied Psychology 60*, 730–735.

83. Payne, R. (1970) "Factor analysis of a Maslow-type need satisfaction questionnaire," *Personnel Psychology 23*, 251–268.

84. Pennings, J. (1973) "Measures of organizational structure: A methodological note," *American Journal of Sociology 79*, 686–704.

85. Porter, L. W. (1962) "Job attitudes in management: I. Perceived deficiencies in need fulfillment as a function of job level," *Journal of Applied Psychology 46*, 375–384.

86. ———. (1964) *Organizational Patterns of Managerial Job Attitudes*, New York: American Foundation for Management Research.

87. ———, and M. M. Henry (1964) "Job attitudes in management: V. Perceptions of the importance of certain personality traits as a function of job level," *Journal of Applied Psychology 48*, 31–36.

88. ———, and E. E. Lawler III (1965) "Properties of organization structure in relation to job attitudes and job behavior," *Psychological Bulletin 64*, 23–51.

89. ———, and V. F Mitchell (1967) "Comparative study of need satisfaction in military and business hierarchies," *Journal of Applied Psychology 51*, 139–144.

90. ———, and Steers, R. M. (1973) "Organizational, work, and personal factors in employee turnover and absenteeism," *Psychological Bulletin 80*, 151–176.

91. Price, J. L. (1972) *Handbook of Organizational Measurement*, Lexington, Mass.: D. C. Heath & Company.

92. Pritchard, R. D., and B. W. Karasick (1973) "The effects of organizational climate on managerial job performance and job satisfaction," *Organizational Behavior and Human Performance 9*, 126–146.

93. Rhinehart, J. B., R. P. Barell, A. S. De Wolfe, J. E. Griffin, and F. E. Spaner (1969) "Comparative study of need satisfactions in government and business hierarchies," *Journal of Applied Psychology 53*, 230–235.

94. Rice, L. E., and T. R. Mitchell (1973) "Structural determinants of individual behavior in organizations," *Administrative Science Quarterly 18*, 56–70.

95. Roberts, K. H., G. A. Walter, and R. E. Miles (1971) "A factor analytic study of job satisfaction items designated to measure Maslow need categories," *Personnel Psychology 24*, 205–220.

96. Ronan, W. W., and E. P. Prien (1973) "An analysis of organizational behavior and organizational performance," *Organizational Behavior and Human Performance 9*, 78–99.

97. Rotter, J. B. (1966) "Generalized expectancies for internal versus external control of reinforcement," *Psychological Monographs 80* (1, Whole No. 609).

98. Runkel, P. J., and H. E. McGrath (1972) *Research on Human Behavior*, New York: Holt, Rinehart and Winston, Inc.

99. Schneider, B., and C. P. Alderfer (1973) "Three studies of measures of need satisfaction in organizations," *Administrative Science Quarterly 18*, 489–505.

100. Schwab, D. P., and M. J. Wallace, Jr. (1974) "Correlates of employee satisfaction with pay," *Industrial Relations 13*, 78–89.

101. Selvin, H. C., and A. Stuart (1966) "Data dredging procedures in survey analysis," *American Statistician 20*, 20–23.

102. Siegel, S. (1956) *Nonparametric Statistics*, New York: McGraw-Hill.

103. Sims, H. P., Jr., and A. D. Szilagyi (1976) "Job characteristic relationships: Individual and structural moderators," *Organizational Behavior and Human Performance 17*, 211–230.

104. Slocum, J. W., Jr. (1971) "Motivation in managerial levels: Relationship of need satisfaction to job performance," *Journal of Applied Psychology 55,* 312–316.
105. Smith, P. C., L. M. Kendall, and C. L. Hulin (1969) *The Measurement of Satisfaction in Work and Retirement,* Chicago: Rand McNally & Company.
106. Starcevich, M. M. (1972) "Job factor importance for job satisfaction and dissatisfaction across different occupational levels," *Journal of Applied Psychology 56,* 467–471.
107. Szilagyi, A. D., H. P. Sims, Jr., and R. T. Keller (1964) "Role dynamics, locus of control, and employee attitudes and behavior," *Academy of Management Journal 19,* 259–276.
108. Tatsuoka, M. M. (1971) *Multivariate Analysis,* New York: John Wiley & Sons, Inc.
109. Theil, H. (1971) *Principles of Econometrics,* New York: John Wiley & Sons.
110. Wahba, M. A., and L. G. Bridwell (1974) "Maslow reconsidered: A review of research on the need hierarchy theory," *Academy of Management Proceedings* pp. 514–520.
111. Wallace, M. J., and P. K. Berger (1973) "The reliability of difference scores: A preliminary investigation of a need deficiency satisfaction scale," *Academy of Management Proceedings* pp. 421–427.
112. Walster, G. W., and T. A. Cleary (1970) "A proposal for a new editorial policy in the social sciences," *American Statistician 24,* 16–19.
113. Waters, L. K., and D. Roach (1973) "A factor analysis of need-fulfillment items designed to measure Maslow need categories," *Personnel Psychology 26,* 185–190.
114. Weiss, D. J., R. V. Dawis, G. W. England, and L. H. Lofquist (1967) *Manual for the Minnesota Satisfaction Questionnaire,* Minneapolis: University of Minnesota, Industrial Relations Center.
115. Weitzel, W., P. R. Pinto, R. V Dawis, and P. A. Jury (1973) "The impact of the organization on the structure of job satisfaction: Some factor analytic findings," *Personnel Psychology 26,* 545–557.